Marko Kölbl, Fritz Trümpi (eds.)
Music and Democracy

The editors invited this volume's authors to contribute their chapters. Each chapter underwent a double-blind peer review process. In total, eighteen independent invited reviewers were involved. The mdwPress coordination and the editors supervised the review process.

Marko Kölbl, Fritz Trümpi (eds.)

Music and Democracy

Participatory Approaches

^m_dwPress

[transcript]

This book was generously funded by

Bibliographic information published by the Deutsche Nationalbibliothek
The Deutsche Nationalbibliothek lists this publication in the Deutsche Nationalbibliografie; detailed bibliographic data are available in the Internet at http://dnb.d-nb.de

Editorial assistant: Karoline Feyertag
Cover layout: Bueronardin
Cover illustration: Dutch pop group Vengaboys perform their song "We're Going to Ibiza" on a stage during a protest against the government in Vienna, Austria, May 30, 2019. Credit: Lisi, Nieser/Reuters/picturedesk.com
Proofread: Jason S. Heilman
Typeset: Nora Schmidt

Print-ISBN 978-3-8376-5657-2
PDF-ISBN 978-3-8394-5657-6
EPUB-ISBN 978-3-7328-5657-2
https://doi.org/10.14361/9783839456576

Contents

Part 3: (Non-)Democratic Participation in Popular Music and Performance Cultures

Part 4: Sonic Implications of Political Changes

Ambivalences in Music and Democracy: Introductory Remarks

Marko Kölbl and Fritz Trümpi

Marko Kölbl is an ethnomusicologist and senior scientist at the Department of Folk Music Research and Ethnomusicology at mdw – University of Music and Performing Arts Vienna. He is specialized in music and dance of minorities and migrant communities with an interest in intersectional, queer-feminist, and postcolonial perspectives.

Fritz Trümpi is a musicologist and associate professor at the Department of Musicology and Performance Studies at mdw – University of Music and Performing Arts Vienna. His research focuses on the history of music industries and musicians' organisations, music & politics, and music culture(s) of the late Habsburg Empire and its successor states.

After Donald Trump's failed re-election as President of the United States of America in fall 2020, the Republicans' out-of-the-blue claims of "electoral fraud" is just one of countless warning signs: to varying extents and degrees, democracy is in great danger all over the world. Already in the early 2000s, Colin Croach noted a subtle but increasing demolition of—but also an increased disinterest in—political participation of the people, which he considered as main characteristics of "post-democracy."[1] However, despite the doubtlessly growing interventions (of growing severity) of political as well as economic elites against liberal and democratic values and structures, it cannot be overlooked that also resistance against limitations on the people's active participation in political life is growing and spreading. Some of these protest movements are globally connected, operating in many parts of the world (such as "Fridays for Future" or "Black Lives Matter"), while others are acting primarily on a country-by-country basis, within specific regions, or even communally.

An illustrative example of regional protests that address the broader political climate is the "Ibiza affaire," to which this book's cover refers. After the

---

1 Colin Crouch, ed., *Coping with Post-Democracy* (Cambridge: Fabian Society, 2000).

infamous Ibiza tapes leaked,[2] the governmental crisis in Austria resulted in public protests that were profoundly shaped by music and dancing. Various musical actors provided the soundscape for political protest, spanning from postmigrant rap to activist choirs. This volume's cover photo captures a historic moment in the course of this governmental crisis. The fact that the eponymous tapes were secretly recorded at a rented *finca* on Ibiza, Spain, resulted in a sudden revival of the 1999 song "We're Going to Ibiza" by the '90s Euro Dance band Venga Boys. The song became the soundtrack of the protest, was used in TV coverage and ranked number one on the Austrian Spotify charts. It achieved definite political significance when Venga Boys performed it from their tour bus in front of the main government's building at Vienna's Ballhausplatz, where an enormous dancing and singing crowd celebrated the expected fall of the government. The song's musical qualities and its topical apoliticality—'90s synthetic club sounds dealing with partying in Ibiza—are not exactly what one would call a prime example of democratic content in music. Precisely the song's trashy aura, however, helped to point out the political critique of cheap corruption and simultaneously showcased contemporary protest culture's entanglement with club culture and party making.

While a rich body of literature has explored in recent years how individuals and groups use music as a resource to achieve social, cultural, and political participation and to bring about social change in society,[3] the present volume specifically focuses on the addressed tensional dichotomy. Its various contributions investigate the manifold ways of music's use by activists, but also by political groups and even governments, exploring emancipative processes and mirroring them with the implementation of nationalist, authoritarian, fascist, or neoliberal political ideas. Furthermore, the volume is also concerned with the promise and myth of democratization through technology in regard to music production, distribution, and reception/appropriation.

---

2   Former Austrian vice chancellor H.C. Strache and his fellow party member Johann Gudenus from the far-right party FPÖ were caught on tape initiating corrupt deals with the supposed niece of a Russian oligarch. The release of the video evoked public civil protests and resulted in the resignation of the two politicians, the dissolution of the government, and subsequent early parliament elections.

3   Above all, we would like to point on the only recently published anthology edited by Robert Adlington and Esteban Buch, *Finding Democracy in Music* (London: Routledge, 2021). Representative of many others, we furthermore point to the important and influential writings of Nancy Love, including *Musical Democracy* (Albany, NY: State University of New York Press, 2006) and *Trendy Fascism: White Power Music and the Future of Democracy* (Albany, NY: State University of New York Press, 2016).

However, the addressed dichotomy—the existence of a causal link between governmental repression and the formation of protest movements—is anything but new. A short look back to the long nineteenth century in Europe, for example, shows this, for instance with regard to the revolutionary acts around 1848 across the continent (and in other parts of the world), when (the not only but predominantly bourgeois) parts of the population revolted against the repressive *ancien régime* (which came back to power after the French Revolution had lost its claims and influence). And these revolutionaries did so not least by using music as an important tool of their political struggle: be it by singing revolutionary songs (as done, among others, by protesting students) or by performing noise ("Charivari") during protest marches, or by composing for the revolution (e.g. the *Revolutions-Marsch* by Johann Strauss Sohn, but also operas like Gustav Albert Lortzing's *Regina*, representing the genre of "opera of freedom"). The revolts of 1848 can therefore, admittedly among many other aspects, also be considered as a musical empowerment of the people, or more precisely, in predominant cases, of the bourgeois protagonists (if not of the bourgeoisie as such), as recently shown in a voluminous anthology edited by Barbara Boisits.[4]

However, the revolutionary frequently threatens to become reactionary: the claims of freedom for the people raised by the revolts' protagonists of 1848 turned soon into severe claims of nationalism, identifying people more and more as national subjects. And again, music served as an important means of communication when nationalist groups tried to press their case, for instance by the men's choral societies that had been flourishing since the mid-nineteenth century.[5] With the rise of nationalist aspirations, the inclusion and exclusion of certain groups among the population also increased, not at least with regard to the production, performance, and consumption of music (of any kind), as (for instance) Philip Bohlman showed in a long-term perspective ranging from the end of the nineteenth century up to the early twenty-first.[6]

---

4   Barbara Boisits, ed., *Musik und Revolution. Die Produktion von Identität und Raum durch Musik in Zentraleuropa 1848/49* (Vienna: Hollitzer, 2013).

5   See, e.g., Sabine Mecking, "Gelebte Empathie und donnerndes Pathos. Gesang und Nation im 19. Jahrhundert," in *Musik—Macht—Staat. Kulturelle, soziale und politische Wandlungsprozesse in der Moderne*, ed. Sabine Mecking and Yvonne Wasserloos (Göttingen: V&R Unipress, 2012), 99–126; Dorothea Redepenning, "'... unter Blumen eingesenkte Kanonen ...'. Substanz und Funktion nationaler Musik im 19. Jahrhundert," in *Das Andere. Eine Spurensuche in der Musikgeschichte des 19. und 20. Jahrhunderts*, ed. Annette Kreutziger-Herr (Frankfurt/Main: Lang, 1998), 225–45.

6   See, e.g., Philip Bohlman, *Focus: Music, Nationalism, and the Making of the New Europe* (New York: Routledge, 2011).

After a first peak of devastating violence in the name of nationalism in World War I and the dissolution of imperial Europe, the establishment of more or less democratic-structured republics across the continent happened only hesitantly and was in many cases short lived. This, by reflecting the role of music within the fragile and ambivalent democratization, marks the starting point of the present volume. The contribution of **David Ferreiro Carballo** deals with the question of how political impacts on bourgeois music culture became implemented within this phase of governmental transition in Spain. He does so with regard to the creation of the National Society of Music, by investigating the repertoire policies of this institution.

What followed, resulting not at least from the republics' weaknesses, which were caused by fragile democratic structures, was the rise and consolidation of fascism. Implemented first in Italy by Mussolini and his henchmen, it soon covered large parts of Europe. Studying fascism shows—until today without comparison—the devastating instrumentalization of governments acting in the name of "the people" while simultaneously excluding any political participation in a democratic sense. Without a doubt, the sphere of music was highly affected by this fascization of politics and society, as numerous scholars were able to show in the recent past, mainly with regard to Nazi Germany (and Austria).[7] In this volume, **Gabrielle Prud'homme** examines the political appropriation of Giuseppe Verdi in Fascist Italy by studying the celebrations surrounding the fortieth anniversary of Verdi's death in 1941. Thereby, the author sheds light on how Mussolini's regime maintained its grip on the commemorations and disseminated a discourse entirely consistent with the fascist political and ideological agenda.

But even under fascist regimes, music did not exclusively fulfil the purposes of the official political agenda. It was, on the contrary, not uncommon to also use music for political protests (albeit for the most part in rather subliminal forms, for fear of repression and persecution); the documented performative acts of the "Swing-Jugend" (Germany) or the "Schlurfs" (Austria) under the Nazi regime may be exemplary here.[8] The same applies to political opposition movements in other totalitarian systems of rule. In her essay on the history of

---

7   To name only a few of the most influential: Oliver Rathkolb, *Führertreu und gottbegnadet. Künstlereliten im Dritten Reich* (Vienna: Österreichischer Bundesverlag, 1991); Erik Levi, *Music in the Third Reich* (Basingstoke: Macmillan, 1994); Pamela Potter, *Most German of the Arts: Musicology and Society from the Weimar Republic to the End of Hitler's Reich* (New Haven: Yale University Press, 1998); Fritz Trümpi, *The Political Orchestra: The Vienna and Berlin Philharmonics during the Third Reich* (Chicago: University of Chicago Press, 2016).

8   See e.g. Wolfgang Beyer and Monica Ladurner, *Im Swing gegen den Gleichschritt. Die Jugend, der Jazz und die Nazis* (Salzburg: Residenz Verlag, 2011).

"bootleg" sound recordings of the twentieth century, **Marsha Siefert** explores the world of *magnitizdat* (as underground music recordings in the Soviet Union were called). She does so by comparing them with "bootleg" opera recordings in the United States, considering both as a way of "democratizing" accesses to music provided by bards (USSR) and music fans (USA).

As implemented in this essay, highlighting the sphere of consumption and distribution of music as a participatory act, and thus as a specific form of artistic practice, adds important perspectives on music and democracy, complementing the more commonly used foci on composing and performing. This understanding obviously meets Christopher Small's concept of "musicking," where both the act of performing and the act of listening are equally considered to be predominant musicological research parameters.[9] In this context, we would like to point not least to the growing field of research that has been dedicated to the manifold aspects of digitalization in/of music.[10] Research on various forms of such "mediamorphosis" include, among others, investigations on the effects for democratization, including possibilities of self-representation, modes of participation for consumers, or business models in music and media. In their contribution, **Raphaël Nowak and Ben Morgan** investigate interactive commercial services within the "digital ecosystem" by placing a critical perspective on "democratization" in its ambivalence, but at the same time by understanding it as a key indicator for evaluating the distribution of music content on streaming platforms.

A few decades before online streaming platforms shaped music consumption, television shows that featured music were central to popular music distribution as well as the public discourses on popular music. These programs were inherently political, as illustrated by **Dean Vuletic** in his text. Vuletic discusses Europe's political split, defined through presumed levels of democracy building on "a longer history of West European cultural prejudice against Central and East Europe" (p. 142). The Intervision Song Contest offered a separate "Eastern" realm for presenting popular music in a competitive format while constituting an arena for the complex dynamics within the chosen regional frame of the singing competition.

Music itself often carries notions of professionalism and elitism that foster a fairly undemocratic image. Specifically, Western classical music's harsh ed-

---

9   Christopher Small, *Musicking: The Meanings of Performing and Listening* (Middletown, CT: Wesleyan University Press, 1998).

10   In the context of music and democracy, cf. especially David Hesmondhalgh, "Have Digital Communication Technologies Democratized the Media Industries?," in *Media and Society*, ed. James Curran and David Hesmondhalgh, 6th ed. (London: Bloomsbury, 2019), 101–20.

ucation system and its high standards of excellence and virtuosity presume a wide range of preconditions seemingly necessary for active musical expression. Similarly, the global pop music scene departs from an understanding of music that is highly professionalized and focuses on idealized individual star figures rather than the collective and social dimensions of music making. However, as a collective and inherently social expression by people notwithstanding their musical educations, instrumental or vocal capabilities, and stylistic preferences, music shows its profoundly democratic qualities. Social movements often rely on democratic ways of musicking that foreground grassroots, "bottom-up" and Do-It-Yourself approaches that help to articulate demands for social justice and challenge political hegemonies.[11] In their contribution, **Milena Dragičević Šešić and Julija Matejić** trace various scenarios of musical activism—"artivism"—in Serbia during the 1990s. The specific contemporary history of the region, the democratic upheavals, and the discussed musical and expressive styles and genres exemplarily showcase music's and art's usage in creating counterpublics, defining citizenship, and enabling participation.

As Dragičević Šešić and Matejić show, instances of musical activism often align their aesthetic preferences and content with their political message. The examples are manifold: Activist choirs that appropriate specific political histories of music for contemporary political struggle,[12] feminist and queer performance groups that contest heteronormative exclusion through musical and bodily aesthetics and/or anti-racist expressions that foreground the identity-political meanings of music and dance. India's anti-caste movement, for example, draws on musical traditions that emphasize a Dalit self-empowerment, contesting racist and classist social orders.[13]

A contrasting example of music's impact is provided by **Ondřej Daniel** in his essay. Daniel's class-sensitive discussion of hardbass, "a predominantly Eastern European electronic dance music style" (p. 158) that spread from Russia in the 2000s, shows how music relates to fast-changing political meanings. Through the example of this unique dance and fashion phenomenon—a "working class mimicry"—Daniel traces the genre's satirical beginnings, its connection to far-right politics, and its subsequent de-politicization.

---

11   See Ursula Hemetek, Marko Kölbl, and Hande Sağlam, *Ethnomusicology Matters: Influencing Social and Political Realities* (Vienna: Böhlau, 2019).

12   See also Ana Hofman, "Disobedient: Activist Choirs, Radical Amateurism, and the Politics of the Past after Yugoslavia," *Ethnomusicology* 64, no. 1 (2020): 89–109.

13   See Rasika Ajotikar, "Reflections on the Epistemic Foundations of Music in Modern India through the Lens of Caste: A Case from Maharashtra, India," in *Ethnomusicology Matters: Influencing Social and Political Realities*, ed. Ursula Hemetek, Marko Kölbl, and Hande Sağlam (Vienna: Böhlau, 2019), 135–62.

Here, music's (anti-)democratic capacities become apparent off the beaten tracks of established musical canons and the global music industry. Regional popular music forms, community-based music traditions, orally transmitted musics, and the like make up the central expressive formats of communities (however they are defined), allowing for democratic meaning within music and dance. Specifically, the music and performance practices of minorities and marginalized groups often aim to challenge and subvert dominant norms and classifications. Since power hegemonies frequently inhibit an appropriate representation of minorities and marginalized groups, the communities in question apply their own expressive agency in contesting subordination. This expressive agency of course encompasses various styles and genres of music and performing arts.

One such particular musical style—Deaf hip hop—is the topic of **Katelyn Best's** chapter. In it, Best shows how musical agency functions within a community that is commonly perceived as voiceless. Her detailed ethnographic account on musical inclusivity through this specific form of hip hop highlights music's efficacy in negotiating social exclusion and structural discrimination. As "sound in Deaf culture is signified across sensory modalities" (p. 239), Deaf hip hop expands the common understanding of music and sound and displays a powerful example of musical participation and the relationship between democracy and music.

Migration and border regimes poignantly illustrate the relationship between democracy and the aforementioned variety of musical and performing practices. Music, here, serves as a tool of diasporic relocation that contests both ethnicization and racialization as well as assimilation and the reduction of cultural rights. In migratory settings, musicking enables translation, defines dynamics of Othering processes, and simultaneously gains meaning in socio-political change in various settings, from diaspora to exile.[14] At the same time, music, and specifically dance, can be useful in propagating ethno-nationalist and gender-stereotypical ideas of ethnicity, as **Rumya Putcha** shows in her text. Drawing on her own positionality and own experience with the transnational South Indian dance education system, she offers meaningful insight into how this ethnically marked performance culture is bound to maintain the classist imaginaries of caste, gender, and ethnicity.

---

14   To name only a few central publications: Philipp Kasinitz and Marco Martiniello, eds., *Ethnic and Racial Studies* 42, Special Issue: "Music, Migration and the City" (2019); Jason Toynbee and Byron Dueck, *Migrating Music* (London: Routledge, 2012); Tina Ramnarine, ed., *Ethnomusicology Forum* 16, no. 1, Special Issue: "Musical Performance in the Diaspora" (2007).

The present volume gathers various and diverse perspectives on the relationships between music and democracy that are based on contributions to the international conference "Participatory Approaches to Music & Democracy," the 2018 edition of isaScience (mdw—University of Music and Performing Arts Vienna). In addition to selected conference participants and keynote speakers, this volume also includes other invited authors that we chose to adequately represent the thematic breadth of political participation, democracy, and music.

References

Adlington, Robert and Esteban Buch. *Finding Democracy in Music.* London: Routledge, 2021.

Ajotikar, Rasika. "Reflections on the Epistemic Foundations of Music in Modern India through the Lens of Caste: A Case from Maharashtra, India." In *Ethnomusicology Matters: Influencing Social and Political Realities,* edited by Ursula Hemetek, Marko Kölbl, and Hande Sağlam, 135–62. Vienna: Böhlau, 2019.

Beyer, Wolfgang and Monica Ladurner. *Im Swing gegen den Gleichschritt. Die Jugend, der Jazz und die Nazis.* Salzburg: Residenz Verlag, 2011.

Bohlman, Philip. *Focus: Music, Nationalism, and the Making of the New Europe.* New York: Routledge, 2011.

Boisits, Barbara, ed. *Musik und Revolution. Die Produktion von Identität und Raum durch Musik in Zentraleuropa 1848/49.* Vienna: Hollitzer, 2013.

Crouch, Colin. *Coping with Post-Democracy.* Cambridge: Fabian Society, 2000.

Hemetek, Ursula, Marko Kölbl, and Hande Sağlam, eds. *Ethnomusicology Matters: Influencing Social and Political Realities.* Vienna: Böhlau, 2019.

Hesmondhalgh, David. "Have Digital Communication Technologies Democratized the Media Industries?" In *Media and Society,* edited by James Curran and David Hesmondhalgh, 6th ed., 101–20. London: Bloomsbury, 2019.

Hofman, Ana. "Disobedient: Activist Choirs, Radical Amateurism, and the Politics of the Past after Yugoslavia." *Ethnomusicology* 64, no. 1 (2020): 89–109.

Kasinitz, Philipp and Marco Martiniello, eds. *Ethnic and Racial Studies* 42, Special Issue: "Music, Migration and the City" (2019).

Levi, Erik. *Music in the Third Reich.* Basingstoke: Macmillan, 1994.

Love, Nancy. *Musical Democracy.* Albany, NY: State University of New York Press, 2006.

———. *Trendy Fascism: White Power Music and the Future of Democracy.* Albany, NY: State University of New York Press, 2016.

Mecking, Sabine. "Gelebte Empathie und donnerndes Pathos. Gesang und

Nation im 19. Jahrhundert." In *Musik—Macht—Staat. Kulturelle, soziale und politische Wandlungsprozesse in der Moderne*, edited by Sabine Mecking and Yvonne Wasserloos, 99–126. Göttingen: V&R Unipress, 2012.

Potter, Pamela. *Most German of the Arts: Musicology and Society from the Weimar Republic to the End of Hitler's Reich*. New Haven: Yale University Press, 1998.

Ramnarine, Tina, ed. "Musical Performance in the Diaspora." Special Issue, *Ethnomusicology Forum* 16, no. 1 (June 2007).

Rathkolb, Oliver. *Führertreu und gottbegnadet. Künstlereliten im Dritten Reich*. Vienna: Österreichischer Bundesverlag, 1991.

Redepenning, Dorothea. "'... unter Blumen eingesenkte Kanonen ...'. Substanz und Funktion nationaler Musik im 19. Jahrhundert." *Das Andere. Eine Spurensuche in der Musikgeschichte des 19. und 20. Jahrhunderts*, edited by Annette Kreutziger-Herr, 225–45. Frankfurt/Main: Lang, 1998.

Small, Christopher. *Musicking: The Meanings of Performing and Listening*. Middletown, CT: Wesleyan University Press, 1998.

Toynbee, Jason and Byron Dueck. *Migrating Music*. London: Routledge, 2012.

Trümpi, Fritz. *The Political Orchestra: The Vienna and Berlin Philharmonics during the Third Reich*. Chicago: University of Chicago Press, 2016.

Part 1:
From Recorded Democracy
to Digital Participation?

Entrepreneurial Tapists

Underground Music Reproduction and Distribution
in the US and USSR, 1960s and 1970s

Marsha Siefert

Abstract: This chapter takes a participatory approach to the reproduction
of live music performance by looking at the history of "bootleg" sound
recordings in two formations during the 1960s and 1970s. The first builds
on the history of how opera lovers, mostly in concert and sometimes in
conflict with formal opera institutions and commercial recording companies, created their own community for reproduced live opera performances
through surreptitious live recording, record producing, distributing, cat-
aloging, trading, and collecting. I will relate these activities to the world
of *magnitizdat*, the live music recordings in the USSR that were also reproduced and circulated through trusted networks. The aim of looking
at both of these twentieth-century forms of music reproduction is to ask
questions about how music listeners responded to perceived limitations of
formal music industries by creating participatory networks that identified,
reproduced, and circulated recorded music that corresponded to their
preferences and ideas about authenticity, aesthetics, and direct experience
before the internet age.

Marsha Siefert[1] is Associate Professor of History at Central European University, Vienna. Her research and teaching focuses on cultural and commu-

---

1   I would like to thank Joe Pearce, the late Ed Wolfe, and Seth Winner of the Vocal
    Record Collectors Society, who have taught me so much about the glories of
    the singing voice. I would also like to thank Yassen Zassoursky for the Melodiya
    albums from a wide variety of Russian music, which opened my sonic world.
    I am indebted to Victor Taki and Alexander Semyonov for helping me obtain
    recordings at Moscow's Gorbushka Market, to Karl Hall for an elusive copy of
    Lysenko's Ukrainian opera, and to Svetlana Kolesnik for a tape recording of
    Schnittke in the days before the explosion of online music. My musical pursuits
    were facilitated by my friends Elena Androunas in Moscow and in Philadelphia,
    the late Joe Pote. This chapter would not have been realized without Fritz
    Trümpi, who encouraged me to return to writing on music history. Finally, I
    would like to thank the two anonymous reviewers for their erudition and careful
    reading of an earlier version of this essay.

nications history, particularly media industries and public diplomacy, from the nineteenth century to the present. Recent published work on Cold War culture appears in *Socialist Internationalism in the Cold War* and *Cold War Crossings*; her most recent edited book is *Labor in State-Socialist Europe, 1945–1989: Contributions to a History of Work*.

As a historian, reading about contemporary discussions of the digital revolution in music, especially the new modes of reproduction and distribution, I could not help but reflect upon these issues in the pre-internet world. Like the stimulating scholarly "rewinding of the phonographic regime,"[2] I, too, fastened onto the role of magnetic tape in revolutionizing post-World War II music and musicking. In music school, I learned about the role of tape technology in music composition and later studied how tape aided song dubbing and soundtrack production in Hollywood film.[3] In life, I encountered innovative uses of magnetic tape for music reproduction and distribution in two otherwise seemingly unrelated practices—American "private" opera recordings and the circulation of Soviet bard song on tape.

One might argue that these two forms from two contrasting, in fact oppositional, political systems of those years are not comparable, or that comparing them must begin from the high politics of capitalism and communism. But I propose to view the phenomena from the point of view of participatory music culture, as was the invitation for the first iteration of this text. Both practices engage people who do not find the established music industry that selects, produces, and distributes sound recordings to be sufficient or inclusive regarding music genre, performers, styles, or aesthetics. Those whom I have called "entrepreneurial tapists" adopted practices from the state or commercial recording industries to create their own sometimes parallel—and even complementary—versions of reproduced musical performances they deemed worthy.

The title of this chapter is emblematic of terms used in the discussion of both of these musical phenomena and practices. Talking about "tapists" builds on the nominative forms in English like artist and vocalist and helps to identify the link between technology and its human agency; paraphrasing Walter Benjamin, the mechanical reproduction of music requires someone to

---

2   Andrea F. Bohlman and Peter McMurray, "Tape: Or, Rewinding the Phonographic Regime," *Twentieth-Century Music* 14, no. 1 (2017): 3–24.
3   Marsha Siefert, "Image/Music/Voice: Song Dubbing in Hollywood Musicals," *Journal of Communication* 45, no. 2 (Spring 1995): 44–64.

produce the "master" copy.[4] Further, as Katz has rightly identified, Benjamin was "wrong" about how recording emancipated music from ritual. As explored here, "reproductions, no longer bound to the circumstances of their creation, generate new experiences, traditions, and indeed rituals, wherever they happen to be."[5]

Recording a music performance for personal use is an allowed form of participation in both societies, but reproducing it for trade is a "gray" area and selling it to consumers accounts for its "entrepreneurial" nature. The appellation of "bootleg" to this genre of reproduced LPs or tapes is also common, although strictly speaking, they are not "bootlegs," since they are not reproducing music that has been "legitimately" issued by official recording entities; quite the contrary. The term "bootleg" came to be used in the commercial recording industry outside of the USSR with reference to unreleased studio recordings, rehearsals, outtakes, alternate versions, and amateur live recordings that are reproduced and sold "illegally"; now in contemporary music it can even be used to sell these versions of a popular artist.[6] Nonetheless, "bootleg" has come to be applied to the reproduction of these recordings for sale or, in the Soviet case, especially in the reproduction of smuggled rock music.[7] Arguably, the term bootleg can be extended to the world of state-sponsored sound recording if private/amateur sound recordings are reproduced and distributed outside the state music recording industry.[8]

And how is it best to refer to and compare the circumstances of their circulation and perhaps even the "ritual" of their communal exchange and listening

---

4   Elaborations of Walter Benjamin's 1935 essay abound in research on sound recording. For an authoritative recent account, see Timothy D. Taylor, "The Commodification of Music at the Dawn of the Era of 'Mechanical Music,'" chapter 3 in his *Music in the World* (Chicago: University of Chicago Press, 2017), 50–73.

5   Mark Katz, *Capturing Sound: How Technology Has Changed Music*, rev. ed. (Berkeley: University of California Press, 2010), 17–18.

6   See, e.g., *Bob Dylan: The Bootleg Series* (Columbia Legacy, 1991–2021), 16 vols.

7   The clearest definition, derived from American popular music, is offered by Lee Marshall, "For and Against the Record Industry: An Introduction to Bootleg Collectors and Tape Traders," *Popular Music* 22, no. 1 (2003): 58; for the economics of tape reproduction, see Anna Kan, "Living in the Material World: Money in the Soviet Rock Underground," in *Dropping Out of Socialism: The Creation of Alternative Spheres in the Soviet Bloc*, ed. Juliane Fürst and Josie McLellan (Lanham, MD: Lexington, 2016), 267, 271, 273.

8   Andrea Bohlman uses the term to describe compact cassette tapes that were circulated in late socialist Poland prior to the Solidarity movement. She suggests that they were precursors to the "bootleg" economy of Solidarity itself. "Making Tapes in Poland: The Compact Cassette at Home," *Twentieth-Century Music* 14, no. 1 (2017): 130.

experience? In the Soviet case, even during Stalinism, the networks among musicians and performers were discussed in terms of official—meaning belonging to the musicians union—and unofficial, for music practices, from composition to performance to reproduction, that took place outside the union's imprimatur.[9] For the commercial recording industry, colorful catchphrases like "piracy on the high Cs" appear regularly along with "the musical underground."[10] Given the culturally overlapping play on words from Dostoevsky's "Notes from Underground," I have chosen to use that term in describing the cultural milieu for both.

The comparison might at first seem spurious—should we not compare forms of popular music, or similar genres at least? In this case, while seemingly far apart, both forms of recorded singing shared values in live performance, relied on an amenity to a taped version, and featured sung performances that, for reasons of content or performance style, would not be appropriate for or appropriated by the official music industry.

Choosing these two forms of underground circulated live vocal performances also helps to give agency, whether in a "democratic" society or "late Soviet socialism," to those who expressed dissatisfaction with the prevailing music industry choices. Their activities in taping live performances and developing appropriate modes for duplication, distribution, listening, and curating illuminate the formation of "trusted" networks of listeners. Admittedly, opera bootleggers and Soviet guitar poets are located in very different formal musical communities, much less political entities. However, by looking for the gray areas and paying attention to practices by these entrepreneurial tapists, we can ask whether there is a similarity in the fluidity and complexity of social relations. By looking at participation in these communities, the goal is to show some "complicity" or at least toleration/cooperation in the formal and informal systems of musical reproduction.

Another reason for choosing these two phenomena—bootleg opera and guitar poetry—is that the choice excludes rock music, which has dominated the analysis of underground music in this period. Not surprisingly, the Soviet and state-socialist rock scene attracted a great deal of attention from the late 1980s and early 1990s until today, as *perestroika* opened the USSR to on-site

---

9   For a useful discussion of these networks see Kiril Tomoff, "'Most Respected Comrade ...': Patrons, Clients, Brokers and Unofficial Networks in the Stalinist Music World," *Contemporary European History* 11, no. 1 (2002): 33–34.

10   Peter Davis uses both terms in his articles: "Piracy on the High Cs," *Music and Musicians* (May 1973): 38–40, and installments of "The Musical Underground: A Brief Look at the Tape Scene," *Musical Newsletter* 6, no. 1 (1976): 17–18.

research.[11] The scholarly focus on rock, especially smuggled recordings of the Beatles and the Rolling Stones, has played into the post-Cold War narrative about "how the Beatles rocked the Kremlin," the name of a widely circulated documentary film,[12] and emphasized music imported from the West. Perhaps the juxtaposition of pirated opera recordings with Soviet-produced "guitar poetry" can reveal participants' motivations and musical desires beyond the Cold War political frame.[13]

This comparison has some other advantages. It allows us to look at the way in which recording technology was used in creative ways to mirror the formal system of record production, distribution, and critique. The materiality of the recordings, whether they are LPs reproduced from tape or reel-to-reel copies, demonstrates how enterprising tapists establish their tapes or LPs as "authentic," documenting the performance, the tapist/producer, and later curated collections.

Of course, the response of the formal recording industry to these informal endeavors varies in each country but, as I will try to show, a certain leniency in both recorded music cultures operated within limits, depending upon who produced and who shared what with whom. In both cases the perceived audience was sufficiently niche that it was not deemed worth pursuing by the authorities except under certain circumstances that will be noted below. Often these same audiences also bought sound recordings marketed through record shops and formal organizations, so the authorities tacitly at least recognized a potential synergy for consumers, buyers, and collectors.

Nonetheless, before proceeding, the stark differences between the music industries—indeed, the political systems and social conditions—of the two Cold War superpowers must be acknowledged. The USSR was a one-party state and cultural industries were state controlled; in the postwar world, the Soviet

---

11 See Timothy W. Ryback, *Rock around the Bloc: A History of Rock Music in Eastern Europe and Soviet Union* (New York: Oxford University Press, 1990); Irina Orlova, "Notes from the Underground: The Emergence of Rock Culture," in *Mass Culture and Perestroika in the Soviet Union*, ed. Marsha Siefert (New York: Oxford University Press, 1991), 66–71; Sabrina P. Ramet, *Rocking the State: Rock Music and Politics in Eastern Europe and Russia* (Boulder, CO: Westview Press, 1994); Thomas Cushman, *Notes from Underground: Rock Music Counterculture in Russia.* (Albany, NY: SUNY Press, 1995); William Jay Risch, ed., *Youth and Rock in the Soviet Bloc: Youth Cultures, Music, and the State in Russia and Eastern Europe* (Lanham, MD: Lexington Books, 2015).

12 *How the Beatles Rocked the Kremlin* (dir. Leslie Woodhead, 2009).

13 For an elaboration, see Ewa Mazierska, "Introduction" in *Popular Music in Eastern Europe: Breaking the Cold War Paradigm*, ed. Ewa Mazierska (London: Springer, 2016), 1–27.

efforts to improve social conditions and provide desired consumer goods were put to the test in various exchanges. These conditions help to make the "West"—even "imagined"—as desirable to many in Soviet society.[14] Decades of research on the cultural Cold War, embracing metaphors like a "cultural contest" and a "nylon curtain,"[15] have emphasized relations conditioned by political systems. Here, focusing on bottom-up, participatory practices does not dismiss these very real differences. However, this essay attempts to look at everyday life as experienced within very real constraints and how active music listeners found ways to create their own cultural practices using the available technologies and creative energies. The perceived power of high politics can sometimes overshadow the vitality and even similarity of bottom-up practices.

The impulse to compare or contextualize the practices is not mine alone. In the introduction to a project on French, Italian, and Soviet "cultures of dissent," the organizers name it a "difficult comparison."[16] In one of the most stimulating analyses of the circulation of *magnitizdat*, literally tape publishing, in the USSR, the phenomenon is described in terms of its Soviet and post-Soviet existence, as well as in comparison to its paper counterpart: *samizdat*.[17] Of the manifestation that I will discuss in this article—"guitar poetry"—another scrupulous commentator recognizes the transnational limits of the genre. By comparing Soviet "guitar poetry" to other examples as a progressive or socialist transnational form, he finds complementary genres in milieus on both sides of the Iron Curtain during the Cold War; however, the songs themselves did not travel due to the linguistic embeddedness of the lyrics.[18] Still, the similarity of

---

14   See, for example, the discussion of the "imagined West" in Gyorgy Péteri, ed., *Imagining the West in Eastern Europe and the Soviet Union.* (Pittsburgh: University of Pittsburgh Press, 2010).

15   Amidst the extensive bibliography on Cold War culture, for "contest," see David Caute, *The Dancer Defects: The Struggle for Cultural Supremacy during the Cold War* (Oxford: Oxford University Press, 2003); for variations on the "iron curtain," see György Péteri, "Nylon Curtain—Transnational and Transsystemic Tendencies in the Cultural Life of State-Socialist Russia and East-Central Europe," *Slavonica* 10, no. 2 (2004): 113–23.

16   Teresa Spignoli and Claudia Pieralli, "Forme culturali del dissenso alle due sponde della cortina di ferro (1956–1991): Problemi, temi e metodi di una difficile comparazione," *Between* 10, no. 19 (2020): i–xxxiv.

17   J. Martin Daughtry, "'Sonic Samizdat': Situating Unofficial Recording in the Post-Stalinist Soviet Union," *Poetics Today* 30, no. 1 (2009): 27–65.

18   Rossen Djagalov, "Guitar Poetry, Democratic Socialism, and the Limits of 1960s Internationalism," *The Socialist Sixties: Crossing Borders in the Second World*, ed. Anne E. Gorsuch and Diane P. Koenker (Bloomington: Indiana University Press, 2013), 148–66.

the phenomena warrants notice.[19] Live opera recordings, on the other hand, derived from one of the earliest transnational music phenomena when the language issue had already been debated and resolved in a variety of ways over the 400 years of opera performance. What will emerge as significant in both cases, as will be discussed, is the authenticity of the performance, whether marred by the risk-taking of live performance or the lack of a conventionally "beautiful voice."

The desire to compare is embodied in the question asked by the editors of the two-volume *Encyclopedia of Informality*: Is Russia a special case? This essay in the encyclopedia, which includes entries on *magnitizdat* as well as other forms of "underground" text and music circulation worldwide, including guerilla radio and bootleg recording, examines the embeddedness of informality and the way in which informality is associated with formal rules. It concludes that bending the rules may be more about social circle and context than about geography or one particular country and that seeking the area between "no but yes" is a way to examine both ambivalence and complexity.[20]

In the discussion that follows, I will describe each genre of bootleg recording in terms of its history and technology, its starred practitioners, its producers and distributors, and its relation to the authorities. The goal will be to see how viewing both practices as participatory can elaborate the concept in music cultures from below—and before digitization.

---

19 A comparison that might yield more similarities would look at the "recordings" of international socialism, such as the fifteen-year run of the US record label Paredon, which between 1970 and 1985 produced fifty albums of protest songs and speeches derived from one founder's friendship with Pete Seeger and Paul Robeson. The label was also produced in New York City, funded "on a shoestring," and obtained some of its material anonymously in "clandestine" ways through an intermediary. A difference with the current phenomenon is that it used a local pressing plant, was funded and distributed openly (although the founders had FBI files), and was not genre specific but political. The inventory was purchased by Folkways Records in 1991. Barbara Dane, "Paredon Records: Reflecting on 50 Years of Paredon" (2020), https://folkways.si.edu/paredon/reflecting.

20 Svetlana Barsukova and Alena Ledeneva, "Concluding Remarks to Volume 2: Are Some Countries More Informal than Others: The Case of Russia," in *The Global Encyclopaedia of Informality* (London: UCL Press, 2018), 2:487–92.

Bootleg Opera Recordings

History and Technology

Record piracy is coexistent with the development of the recording industry in the opening years of the twentieth century.[21] Fledgling sound recording companies dubbed records for distribution under another label and at least one opera fan bootlegged opera performances on cylinders from his prompter's box at the Metropolitan Opera between 1901 and 1904.[22] Edison's cylinder machine was capable of both recording and playback, but lost to the Victor Company's convenience and marketing of playback-only vinyl records.[23] Vocal records dominated due to their acoustic superiority and opera arias, while a small portion of the production, lent legitimacy to the recording industry.

The coming of radio and electric sound recording in the mid-1920s created a new situation for the recording industries and hence for recorded opera as well. "Electric recordings" relied on a microphone for amplifying the vibrations of the singer's voice but were still recorded "live." Radio had an immediate impact in presenting to the public the singing voice "amplified" by the microphone, thereby bringing new-style singers like crooners into the recording limelight. Opera gained its regular, though limited, place on the radio primarily through the "live broadcasts from the Met," which began in 1931. Importantly for pirate records, broadcasts of most radio programs through the 1940s, including the Met Opera broadcasts, were recorded on discs as "soundchecks" and often stored in the corner of a station or network. These soundchecks became a foundation of the opera live recording industry.

Enter magnetic tape in the late 1940s. Originally used for recording film soundtracks, magnetic recording made possible the mixing of tracks from several sound sources.[24] The arrival of magnetic recording meant several things

---

21 For more on the so-called Mapleson cylinders see Robert Angus, "Pirates, Prima Donnas, and Plain White Wrappers. The Record Underground from Mapleson to the Seventies," *High Fidelity* 26 (December 1976): 77–78.

22 Nicholas E. Limansky, *Early 20th Century Opera Singers* (New York: YBK Publishers, 2016), "Introduction."

23 Marsha Siefert, "The Home Audience. Sound Recording and the Marketing of Musical Taste in Early 20th Century America," in *Audiencemaking*, ed. James S. Ettema and D. Charles Whitney (Beverly Hills, CA: Sage, 1994), 186–214; Marsha Siefert, "How the Talking Machine Became a Musical Instrument: Technology, Aesthetics, and the Capitalization of Culture," *Science in Context*, Special Issue: "Technology: Culture, Politics, Aesthetics," ed. Alfred J. Rieber and Marsha Siefert (Summer 1995): 417–50.

24 Steve Jones, "The Cassette Underground," *Popular Music and Society* 14, no. 1 (1990): 75–84.

for those who were to become the opera pirates. First, and most obviously, the availability of consumer reel-to-reel tape recorders meant that for the first time since cylinders, recording live performances *in situ* was practical, even if awkward. Stories of how a reel-to-reel tape recorder could be smuggled into the theater in a briefcase, with the microphone up the raincoat sleeve began in this era.

Ironically, the arrival of magnetic tape in the recording studio gave the new opera pirates a reason for being. Magnetic tape allowed for the manipulation of recording through editing techniques. Rather than "dubbing" an original performance, now a single track could be dubbed, or several performances could be "edited together" to achieve a perfection not always available in nature. One of the most famous studio tinkerings was when Elizabeth Schwarzkopf supplied Kirsten Flagstad's high Cs in her recording of Isolde in the Wagner opera.[25] Opera afficionados felt they could no longer trust what appeared on disc as a "record" of a performance.[26]

The possibility of "over-engineering" also meant that some values, like spontaneity, risk, "presence" (a sound engineering term similar to Benjamin's term "aura"), and operatic vocal excess were devalued in favor of accuracy, con-sistency, and blend achieved, according to opera pirates, through technological tricks. In contrast, the bootleg recordings were valued for being "live." Live performance is "authentic, with all its flaws, where a studio recording is note-perfect but sterile."[27] In live performance, the stakes are higher than if mistakes can be corrected by tape. The flaws, the tempo, the high note held longer, the difficult passage taken faster—these "feats" of live performance become part of the thrill of listening.

Live recordings also circumvented the "legal" limitations of the record-ing industry: singers often had exclusive contracts with individual record companies—RCA, Columbia, etc.—and could not record together even if they sang together onstage. Ideal casts and occasional pairings onstage offered the potential for something new, something extraordinary to emerge on a "hot night," a performance known to opera fans for having superseded the ordinary to a peak experience.[28] Even around 1980, when the record companies began

---

25   Will Crutchfield, "In Opera, 'Live' Is Livelier, but Also Riskier," *New York Times*, July 15, 1990, 44.

26   The record industry also made use of voice substitution in more popular genres. See Marsha Siefert, "Image/Music/Voice," 44–64.

27   Alan G. Ampolsk, "Piracy on the High C's," *New York* (January 29, 1979): 95–96.

28   Crutchfield, "In Opera," 1.

to notice the market for live performances, they patched together various rehearsals and performances, sound-engineered into a whole.[29]

Finally, the pirate tapes of live performance allow for literally "collected memory." Being there—"I heard Callas in Dallas in '56"—is a memory that can be collected and re-collected in its retelling. The recording represents an equally important artifactual memory. It becomes part of the collection, and its very specific musical content is incorporated into the knowledge base that opera lovers share and debate. The act of collecting and the comparison of performances are considered an active, participatory way to be part of opera performance.

Therefore, not only did the bootleg tapes of live performances come to stand, for many of the operagoers of the time, as "real opera," but also the radio broadcasts, both contemporary and the airchecks of the past, took on added value as an "authentic" operatic experience. For a few enterprising men, these tapes became the foundation of a small distribution network that bound together singers, record producers, vocal record collectors, and listeners.

The Singers and their Songs

Tapes of complete live performances of operas were the norm. Some operas were rarely performed, others were obscure. Some were performed with famous conductors, performed with a distinctive cast, featured star singers, or were performed at a major opera house. Some were taped broadcast recordings, so common on the radio from the 1930s.[30] Wagner's "Ring Cycle" was a particular favorite, especially since it was less frequently recorded than Verdi or Mozart.[31] With all this in mind, however, the pirates became known particularly for their multiple recordings of the divas—the star sopranos—especially those who were less available on commercial recordings and who had voices that emphasized their performances as singing actresses.

---

29   Nicholas E. Limansky, *Pirates of the High Cs: Opera Bootlegging in the 20th Century* (New York: YBK Publishers, 2020), 71. In Jan Neckers's review of this book, he adds European details to Limansky's New York-centered descriptions. As he notes, "This is a book for us; avid collectors of pirated recordings from the mid-sixties to the end of the century." http://www.operanostalgia.be/html/L imansky-pirates.html.

30   For the role of the Metropolitan Opera in the hierarchy of performance venues as well as an important source of both commercial and private recordings, see Marsha Siefert, "The Metropolitan Opera and the American Century: Opera Singers, Europe and Cultural Politics," *Journal for Arts Management, Law and Society* 33, no. 4 (Winter 2004): 298–315.

31   Crutchfield, "In Opera," 23.

The one singer who crossed the boundary between the formal opera world of stardom and the pirate kingdom was Maria Callas.[32] At last count, there are at least sixty-five live performances with Callas. While now available on YouTube and remastered CDs, her high E-flat in the triumphal scene of Verdi's *Aida* is one of the frequently shared moments.[33] Other "must-haves" are her bel canto performances in Donizetti's operas.[34] While Callas also formally recorded many operas in the studio, the discussion of her weight and her interpretations backed the large sales of these live pirated recordings. Her voice in particular attracted comment: it was heard as "tortured," or "shrill," or "just plain ugly."[35] The scholarship on Maria Callas and pirate tapes is extensive,[36] but one example may illustrate. The recording company EMI had planned to record Verdi's *La Traviata* in the 1950s; however, they could not include their star, Maria Callas, in one of her most famous roles because she had already recorded it with the Italian label Cetra and was prohibited from recording it with another company for five years. Amidst complicated dealings among companies and agents, it still had not materialized as late as 1968. Into the gap came several pirated recordings that were hunted "with a vengeance," with three pirate labels issuing a live 1955 performance from La Scala, another of a 1952 Mexico City performance, and yet another of a 1958 Covent Garden performance; by the end of 1974 at least four different complete performances had been issued on "private labels."[37]

Magda Olivero, popular in Italy, was a second favorite, her singing available in at least seventy live performances. After dissatisfaction with professional life and the coming of World War II, she retired, but then returned to sing onstage ten years later in 1951. In the United States, she was known by the mid-1960s through her pirate recordings. According to one description, Olivero was willing to "mold, shove, and mangle" her voice "into countless colors and emotions in order to serve the music." She had to find ways to "make her voice

---

32   On the complexity of the stardom of Maria Callas in the American context, see Siefert, "The Metropolitan Opera and the American Century," 307–10.

33   Maria Callas, Act 2 Finale ("Gloria all'Egitto") from *Aida* by Giuseppe Verdi, Mexico, 1951, BJR LP 151, https://www.youtube.com/watch?v=xTjUi_tSzjk.

34   Crutchfield, "In Opera," 23.

35   These adjectives and more are cited in Nina Sun Eidsheim, "Maria Callas's Waistline and the Organology of Voice," *The Opera Quarterly* 33, nos. 3–4 (January 2018): 251.

36   David Hamilton, "Who Speaks for Callas?" *High Fidelity* 29 (January 1979); Anthony Tommasini, "Critic's Notebook: Giving Those Callas Bootleg Tapes a Road Test," *New York Times*, January 9, 2003; Wayne Koestenbaum, "Maria Callas and Her Fans," *Yale Review* 79, no. 1 (1989): 1-20.

37   This story along with subsequent versions, including the 1980 EMI Lisbon *Traviata*, are told by Real La Rochelle, "Maria Callas and La Traviata: The Phantom of EMI," *ASRC Journal* 19, nos. 2–3 (February 1989): 54–61.

beautiful," as her art was often extreme and brutal.[38] Due to these qualities and her rarified repertoire, commercial companies were not willing to make the investment.[39] However, in 1975, at the age of sixty-five, she was invited to sing three performances of Tosca at the Met: "Her prodigious technique and breath control spoke of a bygone era."[40]

During the 1950s and 1960s, the Turkish soprano Leyla Gencer came to be known as "Queen of the Pirates." She was recorded in pirated live performances in over twenty different operas—some in "two salable versions by two rival pirates!"[41] She sang nineteen roles at La Scala between 1957 and 1983 but was often compared unfavorably as "the poor man's Callas" and so was "shamefully neglected by the recording companies."[42] When asked, Gencer was delighted that the pirate recordings exist and "keeps quite a collection [herself], supplied by [her] friends," even though she realizes that the "risk of a bad performance might end up on records."[43] According to the pirates, Gencer was perfect because her "uninhibited dramaticism was, aurally, extremely satisfying."[44] They loved her as "one who prowls a stage like a wild thing confined behind bars." Hurling "imprecations like no one in the business," she was perfect to wear the crown for those who valued singing over the top.[45]

As illustrated by the record catalogs created by the "live opera" record companies, however, the range of taste and popularity extended beyond these soprano divas. To take an example from one undated 1950s newsletter:

> The September release will feature two complete operas and a solo record. First of the operas is Rossini's Zelmira, initially produced in 1822 [...]. The singers, headed by Virginia Zeani,[46] are excellent [...]. Second opera is the most famous production by the Brazilian composer, Antonio Carlos

---

38   Limansky, Pirates, 103.

39   Limansky, Pirates, 100–10.

40   Ira Siff, "Magda Olivero, 104, the Last Great Verismo Soprano, Has Died," Opera News (September 8, 2014).

41   Susan Gould, "Leyla Gencer, Queen of Pirate Recordings," High Fidelity 26 (September 1976): 75. By 2020, over seventy-five of her performances have been reproduced on pirate CDs; Limansky, Pirates, 113.

42   Nicholas E. Limansky, "Vincenzo Bellini: Norma," Opera Quarterly 21, no. 3 (2005): 551–55.

43   Gould, "Leyla Gencer," 75.

44   Limansky, "Vincenzo Bellini," 552. Limansky considered Gencer to be a sort of "bel canto Magda Olivero," 554.

45   Limansky, Pirates, 112.

46   Almost all of Zeani's recordings in sixty-nine major roles were pirates; a commercial recording of selections ("Operatic Recital") from the 1950s was finally commercially issued (Decca 480 8187) over 60 years later in 2015 and reviewed by Scott Barnes in Opera News (March 2015).

Gomes, *Il Guarany*, first produced at Milano in 1870 [...] this can also be recommended without qualm. [...] Had Kirsten Flagstad lived she would have been 70 in July. To commemorate her birthday [...].[47]

Or, to take a later example:

"An Event of Unparalleled Importance!!" For the first time on records, absolutely complete and in very good sound, the famous 1954 La Scala production of Spontini's *La Vestale* [....] Maria Callas was at the height of her musical powers, while her dramatic talents burned more ferociously with each new performance [....] La Callas smolders with dramatic conviction."[48]

Whatever the performance, whomever the singer, one unwritten rule is that a tapist cannot use a tape "to ridicule an artist or to harm a reputation."[49]

Recording, Production, and Distribution Networks

Contextualizing operatic bootleg records in the 1960s and 1970s, especially for the United States, requires a market reality check. In 1974 figures, the proportion of the market allotted to classical music was four percent, with opera a very small subset of these sales.[50] The American center of this bootlegging and dubbing activity was the environs of New York City, with its Metropolitan Opera among its premiere recording sites. But the network of tapists was worldwide. Enterprising producers of "private" opera recordings received tapes of live performances at major opera houses throughout Europe and beyond. Performances were taped in house or from radio broadcasts, and then acquired by the pirates for their special, limited issues. Many tapists who tape for private listening come from the professions, from teachers and doctors to other professions.[51]

Among the first to capitalize this venture was Edward J. ("Eddie") Smith (1931–1984). EJS records copied the practices of a commercial company, including a catalog complete with numbers, different labels, and a newsletter with

---

47 One-page postal announcement for "The Golden Age of Opera." These announcements were obtained from the R&H Clippings Collection of the Lincoln Center for Performing Arts Library, New York City.

48 One-page postal announcement for ERR Recordings, "Available on September 15, 1974, limited amount of sets."

49 Ampolsk, "Piracy," 95.

50 David Bicknell and Robert Philip, "Gramophone," in *The New Grove Dictionary of Music and Musicians*, ed. Stanley Sadie (London: Macmillan, 1980), 7:625. For Great Britain, the figure is ten percent and for Germany, fourteen percent.

51 One source describes a tapist in the "European underground" who is a judge: "he's a real sneak, but his tapes are unbeatable." Ampolsk, "Piracy," 95.

reviews of new releases. He created several labels, such as "The Golden Age of Opera," (1956–71; 566 releases!),[52] Unique Opera Records Corporation (1972–77), A.N.N.A. Record Company (1978–82) and the Special Label issues (1954–81). Each of his labels were printed with a catalog number, e.g., EJS-122D, along with a notice at the bottom: "Private Record Not for Sale." He reissued historic recordings, including Toscanini's earliest Wagner recording with the New York Philharmonic in 1932 (EJS-444A, "The Golden Age of Wagner") and on the other side of the LP included selected opera house recordings from Covent Garden, the Vienna Staatsoper, and the Chicago Opera Company in 1930 (EJS-444B).

His sources were sometimes studio performances or rare broadcast tapes from the interwar period. Many of the singers loaned their own private unissued and broadcast recordings and some set up private concerts in apartments that were recorded in the singers' homes.[53] Smith sold his records in brown paper sleeves with the center cut out to reveal the label. Just as the major record companies like RCA Victor and Columbia, the pirates were able to request small-run custom pressings at various record producing plants, which further muddled relations between the labels and record companies.[54]

At the production site of Ralph Ferrandina, nicknamed "Mr. Tape," a popular New York City producer, the process of copying tapes was impressive. Twenty-six reel-to-reel tape recorders and later twelve double cassette recorders were operating at the same time. Limansky states that all copies were made double-time and of multiple operas. He got used to hearing *Aida* in one ear and *Tosca* in the other, while hustling to fulfill the customers' orders. He was also in charge of mounting the masters, checking the quality, and keeping the tape machines in working order.[55]

Other labels soon joined in the 1970s. Ed Rosen's label (ERR) belonged to a new generation of pirates. Some were hopeful singers who also befriended opera stars; Rosen's collection, for example, began in friendship with the tenor Richard Tucker. Rosen also used mailings, but added more professional packag-

---

52   William Shaman, Edward Joseph Smith, William J. Collins, and Calvin M. Goodwin, EJS, *Discography of the Edward J. Smith Recordings: The Golden Age of Opera, 1956–1971* (Westport, CT: Greenwood, 1994). This first of two volumes of curated descriptions of EJS recordings is 795 pages long, with an introduction illuminating in detail the history of both pirate records and recording enthusiasts.

53   Shaman, et al., EJS, xxix.

54   Raymond R. Wile, "Record Piracy: The Attempts of the Sound Recording Industry to Protect Itself Against Unauthorized Copying 1890–1978," ARSC *Journal* 17, nos. 1–3 (January 1987): 32.

55   Limansky, *Pirates*, 47–49.

ing, libretti, and photographs.[56] New distributors arose carrying many "private labels" and other collectors, like Charles Handelman, advertised "on demand taping" from their private collections.[57]

The private record producers created an informal distribution system with different notions of quantity/profit, different stars, and a different aesthetic for a community that not only purchased but also shared their knowledge and recordings. Information about pirate recordings sometimes surfaced in the press but during the 1960s and 1970s, it was often encoded in otherwise regular catalogs of record and tape sales, ephemeral newsletters, or classified ads. As in other "underground networks," members learned from each other how to recognize traces of this underground distribution system and, indeed, to use the Soviet expression, "read between the lines" in stories about opera stars to find evidence of desirable and available material.

For example, in the late 1970s during the opera season, a one-page weekly newsletter called "Diva" circulated gossip about the Metropolitan Opera and predicted the performances to see (and eventually to tape). An occasional magazine, *Opera Fanatic*, was born from the conjunction of an opera radio show on the Columbia University station, a circulating catalog, and an enterprising disc jockey.

Many members of the musical community made use of these pirate tapes. One tapist recounted that he "tapes on demand," often for performers who are studying roles.[58] But the largest audience—and customers—for the bootleg opera recordings are opera fans and collectors of vocal art, many of whom intersect the official music community as performers, critics, music journalists, radio show hosts, university lecturers, and sound engineers.[59] They are often collectors of tapes and through their detailed description of individual performances—from the interpretation of a given phrase by a given singer to anecdotes of performance disaster—may "leak" information that suggests the existence of a tape, which then adds to its value. Through their program notes and curation, the opera pirates saw themselves as patrons of the arts and as catering to collectors' legitimate demands.[60]

---

56 For more on Ed Rosen and his recordings, see Opera Lounge, http://operalou nge.de/history/opernfanatiker.

57 In requesting tapes of a performer for a birthday present from one of the distributors, I received a printout from an early dot-matrix computer, illustrating the record distributors' adaptation to technologies for maintaining their collection as well as their business.

58 Ampolsk, "Piracy," 96.

59 Peter Davis, "Live Performance Opera—Legal and Otherwise," New York Times, June 10, 1979, 23ff.

60 Angus, "Pirates, Prima Donnas, and Plain White Wrappers," 77.

Important communities of listeners[61] are represented by vocal record collectors. Early in the 1960s, several clubs were formed in New York City that brought together collectors and experts of vocal art, with opera and art song recordings as their primary object. Some focused on the singing itself, such as the Vocal Record Collectors Society,[62] which publishes an annual recording of selections from members' collections. Other collecting communities focus on sound engineering, especially remastering older recordings, with reports published in the ARSC (Association for Recording Sound Collectors) journal. These groups overlap, with recording engineers participating in collectors' meetings and remastering/reissuing collections for institutions like the Lincoln Center Library for the Performing Arts or the Sound Archive at the British Library. These groups also represent the curators of the recordings, especially from the collectors' communities.[63] While the role of collectors is beyond the scope of this chapter, it is worth noting here that the goals of collecting—such as the accumulation of knowledge, systematic classification, as well as "records" of experience—may duplicate the functions that Benjamin feared would be extinguished by mechanical reproduction.[64]

---

61   One community of opera fans that gained attention in the late 1980s and early 1990s was represented by the "opera queens," gay men who attended the opera together and traded in opera knowledge as a form of banter. This opera community was portrayed in the plays of Terence McNally, notably *The Lisbon Traviata*, which chronicled a legendary performance that was rumored only to exist on a pirate tape; see Don Shewey, ed., *Out Front: Contemporary Gay & Lesbian Plays* (New York: Grove, 1988). Soon after the play premiered the tape was discovered and reproduced. Of the books on this fan community most prominent was Wayne Koestenbaum, *The Queen's Throat: Opera, Homosexuality, and the Mystery of Desire* (New York: Poseidon Press, 1992).

62   Joe Pearce, "The Ramblings of a Once Young Record Collector—New World Version," *Record Collector* 63, no. 3 (September 2018): 199–214. *Record Collector* is a London-based magazine begun in 1979.

63   For a taste of the immense expertise of these "vocal historians," see the assessment of the performances of Wagnerian opera in Stockholm according to the Wagnerite perspective, the pure performance perspective, the general opera lover perspective and the vocal historian/collector perspective in Joe Pearce, "Wagner in Stockholm: Great Wagnerians of the Royal Swedish Opera Recordings, 1899–1970." *The Opera Quarterly* 20, no. 3 (2004): 472–505.

64   The standard work on record collecting is Roy Shuker, *Wax Trash and Vinyl Treasures: Record Collecting as a Social Practice* (Oxon: Routledge, 2017), although it is based primarily on collectors of popular music. An insightful study of collecting more generally is Susan Stewart, *On Longing: Narratives of the Miniature, the Gigantic, the Souvenir, the Collection* (Durham, NC: Duke University Press, 1993), see especially chapter 5: "Objects of Desire."

Bootleg Opera and the Authorities

Of course, such taping is illegal. "Bootlegging" (taping a live performance) and "copying" (dubbing tapes for distribution) were explicitly prohibited in the US 1976 copyright law revision and were highly suspect before then.[65] For the most part, however, theater ushers and opera singers regarded the tapists as harmless collectors of private memorabilia. But it is not coincidental that, in the cult French film *Diva* (dir. Jean-Jacques Beneix, 1981), in which a young Parisian opera fan is taping the live stage performance of an opera singer who refuses to record, the two persons sitting behind him are record company executives.[66] Seeking the potential star, enforcing copyright, contracts, and artist royalties all affected into how bootleg opera recordings were tolerated or persecuted at any given time.

The extended network of institutions involved in the production of opera and its recordings have vested interests in the performances recorded, their distribution, and their interpretation. What the pirates record, how they distribute, and how the fans interpret sometimes challenges the hegemony of the opera institutions in controlling these aspects. Everyone from ushers to record executives knew that taping was going on, but the story goes that most in the opera world turned a blind eye toward the practice as long as the trade was in audio tapes and LPs.[67] A couple of circumstances brought about a showdown. First, the arrival of opera videos raised the financial stakes of circulating illegal tapes. Second, in the early 1980s, the Metropolitan Opera Guild, the Metropolitan Opera's official organization of large donors, began to offer selected live broadcasts from their own vault of recordings as premiums for contributions and also began to sell videos of Met performances. They sued to prevent the sale of these recordings in pirated versions. Although the case settled out of court,[68] it scared many underground distributors from advertising

---

65   Edwin McDowell, "Record Pirates: Industry Sings the Blues," *New York Times*, June 30, 1978, D 1, 12.

66   Interestingly, an ethnographic study of people who make and collect bootleg tapes of popular music in the US, from Bruce Springsteen to the Grateful Dead, opens with a detailed description of this same scene in *Diva*, noting only that the singer is American but not that she is singing opera. Memorably, they comment that *Diva* is an "allegory of devotion in an age of technological reproduction." Mark Neumann and Timothy A. Simpson, "Smuggled Sound: Bootleg Recording and the Pursuit of Popular Memory," *Symbolic Interaction* 20, no. 4 (1997): 320.

67   Harvey Phillips, "Psss! I Have Bootlegged 'Norma' for Only...," *New York Times*, September 12, 1971, HF 1.

68   Crutchfield, "In Opera," 23. He also mentioned that one singer—Jessye Norman—initiated proceedings against a "pirate."

their Met Opera recordings.[69] The Met also addressed the problem in an oblique fashion by establishing an archive for taped performances at the New York Public Library for the Performing Arts at Lincoln Center. Citing union contracts and royalties as reasons for the institutional costs of *circulating* these tapes, they made the tapes available for study but not for *collection*. The Metropolitan Opera now has an official "collective memory" but not one capable of being collected. The FBI closed down "Mr. Tape" in 1986, ostensibly because he was marketing "Live from the Met," "Dance in America," and American Ballet Theater performance videos,[70] another of the Lincoln Center performing arts groups.

But a crack in the legal scaffolding appeared abroad. In mid-1970s Italy, copyright bans were lifted from any performances over twenty years old.[71] This ruling is thought to have been tailored to release the live performances of Maria Callas, which could then be marketed in the US without restriction.[72] However, some Italian companies included among their CD collections Metropolitan Opera performances as well, marked in catalogues "not available in the US"[73]

According to one tape owner, there is some degree of guilt at the illegality of the pirate tapes, which encourages them to also purchase commercial recordings. And there is evidence from record store owners and even critics that opera fans are in fact the most knowledgeable buyers of these commercial recordings.[74] Other fans stress that they are performing a service by preserving important performances that would otherwise be lost, an important "collective" and "collected" memory of live performance and, importantly, of the star and less performed repertoire.[75] According to a curator of the EJS collection after enumerating the numerous taped performances still in the vaults of radio stations and opera companies, he affirmed that "there is an unchallengeable right

---

69   A chronological catalog beginning in 1933 of "The Metropolitan Opera on Pirate CD" compiled by Frank Hamilton in 2011 runs to 139 pages. Internet Archive, website captured on 13 September 2019., https://web.archive.org/web/20190 913000208/http://frankhamilton.org/metro/index.html.

70   Limansky, *Pirates*, 68–70. Mr. Tape's arrest was announced in *Opera News*, January 17, 1987, 6; officials seized 6,833 alleged master videocassette tapes.

71   Sam H. Shirakawa, "'Backroom' Reissues of Rare Recordings," *New York Times*, October 21, 1979.

72   Crutchfield, "In Opera," 1.

73   But of course, they were: In the 1980s I was able to purchase one in a local record store and I was able to borrow a full pirate opera vinyl recording of Donizetti's *Poliuto* (MRF-31), with Callas and Franco Corelli, from the local Philadelphia "Free Library." This opera otherwise had not been commercially recorded.

74   Crutchfield, "In Opera," 1.

75   Limansky, *Pirates*, 67.

of afficionados to have access to the great performances of the past."[76] The tapists, producers, and purchasers of live opera recordings in effect were in dialogue with the official, commercial field of opera performance and recording, active participants in creating a community that respected and preserved the performances they valued.

Bootleg Music under Communism

History and Technology

Sound recording began in imperial Russia with record producers from the Victor Company arriving to record Russian singers in the first decade of the twentieth century. Before the October Revolution, Russian bass Feodor Chaliapin had joined Caruso as a "bestseller" for the international Victor Company[77] and three record pressing plants were established in and near Moscow.[78] Concurrently, gramophone records, especially from the international Gramophone Company, were illegally duplicated and distributed, inaugurating a history of musical piracy in Russia.[79] Despite (or perhaps because of) an emphasis on agitational recordings, the Soviet recording industry failed to thrive until the mid-1930s, when the state began production in earnest and increased record production exponentially in the areas of classical music, opera, folksongs, and mass song.[80] Imports from the west, notably jazz, were smuggled to aficionados, some even in the Soviet nomenklatura, through routes later amenable to rock music.[81]

In the late 1940s, intrepid record producers distributed popular music etched on used x-ray films. Hospitals were willing to give them away, because due to their flammability—and several hospital fires—x-ray films had to be

---

76   Bill Collins, "Mining the Musical Underground: Should buried treasures be left exclusively for the pirates?" *High Fidelity* 21 (November 1971): 76.
77   F.W. Gaisberg, *The Music Goes Round* (New York: Macmillan, 1942), 26–34, 69–76.
78   Alexander Tikhonov, "Moll, Kybarth, and Company," Aʀsc *Journal* 22, no. 2 (Fall 1991), 191–99. The Aprelevka plant, established in 1910, became the foundation of the Soviet enterprise.
79   Alexander Tikhonov, "Neizvestnaya 'stoletnyaya voyna': Iz istorii muzykal'nogo piratstva v Rossii" [The Unknown "Hundred Years War": From the history of musical piracy in Russia], *Zvukorezhisser* [Sound Engineer], nos. 3, 4 & 5 (2002), https://www.russian-records.com/details.php?image_id=62731.
80   A.I. Archinov, "A Brief History of the Recording Industry in the Soviet Union," *Journal of Audio Engineering Society* 18, no. 1 (February 1970): 20–22.
81   S. Frederick Starr, *Red and Hot: The Fate of Jazz in the Soviet Union 1917–1991* (New York: Limelight Editions, 1985/1994).

destroyed at the end of each year. These record producers built their own recording machines by rigging a gramophone to a second one with a recording stylus. They worked in secret, making records one at a time. These "bone records" or *Roentgenizdat*, could then be played back on a gramophone.

From the late 1940s, "distributors" of bone records stood outside of the department store GUM or under the Kuznetsky Bridge in Leningrad. Due to the flexibility of the x-ray plates, they could fit twenty-five in each sleeve of their coat! While colloquially called the "ribs of rock," most of the songs recorded featured tangos and popular songs, with a couple of jazz standards.[82] The few Elvis Presley tunes (like "Heartbreak Hotel") represented his vocal balladry not the rhythmic thrust.[83]

X-ray records were linked to "hooliganism" and made illegal in 1958, while some record producers were sent to prison.[84] The ruling may have also been a fallout from the World Festival of Youth and Students, held in Moscow during late summer of 1957, when for the first time live and recorded music of all sorts from all over the world was played and replayed in Moscow. The world's youth was perhaps less impressed with Soviet musical achievements than had been hoped by the authorities and the Soviet youth were perhaps less resistant to the charms of popular western music than decades of Soviet education would have preferred.[85]

The early 1960s saw changes, both organizational and technological, to the Soviet music recording industry. In 1964, the state enterprise Melodiya replaced the All-Union Firm and Studio of Gramophone Recording, uniting under its auspices the sound recording studios located in Moscow, Leningrad, Tallinn, Riga, Tashkent, Vilnius, and Tbilisi, and the manufacturing plants located in the first four cities. Melodiya also controlled the 30,000 retail outlets, wholesaling

---

82 Boris Taigin, "Rastsvet i krakh podpol'noy studii gramzapisi 'Zolotaya Sobaka'" [The rise and fall of the underground recording studio "Golden Dog" (1946–1961)], *Pchela* 20 (May/June 1999), https://cont.ws/@dachnik/430816.

83 Anton Spice, "X-Ray Audio: The Documentary," filmed by P. Heartfield, written by S. Coates and A. Spice, 2016, https://thevinylfactory.com/films/x-ray-audio-soviet-bootleg-records-documentary/.

84 Ryback, *Rock around the Bloc*, 32–33.

85 On music at the 1957 festival, see Pia Koivunen, "Friends, 'Potential Friends,' and Enemies: Reimagining Soviet Relations to the First, Second, and Third Worlds at the Moscow 1957 Youth Festival," in *Socialist Internationalism in the Cold War* (Cham: Palgrave Macmillan, 2016), 219–47; Eleonory Gilburd, *To See Paris and Die: The Soviet Lives of Western Culture* (Cambridge, MA: Belknap Press, 2018), chapter 2. On the importance of educating music listeners to the Soviet modernization efforts, see Elina Viljanen, "Educating the New Listener" in *Philosophical and Cultural Interpretations of Russian Modernisation*, ed. Katja Lehtisaari and Arto Mustajoki (Oxon: Routledge, 2016), 118–35.

branches, and arrangements with external recording companies from the west, such as Emi/Angel and Le Chante du Monde.[86] According to one estimate for the late 1960s, fifty-five percent of all record releases (about 1,200) were from the classical repertoire, although they accounted for only fifteen percent of sales. The rest were about evenly divided between *estrada* and folk music.[87] According to various estimates, by the late 1960s, between 170.5 and 200 million discs were produced per year.[88]

What changed—and challenged this state monopoly on recorded sound— was the affordability and ubiquity of tape recorders in the Ussr The first viable home tape recorders became available—and legal!—in the early 1960s. By 1965, almost half a million tape recorders were produced per year and by 1970, they numbered more than a million annually.[89] Reel-to-reel tape recorders remained the norm, long after tape cassettes became the standard in North America, Europe, and Asia. The reason for this absence is that Melodiya feared that consumers might purchase classical recordings on cassette and then erase them to record what they wished. Even as late as 1984, blank cassette tapes were rare and very expensive.[90]

Magnitizdat, from a combination of the Russian words for "tape recorder" (*magnitofon*) and "publish (*izda(va)t*)," describes a form of copying and self-distributing of tape recordings. The term covers a wide range of music-related practices in the Ussr, from copies of rock albums from the west, music that was considered illegal in the Soviet Union, to home-grown music by Soviet musicians and sanctioned for distribution by the performers but not produced by Melodiya. In fact, according to Troitsky, who wrote about Soviet rock in the late 1980s, some *magnitizdat* recordings were sold right outside the Melodiya

---

86 John R. Bennett, Foreword to *Melodiya: A Soviet Russian LP Discography* (Westport, CT: Greenwood 1981); *Melodia: Celebrating 25 Years of Dedicated Service to the World of Music, 1964–1990*; https://melody.su/melody/history. In 1969, 170.5 to 200 million records were produced per year. Archinov, "A Brief History," 20–22.

87 Pekka Gronow, "Ethnic Music and Soviet Record Industry," *Ethnomusicology* 19, no. 1 (1975): 92–93.

88 Gronow, "Ethnic Music and Soviet Record Industry"; Archinov, "A Brief History," 20–22.

89 Ryback, *Rock around the Bloc*, 44; Brian A. Horne, "The Bards of Magnitizdat: An Aesthetic Political History of Russian Underground Recordings," in *Samizdat, Tamizdat, and Beyond: Transnational Media During and After Socialism*, ed. Friederike Kind-Kovács and Jessie Labov (New York: Berghahn Books, 2013), 175–89.

90 Harlow Robinson, "The Recording Behemoth of Tverskoy Boulevard (On the Soviet Recording Company Melodiya)," *High Fidelity* 36, no. 6 (June 1986): 64–65.

offices, as well as at train stations and other locations.[91] While ribs of rock were distributed in the tens of thousands, *magnitizdat* tapes numbered in the millions.[92]

The Singers and their Songs

Here I focus on one form of *magnitizdat* that epitomized the intimate connection between the vocalist, the performance, and its reproduction: "guitar poetry." In Russian it is called *avtorskaya pesnya* ("author's song," "authored song," or "songwriters' song"). As a genre it is distinguished from other forms of non-classical music like Soviet mass song, composed for individual or chorus, in service of the state;[93] from *estrada*, stage or variety songs; and from folk music.[94] Guitar poetry is also distinguished from *blatnaya pesnya*, songs from the criminal underworld, with which it shares some roots.[95] Importantly, guitar poetry is also distinguished from rock music, especially imported from the west, that also circulated in *magnitizdat*, starting from the late 1960s.[96] The audiences for these forms did not necessarily overlap. As anecdotal evidence suggests,

91   Artemy Troitsky, *Back in the USSR: The True Story of Rock in Russia* (Boston: Faber and Faber, 1987).

92   Yevgeny Yevtushenko, "Magnitofonnaia glasnost," *Nedelia* 18 (1988): 16, http://bard.ru.com/article/8/print_art.php?id=8.14.

93   Gerald Stanton Smith,*Songs to Seven Strings: Russian Guitar Poetry and Soviet "Mass Song"* (Bloomington: Indiana University Press, 1984), chapter 1: "Song in State Service."

94   See, for instance, David MacFadyen, *Red Stars: Personality and the Soviet Popular Song, 1955–1991* (Montreal: McGill-Queen's University Press, 2001), chapter 1: "Soviet Song after Stalin." For a helpful disambiguation of "popular" song in the Soviet context, see Zbigniew Wojnowski, "The Pop Industry from Stagnation to Perestroika: How Music Professionals Embraced the Economic Reform That Broke East European Cultural Networks," *Journal of Modern History* 92, no. 2 (2020): fn. 3.

95   Uli Hufen tells the authoritative story of "criminal" or "underworld" song from its origins in Odessa, with a focus on its most famous practitioner, Arkady Severnyi, but he does not discuss or include guitar poetry. *Das Regime und die Dandys. Russische Gaunerchansons von Lenin bis Putin* (Berlin: Rogner & Berhand, 2010). In his review of the book, Smith argues that *blatnaya pesnya* interpenetrates guitar poetry in both function and music. Gerald Stanton Smith, *Slavonic and East European Review* 89, no. 4 (2011): 731.

96   The bard Bulat Okudzhava persistently distinguishes this genre from the pop song (*estradnaya pesnya*, literally "stage song"), which he uses in 1988 to describe the domestic Russian rock music that emerged. Gerald Stanton Smith, "Okudzhava Marches On," *Slavonic and East European Review* 66, no. 4 (Oct. 1988): 557–58.

rock music tapes overtook bard song for many young people by the early 1970s.[97] In fact, the "textual meaningfulness" of guitar poetry was outright dismissed by one of the major subcultures listening to rock *magnitizdat*—the Soviet hippies.[98] The circulation of guitar poetry represents a particular network of taping, reproduction, and circulation that relied on live vocal performance for its sustenance and participatory community.

The practice of guitar poetry started in Leningrad in the late 1950s when the oldest of the Russian bards, Bulat Okudzhava, began performing his poetry to a seven-string guitar in private apartments. Gerald Stanton Smith, who provides a central and early account, first heard Okudzhava's voice in 1963 when a "fanatical jazz fan" in Leningrad played him an amateur tape. The fan's tape recorder, made in the GDR, was "without a cover; it needed endless cajoling and makeshift repairs."[99] Okudzhava had moved to Moscow, after his parents were "rehabilitated" in 1956, and he joined the Soviet Writer's Union in 1961. His songs were personal and, as a war veteran, anti-war, but not necessarily anti-Soviet, with cryptic references to the Soviet terror in which his father had perished. According to Stites, his performance style was simple and modest and his lyrics always authentic, whether in verses about the Arbat or an old jacket.[100]

However memorable the lyrics, they were received as music, the singing and guitar-playing central to their taped resonance and replication.[101] The acoustic guitar is central to its performance and symbolism. After Stalin's death, the seven-string guitar gained a reputation as a "democratic" instrument among youth.[102] It was also inexpensive, available, portable, and relatively easy to learn

---

97   Zhuk recounts that in Dniepropetrovsk, from the late 1950s, people could pay to record their favorite melodies as holiday greetings in recording salons (*muzykal'naya studya*) on a vinyl disc; by 1965, these recordings included the guitar poets. By 1970, however, ninety percent of the requests were for the Beatles and the Rolling Stones. The record store owner participated in the *magnitizdat* black market. Sergei I. Zhuk, *Rock and Roll in the Rocket City: The West, Identity, and Ideology in Soviet Dniepropetrovsk, 1960–1985* (Washington, DC: Woodrow Wilson Center Press, 2010), 82–84.

98   Juliane Fürst, *Flowers Through Concrete: Explorations in Soviet Hippieland* (Oxford: Oxford University Press, 2021), 243.

99   Smith, *Songs to Seven Strings*, 1.

100 Richard Stites, *Russian Popular Culture: Entertainment and Society since 1900* (Cambridge: Cambridge University Press, 1992), 134.

101 Smith, "Okudzhava Marches On," 553.

102 Danijela Lugarić Vukas, "Living *vnye*: The Example of Bulat Okudzhava's and Vladimir Vysotskii's *avtorskaia pesnia*," *Euxeinos. Culture and Governance in the Black Sea Region* 8, no. 25–26 (2018): fn. 7, 21–22.

to play. [103] For the bards, the seven-string guitar "was the absolute object of the poet's devotion as well as the symbol of his artistic freedom and autonomy."[104] The bards themselves immortalized it in song as the "silver strings,"[105] or as a "faithful companion."[106]

It is also decidedly vocal—and sung. Recited and declaimed public poetry readings mattered then, as did those that briefly flourished in Moscow's Mayakovsky Square in the late 1950s.[107] But the singing voice itself became a marker, an identifier, as well as a dramatic gesture. Platonov describes it as "bad singing," relying on simple melodies, inexpert guitar playing and "untrained, often highly idiosyncratic voices."[108] And yet, it circulated as "sung" and could arguably invoke and evoke older singing traditions that were able to blend oral traditions of performance with aural traditions of song genres that gave *magnitizdat* a longevity as song.

Vladimir Frumkin, a musicologist and Shostakovich scholar, gave shape and legitimacy to guitar poetry as music. His manifesto, "Music and Word,"[109] read at the May 1967 all-Union seminar on the problems of amateur (author's) song, held near the Petushki (Vladimir region), predicted that future historians would turn to guitar poetry as one of the most sensitive indicators of the emancipation of the individual, of the spirit of the inhabitants of Russia, and he urged the many bards present to spread guitar song beyond the cities of Moscow and St. Petersburg. His 1980 publication of Okudzhava's songs offered his appraisal of Okudzhava's significance:

> Before Okudzhava, the Soviet song industry had virtually no competition from within the country [...]. The state monopoly on songs seemed unshak-

---

103   The acoustic guitar was inexpensive in part because the USSR had hoped to encourage its use instead of electric guitars, which were produced in the GDR and Poland and hard to obtain. Engineering students set up a black market of "unofficial manufacturers" in the tens of thousands. See Starr, *Red and Hot*, 195.

104   Lugarić Vukas, "Living *vnye*," fn. 7, 21–22.

105   The title of a Vysotsky song ("Serebryanyye struny").

106   Okudzhava, cited in Vladimir Kovner, "Zolotoy vek magnitizdata" [The golden age of *magnitizdat*, part 1], *Vestnik online* 7, no. 345 (March 31, 2004), http://www.vestnik.com/issues/2004/0331/win/kovner.htm.

107   These informal readings, by poets such as Yevtushenko and Voznesensky, are also important to the personal voice emerging in *magnitizdat*. For more on this poetry, see Donald Loewen, "Blurred Boundaries: Russian Poetry and Soviet Politics during the Thaw," *Russian Literature* 87–89 (January–April 2017): 201–24.

108   Rachel Platonov, "Bad singing: *Avtorskaia Pesnia* and the Aesthetics of Metacommunication," *Ulbandus Review* 9, The 60s (2005/6): 88–89.

109   Vladimir Frumkin, "Muzyka i slovo" [Music and Word], report on a seminar in May 1967, Petushki, Vladimir Region (uploaded December 22, 1997), http://www.ksp-msk.ru/page_42.html.

able. Suddenly it was discovered that one person could compose a song and make it famous, without the Union of Soviet Composers, with its creative sections and department of propaganda, without help of popular singers, choirs and orchestra, without publishing houses, radio and television, film and record companies, editors and censors.[110]

A second singer who anchored the genre is Vladimir Vysotsky, "the unofficial bard of the official word."[111] Vysotsky's career is emblematic of the gray area between a formal and informal relation to the official culture. He is characterized variously not as anti-Soviet but "dangerously un-Soviet," arousing "bureaucratic suspicions" whenever he was formally engaged—as a theater actor, as well as on film and television. Remarkably, before his death he acted in twenty-six television or cinematic films,[112] but it was his guitar poetry that helped propel him to a peculiar kind of celebrity, able to comment on everyday Soviet life in realistic terms—and get away with it![113] He was acquainted with Okudzhava and mentioned him many times in his performances, sometimes dedicating songs to him.[114] He was allowed to record a couple of "safe songs" in the state studio, to be distributed through Melodiya, but his formal albums of guitar poetry were recorded abroad.[115]

The quality of his lyrics is often skeptically evaluated,[116] but as a singer and performer, Vysotsky's influence was considerable. He managed his notoriety by organizing hundreds of unannounced—and unauthorized (!)—"concerts" scheduled in smaller towns to avoid the attention of authorities. His audience

---

110 Vladimir Frumkin, *Bulat Okudzahva: 65 Songs* (Ann Arbor, MI: Ardis, 1980), 15, cited in Ryback, *Rock around the Bloc*, 44.

111 Smith, *Songs to Seven Strings*, 173.

112 Christopher Lazarski, "Vladimir Vysotsky and His Cult," *Russian Review* 51 (1992), 60.

113 It is his commentary on everyday Soviet life, using the terms provided by Soviet ideology, that attracts contemporary commentators in reference to the key work on late Soviet socialism: Alexei Yurchak's *Everything Was Forever, Until It Was No More: The Last Soviet Generation* (Princeton: Princeton University Press, 2006). See also Lugarić Vukas, "Living *vnye*."

114 For a curation of this relationship, based on comments Vysotsky made at his performances, see A.E. Krylov, "Bulat Okudzhava i Vladimir Vysotsky: Istoriya znakomstva" [Bulat Okudzhava and Vladimir Vysotsky: the history of an acquaintance], *Russian Literature* 77, no. 2 (2015): 197–222.

115 The albums he recorded were recorded and published outside the USSR: in Sofia (1975), at RCA in Toronto (1976), and two in Paris (1977); Lida Cope, Natalie Kononenko, Anthony Qualin, and Mark Yoffe, "Sound Recordings in the Archival Setting: Issues of Collecting, Documenting, Categorizing, and Copyright," *Slavic & East European Information Resources* 20, nos. 3–4 (2019): 100, fn. 4.

116 For one summary of the critique, see Lazarski, "Vladimir Vysotsky," 70.

arrived with tape recorders in hand. To give one idea of the extent of these live performances, an online database lists 245 live recordings of his song, "Ia ne lyublyu"—with a high variability; the tapes also include his spoken introduction to a song (avtometaparatekst).[117] These spoken introductions not only created dialogue with the participating audience but also established the particulars of the performance situation, time, and place. These introductions added value to the individual performances and also allowed fans and collectors to develop expertise on the evolution of the singer and his songs. Toward the end of his life, Vysotsky recorded songs "for posterity on quality recording equipment in the homes of Mikhail Shemiakin and Konstantin Mustafidi,"[118] but they did not diminish the value of the live performances for fans and collectors; the ambiance of the "bad recording" was also part of the genre.

Vysotsky's earliest songs were related to the "camps," as gulag prisoners were beginning to share their stories upon their return to Moscow. He also leaned heavily on the genre of "criminal" songs, sometimes crude, and later added dramatic genres to his repertoire, accumulating an oeuvre of 500 to 600 songs.[119] The guitar was central to his composition. According to his mother, he picked up his guitar, immediately played, and never studied, a claim celebrated in the fan lore.[120] Vysotsky believed that writing the verses "with guitar in hand" created more dynamic and effective lyrics, with music emerging "as a final step in the creative process."[121]

Of the major bards, Alexandr Galich's guitar poetry fits best its interpretation as a genre of dissent. Like Okudzhava he was a member of the Soviet Writers Union and like Vysotsky he was involved in filmmaking, being formally trained as an actor but making his living as a screenwriter and member of the Union of Cinematographers. He had traveled to France in the late 1950s to co-write the screenplay for a French-Soviet co-produced film, Nights of Farewell (Tretya molodost', dir. Jean Dréville and Isaak Menaker, 1965) on the life of French-born Russian choreographer Marius Petipa, a sign of privilege in Soviet cultural life. But this was not to last. Galich's first and last public concert was at the March 1968 national festival, sanctioned by the regime—the All-Russia Bard Concert with almost thirty performers. It lasted for three days and attracted 2,000 people, even though it was held far away from the center in

---

117   Cope, et al., "Sound Recordings," 88–91.
118   Cope, et al., "Sound Recordings," 100, fn. 4.
119   Smith's account of the sung antecedents of guitar poetry, range from the eighteenth-century Russian "gypsy" romance, also sung to the seven-string guitar, to the "cruel romance," as well as the criminal song. Smith, Songs to Seven Strings, chapter 4.
120   Lazarski, "Vladimir Vysotsky," 60, fn. 13.
121   Lazarski, "Vladimir Vysotsky," 62.

the Siberian town of Akademgorodok in the Novosibirsk region.[122] Among other songs like "Clouds" and "Ballad on Surplus Value," Galich sang "In Memory of B.L. Pasternak," which "castigated the hypocrisy of the literary establishment that let the great poet's death pass almost unremarked."[123] He was "virtually banned" from singing again in public.[124]

Compared to Okudzhava and Vysotsky, Galich's lyrics to his guitar poetry were more explicitly political. Two of his songs—"Night Watch" and "Stalin"— targeted the latter: "a bastard not a father." While in 1962 Stalin had been discredited, such direct criticism implied criticism of the communist system. His lyrics have also attracted much more analysis and elevation to poetry.[125] According to Garey, "the underground mechanisms that allowed Galich to dodge censors rendered the historical record of performative importance spotty."[126] As Platonov writes of guitar poetry overall,[127] Garey sees Galich's songs as a "dialogue" and emphasizes the communal aspect of the orality and evolution of his sung performance. While other guitar poets, such as Yuri Visbor, Alexander Gorodnitsky, and Yuli Kim, also performed guitar poetry during these years— and were represented in the tape repertoire—Okudzhava, Vysotsky, and Galich remain the most prominent in the genre.

Recording, Production, and Distribution Networks

Even though tape recorders had become available, their quality was not always the highest and increased re-tapings diminished the sound quality significantly.[128] The circumstances of recording and rerecording add to the sonic component of the genre. In Smith's eloquent description:

---

122 Paul R. Josephson, *New Atlantis Revisited: Akademgorodok, the Siberian City of Science* (Princeton: Princeton University Press, 1997), 299–300.

123 Seventeen Moments in Soviet History: An on-line Archive of Primary Sources. Accessed 5 June 2021. http://soviethistory.msu.edu/1956-2/literary-life-at-a-crossroads/in-memory-of-pasternak-1968/; for a translation of the "Ode," see Josephson, *New Atlantis Revisited*, 300–1.

124 Daughtry, "Sonic Samizdat," 40.

125 See, e.g., Smith's introduction to *Songs & Poems by Alexander Galich*, ed. and trans. Gerald Stanton Smith (Ann Arbor, MI.: Ardis, 1983).

126 Amy Garey, "Aleksandr Galich: Performance and the Politics of the Everyday," *Lumina: A Journal of Historical and Cultural Studies* 17 (2011): 1-13.

127 Rachel Platonov, *Singing the Self. Guitar Poetry, Community, and Identity in the Post-Stalin Period* (Evanston: Northwestern University Press, 2012).

128 Soviet sailors and occasional travelers smuggled in preferred Japanese and Western machines that were then resold or traded. Aleksei Yurchak, "Gagarin and the Rave Kids," in *Consuming Russia: Popular Culture, Sex, and Society Since Gorbachev* , ed. Adele Barker (Durham, NC: Duke University Press, 1999), 83.

There is usually considerable surface noise and distortion of sound, and quite wide variations in tape speed—repeated copying on different machines may render a voice quite unrecognizable, converting a baritone into a gabbling contralto; there is range of assorted clunks and pops as the microphone is shifted or bumped; and there is persistent background noise—some of it extraneous, like vehicles passing in the street outside, or the footsteps and voices of neighbors; and some that forms an integral part of the genre ambience—the creak of furniture, the chink of bottle against glass, the coughs and muttered comments, and, most of all, the semi-conspiratorial audience participation: requests, repartee with the singer, warm or bitter laughter, pregnant silence at the conclusion of a particular telling song followed by a bustle of relieved tension-breaking movement and murmuring.[129]

The Leningrad scene[130] is described by Vladimir Kovner, one of the most proficient and prolific tapists. He bought a tape recorder on his first payday in mid-1959 and installed it in his family's room in their communal apartment; he recorded Conover's Voa jazz programs and borrowed old records, taping romances and "gypsy songs" for his collection. In the fall, his friend brought him an Okudzhava recording made at a Leningrad party: "the tape recorder had been under the table and the recording was creepy," but "from that moment his songs became an integral part" of his life. In the early 1960s, Kovner's tapes were played on the radio at lunchtime at the Karl Marx factory where he worked until the party leadership happened to listen. He was also involved in the organization of Okudzhava's first "semi-official" concert in Leningrad arranged by two trade union activists at the Pulkovo Observatory. While it was not the success of later concerts, by the beginning of 1962, Okudzhava's growing popularity was indicated by the strength of the Komsomol newspapers' condemnation of his "permitted" concerts. Therefore, many future recordings were made live in apartments "with a couple of dozen attentive, understanding, loving listeners and, as usual, with a pair of tape recorders." Kovner speaks

---

129 Gerry Smith, "Whispered Cry: The Songs of Alexander Galich," *Index on Censorship* 3, no. 3 (1974): 11.

130 The Leningrad tapists, collectors, and distributors (Frumkin, Kushner, and Kovner) are known through their writings and memoirs published online after their emigration to the US. For more on the Moscow tapists, see Giulia De Florio, "Magnitizdat," in *Alle due sponde della cortina di ferro. Le culture del dissenso e la definizione dell'identità europea nel secondo Novecento tra Italia, Francia e Urss* (1956–1991), ed. Claudia Pieralli, Teresa Spignoli, Federico Iocca, Giuseppina Larocca, and Giovanna Lo Monaco (Florence: goWare, 2019), 335–44, https://www.culturedeldissenso.com.

fondly of borrowing the Grundig tape recorder of his friend, the collector Mikhail "Misha" Kryzhanovsky, as they aimed for quality copies.[131]

Throughout the 1960s and early 1970s, the bards performed their concerts in private apartments and were taped with their permission. Friends were offered the possibility of copying the tapes for their own use for free, usually supplying their own tape. Or tapes could be traded as part of the elaborate system of *blat*, or informal exchange, that operated in Soviet society.[132] Or tapists would become "publishers," distributing tapes hand-to-hand to someone they knew.[133] Sometimes an unannounced concert proved an opportunity for multiple tapings by several audience members, multiplying "master copies" for potential reproduction.

The tapists involved in early commercial operation—to distribute tapes for money—used the sound recording kiosks located in most cities that were established ostensibly to tape legitimate Melodiya records or authorized recordings from Eastern Europe. According to Kan, they were not regulated for a very long time.[134] Homemade tapes of the bards began circulating on a large scale in the major cities, especially among university students, the intelligentsia, and academic elites. As compared to other forms of popular music in circulation, *magnitizdat* recordings of guitar poetry began as essentially an urban phenomenon.[135] Its audience was, in Daughtry's words, "broader and more ideologically diverse," however and extended to music enthusiasts who might not otherwise be involved in *magnitizdat* circles.[136]

The tapes were listened to in private apartments, dorm rooms, and commuter trains. The songs themselves were added to the performance of "tourist songs" on the outdoor student campouts and long hikes that had begun in the late 1950s; admiring amateurs might perform the bard songs live, with guitar, helping to spread the songs, which could then be re-experienced on

131 Kovner, "Zolotoy vek magnitizdata."
132 Although she does not refer specifically to *magnitizdat*, Ledeneva's study of Soviet networking through material objects is the classic exposition: Alena V. Ledeneva, *Russia's Economy of Favours: Blat, Networking and Informal Exchange* (Cambridge: Cambridge University Press, 1998).
133 Vladimir Kovner, "Zolotoy vek magnitizdata" [The golden age of *magnitizdat*, part 2], *Vestnik online*, 8, no. 344 (April 14, 2004), section 6, http://www.vest nik.com/issues/2004/0414/win/kovner.htm.
134 Kan, "Living in the Material World," 267. She also describes a well-developed Moscow system of tape duplication in which an apartment might utilize up to ten tape recorders for rock albums, but it is not clear whether such independent duplicating facilities were operating during the heyday of guitar poetry (271).
135 Laura J. Olson, *Performing Russia: Folk Revival and Russian Identity* (London: Routledge, 2004), 71–72.
136 Daughtry, "Sonic Samizdat," 31.

magnitizdat.[137] Many audience members brought handwritten songbooks to live performances or shared the lyrics in communal settings. In defending the importance of these songs for community participation, Garey remarked that "hundreds of people didn't get together in the woods and sing Beatles songs."[138]

Overall, guitar poetry "evolved not just as a song genre but as a sociocultural phenomenon [that] formed communities that were never entirely within, yet also never outside of the Soviet *kollektiv*."[139] Skirmishes with the authorities, whether in terms of unauthorized concerts or tape distribution, as well as the perceived (and sometimes real) threat of censorship or punishment, may have added cohesion to that community of tapists, their listeners, their collectors, and their imitators. As the official Soviet composer Ivan Dzerzhinsky wrote in 1965, the bards "are armed with magnetic tape. This presents [...] a certain danger since distribution becomes so easy."[140]

The Bards, *Magnitizdat*, and the Authorities

In 1974, when Vladimir Frumkin and his wife left the USSR, he brought among other things a selection of reel-to-reel tape recordings of Okudzhava's performances.[141] He had submitted his tapes to Soviet customs officials who, after several hours returned them with the assurance that they were approved for export. Upon arrival he discovered that the tapes had been de-magnetized and Okudzhava's voice erased, he assumed during their "stay" in customs.[142] This story is repeated by the protagonist as well as others to illustrate various aspects of *magnitizdat*. While undoubtedly a personal loss, Frumkin was not

---

137   Christian Noack, "Songs from the Wood, Love from the Fields: The Soviet Tourist Song Movement," in *The Socialist Sixties: Crossing Borders in the Second World*, ed. Anne E. Gorsuch and Diane P. Koenker (Bloomington: Indiana University Press, 2013), 167–92.

138   Garey, "Aleksandr Galich," 13.

139   Platonov, *Singing the Self*, 4.

140   Cited in Yurchak, "Gagarin," 83.

141   Kryzhanovsky and Kovner prepared these tapes for him. Kovner, "Zolotoy," part 2, section 7.

142   Kovner reports making another set of tapes in 1978 to send abroad, which also disappeared. Later he learned that someone in the American embassy had sent a full set of bard recordings to New York. Vladimir Kovner, "Zolotoy vek magnitizdata" [The golden age of *magnitizdat*, part 3], *Vestnik online* 9, no. 346 (April 28, 2004), section 8, http://www.vestnik.com/issues/2004/0428/win/kovner.htm. In a further irony, he learned that twenty years later, after he himself had emigrated to the US Melodiya Records used Kryzhanovsky's collection of guitar poetry to issue official recordings of the bards' guitar poetry; Kovner, "Zolotoy," part 2, section 7.

prohibited from leaving, demonstrating the relative tolerance of *magnitizdat* compared to its print progenitor, *samizdat*. Like *magnitizdat*, *samizdat* also used an improvised production process and underground distribution system. However, as numerous commentators point out, *samizdat* was most often intensely political and was viewed by its makers and readers in that way.[143] The songs of *magnitizdat*, with the exception of some of Galich's songs, were not apolitical so much as they were un-political, indifferent, or even disinterested. Various trials marked distributors of Soviet *samizdat*, both physical and literal, while as Kovner remarked, "They didn't arrest you for distributing bard songs."[144]

It is not that the leadership liked these songs. But their children "belted out these songs at home and at their dachas with all the power their tape recorders could muster. The leaders themselves listened to them on their own, saying to themselves: 'He's really laying it on thick, the bastard! But that's the truth he's gabbling! Only what's the point? You can't do anything about it anyway.'"[145]

But neither was the practice without risk. Kovner relates a 1965 search of his apartment; while they seemed primarily to be looking for printed *samizdat*, his bard tapes were "for the first, but not the last time" in the hands of the KGB. He was then interrogated and summoned two months later for an "instructive" conversation. He received his tapes back, signed on the back "seized during a search." He was kicked out of his job as a teacher, though allowed to continue working at his factory.[146]

By the early 1970s, the bards themselves were targeted. Phone calls by the authorities to Okudzhava's workplace at *Literaturnaya gazeta* expressed "surprise to have a guitar player working in the poetry section."[147] He was expelled from the Party in 1972 and a book of his verse plus music was withdrawn from a planned publication, so he stopped performing until the late 1970s. Vysotsky was also critiqued for "profiteering" and urged to stop this "illegal entrepreneurial activity" by the influential *Sovetskaya kultura*.[148] It is probably not coincidental

---

143 On *samizdat*, see Peter Steiner, "Introduction: On Samizdat, Tamizdat, Magnitizdat, and Other Strange Words That Are Difficult to Pronounce," *Poetics Today* 29, no. 4 (2008): 613–28; and Daughtry, "'Sonic Samizdat,'" 49–54, among others.

144 Kovner, "Zolotoy," part 2, section 6.

145 Smith, *Songs to Seven Strings*, 98.

146 Three months later, in February 1966, the trial of Sinyavsky and Daniel for publishing their writings abroad (*tamizdat*) began, marking the end of the more tolerant Thaw period. Members of the youth group Kolokol were also prosecuted for *samizdat* distribution; see Sofia Lopatina, "From Komsomol Activists to Underground Reformists: The Leningrad Group Kolokol, 1954–1965" (Master's thesis, Central European University, 2017).

147 Cited in Lugarić Vukas, "Living *vnye*," 22.

148 Ryback, *Rock around the Bloc*, 47–48.

that in 1970 a "Songs Commission" was created within the Writers' Union's Poetry section.[149]

Galich's fate illustrates the price for being openly political. A bootleg copy of his songs was published in Frankfurt in 1969, which he did not disavow; this presumably was the excuse to expel him from the Writers Union in December of 1971 and from the Cinematographers Union the next year; he was forced to emigrate in 1974.[150] In the words of Soviet poet Yevgeny Yevtushenko, writing in 1988, "As soon as Galich began to sing, that is, as soon as he allowed himself to be himself, he turned from a successful dramatist quite acceptable to the bureaucracy to an unwanted person."[151]

Was it, at least in this case, all about politics? In a telling 2008 dialogue between two Soviet émigrés, Vladimir Frumkin and mathematician/poet Boris Kushner, Kushner describes his response to the bards: "the main source of the guitar poetry was not protest at all, but the natural, inherent impulse of creativity in a person [...] *Express yourself.*" Kushner in the early years did not feel the opposition that Frumkin perceived: "There were good, talented songs, there were mediocre ones. And when I sat down to the piano, my favorite melodies arose under my fingers. [...] whether the author was a member of the Composers' Union or not—what did I care."[152]

Yevtushenko also recounts an impromptu concert in his home when Galich and Okudzhava met with the famous Belgian singer Jacques Brel. All sang for each other—and none sang their own songs. "Galich sang old romances, Okudzhava sang carriage songs, and Jacques Brel sang Flemish folk songs."[153] No tape exists, to Yevtushenko's regret, but their choice of repertoire suggests that it was the singing and the songs, the participatory experience, and the "romance" not of the forbidden but of the melody that invigorated these guitar poets of *magnitizdat*.

---

149 Smith, "Whispered Cry," 12.
150 In Paris, Galich joined Radio Free Europe as an announcer and was found dead in 1977; various theories of his death by electrocution—was he plugging in new electronic equipment?—still circulate.
151 Yevtushenko, "Magnitofonnaya glasnost'," 16.
152 "Vladimir Frumkin—Boris Kushner: A Dialogue," *Zametki po yevreyskoy istorii* [Notes on Jewish History] 5, no. 96 (May 2008) and 7, no. 98 (July 2008), http s://berkovich-zametki.com/2008/Zametki/Nomer5/Frumkin1.php.
153 "Vladimir Frumkin—Boris Kushner: A Dialogue."

Some Closing Thoughts:
Participatory Music Culture in the Era of Magnetic Tape

In writing about twenty-first-century hybrid economies of cultural production, Lessig sees western hybrid artistic economies as combining the commercial and the participatory[154]; here we expand these categories to "official" recording, whether commercial or state, to "unofficial recording" and participatory music reproduction and circulation. In both cases there is an economic component: tape recorders and tapes had to be purchased, these tapes, whether reproduced in like form or vinyl, had to be marketed, and some type of economic exchange initiated to maintain the informal system. The personal and participatory nature of both the opera and bardic communities of listeners, enhanced by the entrepreneurial activities of the tapists and distributors, linked the communal value of the live performance to the shared community of listeners to its reproduction.

The aesthetics in both forms stressed its "liveness," its humanness (including frailties and variations), over recording studio perfections. Even sotto voce comments or introductions were part of the dialogue with the audience and by extension the listeners to the recordings. Those valuing live recordings "listen through" the technological flaws to hear the singers and possibly listen more closely as well. Applause on both types of recordings helps to register affect and emotion, even if it breaks the musical spell. The live performance of opera can be listened to as a series of "songs," with applause coming at the end of familiar arias, the composer providing the interludes and recitatives. The curation of both forms—in terms of linking performances to variation in lyric or tone, routine or "over the top"—builds the collector and analyst into the larger community of value surrounding these forms.[155]

The remastering—and redistribution—of these live performances through commercial record companies in the immediate post-Cold War environment built upon the practice in both countries of recording radio broadcasts and reissues in "improved sound" of famous performances. These reissues became a marketing boon with the introduction of remastered and inexpensively produced CDs.[156] With new technologies of streaming and online communities of

---

154 Lawrence Lessig, Remix: Making Art and Commerce Thrive in the Hybrid Economy (London: Penguin, 2008).

155 The way in which individual arias ("songs") aided Pavarotti's rise to fame is chronicled in Marsha Siefert, "The Dynamics of Evaluation: A Case Study of Performance Reviews," Poetics Today 5, no. 1 (Winter 1984): 111–28.

156 For a discussion of the post-Cold War surge in live recordings of famous Soviet musicians, Marsha Siefert, "Re-Mastering the Past: Musical Heritage, Sound Recording, and the Nation in Hungary and Russia," in National Heritage—

fans, the materiality of the vinyl and tape again becomes the property of and important to collectors, who also are curators of the heritage and producers of expert knowledge of the genres. The shaded area of legality of earlier material forms can be supported by the tapists as archivists and historians, supplementing as well as critiquing official recordings. In retrospect, the authorities, too, came to find value in these past performances, reissuing them when the heyday of their stars and performance styles had passed.

In 1990, Okhudzhava restated that the guitar poetry was "not just a song, but also rather a means of communication, a means of dialogue."[157] By recreating "live" performance, the entrepreneurial tapists were able to reconstitute the social relations of production, reproduction, and participation in a parallel recording enterprise. The communities were built through interpersonal rituals of listening together as well as listening separately but with a sense of audience. The trusted networks of distribution, the "romance of the forbidden," the "peer-to-peer" sharing whether at clubs or on campouts, enhanced the participatory quality of both genres.

Ending where I began—with the narrative of Cold War—how much has the "rule of law" discourse, incorporated into the rhetoric of democratization, been once again challenged to allow forms of participatory cultural creation in our current day. Let us leave with an overlapping of these phenomena. Like the timing of Galich's censure, in early 1971 the opera soprano Galina Vishnevskaya received the Order of Lenin and a few months later, her name and voice disappeared from the media. In 1974, she left the USSR with her husband, the cellist Mstislav Rostropovich, after being "hounded by the Soviet authorities for their liberal political views."[158] On November 18, 1993, she came to the Opera Club of Philadelphia and appeared onstage at the Academy of Vocal Arts to present her translated autobiography.[159] During the interview, much was made of her survival and triumph as well as the politicization of her singing abroad. Interspersed in the conversation, held in Italian, some of her recordings were

---

National Canon, ed. Mihály Szegedy-Maszák (Budapest: Collegium Budapest, 2002): 251–80. Leo Records, begun by an "enthusiastic amateur" in 1979 in Newton Abbot, UK, began issuing live performances of Russian free jazz and experimental music already in 1979. They produce "music that refuses to be submitted to the market forces." See http://www.leorecords.com.

157 Video recording of a concert and talk at Middlebury College (Summer 1990), cited in Anatoly Vishevsky, "Timur Shaov and the Death of the Russian Bard Song," *Przegląd Rusycystyczny* 4 (2007): 67.

158 Jonathan Kandell, "Galina Vishnevskaya, Soprano and Dissident, Dies at 86," *New York Times*, December 11, 2012.

159 Galina Vishnevakaya, *Galina: A Russian Story* (New York: Harcourt Brace Jovanovich, 1984).

played by the host, the opera critic Robert Baxter. After the hushed audience listened to an aria recorded at La Scala, she exclaimed, "I have never heard that performance. *Un Pirata?*" The host nodded. Galina smiled.[160]

References

Ampolsk, Alan G. "Piracy on the High C's." *New York*, January 29, 1979, 95–96.

Angus, Robert. "Pirates, Prima Donnas, and Plain White Wrappers. The Record Underground from Mapleson to the Seventies." *High Fidelity* 26 (December 1976): 76–81.

Archinov, A.I. "A Brief History of the Recording Industry in the Soviet Union." *Journal of Audio Engineering Society* 18, no. 1 (February 1970): 20–22.

Barsukova, Svetlana, and Alena Ledeneva. "Concluding Remarks to Volume 2: Are Some Countries More Informal than Others: The Case of Russia." in *The Global Encyclopaedia of Informality*, vol. 2, 487–92. London: UCL Press, 2018.

Bennett, John R. *Melodiya: A Soviet Russian LP Discography.* Westport, CT: Greenwood 1981.

Bicknell, David, and Robert Philip. "Gramophone." In *The New Grove Dictionary of Music and Musicians*, edited by Stanley Sadie, vol. 7, 620–27. London: Macmillan, 1980.

Bohlman, Andrea F. "Making Tapes in Poland: The Compact Cassette at Home." *Twentieth-Century Music* 14, no. 1 (2017): 119–134.

Bohlman, Andrea F., and Peter McMurray. "Tape: Or, Rewinding the Phonographic Regime." *Twentieth-Century Music* 14, no. 1 (2017): 3–24.

Caute, David. *The Dancer Defects: The Struggle for Cultural Supremacy during the Cold War.* Oxford: Oxford University Press, 2003.

Collins, Bill. "Mining the Musical Underground: Should buried treasures be left exclusively for the pirates?" *High Fidelity* 21 (November 1971): 74–76.

Cope, Lida, Natalie Kononenko, Anthony Qualin, and Mark Yoffe. "Sound Recordings in the Archival Setting: Issues of Collecting, Documenting, Categorizing, and Copyright." *Slavic & East European Information Resources* 20, nos. 3–4 (2019): 85–100.

Crutchfield, Will. "In Opera, 'Live' Is Livelier, but Also Riskier." *New York Times*, July 15, 1990.

Cushman, Thomas. *Notes from Underground: Rock Music Counterculture in Russia.* Albany: SUNY Press, 1995.

---

160 The source is my notes from the evening, preserved inside my autographed copy of the autobiography.

Dane, Barbara. "Paredon Records: Reflecting on 50 Years of Paredon." Smithonian Folkways Recordings, 2020. https://folkways.si.edu/paredon/reflecting.

Davis, Peter. "Live Performance Opera—Legal and Otherwise." *New York Times*, June 10, 1979.

———. "Piracy on the High Cs." *Music and Musicians*, May 1973, 38–40.

———. "The Musical Underground: A Brief Look at the Tape Scene." *Musical Newsletter* 6, no. 1 (1976): 17–18.

Daughtry, J. Martin. "'Sonic Samizdat': Situating Unofficial Recording in the Post-Stalinist Soviet Union." *Poetics Today* 30, no. 1 (2009): 27–65.

De Florio, Giulia. "Magnitizdat." In *Alle due sponde della cortina di ferro. Le culture del dissenso e la definizione dell'identità europea nel secondo Novecento tra Italia, Francia e URSS (1956–1991)*, edited by Claudia Pieralli, Teresa Spignoli, Federico Iocca, Giuseppina Larocca, and Giovanna Lo Monaco, 335–44. Florence: goWare, 2019. https://www.culturedeldissenso.com/.

Djagalov, Rossen. "Guitar Poetry, Democratic Socialism, and the Limits of 1960s Internationalism." In *The Socialist Sixties: Crossing Borders in the Second World*, edited by Anne E. Gorsuch and Diane P. Koenker, 148–66. Bloomington: Indiana University Press, 2013.

Eidsheim, Nina Sun. "Maria Callas's Waistline and the Organology of Voice." *The Opera Quarterly* 33, nos. 3–4 (January 2018).

Frumkin, Vladimir. *Bulat Okudzahva: 65 Songs*. Ann Arbor, MI: Ardis, 1980.

———. "Muzyka i slovo" [Music and Word]. Report on a seminar in May 1967, Petushki, Vladimir Region (uploaded December 22, 1997). http://www.ksp-msk.ru/page_42.html.

Fürst, Juliane. *Flowers Through Concrete: Explorations in Soviet Hippieland*. Oxford: Oxford University Press, 2021.

Gaisberg, F.W. *The Music Goes Round*. New York: Macmillan, 1942.

Garey, Amy. "Aleksandr Galich: Performance and the Politics of the Everyday." *Lumina: A Journal of Historical and Cultural Studies* 17 (2011): 1–13.

Gilburd, Eleonory. *To See Paris and Die: The Soviet Lives of Western Culture*. Cambridge, MA: Belknap Press, 2018.

Gould, Susan. "Leyla Gencer, Queen of Pirate Recordings." *High Fidelity* 26 (September 1976): 74–76.

Gronow, Pekka. "Ethnic Music and Soviet Record Industry." *Ethnomusicology* 19, no. 1 (1975): 92–93.

Hamilton, David. "Who Speaks for Callas?" *High Fidelity* 29 (January 1979): 67–71.

Horne, Brian A. "The Bards of Magnitizdat: An Aesthetic Political History of Russian Underground Recordings." In *Samizdat, Tamizdat, and Beyond: Transnational Media During and After Socialism*, edited by Friederike Kind-Kovács and Jessie Labov, 175–89. New York: Berghahn Books, 2013.

Hufen, Uli. *Das Regime und die Dandys. Russische Gaunerchansons von Lenin bis Putin.* Berlin: Rogner & Berhand, 2010.

Jones, Steve. "The Cassette Underground." *Popular Music and Society* 14, no. 1 (1990): 75–84.

Josephson, Paul R. *New Atlantis Revisited: Akademgorodok, the Siberian City of Science.* Princeton: Princeton University Press, 1997.

Kan, Anna. "Living in the Material World: Money in the Soviet Rock Underground." In *Dropping Out of Socialism: The Creation of Alternative Spheres in the Soviet Bloc,* edited by Juliane Fürst and Josie McLellan, 255–76. Lanham, MD: Lexington, 2016.

Katz, Mark. *Capturing Sound: How Technology Has Changed Music,* rev. ed. Berkeley: University of California Press, 2010.

Kandell, Jonathan. "Galina Vishnevskaya, Soprano and Dissident, Dies at 86." *New York Times,* December 11, 2012.

Krylov, A.E. "Bulat Okudzhava i Vladimir Vysotsky: Istoriya znakomstva" [Bulat Okudzhava and Vladimir Vysotsky: the history of an acquaintance]. *Russian Literature* 77, no. 2 (2015): 197–222.

Koestenbaum, Wayne. "Maria Callas and Her Fans." *Yale Review* 79, no. 1 (1989): 1-20.

———. *The Queen's Throat: Opera, Homosexuality, and the Mystery of Desire.* New York: Poseidon Press, 1992.

Koivunen, Pia. "Friends, 'Potential Friends,' and Enemies: Reimagining Soviet Relations to the First, Second, and Third Worlds at the Moscow 1957 Youth Festival." In *Socialist Internationalism in the Cold War,* 219-47. Cham: Palgrave Macmillan, 2016.

Kovner, Vladimir. "Zolotoy vek magnitizdata" [The golden age of *magnitizdat*, part 1]. *Vestnik online* 7, no. 345 (March 31, 2004). http://www.vestnik.com /issues/2004/0331/win/kovner.htm.

———. "Zolotoy vek magnitizdata" [The golden age of *magnitizdat*, part 2]. *Vestnik online* 8, no. 344 (April 14, 2004). http://www.vestnik.com/issue s/2004/0414/win/kovner.htm.

———. "Zolotoy vek magnitizdata" [The golden age of *magnitizdat*, part 3], *Vestnik online* 9, no. 346 (April 28, 2004). http://www.vestnik.com/issue s/2004/0428/win/kovner.htm.

La Rochelle, Real. "Maria Callas and La Traviata: The Phantom of EMI." ARSC *Journal* 19, nos. 2–3 (February 1989): 54–61.

Ledeneva, Alena V. *Russia's Economy of Favours: Blat, Networking and Informal Exchange.* Cambridge: Cambridge University Press, 1998.

Lessig, Lawrence. *Remix: Making Art and Commerce Thrive in the Hybrid Economy.* London: Penguin, 2008.

Limansky, Nicholas E. *Early 20th Century Opera Singers.* New York: Yвк Publishers, 2016.

Limansky, Nicholas E. *Pirates of the High Cs: Opera Bootlegging in the 20th Century.* New York: Yвк Publishers, 2020.

———. "Vincenzo Bellini: Norma." *Opera Quarterly* 21, no. 3 (2005): 551–55.

Loewen, Donald. "Blurred Boundaries: Russian Poetry and Soviet Politics during the Thaw." *Russian Literature* 87–89 (January–April 2017): 201–24.

Lopatina, Sofia. "From Komsomol Activists to Underground Reformists: The Leningrad Group Kolokol, 1954–1965." Master's thesis, Central European University, 2017.

Lugarić Vukas, Danijela. "Living *vnye*: The Example of Bulat Okudzhava's and Vladimir Vysotskii's *avtorskaia pesnia*." *Euxeinos. Culture and Governance in the Black Sea Region* 8, nos. 25–26 (2018): 20–31.

MacFadyen, David. *Red Stars: Personality and the Soviet Popular Song, 1955–1991.* Montreal: McGill-Queen's University Press, 2001.

Marshall, Lee. "For and Against the Record Industry: An Introduction to Bootleg Collectors and Tape Traders." *Popular Music* 22, no. 1 (2003): 57–72.

Mazierska, Ewa. "Introduction." In *Popular Music in Eastern Europe: Breaking the Cold War Paradigm*, edited by Ewa Mazierska, 1–27. London: Springer, 2016.

McDowell, Edwin. "Record Pirates: Industry Sings the Blues." *New York Times*, June 30, 1978.

Neckers, Jan. "Pirates of the High C's (Opera bootlegging in the 20th Century) by Nicholas Limansky." Accessed 5 June 2021. http://www.operanostalgia.be/html/Limansky-pirates.html.

Neumann, Mark, and Timothy A. Simpson. "Smuggled Sound: Bootleg Recording and the Pursuit of Popular Memory." *Symbolic Interaction* 20, no. 4 (1997): 319–41.

Noack, Christian. "Songs from the Wood, Love from the Fields: The Soviet Tourist Song Movement." In *The Socialist Sixties: Crossing Borders in the Second World*, edited by Anne E. Gorsuch and Diane P. Koenker, 167–92. Bloomington: Indiana University Press, 2013.

Olson, Laura J. *Performing Russia: Folk Revival and Russian Identity.* London: Routledge, 2004.

Orlova, Irina. "Notes from the Underground: The Emergence of Rock Culture." In *Mass Culture and Perestroika in the Soviet Union*, edited by Marsha Siefert, 66–71. New York: Oxford University Press, 1991.

Pearce, Joe. "The Ramblings of a Once Young Record Collector—New World Version," *Record Collector* 63, no. 3 (September 2018): 199–214.

———. "Wagner in Stockholm: Great Wagnerians of the Royal Swedish Opera Recordings, 1899–1970." *Opera Quarterly* 20, no. 3 (2004): 472–505.

Péteri, György, ed. *Imagining the West in Eastern Europe and the Soviet Union.* Pittsburgh: University of Pittsburgh Press, 2010.

Péteri, György. "Nylon Curtain—Transnational and Transsystemic Tendencies in the Cultural Life of State-Socialist Russia and East-Central Europe." *Slavonica* 10, no. 2 (2004): 113–23.

Phillips, Harvey. "Psss! I Have Bootlegged 'Norma' for Only..." *New York Times,* September 12, 1971.

Platonov, Rachel. "Bad singing: *Avtorskaia Pesnia* and the Aesthetics of Meta-communication." *Ulbandus Review* 9, "The 60s" (2005/6): 87–113.

———. *Singing the Self. Guitar Poetry, Community, and Identity in the Post-Stalin Period.* Evanston: Northwestern University Press, 2012.

Ramet, Sabrina P. *Rocking the State: Rock Music and Politics in Eastern Europe and Russia.* Boulder, CO: Westview Press, 1994.

Risch, William Jay, ed. *Youth and Rock in the Soviet Bloc: Youth Cultures, Music, and the State in Russia and Eastern Europe.* Lanham, MD: Lexington Books, 2015.

Robinson, Harlow. "The Recording Behemoth of Tverskoy Boulevard (On the Soviet Recording Company Melodiya)." *High Fidelity* 36, no. 6 (June 1986): 64–65.

Ryback, Timothy W. *Rock around the Bloc: A History of Rock Music in Eastern Europe and Soviet Union.* New York: Oxford University Press, 1990.

Shaman, William, Edward Joseph Smith, William J. Collins, and Calvin M. Goodwin. EJS, *Discography of the Edward J. Smith Recordings: The Golden Age of Opera, 1956–1971.* Westport, CT: Greenwood, 1994.

Shewey, Don, ed. *Out Front: Contemporary Gay & Lesbian Plays.* New York: Grove, 1988.

Shuker, Roy. *Wax Trash and Vinyl Treasures: Record Collecting as a Social Practice.* Oxon: Routledge, 2017.

Siefert, Marsha. "How the Talking Machine Became a Musical Instrument: Technology, Aesthetics, and the Capitalization of Culture." *Science in Context,* Special Issue: Technology: Culture, Politics, Aesthetics, edited by Alfred J. Rieber and Marsha Siefert (Summer 1995): 417–50.

———. "Image/Music/Voice: Song Dubbing in Hollywood Musicals." *Journal of Communication* 45, no. 2 (Spring 1995): 44–64.

———. "Re-Mastering the Past: Musical Heritage, Sound Recording, and the Nation in Hungary and Russia." In *National Heritage—National Canon,* edited by Mihály Szegedy-Maszák, 251–80. Budapest: Collegium Budapest, 2002.

———. "The Dynamics of Evaluation: A Case Study of Performance Reviews." *Poetics Today* 5, no. 1 (Winter 1984): 111–28.

———. "The Home Audience. Sound Recording and the Marketing of Musical

Taste in Early 20th Century America." In *Audiencemaking*, edited by James S. Ettema and D. Charles Whitney, 186–214. Beverly Hills, CA: Sage, 1994.

Siefert, Marsha. "The Metropolitan Opera and the American Century: Opera Singers, Europe and Cultural Politics." *Journal for Arts Management, Law and Society* 33, no. 4 (Winter 2004): 298–315.

Siff, Ira. "Magda Olivero, 104, the Last Great Verismo Soprano, Has Died," *Opera News* (September 8, 2014). https://www.operanews.com/Opera_News_Magazine/2014/9/News/Magda_Olivero.html.

Smith, Gerald Stanton. "Das Regime und die Dandys. Russische Gaunerchansons von Lenin bis Putin by Hufen, Uli." *Slavonic and East European Review* 89, no. 4 (2011): 731–33.

———, ed. and trans. *Songs & Poems by Alexander Galich*. Ann Arbor, MI.: Ardis, 1983.

———. *Songs to Seven Strings: Russian Guitar Poetry and Soviet "Mass Song."* Bloomington: Indiana University Press, 1984.

———. "Okudzhava Marches On." *Slavonic and East European Review* 66, no. 4 (Oct. 1988): 553–63.

Smith, Gerry. "Whispered Cry: The Songs of Alexander Galich." *Index on Censorship* 3, no. 3 (1974): 11–22.

Spice, Anton. "X-Ray Audio: The Documentary." Filmed by P. Heartfield, written by S. Coates and A. Spice, 2016. https://thevinylfactory.com/films/x-ray-audio-soviet-bootleg-records-documentary/.

Spignoli, Teresa, and Claudia Pieralli. "Forme culturali del dissenso alle due sponde della cortina di ferro (1956–1991): Problemi, temi e metodi di una difficile comparazion." *Between* 10, no. 19 (2020): i–xxxiv.

Starr, S. Frederick. *Red and Hot: The Fate of Jazz in the Soviet Union 1917–1991*. New York: Limelight Editions, 1985/1994.

Steiner, Peter. "Introduction: On Samizdat, Tamizdat, Magnitizdat, and Other Strange Words That Are Difficult to Pronounce." *Poetics Today* 29, no. 4 (2008): 613–28.

Stewart, Susan. *On Longing: Narratives of the Miniature, the Gigantic, the Souvenir, the Collection*. Durham, NC: Duke University Press, 1993.

Stites, Richard. *Russian Popular Culture: Entertainment and Society since 1900*. Cambridge: Cambridge University Press, 1992.

Taigin, Boris. "Rastsvet i krakh podpol'noy studii gramzapisi 'Zolotaya Sobaka'" [The rise and fall of the underground recording studio "Golden Dog" (1946–1961)]. *Pchela* 20 (May/June 1999). https://cont.ws/@dachnik/430816.

Taylor, Timothy D. "The Commodification of Music at the Dawn of the Era of 'Mechanical Music.'" In *Music in the World*, 50–73. Chicago: University of Chicago Press, 2017.

Tikhonov, Alexander. "Moll, Kybarth, and Company." Arsc *Journal* 22, no. 2 (Fall 1991), 191–99.

———. "Neizvestnaya 'stoletnyaya voyna': Iz istorii muzykal'nogo piratstva v Rossii" [The Unknown "Hundred Years War": From the history of musical piracy in Russia]. *Zvukorezhisser* [Sound Engineer], nos. 3, 4 & 5 (2002). htt ps://www.russian-records.com/details.php?image_id=62731.

Tommasini, Anthony. "Critic's Notebook: Giving Those Callas Bootleg Tapes a Road Test." *New York Times*, January 9, 2003.

Tomoff, Kiril. "'Most Respected Comrade ...': Patrons, Clients, Brokers and Unofficial Networks in the Stalinist Music World." *Contemporary European History* 11, no. 1 (2002): 33–65.

Troitsky, Artemy. *Back in the* Ussr: *The True Story of Rock in Russia*. Boston: Faber and Faber, 1987.

Viljanen, Elina. "Educating the New Listener." In *Philosophical and Cultural Interpretations of Russian Modernisation*, edited by Katja Lehtisaari and Arto Mustajoki, 118–35. Oxon: Routledge, 2016.

Vishnevakaya, Galina. *Galina: A Russian Story*. New York: Harcourt Brace Jovanovich, 1984.

Vishevsky, Anatoly. "Timur Shaov and the Death of the Russian Bard Song." *Przegląd Rusycystyczny* 4 (2007): 67–76.

Wojnowski, Zbigniew. "The Pop Industry from Stagnation to Perestroika: How Music Professionals Embraced the Economic Reform That Broke East European Cultural Networks." *Journal of Modern History* 92, no. 2 (2020): 311–50.

Wile, Raymond R. "Record Piracy: The Attempts of the Sound Recording Industry to Protect Itself Against Unauthorized Copying 1890–1978." Arsc *Journal* 17, nos. 1–3 (January 1987), 18–40.

Yevtushenko, Yevgeny. "Magnitofonnaia glasnost'." *Nedelia* 18 (1988): 16. http:// bard.ru.com/article/8/print_art.php?id=8.14.

Yurchak, Alexei. *Everything Was Forever, Until It Was No More: The Last Soviet Generation*. Princeton: Princeton University Press, 2006.

———. "Gagarin and the Rave Kids." In *Consuming Russia: Popular Culture, Sex, and Society Since Gorbachev*, edited by Adele Barker, 76–109. Durham, NC: Duke University Press, 1999.

Zhuk, Sergei I. *Rock and Roll in the Rocket City: The West, Identity, and Ideology in Soviet Dniepropetrovsk, 1960–1985*. Washington, DC: Woodrow Wilson Center Press, 2010.

New Model, Same Old Stories?
Reproducing Narratives of Democratization in Music Streaming Debates

Raphaël Nowak and Benjamin A. Morgan

Abstract: At the turn of the 2020s, music is largely distributed and consumed via streaming services. This new "moment" in recorded music has attracted a lot of attention from scholars, with the aim of identifying the nature of transformations that are occurring at an economic and/or cultural level. This chapter critically assesses scholarly analyses of music production, distribution, and consumption in the age of streaming services. We note that accounts tend to work with specific assumptions underpinning the association between culture and technology, in particular in relation to the democratization of access. We argue in this chapter that music streaming services become a leitmotiv to anchor discourses about what music should ideally be, thus reproducing narratives that predate the emergence of music streaming.

Raphaël Nowak is a lecturer in Sociology at the University of York. He is a cultural sociologist conducting research on digital technologies and media, music consumption and taste, music genres, and cultural heritage. He is the author of *Consuming Music in the Digital Age* (Palgrave, 2016), co-editor with Andrew Whelan of *Networked Music Cultures* (Palgrave, 2016), and co-author with Sarah Baker and Lauren Istvandity of *Curating Pop* (Bloomsbury, 2019).

Ben Morgan is completing a Ph.D. exploring music streaming services in the Australian music industries at RMIT University. He is a veteran of the US music business and consultant to government institutions who is interested in creative practice across different cultural contexts. Looking ahead, his interest lies in institutional development policy and the global cultural economy in those regions where cultural and media industries are still nascent.

Introduction

At the turn of the 2020s, music is fully integrated within what many call the "platform society."[1] Processes of production, distribution, and consumption are largely operated on, organized around, and mediated by, a number of web-sites, applications, and platforms across computers, phones, and other devices.[2] Interactive on-demand commercial interfaces such as Spotify, Tencent, Apple Music, Boomplay, and Deezer, along with other digital services such as broadcaster Pandora or "alternative platforms" SoundCloud and Bandcamp, have combined to make digital music the primary source of global commercial recording revenue since 2017.[3] Music had already become fully "digitized" in some sense since the advent of peer-to-peer applications in the late 1990s.[4] However, the advent of "digital music commodities"[5] anchors music within the digital realm by providing stable and legal models of distribution that have largely reduced illegal file sharing and arguably threatened the subsistence of "physical" sound carriers. This new "moment" in the digitization of music is centered around usage enclosures and new affordances of often-automated recommendation, which draw on big data and algorithms to organize the distribution and consumption of content. This results in a range of (potentially) novel cultural practices that emerge from these new models of distribution and consumption. Within this broader digital ecosystem, we will focus on the

---

1   José van Dijck, Thomas Poell, and Martijn de Waal, *The Platform Society: Public Values in a Connective World* (New York: Oxford University Press, 2018).

2   We will mostly use "music streaming services" to refer specifically to the commercial interfaces which compensate copyright holders for interactive, on-demand usage. However, it will eventually become important to distinguish whether these services are being framed as new cultural intermediaries, as opposed to novel platforms. Our use of "platform" will rely on the theory of "platformization of cultural production" as used by D. Niebord and T. Poell; see David B. Nieborg and Thomas Poell, "The Platformization of Cultural Production: Theorizing the Contingent Cultural Commodity," *New Media & Society* 20, no. 11 (2018): 4275–92, https://doi.org/10.1177/1461444818769694.

3   David Hesmondhalgh, Ellis Jones, and Andreas Rauth, "SoundCloud and Bandcamp as Alternative Music Platforms," *Social Media + Society* (2019): 1–13, https://doi.org/10.1177/2056305119883429; International Federation of the Phonographic Industry (IFPI), *Global Music Report 2018: State of the Industry* (ifpi.org, 2018), https://www.ifpi.org/ifpi-global-music-report-2018/.

4   David Hesmondhalgh and Leslie Meier, "What the Digitalisation of Music Tells Us about Capitalism, Culture and the Power of the Information Technology Sector," *Information, Communication & Society* 21, no. 11 (2018): 1555–70, https://doi.org/10.1080/1369118X.2017.1340498.

5   Jeremy Wade Morris, *Selling Digital Music, Formatting Culture* (Oakland, CA: University of California Press, 2015), 2–6.

interactive commercial services in which listeners can access the catalogs of most commercial rights holders.

Music streaming is seen as further increasing the omnipresence of music in social life.[6] With the help of algorithms, there is music that can be recommended for, and listened to in, every context of everyday life: playlists such as "Lazy Sunday," "The Stress Buster," or "Songs for Sleeping"[7] have become prominent in how listeners access content. These and other kinds of playlists are often framed as human-curated collections. Meanwhile, user demographic and usage data enclosures are used to construct profiles, which are then used to provide automated recommendations to other similar profiles.[8] While the degree of human decision-making in curation and recommendation is opaque,[9] and even automated algorithmic recommendations are still composed of collective human activity,[10] the streaming services' logic is the prediction of quantified cultural practices: recommendations work with a preexisting set of preferences defined through usage metrics and the assumption that users want to further explore the catalog at their disposal and expand the presence of music in their everyday life.

In this context, a plethora of scholarly research attempts to understand what this model changes. We note that accounts can be summarized along two different yet intertwined objects of analysis: 1) a techno-economic approach that highlights how these streaming services place new key players in charge of music distribution;[11] and 2) a cultural perspective on the "aftermath" of

---

6   Hendrik Storstein Spilker, *Digital Music Distribution: The Sociology of Online Music Streams* (New York: Routledge, 2017), 21–4.

7   All examples are taken from Spotify in April 2020.

8   Robert Prey, "Musica Analytica: The Datafication of Listening," in *Networked Music Cultures: Contemporary Approaches, Emerging Issues*, ed. Raphaël Nowak and Andrew Whelan (London: Palgrave Macmillan UK, 2016), 31–48.

9   Tiziano Bonini and Alessandro Gandini, "'First Week Is Editorial, Second Week Is Algorithmic:' Platform Gatekeepers and the Platformization of Music Curation," *Social Media + Society* 5, no. 4 (2019): 1–11, https://doi.org/10.1177/205630511 9880006; Benjamin A. Morgan, "Revenue, Access, and Engagement via the In-house Curated Spotify Playlist in Australia," *Popular Communication* 18, no. 1 (2020): 32–47, https://doi.org/10.1080/15405702.2019.1649678.

10   Nick Seaver, "Algorithms as Culture: Some Tactics for the Ethnography of Algorithmic Systems," *Big Data & Society* 4, no. 2 (2017): 1–12, https://doi.org /10.1177/2053951717738104.

11   Patryk Galuszka, "Music Aggregators and Intermediation of the Digital Music Market," *International Journal of Communications* 9 (2015): 254–73, https://ijoc. org/index.php/ijoc/article/view/3113/1298; Hesmondhalgh and Meier, "What the Digitalisation of Music Tells Us."

music streaming that questions how people "value" music.[12] At the core of these perspectives lies a particular approach to the nexus of music and democratization. In conducting a critical literature review on scholarship that analyzes the economic and/or cultural aftermath of the emergence of a "platform model" to music distribution and consumption, this chapter interrogates how such scholarship replicates some old myths or stories about what music ought to be— as a valued cultural object for instance and/or as an object worthy of economic retribution for artists. We find that critical discourses on this "new model" are often anchored onto "old stories" regarding the economic and cultural value of music. While we cannot aim to be exhaustive in our review of the literature on the topic, we focus here on accounts that specifically address the issue of "democratization" as a key indicator to evaluate the distribution of music content on streaming platforms. Thus, before critically analyzing each perspective on music streaming, the first section of this chapter is dedicated to defining "democracy" in the relation to accessing music.

What Does "Democratization" Actually Mean in Relation to Accessing Music?

In scholarly work about culture (and its association with technology), democratization can be an important concept that captures either the sweeping historical movement of a greater access to culture that dates back to the post-WWII era or the effects of the introduction of new technologies of communications and consumption on people's access to content. However, as Hesmond-halgh argues, democratization is often raised as a notion but rarely explored in depth.[13] Oftentimes the concept is used without any proper analysis of what it entangles or even suggests. As a result, popular narratives tend to reflect the concerns of specific groups while claiming to speak on behalf of what the technology means for music existentially. Yet, as we intend to show in this section, democratization takes on different and even contradictory meanings.

Yves Evrard distinguishes between two possible definitions of "democratization" by identifying two political positions that he calls "democratization of

---

12   David Arditi, "Music Everywhere: Setting a Digital Music Trap," *Critical Sociology* 45, no. 4–5 (2019): 617–30, https://doi.org/10.1177/0896920517729192; Lee Marshall, "Do People Value Recorded Music?" *Cultural Sociology* 13, no. 2 (2019): 141–58, https://doi.org/10.1177/1749975519839524.

13   See David Hesmondhalgh, "Have Digital Communication Technologies Democratized the Media Industries?" in *Media and Society*, ed. James Curran and David Hesmondhalgh, 6th ed., 101–20 (London: Bloomsbury, 2019).

culture" and "cultural democracy."[14] The democratization of culture refers to a greater access to cultural works for an audience lacking access (for social reasons). It can be initiated or emerge from cultural government policy, economic growth, cultural industry strategy, or a combination of these. Evrard notes that "a mark of success for cultural policy would be a demographic structure for attendance to major artworks that matches that of the total population."[15] The success of the democratization of culture approach is measured by the erasure of the disparities between class, gender, and age groups in the demographics of cultural consumption. By contrast, the second possible definition of democratization refers to what Evrard calls "cultural democracy," defined

> as one founded on free individual choice, in which the role of a cultural policy is not to interfere with the preferences expressed by citizen-consumers but to support the choices made by individuals or social groups through a regulatory policy applied to the distribution of information or the structures of supply.[16]

In this case, the emphasis on individual choices assumes that individuals are either free to choose content that pleases them, or that they ought to be free to do so. The dichotomy between the two different positions is "rooted in fundamental philosophical debates"[17] and is useful to uncover the political positions behind critical scholarships on music and technologies, particularly in relation to the most recent development of music streaming.

In cultural studies, the democratization of culture position can be found for instance in the writings of Theodor W. Adorno, where lower strata of a society (the "masses") who consume popular culture are seen as dominated and passive.[18] The solution to achieve "emancipation" is found in an access to high culture, which heightens the senses. Adorno defends an argument that popular culture is bad because it is repetitive and standardized.[19] A more thorough and measured approach to the democratization of culture is found in Pierre Bourdieu's illustrious investigation of French cultural practices.[20] In contrast with Adorno, Bourdieu argues that it is the social organization that

---

14   Yves Evrard, "Democratizing Culture or Cultural Democracy?" *Journal of Arts Management, Law, and Society* 27, no. 3 (1997): 167–75, https://doi.org/10.1080/10632929709596961.

15   Evrard, "Democratizing Culture or Cultural Democracy?," 167–68.

16   Evrard, "Democratizing Culture or Cultural Democracy?," 168.

17   Evrard, "Democratizing Culture or Cultural Democracy?," 169.

18   Theodor W. Adorno, *Current of Music. Elements of a Radio Theory* (Cambridge: Polity, 2009), 92–113.

19   Adorno, *Current of Music*, 153.

20   Pierre Bourdieu, *Distinction: A Social Critique of the Judgment of Taste* (London: Routledge, 1984).

deems popular culture bad. Here again, cultural content is denoted with status on a hierarchy from high and legitimate to low and dominated. On the other hand, the democracy of culture position implies "a network [...] of independent units"[21] and is exemplified by scholarly accounts that emphasize the "choices," or at least the relative autonomy, of cultural groups, such as in subcultural theory.[22]

We briefly mention these accounts as a way to highlight how their positions—if not fully disclosed—have been discussed and situated within the paradigms established by Evrard, who notes fundamental philosophical debates behind each position are concerned with theories of aesthetics:

> The main basis for this dichotomy lies in the difference between beauty and aesthetics. In the [case of the democratization of culture position], there are objective, universal norms present in the work of art, which give it its value. Democratization would seek to disseminate these norms or create a universal canon. By contrast the theory of aesthetics [...] bases value on the pleasure or satisfaction derived from contemplating a work of art or attending a performance, that is, the subjective judgment of taste. Even though the exercise of judgment is universal, the outcome is not, and this leads to different choices that may be observed and analysed.[23]

The issue underpinned by the two perspectives on democratization questions a particular approach to the value of culture: do objects possess an objective aesthetic value? Or does the aesthetic value subjectively emerge through interactions with the object?

With regard particularly to music and technologies, we find that authors' positions on culture are not always (fully) disclosed, but rather subsumed and hidden behind more micro foci. However, from our critical review of the literature, we find arguments relating to the cultural democracy position in the fields of popular music studies, science and technology studies, cultural studies, and sociology. In fact, we can trace a genealogy of different positions that have had academic currency and momentum over time. Simon Frith suggests that scholarly discourses on music and aesthetics have successively moved from the position "if it's popular it must be bad" (as in Adorno), to the position "if it's popular it must be bad, unless it's popular with the right people" (as in subcultural theory), and finally to the position "if it's popular it must be good!" (as in em-

---

21   Evrard, "Democratizing Culture or Cultural Democracy?," 170.

22   See for example Dick Hebdige, *Subculture: The Meaning of Style* (London: Methuen, 1979).

23   Evrard, "Democratizing Culture or Cultural Democracy?," 168.

pirical accounts of listening).[24] The more celebratory perspective corresponds to a cultural democracy position whereby individuals exercise free choice over what music they produce, distribute, and listen to, assisted by the technological evolution of recorded music, often seen as detrimental to the question of access. The advent of music streaming services somehow reconfigures scholarly perspectives on music. We find that the notion of democratization acts as the backdrop of contemporary accounts critically evaluating what music streaming has economically or culturally changed to the realm of recorded music. The next section focuses on the economics of music streaming.

Artists, Producers, and the Economics of Music Streaming

Music streaming has become the dominant source of global revenue from recordings.[25] Its structural configuration has seen the emergence of "new players" in charge of music distribution and playback,[26] though the market dominance of oligopolistic rights holders has never been undermined.[27] The question is not of ownership or market share of copyright revenue, but of whether or not these new players have made the economic structures of music distribution more or less democratic.

A range of discourses engage this question through lenses such as rates of payment to rights holders,[28] broad revenue flows across sectors,[29] or subscrip-

---

24   Simon Frith, "The Good, the Bad, and the Indifferent: Defending Popular Culture from the Populists," *Diacritics* 21, no. 4 (1991): 102–4, https://www.jstor.org/stable/465379.

25   IFPI, *Global Music Report 2018*.

26   Galuszka, "Music Aggregators"; Hesmondhalgh and Meier, "What the Digitalisation of Music Tells Us."

27   Peter Tschmuck, *The Economics of Music* (Newcastle upon Tyne: Agenda Publishing, 2017), 86.

28   Lee Marshall, "'Let's Keep Music Special. F—Spotify:' On-demand Streaming and the Controversy over Artist Royalties." *Creative Industries Journal* 8, no. 2 (2015): 177–89, https://doi.org/10.1080/17510694.2015.1096618; Rethink Music Initiative (Berklee Institute of Creative Entrepreneurship). "Fair Music: Transparency and Payment Flows in the music industry," 2015, https://www.rethink-music.com/research/fair-music-transparency-and-payment-flows-in-the-music-industry.

29   Jason B. Bazinet, Kota Ezawa, Mark May, Thomas A Singlehurst, Jim Suva, and Alicia Yap, *Putting The Band Back Together: Remastering the World of Music*. Citi GPS: Global Perspectives & Solutions, 2018, https://www.citivelocity.com/citigps/music-industry/; Alan B. Krueger, *Rockonomics: A Backstage Tour of What the Music Industry Can Teach Us about Economics and Life* (New York: Currency, 2019).

tion price[30] as measures of the economic harm—or democratic potential—of music streaming. Though all revenue-based arguments provide only a partial perspective, they overall paint a picture where music streaming benefits consumers and the rights holders of catalogues and mass hits, while implying that recording artists and songwriters are suffering from a disappearance of income. As Hesmondhalgh points out, these critical economic arguments rely on a "dubious" focus on rates of payment to rights holders, which present claims of an overall decline in conditions for musicians, while "it seems clear that the current system retains the striking inequalities and generally poor working conditions that characterized its predecessors."[31] When asking whether streaming is more or less democratic from an economic perspective, we must first recognize that the recording industry has long been premised on widespread economic failure and rare lucrative mass success, where revenue is top-heavy and most recordings do not cover their investment costs.[32] We focus our attention to two types of perspectives in this section—those exploring royalty payments and those assessing access to the marketplace.

Royalty Payments as the Economic Measure of Fairness

A commonly attempted approach to answer this question is purely financial and concerns royalty payments to recording artists. Arguments about music streaming in journalistic and vernacular accounts center around concepts of "fairness" and "transparency,"[33] with the rate of payment to rights holders for

---

30 Matt Brennan, and Kyle Devine, "The Cost of Music." *Popular Music* 39, no. 1 (2020): 43–65, https://doi.org/10.1017/s0261143019000552.

31 David Hesmondhalgh, "Is Music Streaming Bad for Musicians? Problems of Evidence and Argument," *New Media and Society* (September 2020): 1–18, http s://doi.org/10.1177/1461444820953541.

32 Lee Marshall, "The Structural Functions of Stardom in the Recording Industry," *Popular Music and Society* 36, no. 5 (2013): 578–96, https://doi.org/10.1080/0 3007766.2012.718509.

33 Adjacent to these more high-profile arguments around rates of payment lie discussions around the "transparency" of how payments are handled; see Paul Resnikoff, "Welcome to the 'Royalty Black Box,' the Music Industry's $2.5 Billion Underground Economy," *Digital Music News* (blog), August 3, 2017, https://www.digitalmusicnews.com/2017/08/03/music-industry-royal ty-black-box/. For an in-depth exploration of the concept of "transparency," see Jay Mogis, "Transparency, Technology and Trust: Music Metrics and Cultural Distortion" (Ph.D. diss., Queensland University of Technology, 2020). We focus on "fairness" in this chapter.

usage of songs and recordings receiving particular attention.[34] While these outputs impact holders of sound recording and song copyrights, it is common to see rhetorical arguments reduced to how musicians and songwriters are paid by commercial streaming services. Two discursive subtleties are important to note here: the framing of these firms paying "musicians" and "songwriters" as opposed to "copyright owners" or "rights holders," and a frequent comparison of digital streaming's usage-based revenue calculations to the older sales model of purchasing a personal copy of a recording for unlimited personal use. These strategies are used to imply that streaming services (Spotify in particular)[35] are unfair to musicians broadly and in need of more "democratization." However, these critical accounts typically present comparisons to the larger amounts paid for ownership for unlimited use as a sufficient demonstration of past systems being more lucrative, and also often imply that the streaming services pay royalties to artists, not rights holders. Even well-argued institutional research papers on the topic of streaming revenue rates use "fairness" and "transparency" uncritically.[36] Moreover, the discursive focus on how musicians are compensated often completely neglects the issue of how record labels and publishers compensate the creators under contract. In many instances, critiques of Spotify's rates of payments resemble older political economy arguments directed at the dominant record labels and publishers on whom their production, and ultimately their livelihoods, ostensibly depend.[37] When looking at the rates paid to copyright holders by Spotify, the oligopolistic powers remain significantly involved in the negotiation of how much is paid for copyright usage. The systemic role of record labels, publishers, and collecting societies in negotiating rates and paying royalties is often ignored.

Obfuscated elements of complex revenue structures further problematize arguments about payment rates. Rates paid to rights holders are based on sharing the revenue Spotify receives from subscriptions and advertisers in a territory, and the particular amounts paid to the rights holders are dependent

---

34 Marshall, "'Let's Keep Music Special. F—Spotify'"; Aram Sinnreich, "Slicing the Pie: The Search for an Equitable Recorded Music Economy," in *Business Innovation and Disruption in the Music Industry*, ed. Patrik Wikström and Robert DeFillippi (Cheltenham: Edward Elgar Publishing, 2016), 153–74.

35 When it comes to revenue and access controversies, Spotify has been the primary target and will be the main example. For a critical history of the company, see Maria Eriksson et al., *Spotify Teardown: Inside the Black Box of Streaming Music* (Cambridge, MA: Isc Press, 2019).

36 Rethink Music Initiative, "Fair Music."

37 Steve Chapple and Reebee Garofalo, *Rock'n'roll is Here to Pay: The History and Politics of the Music Industry* (Chicago: Nelson-Hall, 1977); Aram Sinnreich, *The Piracy Crusade* (Boston: University of Massachusetts Press, 2013).

on a variety of factors, of which we will mention only a few. The record label or aggregator service which has uploaded the recordings will have negotiated their own specific deal with Spotify, often under a non-disclosure agreement. The performance rights organizations responsible for the collection of song royalties (which are defined differently around the world) negotiate the rate for their catalog in each territory. In different countries, copyright laws and structures will impact who can collect which rights and who can negotiate for those rights holders. Publishing mechanical royalty payments are handled quite differently in the Usa than in other countries, for example, with the government directly involved in setting the rates. Since Spotify's revenue pool is shared, paying more to one group of rights holders means less revenue for others. Ultimately, the rates paid to rights holders or aggregators per stream vary considerably. Demanding one group (songwriters for example) to be paid higher rates is arguing, in essence, that other groups (recording rights holders) should be paid less.

A second critical point concerns the deals between rights holders and musicians, including issues of artist royalty payments. The question of what a musician will be paid quickly becomes a query of who they work with. Record labels, aggregators, performance rights organizations, and even managers of the world's most popular artist brands all compete with each other for their share of the available revenue from the platforms. Revenue studies will obtain different results based on methodology and sample. Still, even if a broader picture among groups can be seen in these large studies, given the heterogeneous concerns of performing musicians, songwriters, recording engineers, managers, rights holders, concert promoters, and countless other stakeholder groups involved in the music business, the search for a grand narrative of democratization or democracy upon which everyone can agree will remain elusive using rates of payment.

Access to the Marketplace

A second measure of the economic impact induced by music streaming is the one of access to the marketplace. In that sense, music streaming represents a major structural shift. Digital technology allows musicians to produce and distribute their recordings with relative ease, especially in the context of the transition from the ownership model to access.[38] The historical difficulty for producers to get releases into retail stores alongside that of major-label albums was famously the concern of smaller record labels and unsigned artist brands

---

38   Patrik Wikström, *The Music Industry: Music in the Cloud.* 3rd ed. (Medford, MA: Polity Press, 2020).

in the pre-internet area, when recording was prohibitively expensive and main-stream (physical) distribution dominated by the major labels. Nowadays, any producer can pay a small fee to put their music into the streaming platform catalogues and receive some revenue for it. Spotify has reported that over 40,000 songs are uploaded to their ecosystem each day and the vast majority of recordings will fail to generate enough usage and revenue to pay for this fee.[39] One example of a new narrative is home recording artist Steve Benjamins,[40] who claims that he collects $400 per month without playing live, and his streams are driven through Spotify's playlists and automated algorithmic recommendation tools. Benjamins does not work with a record label or hire other musicians. If we are to take this case as indicative of a modest new revenue structure (rather than hyperbole more in line with the viral myth that intermediaries are no longer needed), it points towards a production strategy created by platformization which is in fact more "democratic" from a systemic perspec-tive. The case shows that Spotify's discovery tools have created opportunities for a production method and level of investment which previously would not have found an audience at scale. And being that this is something new, which threatens existing revenue structures and incumbents, it is to be expected that status quo interests will resist or challenge the legitimacy of these kinds of stories as outliers, or the music as inauthentic. Admittedly, Benjamins provides an example of a specific narrative that has been difficult to confirm. Bearing this in mind, stories such as that of Benjamins should not necessarily be taken as proof of a new structure that is easily accessible to all, but rather a need for more research into how prevalent and accurate these new kinds of narratives actually are.

Coming on top of the question of "access" is the issue of "visibility" of recordings in the crowded marketplace of the digital music commodity. In order to get deeper inside the concept of "access" and what has and has not shifted, we look at the words of musician and activist Jenny Toomey, founder of the Future of Music Coalition, when internet technology was just beginning to affect structures of music industries in 2001:

> Do traditional music business models serve musicians? In my opinion, aside from the cultural legitimization that comes with signing a major label deal,

---

39   Tim Ingham, "Nearly 40,000 Tracks Are Now Being Added to Spotify Every Single Day," *Music Business Worldwide* (blog), April 29, 2019, https://www.mus icbusinessworldwide.com/nearly-40000-tracks-are-now-being-added-to-sp otify-every-single-day/.

40   Steve Benjamins, "How Spotify & Discover Weekly Earns Me $400 / Month," *Steve Benjamins* (blog), March 14, 2019, https://www.stevebenjamins.com/bl og/spotify-and-discover-weekly.

> there are three need-based reasons why musicians sign major labor deals. The first one is *access to resources* [...]. The second reason is *access to distribution* [...]. The final reason that artists are signing these deals is *access to promotion*.[41]

It is the second of these three forms of access, that of distribution in the sense of delivery from producer to listener, which streaming platforms have solved brilliantly. The access to promotion is related to how "discovery" works within the streaming interface and is the most interesting to explore. Generating sufficient interest in a song or artist brand to make them fashionable still requires investment and expertise. Regardless of their access to catalogues, producers face a saturated space where everyone aims at attracting users' attention on platforms, with, in return, a lot of content that is never listened to. Streaming services have created infomediary ecosystems which mine, monitor, and mediate the way songs are used and presented.[42] From the perspective of an artist brand, record label, or publisher wishing to see recordings promoted within the digital music commodity interface, the opaque nature of the sociotechnical intermediary easily leads to suspicion of influence on the process being wielded by the oligopolistic powers. The skepticism of oligopolies' influence on the promotion/discovery process can be seen as the need for Spotify to democratize its access to promotion. This again extends old logics about corrupt or entrenched gatekeepers who are not being "fair" to artist brands or songs which are lacking in capital. The alternate view, which is only more recently starting to emerge through high-profile cases such as Chance the Rapper[43] or more obscure ones like Benjamins, is that there are niches where unsigned artist brands earn revenue without the reliance on record labels, other promotional services, or even performing concerts.

From our brief exploration of the economic aspect of the music streaming model, we note that the focus either on royalty payments or on access to the marketplace produces different results in the evaluation of said model as a potential for a more democratic popular music market. Pointing out the micro-payments of commercial streaming services or the new possibilities for unsigned "amateur" artists to share their content on streaming platforms are

---

41   Jenny Toomey, "The Future of Music," *Texas Intellectual Property Law Journal* 10, no. 2 (2001): 227, https://heinonline.org/HOL/LandingPage?handle=hein.jour nals/tipjl10&div=13.

42   Jeremy Wade Morris, "Curation by Code: Infomediaries and the Data Mining of Taste," *European Journal of Cultural Studies* 18, no. 4–5 (2015): 446–63. https://doi.org/10.1177/1367549415577387.

43   Tom Johnson, "Chance the Rapper, Spotify, and Musical Categorization in the 2010s," *American Music* 38, no. 2 (2020): 176–96, https://doi.org/10.5406/ame ricanmusic.38.2.0176.

only examples of structural reconfigurations in the production and distribution of popular music. Moreover, framing debates about revenue rates as directly between artists/songwriters and the services extends old logics around the ideology of stardom, which seek to conceal the professional mechanisms and labor involved in the commercialization of recordings and artist brands.[44] Under this ideology, success is due to the amazing charisma and talent of artist personas, while failure is accepted as the natural outcome for those who lack those rare gifts or who fail to connect with the right stakeholders who can nurture and develop them. This both hides the role of music business workers and distances their effort from the outcomes.

When particular stories of economic success or failure become the basis upon which to construct an evaluative narrative of streaming music, then we find that these narratives are in fact rooted in other assumptions as to what an *ideal* situation should resemble, but which are never fully established and fail to acknowledge the underlying design of recording industries to overproduce in search of a few stars, alongside the mass failure of most commercial releases and artist brands. In the case of royalty payments, what would a "fair" redistribution consist of, and to whom should it be paid? In the case of the streaming marketplace, who should be able to put their music into the ecosystem and benefit from it? Here is where the perspective of the "platformization of cultural production" becomes helpful.[45] Should artist brands and songwriters optimize their production for the platform, as opposed to the audience or individual listener? Whether "platformization" is seen as positive or negative for the music industries broadly relates to the question: should commercial sustainability continue to be contingent upon stakeholder experts and intermediaries to locate and develop stars and hit songs, especially given the high rate of failure? We argue that different answers to these questions can be uncovered, and they are determined by the particular approach that authors have of music and its relationship to either a democratization of culture or cultural democracy paradigm.[46] In the next section, we continue on our critical overview of accounts framing music streaming's *changes*, but this time, in cultural terms.

Audiences and the Cultural Aftermath of Music Streaming

Besides economic perspectives on how music streaming *changes* how artists and producers distribute their music, more recent discussions move towards

---

44   Marshall, "The Structural Functions of Stardom in the Recording Industry."
45   Nieborg and Poell, "The Platformization of Cultural Production."
46   Evrard, "Democratizing Culture or Cultural Democracy?"

the "cultural" aftermath of the streaming model. To some authors, the question is laid out as follows: "what has streaming done to music's value?"[47] This interrogation underpins how the technological and economic configuration of music streaming changes, or contributes to change, the value of music as cultural content.

Taste and Consumption Practices

With the shift towards audience studies in the 1970s and 1980s, consumers of culture have been described as possessing a certain autonomy.[48] Scholarly accounts of audiences' *ways of doing* align with a cultural democracy position.[49] In the case of music, this translates into the following question: "what does [music] make people do?"[50] When interrogating audiences, scholars do not focus on the type of cultural content that is listened to as much as they question 1) the contexts within which listening practices are "performed," and 2) what happens within the interactions with music, with the idea that music represents a "capacity for social action."[51] As such, listening *practices* are discussed in relation to how affective outcomes emerge. Music is understood in relation to its use value, meaning that it is *valued* by consumers, and therefore socially *valuable*, because it enables, accompanies, and affects.

In the age of music streaming, the presence of music in everyday life is said to increase.[52] Streaming services ensure a continuous musical flow by providing a playlist that fits every aspect of one's daily routine. The technological means to access and listen to music are understood as offering more options to manage an everyday accompaniment of music. A cultural democracy approach to music considers listeners as competent in their choices of music content that is suited to the different listening practices carried on in their everyday life, in direct contrast to the recording industry view that experts and intermediaries are

---

47   See, among others, David Arditi, "Music Everywhere"; Hesmondhalgh and Meier, "What the Digitalisation of Music Tells Us"; Marshall, "Do People Value Recorded Music?"

48   David Looseley, "Antoine Hennion and the Sociology of Music," *International Journal of Cultural Policy* 12, no. 3 (2016): 341–54, https://doi.org/10.1080/102 86630601020611.

49   E.g. Evrard, "Democratizing Culture or Cultural Democracy?"

50   Antoine Hennion, "Musiques, Présentez-vous! Une Comparaison entre le Rap et la Techno," *French Cultural Studies* 16 (2005): 121, https://doi.org/10.1177%2F0 957155805053702.

51   Tia DeNora, *Music in Everyday Life* (Cambridge: Cambridge University Press, 2000), 153.

52   See Spilker, *Digital Music Distribution: The Sociology of Online Music Streams*, 21–4.

needed to help listeners choose "the best music." Automated algorithms that organize recommendations present the potential to increase individuals' access to music, for instance through suggestions of automated playlists that aim at capturing a particular mood. However, algorithms construct user profiles on the basis of a pre-existing repertoire of preferences and proximity with other users.[53] In that regard, music streaming cannot necessarily be seen as the tool that will transform every user's taste one way or another. The aim of the commercial services is to get users to pay a monthly subscription. They do so by deploying algorithms that suggest content that must feel new, but also cannot be too different from the songs they usually listen to.

The process for artists to feature in playlists on streaming platforms is somewhat opaque, and it has been recently reported that rights holders attempt to influence playlist curators through "pitching" releases.[54] With algorithmic tools also involved, the curation of playlists is still seen as a new version of pitching radio programmers, magazine editors, or record store retailers to feature certain songs or releases over others. For producers unable to get their songs onto these playlists, the process seems unfair and in need of democratization. These criticisms echo old narratives of the corrupt influence of radio promotion companies and major labels.[55] The extension of older recording industry concepts frames these tools of recommendation and curation as new sociotechnical intermediaries which are needed to add value to songs, and can be influenced through strategic campaigns of influence, extending the old logics around publicity, promotion, and marketing. In this frame, the producers are still optimizing music for audiences. Alternately, the platformization view would portray these same streaming services as platforms: novel structures which require different production approaches than cultural intermediaries. This view also constrains the formerly vital role of recording industry stakeholders in favor of the platforms. Whether seen as new versions of old intermediaries, or as novel platforms, the end result is that the way artist brands, albums, and songs are selected into playlists and other automated recommendation features is a process that remains curated and mediated for users. Now the question is whether this very process of curation and mediation is seen as a necessary form of imposition of certain artists and songs onto users' everyday listening practices or a mere suggestion as to what content can be a better fit with what everyday activity.

---

53   Prey, "Musica Analytica."
54   Morgan, "Revenue, Access, and Engagement."
55   Fredric Dannen, Hit Men: Power Brokers and Fast Money Inside the Music Business (Sydney: Muller, 1990).

The importance of music streaming as a mode of music consumption raises an important theoretical conundrum. Eric Drott for instance argues that even the desire to consume new music needs to be manufactured, implying that the urge to hear new music is itself fabricated in the interest of platform capitalism.[56] David Arditi goes further by arguing that the ubiquity of music as organized by streaming platforms means that we are "inundated" with music.[57] The "digital music trap" commodifies our everyday existence, turns music consumers into music users, and makes us pay for music with cash or data for access to a platform. Arditi's critique of music streaming aligns with a democratization of culture perspective, whereby the techno-cultural infrastructure (here, streaming services) entraps and dominates its users by imposing a continuous stream of music.

A cultural democracy perspective would instead highlight how streaming platforms enable (to some extent) different "independent units"[58] to better connect and feed each other's taste and practices. Moreover, the autonomy of music consumers means that they are given more opportunities—through access to a large catalog of music content—to find the music that is better suited to their everyday tasks and with the aim of an affective outcome. The opposition between the two paradigms points to a different approach to the issue of the value of music in the age of streaming, which we explore more closely in the next section.

Music's Presence, Listeners' Attention ... and Regimes of Cultural Value

The issue of the value of music has recently become of prominent significance across scholarly publications.[59] The question is not so much about whether the cultural value of music has evolved over time, since we can simply point to the historical and cultural evolution of popular music, its division and development into various genres, its increasing presence within societies, and the evolution of technologies that enable humans to produce, distribute, and consume it. Instead, the question lies in whether the increasing "ubiquity" of music transforms how we value it in a non-econometric sense, or: does the presence of music in contemporary capitalistic societies—and especially mediated by streaming services—make it more valuable to *people*, or less valuable?

---

56   Eric Drott, "Why the Next Song Matters: Streaming, Recommendation, Scarcity," *Twentieth-Century Music* 15, no. 3 (2018): 325–57, https://doi.org/10.1017/s147 8572218000245.

57   David Arditi, "Music Everywhere," 617–18

58   Evrard, "Democratizing Culture or Cultural Democracy?," 170.

59   See, among others, David Arditi, "Music Everywhere"; Hesmondhalgh and Meier, "What the Digitalisation of Music Tells Us."

While we witness a resurgence of publications on the issue of music's cultural value, and particularly in relation to its association with streaming platforms, we first need to ask whether music streaming constitutes a point of rupture. Of course, all authors would point to the genealogy of digital music as laying the grounds for the current organization of music streaming. Nevertheless, there may be something specific to music streaming in the age of platform ecosystems which would tip the issue "over the line." For instance, while Arditi acknowledges that recorded music has always been a commodity, the current techno-economic infrastructure, which he analyses as a "digital music trap," further commodifies music. He writes: "the digital music trap allows for the perpetual exploitation of listening-labor through the expanded means of music consumption."[60] Likewise, in Hesmondhalgh and Meier's cultural history of the evolution of digital music, we find that the third "moment" that is characterized by the dominance of IT companies may result in a "loss" of "music's power."[61]

In those critics, we note two dominant issues that are somewhat located into the technological infrastructure of music consumption: first, there is a loss of music's economic value (we no longer pay for units); second, the ubiquitous background presence of music means we do not pay attention to it, which reduces its emotional force. On that later point, Lee Marshall draws on a neo-classical approach to value (stipulating that people need to be "aware" of objects) and notes that "the idea of ubiquitous listening can contribute to an explanation as to why many individuals may not view music as particularly valuable, especially given that, by definition, this kind of musical experience exists on the periphery of an individual's consciousness."[62] Tying those two issues together, he adds that "it is not difficult to see why peripheral awareness of low-intensity musical experience may result in most people thinking that music is not worth paying for, or at least not paying much for."[63] A key concept that is present across the accounts of Arditi, Hesmondhalgh and Meier, and Marshall is the one of the "average listener," which somehow enables them to speak on behalf of a disembodied collective of individuals. In that regard, the issue of music's ubiquity is understood as having a direct correlation with the one of "attention," which is itself constructed as a monolith: background music means "no attention." Such critics are reminiscent of the democratization paradigm, whereby music listeners are constructed as a whole body of passive consumers.[64]

---

60   Arditi, "Music Everywhere: Setting a Digital Music Trap," 625.
61   Hesmondhalgh and Meier, "What the Digitalisation of Music Tells Us," 1568.
62   Marshall, "Do People Value Recorded Music?," 153.
63   Marshall, "Do People Value Recorded Music?," 153.
64   See Evrard, "Democratizing Culture or Cultural Democracy?," 171.

The cultural democracy approach to music as defended by the likes of Hennion or DeNora emphasizes the emotional forces of music as experienced by competent and active individuals.[65] To David Looseley, this is a narrative about music's "expressive value."[66] Although authors in this paradigm largely fail to provide a true perspective on how technological means to music consumption play a critical part in how individuals access and listen to music,[67] there is an underlying assumption that technologies such as CDs, MP3 files, and now streaming platforms do not "dominate" consumers as much as they offer pathways through which musical explorations are possible. While this perspective provides very little insight on the actual structural organization of music distribution, it directly opposes the view that music's emotional force results from a domination from the top, a rather philosophical challenge to the anxiety about the need for intermediaries to help identify appropriate canons. Instead, it considers individuals' affective responses to music as the basis upon which any discourse on music's emotional force and cultural value becomes possible.

The different perspectives on value certainly make the two paradigms (democratization of culture and cultural democracy) quite apparent in how different authors approach the issue of music's contemporary value. The question that remains is the actual role that is to be attributed to streaming platforms in the changes (for better or worse) to music's cultural value. As Marshall contends, "it is possible that new digital technologies have simply revealed some of the underlying social dynamics of music listening rather than causing any kind of cultural devaluation."[68] What is certain, however, is that those conversations will continue to develop over the coming years.

Conclusion

The current state of recorded music, which is largely organized around music streaming, has attracted a great deal of attention from scholars. In this chapter, we have attempted to critically discuss some of the accounts that evaluate the "nature" of current transformations to the production, distribution, and consumption of music. By deploying Evrard's dichotomy of positions towards

---

65 See Hennion, "Musiques, Présentez-vous! Une Comparaison entre le Rap et la Techno" or DeNora, *Music in Everyday Life*.
66 Looseley, "Antoine Hennion and the Sociology of Music," 343.
67 Raphaël Nowak, *Consuming Music in the Digital Age. Technologies, Roles and Everyday Life* (Basingstoke: Palgrave Macmillan, 2016).
68 Marshall, "Do People Value Recorded Music?," 153.

culture and its status, we are able to understand how these accounts are actually situated within particular logics, which in turn betray particular expectations about the relationship between music and contemporary society. We note that following the emergence of audience studies in the 1970s and 1980s,[69] and particularly from the 1990s, the cultural democracy paradigm has dominated certain research fields. Led notably by sociologists such as DeNora and Hennion, who have contributed to new knowledge about music and its emotional forces, this approach has certainly influenced a particular strain of music research. In opposition, we witness a rising tide of critics that question positivist conclusions about music's presence in contemporary societies.[70] The current state of music distribution and consumption based on streaming provides an ideal culprit to point to the limitations of the cultural democracy paradigm and/or to argue against its main conclusions. We here want to conclude with two main ideas from our critical evaluation of accounts on music and streaming:

First, we note that analyses of music streaming tend to deploy particular examples or stories to base a discursive evaluation of the *whole* situation. However, depending on what the analyses focus on—be it royalty payments, access to the marketplace, attention paid to music—the evaluations of the current situation differ. We argue that the focus on one stakeholder perspective, personal narrative (of success or failure), or technological location to construct a critical evaluation of the current music streaming ecosystem fails to capture the complexity of the political, social, and cultural organizations that enable these very stories to emerge and infrastructures to exist, disseminate, and become successful in the first place. Rather than providing a finite point, these stories are in need of further scrutiny because they are in fact passageways to explore the political and social organization that enables them.

Second, even if they can remain somewhat concealed, ideas are carried in each account concerning for example what music *ought* to be, who *ought* to be remunerated for it, and how it *ought* to be listened to. Streaming services become a leitmotif to construct a critical narrative as to why music becomes something that it should *ideally* not be, and in that regard, we argue that such accounts convey "old stories" about an ideal state of music as an economic and/or cultural object. Those critics evaluate the current state of music against an invisible benchmark, inasmuch as they do not clearly state what the reference point is. Thus, to those critics, we ask the following questions (among many others): With regard to the economics of streaming, what would a "fair" redistribution of royalty payment resemble? Who should receive less in order

---

69   Looseley, "Antoine Hennion and the Sociology of Music."
70   Primarily from the 2000s, and for instance through the work of David Hesmond-halgh.

to compensate those who "deserve" more, and who should be entitled to judge this? When it comes to culturally valuing music, what does paying attention to music actually mean? What are the conditions within which it can happen? While we certainly do not wish to argue against the very legitimacy of deploying a critical evaluation of music streaming, we would instead invite authors to more clearly establish what the counterpart to a bad situation is. In the absence of such discourse, we are instead left with the perspective of the onlooker as constitutive of what music—its economic and cultural value—is.

References

Adorno, Theodor W. *Current of Music. Elements of a Radio Theory.* Cambridge: Polity, 2009.

Arditi, David. "Music Everywhere: Setting a Digital Music Trap." *Critical Sociology* 45, no. 4–5 (2019): 617–30. https://doi.org/10.1177/0896920517729192.

Bazinet, Jason B., Kota Ezawa, Mark May, Thomas A Singlehurst, Jim Suva, and Alicia Yap. *Putting The Band Back Together: Remastering the World of Music.* Citi Gps: Global Perspectives & Solutions, 2018. https://www.citivelocity.com/citigps/music-industry/.

Benjamins, Steve. "How Spotify & Discover Weekly Earns Me $400 / Month." *Steve Benjamins* (blog). March 14, 2019. https://www.stevebenjamins.com/blog/spotify-and-discover-weekly.

Bonini, Tiziano, and Alessandro Gandini. "'First Week Is Editorial, Second Week Is Algorithmic:' Platform Gatekeepers and the Platformization of Music Curation." *Social Media + Society* 5, no. 4 (2019): 1–11. https://doi.org/10.1177/2056305119880006.

Bourdieu, Pierre. *Distinction: A Social Critique of the Judgment of Taste.* London: Routledge, 1984.

Brennan, Matt, and Kyle Devine. "The Cost of Music." *Popular Music* 39, no. 1 (2020): 43–65. https://doi.org/10.1017/S0261143019000552.

Chapple, Steve, and Reebee Garofalo. *Rock'n'roll is Here to Pay: The History and Politics of the Music Industry.* Chicago: Nelson-Hall, 1977.

Dannen, Fredric. *Hit Men: Power Brokers and Fast Money Inside the Music Business.* Sydney: Muller, 1990.

DeNora, Tia. *Music in Everyday Life.* Cambridge: Cambridge University Press, 2000.

DiCola, Peter. "Money from Music: Survey Evidence on Musicians' Revenue and Lessons about Copyright Incentives." *Arizona Law Review* 55, no. 2 (2013): 301–70. https://ssrn.com/abstract=2199058.

Drott, Eric. "Why the Next Song Matters: Streaming, Recommendation, Scarci-

ty." *Twentieth-Century Music* 15, no. 3 (2018): 325–57. https://doi.org/10.1
017/s1478572218000245.

Eriksson, Maria, Rasmus Fleischer, Anna Johansson, Pelle Snickars, and Patrick
Vonderau. *Spotify Teardown: Inside the Black Box of Streaming Music*. Cambridge, MA: MIT Press, 2019.

Evrard, Yves. "Democratizing Culture or Cultural Democracy?" *Journal of Arts
Management, Law, and Society* 27, no. 3 (1997): 167–75. https://doi.org/10.
1080/10632929709596961.

Frith, Simon. "The Good, the Bad, and the Indifferent: Defending Popular
Culture from the Populists." *Diacritics* 21, no. 4 (1991): 101–15. https://www
.jstor.org/stable/465379.

Galuszka, Patryk. "Music Aggregators and Intermediation of the Digital Music
Market." *International Journal of Communications* 9 (2015): 254–73. https:/
/ijoc.org/index.php/ijoc/article/view/3113/1298.

Hebdige, Dick. *Subculture: The Meaning of Style*. London: Methuen, 1979.

Hennion, Antoine. "Musiques, Présentez-vous! Une Comparaison entre le Rap
et la Techno." *French Cultural Studies* 16 (2005): 121–34. https://doi.org/10
.1177%2F0957155805053702.

Hesmondhalgh, David. "Have Digital Communication Technologies Democratized the Media Industries?" In *Media and Society*, edited by James Curran
and David Hesmondhalgh, 6th ed., 101–20. London: Bloomsbury, 2019.

———. "Is Music Streaming Bad for Musicians? Problems of Evidence and
Argument." *New Media and Society* (September 2020): 1–18. https://doi.o
rg/10.1177/1461444820953541.

Hesmondhalgh, David, Ellis Jones, and Andreas Rauth. "SoundCloud and Bandcamp as Alternative Music Platforms." *Social Media + Society* (October 2019):
1–13. https://doi.org/10.1177/2056305119883429.

Hesmondhalgh, David and Leslie Meier. "What the Digitalisation of Music Tells
Us about Capitalism, Culture and the Power of the Information Technology
Sector." *Information, Communication & Society* 21, no. 11 (2018): 1555–570. h
ttps://doi.org/10.1080/1369118X.2017.1340498.

International Federation of the Phonographic Industry. *Global Music Report
2018: State of the Industry*. 2018. https://www.ifpi.org/ifpi-global-music-
report-2018/.

Ingham, Tim. "Nearly 40,000 Tracks Are Now Being Added to Spotify Every
Single Day." *Music Business Worldwide* (blog). April 29, 2019. https://www.
musicbusinessworldwide.com/nearly-40000-tracks-are-now-being-add
ed-to-spotify-every-single-day/.

Johnson, Tom. "Chance the Rapper, Spotify, and Musical Categorization in the
2010s." *American Music* 38, no. 2 (2020): 176–96. https://doi.org/10.5406/
americanmusic.38.2.0176.

Krueger, Alan B. *Rockonomics: A Backstage Tour of What the Music Industry Can Teach Us about Economics and Life.* New York: Currency, 2019.

Looseley, David. "Antoine Hennion and the Sociology of Music." *International Journal of Cultural Policy* 12, no. 3 (2016): 341–54. https://doi.org/10.1080/10286630601020611.

Marshall, Lee. "The Structural Functions of Stardom in the Recording Industry." *Popular Music and Society* 36, no. 5 (2013): 578–96. https://doi.org/10.1080/03007766.2012.718509.

———. "'Let's Keep Music Special. F— Spotify:' On-demand Streaming and the Controversy over Artist Royalties." *Creative Industries Journal* 8, no. 2 (2015): 177–89. https://doi.org/10.1080/17510694.2015.1096618.

———. "Do People Value Recorded Music?" *Cultural Sociology* 13, no. 2 (2019): 141–58. https://doi.org/10.1177/1749975519839524.

Mogis, Jay. "Transparency, Technology and Trust: Music Metrics and Cultural Distortion." Ph.D. diss., Queensland University of Technology, 2020. https://doi.org/10.5204/thesis.eprints.199497.

Morgan, Benjamin A. "Revenue, Access, and Engagement via the In-house Curated Spotify Playlist in Australia." *Popular Communication* 18, no. 1 (2020): 32–47. https://doi.org/10.1080/15405702.2019.1649678.

Morris, Jeremy Wade. "Curation by Code: Infomediaries and the Data Mining of Taste." *European Journal of Cultural Studies* 18, no. 4–5 (2015): 446–63. https://doi.org/10.1177/1367549415577387.

———. *Selling Digital Music, Formatting Culture.* Oakland, CA: University of California Press, 2015.

Mulligan, Mark. "Recorded Music Revenues Hit $21.5 Billion in 2019." *Music Industry Blog* (blog). March 5, 2020. https://musicindustryblog.wordpress.com/tag/record-label-market-shares-2019/.

Nieborg, David B., and Thomas Poell. "The Platformization of Cultural Production: Theorizing the Contingent Cultural Commodity." *New Media & Society* 20, no. 11 (2018): 4275–92. https://doi.org/10.1177/1461444818769694.

Nowak, Raphaël. *Consuming Music in the Digital Age. Technologies, Roles and Everyday Life.* Basingstoke: Palgrave Macmillan, 2016.

Prey, Robert. "Musica Analytica: The Datafication of Listening." In *Networked Music Cultures: Contemporary Approaches, Emerging Issues*, edited by Raphaël Nowak and Andrew Whelan, 31–48. London: Palgrave Macmillan UK, 2016.

Resnikoff, Paul. "Welcome to the 'Royalty Black Box,' the Music Industry's $2.5 Billion Underground Economy." *Digital Music News* (blog). August 3, 2017. https://www.digitalmusicnews.com/2017/08/03/music-industry-royalty-black-box/.

Rethink Music Initiative (Berklee Institute of Creative Entrepreneurship). "Fair

Music: Transparency and Payment Flows in the music industry." 2015. http
s://www.rethink-music.com/research/fair-music-transparency-and-p
ayment-flows-in-the-music-industry.

Seaver, Nick. "Algorithms as Culture: Some Tactics for the Ethnography of
Algorithmic Systems." *Big Data & Society* 4, no. 2 (2017): 1–12. https://doi
.org/10.1177/2053951717738104.

Sinnreich, Aram. *The Piracy Crusade*. Boston: University of Massachusetts Press,
2013.

———. "Slicing the Pie: The Search for an Equitable Recorded Music Economy."
In *Business Innovation and Disruption in the Music Industry*, edited by
Patrik Wikström and Robert DeFillippi, 153–74. Cheltenham: Edward Elgar
Publishing, 2016.

Spilker, Hendrik Storstein. *Digital Music Distribution: The Sociology of Online
Music Streams*. New York: Routledge, 2017.

Thomson, Kristin. "Roles, Revenue, and Responsibilities: The Changing Nature
of Being a Working Musician." *Work and Occupations* 40, no. 4 (2013): 514–25.
https://doi.org/10.1177/0730888413504208.

Toomey, Jenny. "The Future of Music." *Texas Intellectual Property Law Journal*
10, no. 2 (2001): 221–43. https://heinonline.org/HOL/LandingPage?handl
e=hein.journals/tipj10&div=13.

Tschmuck, Peter. *The Economics of Music*. Newcastle upon Tyne: Agenda
Publishing, 2017.

van Dijck, José, Thomas Poell, and Martijn de Waal. *The Platform Society: Public
Values in a Connective World*. New York: Oxford University Press, 2018.

Wikström, Patrik. *The Music Industry: Music in the Cloud*. 3rd ed. Medford, MA:
Polity Press, 2020.

Part 2:
Political Impacts of Bourgeois Music Culture

The National Society of Music (1915–1922) and the Ambivalent Democratization of Music in Spain

David Ferreiro Carballo

Abstract: The Spanish National Society of Music was founded in 1915 with a double objective: first, to define, once and for all, the musical identity of the country; and second, to create a space where composers and musicians could develop their artistic careers. In this sense, both the society's self-denomination as "national," and its apparent integrating nature suggest a clear attempt to democratize Spanish music. However, the present paper shows that the reality was completely different. Yet, by analyzing the society's internal ideology, by describing its policy for selecting the repertoire of the concerts, and by examining its actual social impact, I demonstrate that the National Society of Music was a non-democratic institution with an elitist understanding of the art. This reality strongly contrasts its typically idealized conception and will allow the reader to understand its disappearance in 1922, after only seven seasons of activity.

David Ferreiro Carballo holds a Ph.D. in Musicology (2019) and a master's degree in Spanish and Hispano-American music from the Complutense University of Madrid (2015). His lines of research focus around Spanish music and musicians of the nineteenth and twentieth centuries.

At the beginning of the 1910s, some of the most influential Spanish composers and performers who were developing their artistic careers in the country started to demand an improvement in their work situation. Their primary complaints focused around the little attention that institutions devoted to musical diffusion—especially the Philharmonic Societies—were paying to their music. In such a way, the press and the specialized magazines became a forum for debate on this issue, and the point of no return was the manifesto signed in August of 1911 by the composer Rogelio Villar. Within his writing, not only did he manage to summarize the claims of the moment, but he also proposed, as a solution, the creation of the National Society of Music, as we can read in the following extract from the aforementioned manifesto:

> The Spanish composers who cultivate composition for the love of the art, as [a] sort of apostolate, since in Spain, currently, it is not possible to aspire

to make a living from this art, [we] spend our lives regretting, rightly, the shortage of concerts of chamber and symphonic music, the little importance that is given among us to musical art, the lack of a national lyrical theater, the need for a concert hall, [the absence of] intelligent criticism, the little interest for good music and the lack of protection, the almost abandonment and indifference that the government shows for this art, [and] the unpatriotic work of musical societies that, like the Madrilenian Philharmonic, [...] do little or nothing for Spanish music and musicians.

As composers, we would remedy our already chronic ills [...] by constituting a National Society of Music, like the French, or the Italian, dedicated, if not exclusively, with the specialty of promoting the love of our music, organizing concerts of works by Spanish composers, executed by artists and groups of the country. [...] There is no other solution: [...]. Anything other than founding a National Society for the purpose indicated, by means of a sincere union between the composers, will be wasting time and crying out to the moon [...].[1]

Therefore, and after four years of fierce discussions between musicians and members of Philharmonic Societies, the final establishment of the National Society of Music in 1915 promised a solution for two longstanding problems plaguing the Spanish musical milieu. Firstly, there was a need to define the country's musical identity, which translated into a strong concern about the development of Spanish music and its integration into the international context. Secondly, the musical canon was dissociated from new music, which had difficulties finding its way into the musical circuit and to the audience. Yet during the Society's years of activity (1915–1922), a strong cultural restoration was going on in Spain in which music was placed, at last,

---

1   "Los compositores españoles que cultivamos la composición por amor al arte, como [una] especie de apostolado, pues en España, por ahora, no puede aspirarse a vivir de este arte, pasamos la vida lamentándonos, con razón, de la escasez de conciertos de música de cámara y sinfónica, de la poca importancia que se da entre nosotros al arte musical, de la falta de un teatro lírico nacional, de la necesidad de una sala de conciertos, de una crítica inteligente, de la poca afición a la buena música y de la falta de protección, del casi abandono e indiferencia que el estado tiene por este arte, de la labor poco patriótica de las sociedades musicales que, como la filarmónica madrileña, [...] poco o nada hacen por la música y músicos españoles. Los compositores remediaríamos nuestros ya crónicos males [...] constituyendo una Sociedad Nacional de Música, como la francesa, o como la italiana, dedicada, si no exclusivamente, con especialidad a fomentar la afición a nuestra música, organizando conciertos de obras de compositores españoles, ejecutadas por artistas y agrupaciones del país. [...] No hay otra solución: [...] Todo lo que no sea fundar una Sociedad Nacional con el fin indicado por medio de una unión sincera de los compositores será perder el tiempo y clamar a la luna [...]." Rogelio Villar, "Sociedad Nacional de Música," *Revista musical* [Bilbao], no. 8 (August 1911): 194 (author's translation).

at the height of the other arts in importance and consideration.[2] Moreover, as I will discuss later on, this issue was part of a larger debate in Spanish politics and society on how to reform the country after the "Disaster of 1898"—a term employed to denominate the loss, in 1898, of the last colonies of Cuba and the Philippines—and how to proceed during the World War I.

Consequently, and following the essential premises of its own constitution, the Society introduced a wide range of old and new repertoire by Spanish composers, as well as pieces created by foreign musicians following the new European musical practices. In this sense, both the Society's identity as "national" and its apparent integrating nature suggest a clear attempt to democratize Spanish music, giving a space reclaimed by composers and performers, but also opening up the musical circuit to a wider array of audiences through concerts. Indeed, this was the first amendment of its own Book of Regulation:

> Art. I. With the name of *Sociedad Nacional de Música* is created one in this Court, which object is, firstly, to promote the musical creation and to procure that the music produced is performed and edited. By the same token, it would also be the object of the Society everything that, in addition to the first objective, means culture and promotion of the music.[3]

However, and after researching this transcendental institution,[4] a crucial question arises: Was this attempt at democratization a real priority for the direction of the National Society of Music?

Hence, throughout this paper, I explore and answer this question by studying how the internal ideology of the National Society of Music and its social impact affected its active involvement in disseminating music. First, I analyze the cultural context and the ideological and aesthetic debates generated at the very moment of its foundation. Second, I address one issue related to its operation: the selection of the repertoire. Finally, I examine the typology of its members and the opinions of the critics. In doing so, I show that the National

---

2   María Nagore, Leticia Sánchez de Andrés, and Elena Torres, eds., *Música y cultura en la Edad de Plata (1915–1939)* (Madrid: Instituto Complutense de Ciencias Musicales, 2009).

3   " Art. I. Con el título de *Sociedad Nacional de Música* se constituye una en esta corte una cuyo objeto es, en primer término, el de fomentar la creación musical y procurar que la música producida sea publicada en conciertos y ediciones. Será asimismo objeto de la sociedad todo aquello que, además de este primer objetivo, signifique cultura y fomento de la música." *Reglamento* [Book of Regulation], Madrid, Biblioteca de la Real Academia de Bellas Artes de San Fernando, Legacy of Bartolomé Pérez Casas, signature M-3383 (author's translation).

4   David Ferreiro Carballo, "La Sociedad Nacional de Música (1915–1922): Historia, Repertorio y Recepción" (Master's thesis, Universidad Complutense de Madrid, 2015).

Society of Music was a non-democratic institution with an elitist understanding of the art—a reality that strongly contrasts its typically idealized conception.

The Context and the Origin of the Ideology

The members of the National Society of Music projected inside the institution an aesthetic conflict between two external cultural powers: France and Germany. Musicologist Samuel Llano, in his book *Whose Spain?*,[5] has explored this issue in depth, putting on the table the influence of France in the configuration of the face of Spanish musical identity, which had been the most visible up until the present. Paraphrasing his own words, the first two decades of the twentieth century show a change in the mentality of French intellectuals who, in their cultural studies of Spain, captured concerns over the military and cultural hegemony of Germany, who had won the Franco-Prussian War in 1870. Consequently, they ended up building an image of Spain that is based on its Latin essence and is described by a very strong anti-Teutonic character, especially within the musical milieu. In this sense, Spain was considered within their writings to be the best cultural allied of France against Germany, and this reality—which will be crucial to understand the operation of the Spanish National Society of Music—is summarized by Samuel Llano as follows:

> The early decades of the twentieth century witnessed a significant change in how Spain was situated on the French intellectual horizon. At that moment, Spain ceased to be mostly regarded as an exotic corner of Europe, and was increasingly being used as a discursive site on which to project shared anxieties over the definition of a French identity. Although the popular imaginaries mostly relied on nineteenth-century "exotic" stereotypes of Spain, French intellectuals started to reflect their concerns over Germany's military power and cultural hegemony in their studies about Spanish culture, literature, music and the arts. This phenomenon stemmed from the fact that, unlike Spain, Germany had represented a military, diplomatic, economic and cultural rival since at least the mid-nineteenth-century.[6]

Hence, before 1914 in France, the French intelligentsia wrote a set of anti-German discourses based on the idea of a union between all nations with a Latin tradition. Once again using Llano's words, for the French, Spain rapidly assumed the status of a "cultural periphery, or [even] more particularly, a satellite of France."[7] Some years later, immediately after the outbreak of World War I in

---

5   Samuel Llano, *Whose Spain?* (New York: Oxford University Press, 2013).
6   Llano, *Whose Spain*, 3.
7   Llano, *Whose Spain*, 12. In addition to Llano's discussion, the ideological development of French music in the pre-war time was also analyzed by Barbara

1914, the idea of Spain as an appendix of France became more pronounced and was supported by the most celebrated French Hispanists of the time, who continued with the idea of considering the adjacent country as a major cultural ally against Germany. Within the musical sphere, Henri Collet stands out as a leading French intellectual during this period, and Llano summarizes his ideas in the following manner: "[Collet] argues that the Spanish national musical school exists only thanks to the support and encouragement of French musicians, who have instilled a sense of national pride in their Spanish counterparts."[8] In addition to that, the Spanish musicians who were studying in France contributed themselves to the consolidation of this artificial stance. A good example of this is the testimony of the Spanish composer Manuel de Falla, who wrote in a letter addressed to the painter Ignacio Zuloaga: "referring to my profession, my homeland is Paris."[9]

From my discussion above, a reality that was important for the constitution of the National Society of Music emerges: a sizable majority of the Spanish composers from the beginning of the twentieth century had chosen Paris for studying with the masters of the French school. Not only did they learn French musical techniques but also assumed and integrated the anti-German discourses that I have mentioned. Once World War I began in 1914, these musicians returned to Spain with a clear aesthetic point of view and were ready to defend the principles instilled in their minds by French propaganda. If this was not enough, due to the neutrality of Spain during the Great War, French Hispanists could keep in touch with the principal Spanish musicians of the time, which made it possible for them to maintain their influence during the years of activity of the National Society of Music (1915–1922).

However, in those years Madrid was also going through the last peak of the Wagnerism, especially after the first premiere of *Tristan und Isolde* in the Royal

---

Kelly, *Music and Ultra-Modernism in France. A fragile Consensus*, 1913–1939 (Woodbridge: The Boydell Press, 2013).

8   Llano, *Whose Spain*, 38.

9   "*Para cuanto se refiere a mi oficio, mi patria es París.*" Letter from Manuel de Falla to the painter Ignacio Zuloaga, dated in Granada on February 12, 1923 (author's translation). The whereabouts of the original are unknown. There is a copy in Granada (Spain), Fundación y Archivo Manuel de Falla, folder of correspondence 7798. Of course, this quotation is only a direct example to illustrate here Falla's aesthetic thought. However, this issue has been deeply studied by other scholars, such as Michael Christoforidis, "Aspects in the Creative Process in Manuel de Falla's *El retablo de Maese Pedro* and Concerto" (Ph.D. diss., University of Melbourne, 1997); Carol Hess, *Manuel de Falla and the Modernism in Spain*, 1898–1936 (Chicago: University of Chicago Press, 2001); and Elena Torres Clemente, *Las operas de Manuel de Falla: de* La vida breve *a* El retable de Maese Pedro (Madrid: Sociedad Española de Musicología, 2007).

Theater, in 1911,[10] which meant that some composers supported the German musical influence. Of course, this reality reveals a larger debate that comes from the so-called "Disaster of 1918." Yet, after losing the colonies of Cuba and Filipinas, Spain initiated a process of political and cultural regeneration in order to integrate the country inside Europe. The outbreak of World War I took place in the middle of this process, when nothing was completely defined. In consequence, Spain—which at the moment was not important to the other European nations—faced a military conflict without a clear ideological position, and have to decide among three proposals derived from the war: the parliamentary monarchy of Great Britain, the French Republic, and the authoritative monarchy of Germany.[11] The problem was that the political tendencies and the artistic influences of the Spanish intelligentsia did not match: for example, a political supporter of France could also be a cultural supporter of Germany, and vice versa. This is just one reason why the apparent neutrality of Spain was much more complex than the simple fact of not participating in the actual war.[12] This also applies in particular to the musical milieu and, especially, to the National Society of Music. Hence, the ingredients for an internal aesthetic conflict within the institution were on the table.

Indeed, the cultural and social tensions that I have outlined allowed the coexistence of two opposed aesthetic models within the Artistic Committee of the National Society of Music: on the one hand, those who had returned from Paris, represented by Manuel de Falla, brought with them a Francophile agenda influenced by the style of Claude Debussy. Therefore, they built a musical identity based on Spanish popular sources subjugated to the symbolistic modal harmonies of Debussy's model. On the other hand, there was a group of musicians with Conrado del Campo at the forefront,[13] which projected prac-

---

10   To go deeper into the influence of Wagner in Madrid between 1900 and 1914, see Paloma Ortiz de Urbina Sobrino, "La recepción de Richard Wagner en Madrid (1900–1914)" (Ph.D. diss., Universidad Complutense de Madrid, 2003).

11   To go deeper into this issue, see Maximiliano Fuentes Codera, *España en la Primera Guerra Mundial. Una movilización cultural* (Madrid: Akal, 2014).

12   The cultural and political tensions generated in Spain during World War I between neutrals, allies, and Germanophiles were studied in depth by Andreu Navarra Ordoño, 1914. *Aliadófilos y germanófilos en la cultura Española* (Madrid: Cátedra, 2014).

13   Conrado del Campo was, together with Manuel de Falla, one of the most important composers of the time, not only because of the inherent quality of his prolific catalogue, but also due to the influence of his aesthetic ideas on his students at the Conservatory of Madrid, where he taught composition from 1915 onwards. For more about this important figure, I recommend two main sources: 1) Ramón García Avello, "Campo Zavaleta, Conrado del," in *Diccionario de la música española e hispanoamericana* (Madrid: SGAE, 1999–2002), 2:982–93;

tices from the second half of the nineteenth century and combined them with more advanced gestures, textures, and harmonies that were employed by other German composers of the time. Thus, they created an alternative vision of the Spanish musical identity which also made use of material stemming from traditional music, but hybridized them with a German influence combined with the strong Wagnerian heritage that had been developed during the first fifteen years of the twentieth century. Despite the fact that this situation was general within the Spanish musical milieu, it ended up conditioning the operation of the National Society of Music, as I will demonstrate.

The Programmed Repertoire

Of course, this aesthetic confrontation was reflected in the musical programming of the National Society of Music. In this sense, during its seven seasons of activity (1915–1922), the institution organized a total of 82 concerts in which an approximate number of 754 musical pieces were performed, as it is shown on Table 1.

After having carried out a systematic study of the National Society's programming in the aforementioned study,[14] it is possible to state that, in general, the society was quite integrating: despite the internal ideological inclination that I will explain later, they put together, to a greater or lesser extent, a very rich variety of musical styles. In this sense, the concerts included pieces that are modern and canonical; Spanish and foreign; solo, chamber, and orchestral. In addition, performers ranged from musicians known primarily in Spain to artists with international reputations. This was explained by the secretary of the institution, Adolfo Salazar, who wrote in 1919—when the institution had already overcome the middle-point of its activity—an accurate summary of the Society's programming that, as a matter of fact, completely matches with my analysis:

> The Society has given 61 concerts, in which 338 Spanish works have been performed, premiering 157 of them. The number of foreign [compositions] is approximately the same: 387, with 171 at the first hearing. Among the authors, most of them current, we can find French, English, Italians, Bohemians, Hungarians and Russians. The works range from the grand orchestra to solo piano, [and] there have been "concert versions" of lyric theater, symphonies, suites, symphonic poems, sextets, quintets, quartets, trios and sonatas for bow and wind instruments; [and] celebrated virtuoso

---

2) David Ferreiro Carballo, Conrado del Campo y la definición de una nueva identidad lírica española: *El final de don Álvaro* (1910–1911) y *La tragedia del beso* (1911–1915) (Ph.D. diss., Universidad Complutense de Madrid, 2019).

14 Ferreiro, *La Sociedad.*

		1915	1915-16	1916-17	1917-18	1918-19	1919-20	1920-21
					Seasons (years)			
	I	7	4	18	14	16	17	12
	II	11	5	3	15	4	10	16
	III	7	4	9	3	12	3*	3
	IV	9	3	10	12	11	4*	10
	V	11	10	5	13	7	2*	4
	VI	19	15	4	4	7	-*	11
Concerts	VII	11	11	19	8	9	5	11
	VIII	3	8	8	6	5	19	11
	IX	-	11	4	4	9	6	9
	X	-	21	4	18	20	3	5
	XI	-	4	10	4	17	4	-
	XII	-	16	13	11	13	-	-
	XIII	-	9	11	7	5	-	-
	XIV	-	-	18	-	-	-	-
Total		754	78	121	136	119	135	73*	92

Table 1: Seasons, concerts, and number of pieces programmed by the National Society of Music during its seven years of activity (1915-1922). Author's elaboration based on the historical sources mentioned below. The Roman numerals in the left column refer to each concert throughout the corresponding season, as is indicated in the top row. The Arabic numerals in the columns, in turn, represent the number of pieces performed in each of these concerts. The data comes from the official concert programs, which I accessed in two important Spanish archives: the Fundación y Archivo Manuel de Falla, located in the city of Granada, and the Biblioteca de la Real Academia de Bellas Artes de San Fernando, located in Madrid. Notwithstanding, notice that the Arabic numbers marked with an asterisk in the sixth season (1919-20) are approximative and based on historical newspapers, since it was not possible to locate the actual programs of concerts III, IV, V, and VI.

and emerging artists have paraded for their stage (the sessions were held in the concert hall of the Ritz hotel).[15]

However, if we focus our attention on the names of the composers that were programmed on the concerts of the society, we see its actual aesthetic tendency. First of all, let us take a look at the general top ten:

Name	Pieces programmed
Claude Debussy	61
Enrique Granados	32
Isaac Albéniz	25
Frederick Chopin	23
Wolfgang Amadeus Mozart	17
César Franck	17
Gabriel Fauré	17
Rogelio Villar	17
Manuel de Falla	16
Maurice Ravel	16

Table 2: The ten most programmed composers of the National Society of Music during its seven seasons (1915–1922). Author's elaboration based on the historical sources mentioned above.

As it is possible to see in Table 2, Claude Debussy is first in the ranking (8.1%), with more than twice the number of pieces as the next composer. Debussy is followed by Enrique Granados (4.4 %) in second place and Isaac Albéniz (3.3%) in third—two composers who are considered to be aesthetic precursors of Manuel Falla and are also very close to the Francophile style, especially Isaac Albéniz[16].

15 "La Sociedad lleva dados 61 conciertos, en los que ha interpretado 338 obras españolas, estrenando 157 de ellas. El número de extranjeras es aproximadamente igual: 387, con 171 en primera audición. Entre los autores, en su mayoría actuales, figuran franceses, ingleses, italianos, bohemios, húngaros y rusos. Las obras van desde la gran orquesta al piano solo, ha habido "versiones de concierto" de obras teatrales, sinfonías, suites, poemas sinfónicos, sextetos, quintetos, cuartetos, tríos y sonatas para instrumentos de arco y viento; han desfilado por su sala (las sesiones se celebraban en la sala de conciertos del hotel Ritz) virtuosos célebres y artistas incipientes." Adolfo Salazar, "El año musical, balance de la temporada," La lectura [Madrid], no. 5 (May 1919): 341 (author's translation).

16 For more information about the Francophile style of Isaac Albéniz, see Walter Aaron Clark, Isaac Albéniz. Portrait of a Romantic (Oxford: Oxford University Press, 1999).

Next, two canonical musicians show up, F. Chopin (3.1%) and W.A. Mozart (2.3%), who, more than representing their own nations, are symbols of a musical past with a different set of aesthetic implications. Following this pair are Cesar Franck (2.3%) and Gabriel Fauré (2.3%), two of the most important masters of the French school prior to Debussy. They are followed by Manuel de Falla (2.2%) and, somewhat unexpectedly, Rogelio Villar (1875–1937)—a Spanish composer linked to the German tradition (2.3%)[17]. The reason for Villar's appearance might lie in the fact that, as I showed at the beginning of this chapter, he was the first promoter of the institution and had a close connection with Falla and the secretary Adolfo Salazar, especially with the latter, with whom he was in charge of the *Revista musical hispano-americana*. Finally, this top ten list is closed by another leading figure of the French milieu, Maurice Ravel (2.2%). Hence, as we can see, there is a prominent and evident relationship with French music.

However, we can go even further, since shifting the attention to the ten most programmed Spanish composers results in a more or less similar outcome, as demonstrated in Table 3.

Name	Pieces programmed
Enrique Granados	32
Isaac Albéniz	25
Rogelio Villar	17
Manuel de Falla	16
Antonio Soler	16
Joaquín Turina	13
Juan Manén	9
Joaquín Larregla	8
Óscar Esplá	8
Conrado del Campo	7

Table 3: The ten most programmed Spanish composers of the National Society of Music during its seven seasons (1915–1922). Author's elaboration based on the aforementioned historical sources mentioned above.

The first four, as is evident, are the same Spaniards included in the previous table (Table 2). They are followed by Antonio Soler (2.2%), representative of a

---

17   For more about this important critic and Spanish composer, see: Enrique Franco, "Villar, Rogelio del," in *Diccionario de la música española e hispanoamericana* (Madrid: SGAE, 1999–2002), 10:934–38.

musical past that was highly admired by Falla during his neoclassical period.[18] Moreover, Joaquín Turina (1.7%) and Óscar Esplá (1.1%) are both, once again, related to the Francophile style.[19] Rogelio Villar (2.3%) and Conrado del Campo (1%) also sneak into the list, the latter being a member of the Artistic Committee and, therefore, possessing a certain (but not too much) influence on the programming. Hence, the principal conclusion is evident: at least on an internal level, the aesthetic battle between the musical supporters of the Francophiles and the Germanophiles was clearly won by the French, since they had a stronger presence in the concerts programmed by the institution between 1915 and 1922. As it could not be any other way, this triumph was translated into a positive valuation of the Francophile group and into an ulterior and exclusive historiographic treatment of them, since Spanish musicology has ignored the German-influenced side of our musical identity. Fortunately, this mistake is already being rectified by Spanish musicology.

---

18   Antonio Soler (1729–1783) was the chapel master of the monastery of San Lorenzo del Escorial, a city very close to Madrid, and one of the leading figures of Spanish music in the eighteenth century. For more about this important composer, see Paulino Cepedón, "Soler y Ramos, Antoni," in *Diccionario de la música española e hispanoamericana* (Madrid: SGAE, 1999–2002), 9:1122–31.

19   Joaquín Turina (1882–1949) was, together with Manuel de Falla and Conrado del Campo, one of the most important and influential Spanish composers during the first half of the twentieth century. For more about this composer, I recommend two important sources: 1) Mariano Pérez Gutiérrez, "Turina Pérez, Joaquín," in *Diccionario de la música española e hispanoamericana* (Madrid: SGAE, 1999–2002), 10:513–25; and 2) Tatiana Aráez Santiago, "La etapa parisina de Joaquín Turina (1905–1913): construcción de un lenguaje nacional a partir de los diálogos entre Francia y España" (Ph.D. diss., Universidad Complutense de Madrid, 2019). Óscar Esplá (1886–1976) was a Spanish composer very close, personally and stylistically, to Manuel de Falla and the Francophile aesthetic side. For more, see Enrique Franco, "Esplá Triay, Oscar," in *Diccionario de la música española e hispanoamericana* (Madrid: SGAE, 1999–2002), 4:786–94. Juan Manén (1883–1971) was a Catalan violinist, conductor, and composer influenced by the style of Richard Wagner and Richard Strauss. For more, see Francesc Cortès i Mir, "Manén i Planas, Juan," in *Diccionario de la música española e hispanoamericana* (Madrid: SGAE, 1999–2002), 7:91–93. Joaquín Larregla (1865–1945) was a composer born in the north of Spain (Navarra) who implemented in his oeuvre the folkloric traditional materials of his region. For more, see Antonio Iglesias, "Larregla Urbieta, Joaquín," in *Diccionario de la música española e hispanoamericana* (Madrid: SGAE, 1999–2002), 6:766–67.

Typology of the Members: Propaganda, Exclusivity, and Social Impact

Not only was this victory the product of a friendly cultural exchange within the Francophile group, but it was also supported internally by the two main leaders of the society—president Miguel Salvador[20] and, especially, secretary Adolfo Salazar, who was also a composer, but, above all, a very influential and vehement musical critic. In this sense, I have to highlight the role of Salazar as the principal source of musical propaganda that was crucial in tipping the aesthetic scales toward the French side. As musicologist Elena Torres puts it, when Adolfo Salazar met Manuel de Falla in person, he became one of the biggest supporters of the Andalusian composer, announcing him as "the savior of Spanish music."[21] This attitude was fully integrated into his duties as a secretary, and, as Mexican musicologist Consuelo Carredano states in her dissertation about Salazar, it was within the National Society of Music where he first proved his capacity for musical influence.[22]

One of Salazar's most notable efforts can be seen in the program notes he wrote for each concert, which can be considered as authentic propaganda in favor of the Francophile side. For the concert on November 29, 1916,[23] the National Society had programmed together the orchestral version of Manuel

20   The importance of Miguel Salvador in understanding the development of Spanish music during the first third of the twentieth century is crucial. In addition to his musical activity as an amateur pianist and composer, he was also a very influential politician and cultural manager, as director of the National Society of Music (1915–1922), founder of the Orquesta Filarmónica de Madrid (1915), and finally, during the second republic (1931–1939), executive member of the Junta Nacional de Música, an institution which belonged to the Spanish Government. For more on this figure, see Emilio Casares Rodicio, "Salvador Carreras, Miguel," in *Diccionario de la música española e hispanoamericana* (Madrid: Sgae, 1999–2002), 9:627.

21   Elena Torres Clemente, "La imagen de Manuel de Falla en la crítica de Adolfo Salazar," in *Música y cultura en la Edad de Plata (1915–1939)*, ed. María Nagore, Leticia Sánchez de Andrés, and Elena Torres Clemente (Madrid: Iccmu, 2009), 265–85.

22   Consuelo Carredano, "Adolfo Salazar: pensamiento estético y acción cultural (1914–1937)" (Ph.D. diss., Universidad Complutense de Madrid, 2006). In addition to these last two sources, I also recommend the most recent book on Adolfo Salazar: Francisco Parralejo Masa, *El músico como intelectual. Adolfo Salazar y la creación del discurso de la vanguardia musical española (1914–1936)* (Madrid: Sociedad Española de Musicología, 2019).

23   Program notes for the concert celebrated on November 29, 1916. Madrid, Biblioteca de la Real Academia de Bellas Artes de San Fernando, collection "Bartolomé Pérez Casas," reference M-3383.

de Falla's *El amor brujo* and Manuel Manrique de Lara's Symphony in D minor, representative examples of the two aesthetic models: Francophile and Germanophile, respectively. In his program notes for the concert, Salazar introduces the first composition as a musical piece in which Falla "adopts an extremely new technique and a way of expression, to whose first advances alone are we just started to get accustomed."[24] Contrastingly, he describes Manrique de Lara's symphony as "a spiritual decadence or regression to a less refined state of sensibility than that of Wagner."[25] Thus, as we can see, the secretary of an institution that is supposed to be democratic and impartial with the Spanish repertoire it programs is defending his own aesthetic stand.

Hence, it is very evident that Salazar's program notes represent a slanted and highly tendentious set of documents which—due to their widespread public nature and availability—turned the National Society of Music into one of the most active driving forces of musical propaganda of the time. In addition, I must underline the consequences of such propaganda. Despite the fact that the works of both Falla and Manrique de Lara are considered to be of high quality today, the two composers did not secure the same status in history: Falla has always received more favor in historiographical discourses. This unequal treatment—and, of course, the situation of Manrique de Lara can be extrapolated to the rest of the composers with the same aesthetic profile—is a result of the strong impact of the general media spider web that reached into different places, including the National Society of Music.[26]

In this sense, all the matters treated to this point reflect an evident attempt by the majority sector of the National Society of Music to impose their ideals and to have influence over the musical taste of the audience, a fact that reveals a non-democratic agenda. Indeed, there is no doubt that not only were the propagandistic discourses generated in France against Germany assumed by a large majority of Spanish musicians, but they were also the catalyst for the exclusive historical prevalence of the Francophile model of musical identity that stems from themselves. Notwithstanding, the historical testimonies prove that, actually, the capacity of the National Society to change the aesthetic

---

24   "*Adopta una técnica y modo de expresión novísimos, a cuyos solos primeros avances empezamos a acostumbrarnos.*" (Author's translation).

25   "*una decadencia espiritual, o una regresión a un estado de sensibilidad menos refinado que el de Wagner.*" (Author's translation).

26   The importance of Manuel Manrique de Lara has recently been reevaluated by Spanish musicology by means of a book that won the National Award of Musicology in 2014: Diana Díaz González, *Manuel Manrique de Lara (1863–1929). Militar, crítico y compositor polifacético en la España de la Restauración* (Madrid: Sociedad Española de Musicología, 2015).

inclinations of the immediate audience was quite limited and remains reduced to its internal French-related circle.

First of all, the Society focused its attention on a very limited social spectrum. On the one hand, in order to be a member of the institution, it was necessary to reside in Madrid, as one can read on its Book of Regulation.[27] This fact alone shows an evident contradiction with the adjective "national" included within its own name. On the other hand, within their lists of members, it is possible to find three different social groups, all of which belong to the Madrilenian upper class: 1) the most prominent musicians, 2) the most prestigious intellectuals, and 3) the aristocracy and the highest social classes of the city. This element, which the press used to refer to as "a very distinguished audience" or "the most important of the Madrilenian milieu," reveals the image of a very exclusive institution that did not welcome ordinary people. Finally, once again regarding the repertoire, it is very significant that the National Society always refused to include in its concerts the *zarzuela*, a kind of musical spectacle that was appreciated by all social classes. All of these elements together confirm that the institution, its programming, and membership cannot be considered as democratic: the National Society of Music ignored the most popular genre of the time (*zarzuela*); marginalized German-influenced composers; and, finally, excluded not only the popular audiences of Madrid, but also those from the rest of the country.

Second of all, the main foundational principles of the institution were not ignored but understood in a very particular way in order to favor the propagandistic interests that I have outlined. This issue can be observed through the historical press: its study reflects the social impact of the institution as well as the consequences of its decisions. Initially, and no matter the ideological inclination of each newspaper, the National Society of Music was welcomed with a great deal of enthusiasm. A good example of this is the following newspaper clipping from *La Correspondencia de España*, published on February 6, 1915:

> It is undeniable that we are walking with firm steps toward the revival of the Spanish music. This fact is clearly proved by the recent success of Spanish composers, such as Turina, Falla, Pérez Casas, Guridi, Conrado del Campo, Vives, Casals, Villar, Usandizaga, Viñes, Óscar Esplá and many other youths that with their talent and enthusiasm are strengthening this flattering hope. [...] Another piece to underline what we are saying is the foundation of the National Society of Music, whose main objective is—according to its Book of

---

27   Book of Regulation, conserved in Madrid, Biblioteca de la Real Academia de Bellas Artes de San Fernando, collection "Bartolomé Pérez Casas," reference M-3383.

Regulation—to promote the musical creation and to ensure that the music thus produced would be published in concerts and editions.[28]

In this excerpt, we must focus our attention on a special element: the insistence on linking the National Society with the resurrection of the Spanish music, which allows us to situate the institution within the Spanish cultural regeneration—already introduced at the beginning of this chapter—during the first three decades of the twentieth century. Notably, evidence of the aesthetic confrontation are not yet present in this review, since the writer names both groups of musicians: Francophiles, with Falla and Turina, and Germanophiles, with Del Campo and Villar, among many others.

Over the years, the ideological inclination of the National Society became more evident, and, consequently, the first critical voices against the institution appeared. One of the most representative instances was Rogelio Villar who, as we can read in the following excerpt from a musical magazine, did not hesitate in pointing out the lack of space for Spanish composers within the National Society of Music:

Another thing that I really hate in some of my friends of the National [Society] is what I designate as an excessive effusiveness for the so-called new music [...] and for some of its performers, which is highly detrimental for our production. They do not realize the damage they make [...] and the confusion they cause in the audience, which can be one of the reasons why they lose all appreciation of our music, being imposed as a kind of art that they are not able to understand.[29]

---

28 "Es indudable que se camina con firme paso hacia el resurgir de la música española. Con toda claridad lo dicen los recientes triunfos de compositores españoles, como Turina, Falla, Pérez Casas, Guridi, Conrado del Campo, Vives, Casals, Villar, Usandizaga, Viñes, Óscar Esplá y otros muchos jóvenes que con su talento y entusiasmo van robusteciendo esa esperanza halagadora. [...]. Otra pieza de convicción de cuanto decimos es la creación de la Sociedad Nacional de Música, cuyo objeto es en primer término —según dice su Reglamento— el de fomentar la creación musical y procurar que la música producida sea publicada en conciertos y ediciones." "Sociedad Nacional de Música," La Correspondencia de España, Madrid, February 6, 1915: 5 (author's translation).

29 "Otra cosa que deploro de veras en algunos de mis amigos de la Nacional es lo que yo califico de excesiva efusión por la música llamada nueva [...] y por alguno de sus intérpretes, que tanto perjudica a nuestra producción. No se dan cuenta del daño que hacen [...] y de la desorientación que producen en el público, que puede ser causa de que pierda la poca afición que tiene por nuestra música, imponiéndole un arte que no suele ser capaz de comprender." Rogelio Villar, "A mis amigos de la Sociedad Nacional," Revista musical hispano-americana [Madrid], no. 12 (1916): 5–6 (author's translation).

However, this fact must be situated in context: what Villar is really exposing is that the musicians who do not support the Francophile side are being intentionally ignored by the National Society of Music, as we already know. In addition, the other main problem of the institution comes into light: its favoring of radical tendencies and excessive usage of musical vanguards, which will become the central aesthetic issue during the next decade.

All of these problems—the excessive praise of vanguards, the personal influences, and the unilateral propaganda—were summarized in the memoirs of Carlos Bosch, who was the first Secretary of the National Society of Music and who ended up succumbing to the power of Adolfo Salazar, as can read in the following extract:

> One of the causes that spoilt our "National [Society]" was the abuse, in all of the concerts, of these *avant-garde novelties*, which were rejected by a big majority of the members. The decisions about the music to be performed were made without careful consideration: they mixed some very thoughtful pieces with other new monstrosities and, as it usually happens in such cases, *personal influences* were imposed with a damaging and very destructive bias.[30]

These codes of conduct caused an institutional crisis that signified the gradual decline of the institution. In consequence, little by little, the National Society of Music lost the favor of its members who did not identify with the musical selections, and also the support of the Germanophile side of the Artistic Committee. On the other side, and despite Salazar's efforts to protect the institution, the press during the last years notably reduced their coverage to mere descriptions of the concerts without relevant content, diverting the attention away from an institution that had already lost its social impact.[31]

---

30 "*Una de las causas que malograron nuestra 'Nacional' fue esa exageración de novedades vanguardistas que se ejecutaban en todos los conciertos, a lo que se resistían la mayor parte de los asociados. Eso se hacía, además, sin verdadera excogitación* [sic] *escrupulosa: se mezclaban obras de enjundia creadora con meros engendros de nuevo cuño y, según ocurre en tales casos, se imponían influencias personales y se agudizó un partidismo nocivo, de gérmenes destructivos.*" Carlos Bosch Herrero, *Mnème. Anales de música y sensibilidad* (Madrid: Espasa-Calpe, 1942), 82 (author's translation); emphasis mine.

31 A comprehensive analysis of the presence of the National Society of Music in the historical press was conducted in Ferreiro, *La Sociedad.*

Conclusions

Having arrived to this point, the main conclusion is evident: not only was the National Society of Music an institution with the aim of musical diffusion, but also it was involved in the cultural and aesthetic debates of the time and, especially, in the process of cultural regeneration through which the country was living. The analysis of its musical programming can be understood as an immediate indicator of this issue, considering that it has revealed an aesthetic inclination toward the Francophile model. In this sense, although at the beginning they tried a confluence of musical tendencies, over the time it became completely sectarian. As I have demonstrated, the main agent in charge of making this mechanism works was Salazar, who used his own program notes as a means of propaganda. This was done with a triple objective: first, to defend the Francophile model and the figure of Manuel de Falla; second, to stop the development of German-influenced music in Spain after World War I; and third, to guide and influence the audience's musical interests.

However, and despite Salazar's efforts, the outcome was not as expected. This was due to three reasons: first, because the institution limited its own impact to a very small and exclusive sector of the society; second, because the real tastes of their audience were ignored by means of the repudiation of the most popular Spanish lyric theatre, the *zarzuela*; and finally, because the National Society, eventually, alienated its own members, who no matter how exclusive they were, did not support the programming of a certain musical aesthetic or the excessive predomination of the vanguards, which, paradoxically, entered Spain thanks to this institution. Hence, the conclusion becomes evident: even though the National Society of Music was created in order to integrate every aspect of Spanish music, its development reveals a non-democratic tendency with the aim of stopping the influence of German culture (a consequence of World War I) and consolidating a Spanish musical identity related to the French aesthetic.

This last aspect leads us to an interesting conclusion directly related to the cultural consequences of World War I in Spain: a large part of the institution's members, mostly the aristocracy, came to the National Society from the Wagnerian Association of Madrid, which had disappeared in 1914. Their entry into the National Society of Music can be perfectly understood as an attempt to dissociate themselves from the German side during the years of conflict, but not because they truly liked the new Francophile aesthetic and the vanguardism imposed by the National Society. A good proof of this consists in the fact that this group started leaving the institution once the war was over.

To conclude, all of these issues confirm that the institution did not have its hypothetical and presupposed democratic effects. Its capacity for the musical indoctrination of the society was reduced to its internal circle and to a limited and exclusive number of members who remained until the end. Nevertheless, we also have to recognize their undeniable merits related to musical diffusion, since it was thanks to its activity that the vanguards could enter Spain and become the inspiration for the composers of the next period—the so-called "Generation of '27." In this sense, the aftermath of the Society's activities would be positive because, despite the elitism and the sectarianism, and putting away the aesthetic debates, the musical diffusion was transcendental for the cultural and musical regeneration that took place in Spain during the first third of the twentieth century.

References

Aráez Santiago, Tatiana. "La etapa parisina de Joaquín Turina (1905–1913): construcción de un lenguaje nacional a partir de los diálogos entre Francia y España." Ph.D. diss., Universidad Complutense de Madrid, 2019.

Bosch Herrero, Carlos. *Mnème. Anales de música y sensibilidad*. Madrid: Espasa-Calpe, 1942.

Casares Rodicio, Emilio. "Salvador Carreras, Miguel." In *Diccionario de la música española e hispanoamericana*, vol. 9, 629. Madrid: SGAE, 1999–2002.

Carredano, Consuelo. "Adolfo Salazar: pensamiento estético y acción cultural (1914–1937)." Ph.D. diss., Universidad Complutense de Madrid, 2006.

Cepedón, Paulino. "Soler y Ramos, Antoni." In *Diccionario de la música española e hispanoamericana*, vol. 9, 1122–31. Madrid: SGAE, 1999–2002.

Clark, Walter Aaron. *Isaac Albéniz. Portrait of a Romantic*. Oxford: Oxford University Press, 1999.

Cortès i Mir, Francesc. "Manén i Planas, Juan." In *Diccionario de la música española e hispanoamericana*, vol. 7, 91–93. Madrid: SGAE, 1999–2002.

Christoforidis, Michael. "Aspects in the Creative Process in Manuel de Falla's *El retablo de Maese Pedro* and Concerto." Ph.D. diss., University of Melbourne, 1997.

Díaz González, Diana. *Manuel Manrique de Lara (1863–1929). Militar, crítico y compositor polifacético en la España de la Restauración*. Madrid: Sociedad Española de Musicología, 2015.

Ferreiro Carballo, David. "La Sociedad Nacional de Música: historia, recepción y repertorio." Master's thesis, Universidad Complutense de Madrid, 2015.

———. "Conrado del Campo y la definición de una nueva identidad lírica española: *El final de don Álvaro* (1910–1911) y *La tragedia del beso* (1911–1915)." Ph.D. diss., Universidad Complutense de Madrid, 2019.

Franco, Enrique. "Esplá Triay, Oscar." In *Diccionario de la música española e hispanoamericana*, vol. 4, 786–94. Madrid: Sgae, 1999–2002.

———. "Villar, Rogelio del." In *Diccionario de la música española e hispanoamericana*, vol. 10, 934–38. Madrid: Sgae, 1999–2002.

Fuentes Cordera, Maximiliano. *España en la Primera Guerra Mundial. Una movilización cultural*. Madrid: Akal, 1914.

García Avello, Ramón. "Campo Zavaleta, Conrado del." In *Diccionario de la música española e hispanoamericana*, vol. 2, 982–93. Madrid: Sgae, 1999–2002.

Hess, Carol. *Manuel de Falla and Modernism in Spain, 1898–1936*. Chicago: University of Chicago Press, 2001.

Iglesias, Antonio. "Larregla Urbieta, Joaquín." In *Diccionario de la música española e hispanoamericana*, vol. 6, 766–67. Madrid: Sgae, 1999–2002.

Kelly, Barbara. *Musica and Ultra-Modernism in France. A fragile Consensus, 1913–1939*. Woodbridge: Boydell Press, 2013.

Llano, Samuel. *Whose Spain?* New York: Oxford University Press, 2013.

Nagore, María, Leticia Sánchez de Andrés, and Elena Torres, eds. *Música y cultura en la Edad de Plata (1915–1939)*. Madrid: Instituto Complutense de Ciencias Musicales, 2009.

Navarra Ordoño, Andreu. 1914. *Aliadófilos y germanófilos en la cultura española*. Madrid: Cátedra, 1914.

Ortiz de Urbina, Paloma. "La recepción de Richard Wagner en Madrid (1900–1914)." Ph.D. diss., Universidad Complutense de Madrid, 2003.

Parralejo Masa, Francisco. *El músico como intelectual. Adolfo Salazar y la creación del discurso de la vanguardia musical española (1914–1936)*. Madrid: Sociedad Española de Musicología, 2019.

Pérez Gutiérrez, Mariano. "Turina Pérez, Joaquín." In *Diccionario de la música española e hispanoamericana*, vol. 10, 513–25. Madrid: Sgae, 1999–2002.

Salazar, Adolfo. "El año musical, balance de la temporada 1918-19." *La lectura* [Madrid], no. 5 (May 1919): 339–49.

Torres Clemente, Elena. "La imagen de Manuel de Falla en la crítica de Adolfo Salazar." In *Música y cultura en la Edad de Plata (1915–1939)*, edited by María Nagore, Leticia Sánchez de Andrés y Elena Torres Clemente, 265–85. Madrid: Iccmu, 2009.

———. *Las óperas de Manuel de Falla: de La vida breve a El retablo de Maese Pedro*. Madrid: Sociedad Española de Musicología, 2007.

Villar, Rogelio. "A mis amigos de la Sociedad Nacional." *Revista musical hispano-americana* [Madrid], no. 12 (1916): 5–6.

———. "Sociedad Nacional de Música." *Revista musical* [Bilbao], no. 8 (August 1911): 194–96.

Verdi at the Heart of the Dictatorship
A *celebrazione verdiana* Among Fascists

Gabrielle Prud'homme

Abstract: This chapter examines the political appropriation of Giuseppe Verdi in Fascist Italy through a study of the celebrations commemorating the fortieth anniversary of his death in 1941. More specifically, it provides an analysis of the Verdi Year through the lens of a landmark event held among fascist officials at the Academy of Italy in Rome, the heart of the regime's intellectual power, in June 1940—a few days before Italy's entry to war. By reconstructing the structure and the reception of the event, I shed light on how Mussolini's regime maintained its grip on the commemorations and disseminated a discourse entirely consistent with the fascist political and ideological agenda. By insisting on Verdi's patriotic image, exploiting the nationalist topoi conveyed in his operas, emphasizing his peasant origins, and exalting his Italianness, party intellectuals nurtured a Verdian myth that enhanced the Fascist political and totalitarian project.

Gabrielle Prud'homme is a Ph.D. candidate in musicology at the University of Montréal and the University of Music and Performing Arts in Vienna, as well as a member of the Canada Research Chair in Music and Politics. Supported notably by the Social Sciences and Humanities Research Council of Canada (Sshrc) and the German Academic Exchange Service (Daad), her thesis explores the reception of German-speaking composers in the light of musical commemorations in post-war Austria and Germany.

The fortieth anniversary of Giuseppe Verdi's death in 1941 impregnated the fascist musical calendar with a series of commemorative events throughout the peninsula. From mid-1940 to the end of 1941, speeches, official ceremonies, exhibitions, opera productions and concert series succeeded one another in which a great number of Italian intellectuals, artists and politicians among the most influential took part. The Verdi Year (*Anno verdiano*) proved to be a significant display of cultural propaganda with more than a hundred events held both in Italy and abroad, and which responded to the Duce's own will to celebrate a figure carefully molded on the fascist political and totalitarian project.

Such a pronounced infatuation stemmed from the ideal figure that Verdi represented. As the "bard of the Risorgimento," he embodied both the expression of Italian patriotism and cultural primacy, in addition to his undisputed popularity as one of the most frequently performed composers throughout the *ventennio* (1922–1943).[1] Fascist authorities therefore took advantage of the composer's prominence and exploited his anniversary as a powerful tool to support the legitimacy of their political power, at a pivotal moment when the regime was engaging Italy in a conflict alongside Nazi Germany. The end of Italy's non-belligerency formalized by Mussolini on June 10, 1940—a few days after the first major Verdi event in Rome—was indeed greeted by the Italians without enthusiasm and mobilized a nation whose military capacity was fundamentally weak, by no means in accordance with the Duce's ambitious expansionist aims.[2] Erected as a quintessential icon of Italian cultural superiority, Verdi served as an ideal pretext to praise the glorious past of the peninsula, set connections with contemporary Italian life, and testify to the greatness of a nation that intended to go on a crusade against "Western plutocracies" and establish its domination over the Mediterranean basin. Celebrating Verdi thus enabled the fascist government to reassert its ideological orientation through the dissemination of a figure in line with the ideals of the regime.

This phenomenon has only been briefly addressed; although some studies have dealt with the musical *ventennio*,[3] few of them were devoted to the instrumentalization of Verdi under Mussolini's regime, and even fewer to the political implications of the 1941 anniversary. Various publications have touched on the 1941 commemorations, but only briefly, focusing instead on the media,[4]

---

1   Fiamma Nicolodi, *Musica e musicisti nel ventennio fascista* (Florence: Discanto, 1984), 25.

2   Philippe Foro, *L'Italie fasciste* (Paris: Armand Colin, 2006), 175–77.

3   See for instance Stefano Biguzzi, *L'orchestra del Duce: Mussolini, la musica e il mito del capo* (Turin: Utet, 2004); Charlotte Ginot-Slacik and Michela Niccolai, *Musiques dans l'Italie fasciste: 1922–1945* (Paris: Fayard, 2019); Roberto Illiano, ed., *Italian Music During the Fascist Period* (Turnhout: Brepols, 2004); Stephanie Klauk, Luca Aversano, and Rainer Kleinertz, eds., *Musik und Musikwissenschaft im Umfeld des Faschismus: Deutsch-italienische Perspektiven* (Sinzig: Studio Verlag, 2015); Fiamma Nicolodi, *Musica e musicisti nel ventennio fascista* (Florence: Discanto, 1984); Harvey Sachs, *Music in Fascist Italy* (New York: Norton, 1987); Jürg Stenzl, "Fascismo—kein Thema?," in *Musikforschung Faschismus Nationalsozialismus: Referate der Tagung Schloss Engers (8. bis 11. März 2000)*, ed. Isolde von Foerster et al. (Mainz: Are Verlag, 2001), 143–50; Jürg Stenzl, *Von Giacomo Puccini zu Luigi Nono: Italienische Musik 1922–1952: Faschismus, Resistenza, Republik* (Büren: Knuf, 1990).

4   See Marco Capra, *Verdi in prima pagina: Nascita, sviluppo e affermazione della figura di Verdi nella stampa italiana dal XIX al XXI secolo* (Lucca: Libreria

on regional celebrations,[5] or on the topoi conveyed during the *Anno verdiano* and their echoes after the war.[6] This chapter proposes to deepen the reflection through a different and complementary approach, more specifically by studying the festivities through the lens of the inauguration of an exhibition of memorabilia (*mostra verdiana*) at the Academy of Italy in Rome in June 1940 in the presence of the Duce, as a landmark event of the Verdi anniversary. By reconstructing the structure of this event and analyzing its reception in the Italian media landscape of the time, I intend to shed light on how the fascist regime got involved in the organization of a highly politicized cultural event that exemplified the means used throughout the *Anno verdiano* to maintain political and ideological control over the commemorations.

This close focus also allows the identification of the discursive dominant themes that have been emblematic of those conveyed throughout 1941 and the strategies that served to disseminate a discourse entirely consistent with the fascist political agenda, at a time when the dictatorship became even more repressive, both culturally and socially—a tightening that occurred in the 1930s and intensified through its alignment on Nazi Germany.[7] This approach seeks

---

musicale italiana, 2014); Claudia Polo, *Immaginari verdiani: Opera, media e industria culturale nell'Italia del XX secolo* (Milan: Ricordi, 2004).

5   For the commemorations held at the Academy of Italy in Rome, see Paola Cagiano and Susanna Panetta, "Giuseppe Verdi e l'Accademia dei Lincei: Percorsi e vicende," in *Verdi e Roma*, ed. Olga Jesurum (Rome: Accademia nazionale dei Lincei, 2015), 429–56. For a survey of the Verdi anniversary in Parma, see Marco Capra, "Tra modernismo e restaurazione: La vita musicale a Parma nel ventennio fascista," *Storia di ieri: Parma dal regime fascista alla liberazione (1927-1945)* (Parma: Istituzione biblioteche del comune di Parma, 2011), htt ps://www.comune.parma.it/dizionarioparmigiani/ita/La%20vita%20musical e.aspx?idMostra=49&idNode=380. For the reception of the Verdi Year beyond the Alps, see Gundula Kreuzer, *Verdi and the Germans: From Unification to the Third Reich* (Cambridge: Cambridge University Press, 2010), particularly 229– 36; and Fiamma Nicolodi, "Mitografia verdiana nel primo Novecento," in *Verdi Reception*, ed. Lorenzo Frassà and Michela Niccolai (Turnhout: Brepols, 2013), 70.

6   See Nicolodi, "Mitografia verdiana," 58–75; Birgit Pauls, *Giuseppe Verdi und das Risorgimento: Ein politischer Mythos im Prozess der Nationenbildung* (Berlin: Akademie Verlag, 1996), in particular the chapter "Der politische Mythos Verdi im faschistischen Schulbuch und bei Mussolini," 305–10. For echoes of the 1941 anniversary in post-war Italy, see Harriet Boyd-Bennett, *Opera in Postwar Venice: Cultural Politics and the Avantgarde* (Cambridge: Cambridge University Press, 2018). See the second chapter "A *Futura Memoria*: Verdi's *Attila*, 1951": 61– 90, and more specifically 64, 74–75.

7   See Fiamma Nicolodi, "Aspetti di politica culturale nel ventennio fascista," in *Italian Music During the Fascist Period*, ed. Roberto Illiano (Turnhout: Brepols,

to examine this circumscribed event as a microcosm that exemplifies the mechanisms underlying the instrumentalization of musical heritage by authoritarian political forces through commemorations intended to integrate a creator into the dominant ideology. The analysis presented in this chapter draws from a wide range of journalistic and archival sources, including newspapers, cultural periodicals, commemorative books published in the wake of the festivities, and archival material (especially the documents gathered at the Archivio dell'Accademia nazionale dei Lincei in Rome).[8]

Ultimately, this study aims to question the role of political, but also intellectual and artistic figures in the development of a narrative that supported the political power, while illustrating how a public discourse of commemoration could be used to promote and disseminate an ideology based on ultranationalism, hegemony, and oppression. The *Anno verdiano* of 1941 therefore serves as an example of anti-democracy: it allows us to examine the mechanisms by which the political power—in this case, not a shared and balanced power, but a centralized and absolute one—succeeded in keeping its sway over the cultural heritage.

The Verdi Year, "Per la volontà del Duce"[9]

The *Anno verdiano* was not the only anniversary that occurred under the fascist regime, far from it. Essential to the dictatorship,[10] commemorations were abundant during the *ventennio* and served to create experiences of collectivity aimed at nurturing the process of cultural and national cohesion and increasing adherence to the Duce's political project. Remembering was also an integral part of the regime's strategy to celebrate the national heritage, provide an official and ideologically convenient interpretation of the past, and legitimize the

2004), 97; and Emilio Gentile, *Qu'est-ce que le fascisme? Histoire et interprétation* (Paris: Gallimard, 2004), 56–59.

8   The collection *Ufficio tecnico* has been essential for documenting the Verdi exhibition organized in June 1940 at the Academy of Italy in Rome. See Archivio Accademia d'Italia, Ufficio tecnico, b. 11, fasc. 58.

9   "Per il genio e la volontà del Duce." "Il Duce inaugura all'Accademia d'Italia la mostra di autografi e cimeli verdiani," *Gazzetta di Venezia*, June 5, 1940, 5; "Per la volontà e con la personale partecipazione del Duce." Alceo Toni, "Mussolini inaugura all'Accademia d'Italia la Mostra dei cimelî verdiani," *Il Popolo d'Italia*, June 5, 1940, 4.

10 Mabel Berezin, "The Festival State: Celebration and Commemoration in Fascist Italy," *Journal of Modern European History* 4, no. 1 "Dictatorship and Festivals" (2006), 71–72.

authority of the official power. As a "festival state,"[11] fascist Italy was the scene
of an intense commemorative activity; Italian cultural life was punctuated by
several tributes paid to the patriarchs of the peninsula, all of them transformed
into national heroes. In this regard, the fiftieth anniversary of Garibaldi's death
in 1932 reached a high point, on the occasion of which a "commemorative
spectacle"[12] largely orchestrated by the Duce unfolded and contributed to the
institutionalization of a fascist historic imaginary.[13] Several other figures of the
past were at the heart of commemorative attention, such as Mantegna in 1931,
Bellini and Horace in 1935, Giotto and Leopardi in 1937, Galileo, Livy, and Rossini
in 1942, and Monteverdi in 1943. The Verdi anniversary of 1941 therefore took
place in this mosaic of commemorative events and proved to be a highlight
of Italy's musical life in wartime. Celebrated in great style, the *Anno verdiano*
stemmed from the Duce's personal will and unfolded over more than a year,
turning out to be the peak of the political appropriation of the composer under
fascism.

Mussolini's intention of celebrating Verdi was shared through a communiqué from the General Directorate for the Theatre (*Direzione generale per
il teatro*)—under the aegis of the Ministry of Popular Culture (*Ministero della
cultura popolare*)[14]—addressed to the opera houses on August 20, 1940, decree-
ing the programming of a Verdi opera on January 27, 1941, the anniversary of
the composer's death, in order to "solemnly" remember the "great Maestro."[15]
This intention was then published in the press; the communiqué's content was

---

11   See Berezin, "The Festival State": 60–74.
12   Claudio Fogu, *The Historic Imaginary: Politics of History in Fascist Italy*, Toronto,
     University of Toronto Press, 2003: 74.
13   For an in-depth analysis of the *cinquantenario garibaldino*, see Fogu, *The
     Historic Imaginary*, mainly chapters 3 to 5.
14   The Theater Inspectorate (*Ispettorato del teatro*), which later became the
     Directorate for the Theatre, was founded in 1935 with the aim of creating
     a centralized structure to coordinate and control cultural activities. The
     Inspectorate operated under the Ministry of Press and Propaganda (*Ministero
     per la stampa e la propaganda*), which in 1937 became the Ministry of Popular
     Culture. See Nicolodi, *Musica e musicisti nel ventennio fascista*, 17.
15   "*Il Duce ha espresso il desiderio che la figura e le opere di Giuseppe Verdi siano
     messe maggiormente in luce nella vita musicale italiana. Poiché il 27 gennaio
     p.v. si compiono 40 anni dalla morte del grande Maestro, si dispone che tutti
     gli enti che a quella data hanno in corso la normale stagione commemorino
     solennemente l'anniversario con l'esecuzione in tal giorno di un'opera verdiana.*"
     Circolare della Direzione generale per il teatro (Ministero della cultura popolare,
     Div. II, Sez. I, prot. 16519), 20 agosto 1940 agli enti autonomi dei teatri lirici. Cited
     in Nicolodi, "Mitografia verdiana," 69. All translations are the author's unless
     otherwise specified.

essentially reproduced, to which information regarding the program was added: the forthcoming commemorative cycle organized by the Ministry of Popular Culture at the Teatro Reale dell'Opera in Rome was publicized, during which Verdi's operas of "popular character" were to be presented. The announcement appeared in Italy's leading newspapers, including *Corriere della Sera* (Milan), *Il Popolo d'Italia* (Rome), *La Stampa* (Turin), in regional newspapers (as *Gazzetta di Venezia*, Venice), and in music periodicals such as *Il Musicista* (published by the National Fascist Union of Musicians in Rome), *Musica d'oggi* (Milan), and *La Rassegna musicale* (Rome):

> The Duce has ordered that the great figure and the work of Giuseppe Verdi be worthily commemorated and celebrated on the occasion of the fortieth anniversary of the death of the Maestro, which will take place on January 27 of the year XIX.[16]
>
> The Ministry of Popular Culture has therefore elaborated a series of special commemorative events that will begin next October in Rome at the Teatro Reale, before the usual winter opera season, where there will be some representations of Verdi's popular works. *I Vespri siciliani*, *La Forza del destino*, *Il Trovatore*, *Otello*, and *Falstaff* will be represented (in daytime and at affordable prices); conductors will be Serafin, De Fabritiis and Bellezza.
>
> Then, a solemn Verdian celebration will take place in most Italian opera houses, including self-governing theaters (*enti autonomi*),[17] on the evening of January 27. Theaters that usually start their season after that date will host a celebration during their performances.
>
> Even the most important Italian concert societies, headed by the Institution of the concerts of the Reale Accademia di Santa Cecilia in Rome, and that of the Teatro Vittorio Emanuele II in Florence, will celebrate Verdi with a great vocal-symphonic concert.
>
> Ultimately, conferences illustrating the life and work of the great Maestro

---

16   In 1925, Mussolini decreed the "fascist era" and established a Fascist calendar, which he began in October 1922, on the day after the March on Rome. All official documents had to be dated in such a way as to add the fascist year in Roman numerals following the year of the Gregorian calendar. In the above case, January 27, 1941, belonged to the nineteenth year of the fascist era, hence the number XIX.

17   *Enti autonomi* were state-subsidized theaters. Previously managed by impresarios, theaters started to be run as *enti autonomi* in the 1920s, beginning with the Teatro alla Scala (1920), followed by the Teatro Reale dell'Opera in Rome (1929) and all major theaters of the peninsula (Bologna, Florence, Genoa, Naples, Palermo, Turin, Trieste, Venice, and Verona). This standardization responded to the fascists' will to exercise a more effective political control while maintaining an artistic quality "worthy of the Italian tradition." See Fiamma Nicolodi, "Il sistema produttivo dall'Unità a oggi," in *Storia dell'opera italiana*, ed. Lorenzo Bianconi and Giorgio Pestelli (Turin: Edizioni di Torino, 1987), 4:194–201.

will be held in the most important cities of Italy; the same will be done abroad in Cultural Institutes and at the Dante Alighieri Society.[18]

Following the press release, many state-subsidized theaters (*enti lirici*) engaged in celebrating Verdi with great fanfare: the Teatro Reale dell'Opera in Rome held two cycles dedicated to the composer in the fall of 1940 and 1941, in addition to two commemorative concerts on January 29 and 31, 1941; because of the composer's Parmesan origin, the Teatro Regio in Parma organized a Verdi season (*stagione verdiana*) and hosted an exhibition of memorabilia from January 27 to February 25, 1941; *Falstaff* and *La Traviata* were staged at the Teatro Carlo Felice in Genoa and at the Teatro San Carlo in Naples, respectively, on January 27, 1941; the Teatro alla Scala presented a concert on January 30 and February 2, 1941; the Teatro La Fenice organized in collaboration with the Fascist Union of Musicians of Venice a commemorative concert on February 2, 1941; the Teatro comunale in Florence presented a ceremony (*celebrazione*

---

18   "*Il Duce ha disposto che la grande figura e l'opera di Giuseppe Verdi siano degnamente rievocate e celebrate in occasione del 40° anniversario della morte del Maestro, che cade il 27 gennaio dell'anno XIX.*

Il Ministero della Cultura popolare ha pertanto predisposto un ciclo di speciali manifestazioni celebrative che avrà inizio nel prossimo ottobre in Roma, dove, al Teatro Reale, prima della consueta stagione lirica invernale, avranno luogo alcune rappresentazioni di opere verdiane a carattere popolare. Si rappresenteranno (in recite diurne ed a prezzi popolari) I Vespri siciliani, La Forza del destino, Il Trovatore, Otello e Falstaff; direttori i maestri Serafin, De Fabritiis e Bellezza.

La sera del 27 gennaio poi, nel maggior numero dei teatri lirici italiani, compresi quelli degli Enti autonomi, avrà luogo la solenne celebrazione verdiana. Quei teatri che iniziano di consueto la loro stagione dopo tale data, terranno invece la celebrazione durante il corso dei loro spettacoli.

Anche le più importanti società italiane di concerti, con a capo l'Istituzione dei concerti della R. Accademia di S. Cecilia, di Roma, e quella dell'Ente autonomo del Teatro Vittorio Emanuele II di Firenze, celebreranno Verdi con un grande concerto sinfonico vocale.

Nelle più importanti città d'Italia saranno infine promosse conferenze illustranti la vita e l'opera del grande Maestro; analogamente si farà all'estero presso gli Istituti di cultura e le sezioni della 'Dante Alighieri.'" See "Notizie," *Musica d'oggi* 22, no. 8–9 (August–September 1940): 254. The text has been slightly modified to be published in several newspapers of the peninsula, such as *La Stampa* ("Il 40° anniversario della morte di Giuseppe Verdi," *La Stampa*, August 23, 1940, 3); *Corriere della sera* ("Il 40° della morte di Verdi: Un ciclo di manifestazioni celebrative," *Corriere della sera*, August 23, 1940, 4); *Gazzetta di Venezia* ("Il Duce per la celebrazione di Verdi," *Gazzetta di Venezia*, August 23, 1940, 3); *Il Musicista* ("Celebrazioni verdiane," *Il Musicista* 7, no. 11 (August 1940): 168); and *La Rassegna musicale* ("Notizie e informazioni," *La Rassegna musicale* 13, no. 7–8 (July–August 1940): 325).

verdiana) "under the auspices of the Ministry of Popular Culture"[19] on January 24, 1941, during which the orchestra and choir of the Maggio musicale fiorentino performed the *Messa da Requiem*.

The *Requiem* was also at the heart of a large-scale concert under the direction of high-profile conductor Victor De Sabata at the Basilica Santa Maria degli Angeli in Rome on December 14, 1940. The event brought together 150 performers from the Rome and Turin Radio Orchestras, a choir of 250 singers and eminent soloists: Maria Caniglia, Ebe Stignani, Beniamino Gigli, and Tancredi Pasero. Reportedly, more than four thousand people attended the ceremony, including several personalities from the music and political scene, such as the Minister of Popular Culture Alessandro Pavolini and the German ambassador Hans Georg von Mackensen—who earlier that day inaugurated the new headquarters of the Italian-German Association in Rome in the presence of fascist and Nazi officials. As a highlight of the Verdi Year, the *Requiem* in Santa Maria degli Angeli was broadcast on national radio (*Ente Italiano per le Audizioni Radiofoniche*, EIAR) and was preceded by a commemorative speech delivered on air by the fascist official Roberto Farinacci.

This event testified to Rome's significance throughout the *Anno verdiano*, both in terms of the number and the prominence of the celebrations; the capital hosted several ceremonies, both popular and official, which served to illustrate the Eternal City's dynamism and nurture the myth of *romanità*.[20] The Duce indeed aimed to restore Rome's status as an imperial capital and transform the city as a showcase for the fascist state, the ultimate symbol of Mussolini's regime.[21] It was also in Rome that the first major Verdi event was launched, the political significance of which set the tone for subsequent festivities.

---

19   "*Celebrazione verdiana, sotto gli auspici del Ministero della Coltura popolare.*" Aloma Bardi and Mauro Conti, eds., *Teatro comunale di Firenze: Catalogo delle manifestazioni 1928–1997* (Florence: Le Lettere, 1998), 80.

20   The cult of *romanità*—romanness—aimed at celebrating the ancient Roman past as a common heritage and arose from Mussolini's will to restore the former glory of the Romans in Italy. See Andrea Giardina, "The Fascist Myth of Romanity," *Estudos Avançados* 22, no. 62 (2008): 55–76.

21   John Agnew, "'Ghosts of Rome': The Haunting of Fascist Efforts at Remaking Rome as Italy's Capital City," *Annali d'Italianistica* 28 (2010), 179; Maria Rosa Chiapparo, "Le mythe de la 'Terza Roma' ou l'immense théâtre de la Rome fasciste," *Nuovo rinascimento* (May 17, 2004), 20, 22–23, http://www.nuovorina scimento.org/n-rinasc/saggi/pdf/chiapparo/roma.pdf.

The *Anno verdiano*'s Prologue: *La Mostra verdiana*

Precisely six days before Mussolini declared war on England and France from his balcony on the Palazzo Venezia, a handful of fascist intellectuals welcomed the Duce and his disciples on June 4, 1940, to inaugurate the *mostra verdiana*, an exhibition of memorabilia set up at the Villa Farnesina, seat of the Academy of Italy. As the "regime's highest cultural institution,"[22] the Academy was founded by Mussolini in 1929 "in order to preserve the national purity of Italian culture"[23] and whose objective was to subject the Italian intelligentsia to political power.[24]

The event arose from a donation of 365 letters written between 1859 and 1890 by Verdi to Senator Giuseppe Piroli (1815–1890) offered by Piroli's heirs to the Duce, who then granted them to the institution in 1940. The *mostra*'s elaboration was entrusted to the Verdian scholar Alessandro Luzio, historian and academician, who was in the process of editing Verdi's correspondence. Luzio conceived the exhibition in order to highlight the material recently acquired by the Academy (section entitled *Carteggi*), which also served to advertise the first two volumes of Verdi's *Carteggi* he previously edited.[25] The selection of the documents and their configuration announced various topoi that were to be exploited throughout the *Anno verdiano*, notably by themes devoted to the composer's political involvement (subsections entitled "Verdi's politics"; "Verdi deputy and senator"), his peasant identity ("Rural Verdi"), and his humanness ("Verdi philanthropist").[26] In addition, the exhibition included scores, manuscripts, and several depictions of the composer.[27]

Luzio was also a key figure at the *mostra*'s opening on June 4, 1940, having delivered an inaugural speech whose content revolved around Mussolini's re-

---

22 "*Massima istituzione culturale del Regime.*" "Il Duce inaugura all'Accademia d'Italia la mostra di autografi e cimeli verdiani," *Gazzetta di Venezia*, June 5, 1940, 5.

23 "*Allo scopo di conservare la purezza nazionale della cultura italiana.*" Nicolodi, "Mitografia verdiana," 61.

24 For an extensive study on the Academy of Italy, see Marinella Ferrarotto, *L'Accademia d'Italia: Intellettuali e potere durante il fascismo* (Naples: Liguori, 1977).

25 The publication was interrupted by the war; the last two volumes of Luzio's edition were published posthumously in 1947. See Alessandro Luzio, ed., *Carteggi verdiani* (Rome: Reale Accademia d'Italia/Accademia dei Lincei, 1935–1947).

26 "*La politica di Verdi*"; "*Verdi deputato e senatore*"; "*Verdi rurale*"; and "*Verdi benefattore.*" See Cagiano and Panetta, "Giuseppe Verdi e l'Accademia dei Lincei," 443.

27 "Mostra verdiana," Archivio Accademia d'Italia, Ufficio tecnico, b. 11, fasc. 58.

cent donation.[28] After personally thanking the Duce for having "offered the most splendid testimony of his [Verdi's] aesthetic, moral and political importance,"[29] the academician pointed out the guiding threads of the correspondence between Verdi and Piroli, in order to portray a composer particularly well suited to his audience: an intrinsically Italian musician of "humble origins"[30] who "praised his peasant roots,"[31] a patriot who served his country both as an artist and as a deputy, and who vehemently shared his dissatisfaction with the government, outraged at the "inability of the rulers"[32] to adequately protect culture and agriculture.

This polysemic depiction enabled a reinterpretation of Verdi's persona in light of the *ventennio* and the forging of teleological links between fascist policies and the composer's convictions. By stressing the idea that the Duce was the head of state foreseen by Verdi to stimulate Italy's artistic and socio-economic life, Luzio suggested that the composer had anticipated, and even wished for, the fascist takeover. Luzio's assertions, however, must be nuanced; as musicologist Fiamma Nicolodi pointed out, Verdi expressed the need for a bigger involvement of the state, notably in the music scene, but he never considered the control of opera houses as was exercised by the fascist regime.[33]

---

28   Luzio's speech was published by the Academy of Italy in the collection "*celebra-zioni verdiane*," which brought together several speeches given by Academicians throughout the Verdi anniversary. The series included Arturo Farinelli, *Giuseppe Verdi e il suo mondo interiore: Discorso per il quarantennio della morte tenuto alla Reale Accademia d'Italia il 19 febbraio 1941–XIX* (Rome: Reale Accademia d'Italia, 1941); Angelo Gatti, *L'italianità di Giuseppe Verdi: Discorso per il quarantennio della morte tenuto nella Casa di riposo dei musicisti in Milano il 27 gennaio 1941–XIX* (Rome: Reale Accademia d'Italia, 1941); Alessandro Luzio, *Per Giuseppe Verdi: Discorso inaugurale della mostra verdiana alla presenza del Duce nella sede della Reale Accademia d'Italia, 4 giugno 1940–XVIII* (Rome: Reale Accademia d'Italia, 1940); and Francesco Orestano, *Giuseppe Verdi mediterraneo e universale: Discorso per la settimana verdiana di Monaco di Baviera pronunziato il 5 febbraio 1941–XIX nella Münchner Künstlerhaus* (Rome: Reale Accademia d'Italia, 1941).

29   "*Nè poteva giungere sotto auspici più fausti, quando Voi, Duce, [...] offrite la testimonianza più splendida della sua importanza estetica, morale, politica.*" Luzio, *Per Giuseppe Verdi*, 6.

30   "*Umili origini.*" Luzio, *Per Giuseppe Verdi*, 5.

31   "*Si gloriava della sua origine contadinesca.*" Luzio, *Per Giuseppe Verdi*, 11.

32   "*Incapacità dei governanti.*" Luzio, *Per Giuseppe Verdi*, 11.

33   Nicolodi, "Mitografia verdiana," 52, fn. 55.

Figure 1: Alessandro Luzio (right) delivering the opening address of the *mostra verdiana* alongside the president of the Academy of Italy Luigi Federzoni (on his right) in the presence of the Duce (left) and fascist intellectuals. Source: Alessandro Luzio, *Per Giuseppe Verdi*, 22-23. Courtesy of the Archivio dell'Accademia nazionale dei Lincei.

Figure 2: Guests, led by the president of the Academy of Italy Luigi Federzoni (right) alongside Mussolini (center), moving towards the concert in the gardens of the Villa Farnesina. Source: see Figure 1.

Listened to by the Duce with "keen interest,"[34] Luzio's speech ended on a nationalist tone, declaring that the ceremony was an "omen of power, of glory to which the renewed nation yearned."[35] The guests then viewed the exhibition and attended a brief concert in the gardens of the Villa Farnesina with the orchestra of the Accademia di Santa Cecilia under the baton of conductor Bernardino Molinari—a fundamental figure in Roman musical life whose enthusiasm for fascism was well known.

Figure 3: Guests (including the Duce, in the front row) attending the concert performed by the orchestra of the Accademia di Santa Cecilia in the gardens of the Villa Farnesina. Source: see Figure 1.

The concert included symphonic excerpts from Verdi's operas: an unpublished sinfonia from *Aida*, the prelude of *La Traviata*'s last act, and the sinfonia from *I Vespri siciliani*. The repertoire was emblematic of the *Anno verdiano*'s musical choices, consisting of works belonging to Verdi's stylistic maturity that were well known and appreciated by the public. *Aida* was particularly well suited to a Roman audience, being the most performed opera at Rome's Teatro

---

34   "*Vivissimo interesse.*" "Il Duce inaugura la Mostra dei cimeli verdiani," *Corriere della Sera*, June 5, 1940, 3. Also in other newspapers, such as "Il Duce inaugura all'Accademia la mostra dei cimeli Verdiani," *La Stampa*, June 5, 1940, 4; and "Il Duce inaugura all'Accademia d'Italia la mostra di autografi e cimeli verdiani," *Gazzetta di Venezia*, June 5, 1940, 5.

35   "*Auspicio di potenza, di gloria, a cui ha diretto la rinnovellata nazione.*" Luzio, *Per Giuseppe Verdi*, 7.

Costanzi (which became the Teatro Reale dell'Opera in 1928) from 1900 to 1950.[36] Its then unpublished sinfonia[37] had been composed for the Italian premiere on February 8, 1872, at the Teatro alla Scala with an intention to replace the opera's prelude as premiered in Cairo on December 24, 1871. Having decided to keep the original prelude, however, Verdi withdrew the sinfonia in Sant'Agata, a decision that kept the score in obscurity.[38] We owe its rediscovery to Toscanini, who transcribed the music in 1913 from the original manuscript and premiered the sinfonia with the Nʙᴄ Symphony Orchestra on March 30, 1940. Then deeply hostile to Mussolini's regime and exiled in the United States, Toscanini most likely had the aim of reducing the significance of the concert at the Academy as a national premiere.[39] The incident was touched upon in the press by Alceo Toni, who condemned in Il Popolo d'Italia the "questionable indiscretion of a great conductor"[40] for having brought the work in the United States.

Of great popularity, La Traviata was among the operas most often performed during the Anno verdiano. Announcing Violetta's resignation in the face of her inevitable death, the prelude to the last act served to illustrate Verdi's sensitivity and the powerful musical narrativity of his operas, notions that permeated the celebrative rhetoric of 1941. I Vespri siciliani also received considerable attention throughout the anniversary, especially in Rome; in addition to the sinfonia presented at the Academy, the opera opened the ciclo verdiano organized by the Ministry of Popular Culture at the Teatro Reale dell'Opera in October 1940, a series of operas bringing together works of "popular character," as seen above. At the Academy, I Vespri's sinfonia had replaced the overture to La Forza del destino originally programmed for the concert,[41] which was probably considered too tormented to conclude the ceremony. I Vespri must have been appealing for its military nature (exemplified in the sinfonia with an omnipresent snare drum) and for its plot, which progresses towards the

---

36   Nicolodi has shown that the ten operas most frequently performed at the Teatro Costanzi in Rome from 1900 to 1950 were Aida, Tosca, La Bohème, La Traviata, Rigoletto, Madama Butterfly, Mefistofele, Carmen, Il Barbiere di Siviglia, and Cavalleria rusticana. See Fiamma Nicolodi, "Musica a Roma nella prima metà del '900," Analecta musicologica 45 (2011), 494.

37   Pianist and musicologist Pietro Spada edited the sinfonia in 1977 (Milan, Suvini & Zerboni). See Antonio Rostagno, "Ouverture e dramma negli anni Settanta: Il caso della Sinfonia di Aida," Studi verdiani 14 (1999): 22.

38   Rostagno, "Ouverture e dramma negli anni Settanta," 20–21.

39   Rostagno, "Ouverture e dramma negli anni Settanta," 21–22; Cagiano and Panetta, "Giuseppe Verdi e l'Accademia dei Lincei," 446–50.

40   "Discutibile indiscrezione di un grande direttore d'orchestra." Alceo Toni, "Mussolini inaugura all'Accademia d'Italia la Mostra dei cimeli verdiani," Il Popolo d'Italia, June 5, 1940, 4.

41   Cagiano and Panetta, "Giuseppe Verdi e l'Accademia dei Lincei," 446.

Figure 4: Orchestra of the Accademia di Santa Cecilia under the baton of conductor Bernardino Molinari. Source: see Figure 1.

massacre of French troops by Sicilian patriots (which is already announced in the overture by the thematic choice). A few days before Italy's invasion of France, the parallelism was explicit, although not exploited by the press.

After the concert, the ceremony concluded with the departure of the Duce and his disciples to the musical background of *Giovinezza*, the official fascist anthem. The event, which unfolded in about an hour, was methodically planned; the archives at the Academy indicate, among other things, that the time allotted to Luzio's speech was greater than the duration of the concert[42] — a configuration that testified to the primacy of words rather than sounds to share politically and ideologically charged ideas. Moreover, the structure of the ceremony was a common formula during the *Anno verdiano* (although the musical material was generally more extensive); the majority of the commemorative events took the form of concerts featuring excerpts from Verdi's operas, preceded by speeches delivered by members of Italian cultural and/or political life. This type of event had been included in the calendar of many opera houses and cultural institutions, as well as in conservatories and music schools throughout the peninsula, aiming at reaching and involving young musicians in the celebration. This strategy allowed the creation of a politicized discursive landscape into which Verdi's music was inserted, thus adding an additional semantic layer to the musical event.

---

42   Letter to the Cancelliere, May 15, 1940, Archivio Accademia d'Italia, Ufficio tecnico, b. 11, fasc. 58.

The event received considerable media coverage; reports were published the following day in leading newspapers of the time, such as *Corriere della sera*, *Il Popolo d'Italia*, and *La Stampa*, as well as in the newsreel series *Cinegiornale Luce* a week later. These covers appeared in media in which military news prevailed, at a time when the Duce and his party were preparing the nation for an imminent war. The exploits of the Wehrmacht abounded in all the newspapers of the peninsula, encouraging Italian participation; the headline "Mussolini's war" appeared on the front page of the June 5, 1940, issue of *Il Popolo d'Italia*, while the *Corriere della sera* published an article entitled "The Axis mission for the future of Europe and the world" below the report of the ceremony at the Academy.[43] The *Cinegiornale Luce* of June 11, 1940, (when Italy was at war) was mostly dedicated to military strength; the segment covering the *mostra verdiana* was coupled with reports glorifying the crushing victories of the Reich and the military power of befriended nations (Japan, Hungary, and Romania).

Almost entirely identical, the press reviews seemed to have stemmed from a common source—which probably came from the General Directorate for the press (*Direzione generale per la stampa*), an organ of the Ministry of Popular Culture whose task was to control and synchronize media content—except for *Il Popolo d'Italia*, which also featured a review by music critic Alceo Toni. This phenomenon bears witness to the lack of diversity that arose from the discursive landscape of the *Anno verdiano*; the media apparatus, entirely controlled by the regime, conveyed a fundamentally homogeneous discourse. This was a reality inherent to the fascist totalitarian project, where the establishment of an authoritarian media system and the imposition of censorship standardized the communicative tools and gradually suppressed the freedom of speech.[44]

Both written and audiovisual reports revolved around the Duce; by stressing his "generous" donation, the media presented a patron of the arts and a music lover, a genuine "enlightened despot." This depiction perpetuated the image of *Mussolini musicista* (Mussolini musician) which had been disseminated throughout the *ventennio* and portrayed the ruler as an amateur violinist and music connoisseur.[45] In addition to nurturing the cult of a charismatic leader

---

43 "Guerra mussoliniana," *Il Popolo d'Italia*, June 5, 1940, 1; "La missione dell'Asse per l'avvenire dell'Europa e del mondo," *Corriere della sera*, June 5, 1940, 3.

44 For comprehensive studies on censorship in the publishing industry under Mussolini's regime, see for instance Guido Bonsaver, *Censorship and Literature in Fascist Italy* (Toronto: University of Toronto Press, 2007) and Nicola Tranfaglia, *La stampa del regime 1932–1943: Le veline del Minculpop per orientare l'informazione* (Milan: Bompiani, 2005).

45 The figure of a musician dictator was nurtured throughout the *ventennio*, an emblematic case of which being *Mussolini musicista*, published in 1927 in the collection "Mussolinia." Written by musicologist Raffaello De Rensis, the booklet

(inherent to fascist politics and its totalitarian logic), presenting a statesman mindful of the culture conveyed the idea that fascism was not only violence and domination,[46] especially in the context of a stricter repression in the arts and at a time when the media landscape was largely dominated by military news. This strategy also served to convey the image of a Duce in complete control of Italy's governance, who, despite the political uncertainty, yet supported the arts.

The reviews also testified to the hermetic and formal nature of the event (visually represented by ritualistic gestures such as the Roman salute); it consisted of an official ceremony reserved for high-ranking members of the regime who paid tribute to one of their own. This elitism contradicted Mussolini's will to celebrate Verdi through commemorations geared towards the entire population, an intention that was echoed in numerous "popular" events, notably under the aegis of the Opera nazionale dopolavoro (National Afterwork Club), an organization created under the regime to coordinate workers' leisure time. One can see the ambiguity of the regime's populist trends; despite an apparent proximity to the people, fascism remained exclusive.

The diversity of the media outlets allowed the scope of the coverage to increase; while print media paid predominant attention to Luzio's speech, the newsreels focused on the exhibition and on the concert (with no reference to the discourse). The conciseness of the musical comment in the press was emblematic of the treatment of music during the Anno verdiano, whereas critical assessments were generally limited to a few laudatory remarks about the performance. Such an approach testifies to the paralysis of music criticism that occurred during the anniversary, be it for the celebrative context or the censorship that prevailed in the print media.

The extent of the media coverage testifies to the role given to the media apparatus to document the festivities throughout the Anno verdiano, with a clear predominance of the press. As Claudia Polo has shown, the radio was significantly less exploited to disseminate Verdi-related content due to the war effort[47]—which probably also explains the scarcity of the composer's ap-

---

aimed to extol the musical qualities of the Duce in order to portray him as a sensitive music lover and a seasoned violinist. See Raffaello De Rensis, Mussolini musicista (Mantua: Paladino, 1927).

46   Roberto Illiano and Massimiliano Sala, "The Politics of Spectacle: Italian Music and Fascist Propaganda," Musikologija/Musicology 12 (2012), 15.

47   Only three Verdi operas were broadcast during the 1941 anniversary (Un Ballo in maschera on May 15, Il Trovatore on June 21, and Aida on July 19). By comparison, six operas were broadcast in 1931 and 24 in 1951, on the occasion of the thirtieth and fiftieth anniversary of the composer's death. See Polo, Immaginari verdiani, 90–92.

pearances on film in 1941.[48] The press was consequently an essential organ for the dissemination of the celebrations; the writings allowed to reach a much wider and diversified audience than that of the concert halls and broadened the scope of the discursive elements associated with the commemorations. The importance given to the print media also demonstrated Mussolini's recognition of the medium's potential to reach the general population and his use of it as a significant tool for propaganda.[49]

"Anticipando le realizzazioni dell'Italia fascista":[50] Verdi as Forerunner of Fascism?

The ceremony at the Academy of Italy laid the foundations of a rhetoric that thrived throughout the Verdi anniversary and that was entirely coherent with the fascist political agenda. Aspects of Verdi's biography that suited the regime were amplified, such as his patriotism and his Italianness, which proved to be two fundamental leitmotifs of the celebrative discourse. The recurrent depiction of Verdi as a "rural man" also prevailed and helped to make the composer an archetype of the new Italian, thus subtly promoting the myth of the "new man," an Italian regenerated by the "anthropological revolution" undertaken under the *ventennio*.[51] Unsurprisingly, other dimensions of Verdi's biography were overlooked, such as his belonging to the liberal bourgeoisie or his yearning for freedom of speech (which he found in France, unlike Northern Italy, where censorship was imposed by foreign occupation). Such unsuitable notions for fascist authorities were carefully erased from the dominant discourse.

---

48   In addition to the *Giornale* dedicated to the *mostra verdiana*'s inauguration in June 1940, the state-owned Istituto Luce produced *Giornali* on the Casa di riposo per musicisti, Verdi's resting place and a home for retired musicians set up on the composer's initiative, and on the commemoration held in Busseto in January 1941. See Istituto nazionale Luce, "Milano—Una visita alla Casa di Riposo per musicisti e cantanti," *Giornale Luce* C0111, January 21, 1941; Istituto nazionale Luce, "La gloria di Giuseppe Verdi celebrata a Busseto, città natale del Maestro," *Giornale Luce* C0014, January 31, 1941.

49   Pierluigi Allotti, *Giornalisti di regime: La stampa italiana tra fascismo e antifascismo (1922–1948)* (Rome: Carocci, 2012), 23.

50   "L'alta intuizione che il Verdi portava anche nei problemi sociali ed economici della Nazione, anticipando nel pensiero e più ancora nella auspicazione, quelle che sono state poi, per il genio e la volontà del Duce, la realizzazione dell'Italia Fascista, in ogni campo delle attività e pratiche del nostro popolo." "Il Duce inaugura all'Accademia la mostra dei cimeli Verdiani," *La Stampa*, June 5, 1940, 4.

51   Gentile, *Qu'est-ce que le fascisme*, 354–55.

Verdi the Italian

Celebrating Verdi involved making the composer the ultimate expression of the national spirit; by presenting his figure and his work as a testimony to the richness of Italy's cultural heritage, the organizers intended to promote Italian cultural superiority and thus nurture the nationalist sentiment—a crucial knot of fascist politics. The composer's Italianness was fundamental to Luzio's inaugural speech at the Academy, which referred to Verdi as an "Italic genius, complete and multifaceted" ("italic" referring to the ancient tribes from which stemmed the Romans, a mindfully selected term) and sustained that he "eminently possessed the virtues of the race."[52]

The review of the event written by musicologist Alceo Toni, a fervent fascist adherent and music critic for *Il Popolo d'Italia*, emblematically illustrates the ubiquitous nationalism that permeated the literature during the Verdi anniversary. Claiming that "Verdi loved and served Italy with an Italian conscience and sentiment that are unique to national saints and patriarchs,"[53] Toni argued that the letters displayed at the *mostra* illustrated the composer's commitment to his homeland, as well as his "distinctly francophobic"[54] temperament. Toni reasserted Verdi's Italianness in music, maintaining that the sinfonia from I *Vespri siciliani* was "revolutionary Italian"[55] (*rivoluzionaria italianissima*), although the work was composed according to the genre of grand opéra, originally on a French libretto, and for the Parisian stage.

Evidently magnified, Verdi's antipathy toward France had been highlighted throughout the *Anno verdiano*.[56] Yet despite some degree of ambivalence, the composer "remained in fundamental sympathy with France,"[57] according to historian and musicologist John Rosselli; he noticeably felt comfortable in Paris[58]

---

52   "*Come ogni Genio italico, completo e poliedrico, Verdi possedeva in grado eminente le virtù della razza.*" Luzio, Per Giuseppe Verdi, 6.

53   "*Verdi ha amato e servito l'Italia con una coscienza e un sentimento italiani che sono soltanto dei Santi e Patriarchi nazionali.*" Toni, "Mussolini inaugura all'Accademia d'Italia la Mostra dei cimeli verdiani," 4.

54   "*Nelle lettere è messa in evidenza sintetica la bontà, l'italianità, il patriottismo verdiano, così marcatamente francofobo.*" Toni, "Mussolini inaugura all'Accademia d'Italia la Mostra dei cimeli verdiani," 4.

55   "*La sinfonia [...] rivoluzionaria italianissima dei* Vespri siciliani." Toni, "Mussolini inaugura all'Accademia d'Italia la Mostra dei cimeli verdiani," 4.

56   See for instance Roberto Farinacci, "Celebrazione di Verdi," in Verdi: Studi e memorie, ed. Giuseppe Mulè (Rome: Istituto Grafico Tiberino, 1941) 13–14.

57   John Rosselli, The Life of Verdi (Cambridge: Cambridge University Press, 2000), 122.

58   Anselm Gerhard, "Verdi-Bilder," in Verdi Handbuch, 2nd ed., ed. Anselm Gerhard and Uwe Schweikert (Stuttgart: Metzler, 2013), 20.

and appreciated the freedom and anonymity it provided, besides having shown his openness to French musical expressions. Toni's chauvinist narrative seems to have stemmed from an ambition to overshadow any foreign influence in Verdi's work, or even to undermine the future enemy. It supported the dominant discourse, which advocated the idea that Verdi was an Italian musician *par excellence* who only drew from the legacy of great Italian masters through operatic works (the ultimate Italian musical genre) created on Italian poetry (the means of expression of the Italian people).

Verdi the Patriot

Verdi's Italianness was also discussed in terms of his patriotism, which stemmed from a reignited interest in the "political" Verdi since the beginning of the *ventennio* and aimed at putting the patriotic convictions of the composer at the service of the fascist ideology. Presenting an artist devoted to a "religiously worshiped"[59] homeland, Luzio asserted that a palpable testimony to Verdi's political engagement was his decision to become a member of the parliament "by mere submission to Cavour's wish"[60] (proof of an absolute allegiance to the head of state), but also through his involvement in the Risorgimento. Similarly, Alceo Toni stated in *Il Popolo d'Italia* that "Giuseppe Verdi was a landmark of Italianness in the period of our Risorgimento: a propelling force of patriotic enthusiasm in the ardor of his songs, in words and works of virile devotion, with a remarkable Italian pride and passion."[61]

Approaching Verdi through the lens of the Italian unification movement had always been common in the literature, although scholarship has recently shown that the making of Verdi as "bard of the Risorgimento" occurred primarily after unification.[62] The parallel was nonetheless exuberantly exploited during

---

59   "Prò della Patria, dell'arte, religiosamente adorate." Luzio, Per Giuseppe Verdi, 6.
60   "Verdi, per sola sommissione al desiderio di Cavour, accettò la deputazione politica." Luzio, Per Giuseppe Verdi, 17.
61   "Giuseppe Verdi fu segnacolo d'italianità nel periodo del nostro Risorgimento: una forza propulsiva di entusiasmi patriottici nell'ardore dei suoi canti, nella parola e nell'opera di virile dedizione, con una fierezza e una passione italiana esemplari." Toni, "Mussolini inaugura all'Accademia d'Italia la Mostra dei cimeli verdiani," 4.
62   See in particular Roger Parker, Leonora's Last Act: Essays in Verdian Discourse (Princeton: Princeton University Press, 1997) and "Arpa d'or de' fatidici vati": The Verdian Patriotic Chorus in the 1840s (Parma: Istituto nazionale di studi verdiani, 1997); Birgit Pauls, Verdi und das Risorgimento: Ein politischer Mythos im Prozess der Nationenbildung (Berlin: Akademie Verlag, 1996); Mary Ann Smart, "Verdi, Italian Romanticism, and the Risorgimento," in The Cambridge Companion to Verdi, ed. Scott L. Balthazar (Cambridge: Cambridge University Press, 2004), 29–45. For more recent accounts, see Roger Parker, "Verdi Politico: A Wounded

the 1941 celebrations; Verdi was depicted as a leading figure of the movement, an "*aiodos* of the Risorgimento"[63] who fought against the oppressor with an "indisputably national"[64] music. His early operas, such as *Nabucco, Ernani, Attila,* and *La Battaglia di Legnano*, were often referred to as illustrating the patriotic fervor of a composer who, through politically charged plots, shed light on the subjugation of the Italian people under foreign yoke. Although they did not arouse much enthusiasm on stage, having been sparsely performed during the *Anno verdiano*, these operas were frequently mentioned in writings and speeches as testifying to Verdi's significance in the risorgimental epic, as fascist official Roberto Farinacci argued in his discourse broadcast on national radio (Eɪᴀʀ) in December 1940:

> The audacious allusions in *Ernani*, the heroism and love of the homeland in *Giovanna d'Arco*, the remote temerity in *La Battaglia di Legnano*, the hatred and anger against the foreigner in *I Vespri*, the glory of ancient republics in *Simon Boccanegra*, the invocation to Italy in *Attila*, are the voices of the soul and faith of this great man of the people (*popolano*) of Italy with an impetuous and generous heart, of this hero of the Risorgimento, powerful as Garibaldi with his sword on the battlefields.[65]

Exalting the myth of Italy's unification allowed the authorities to take advantage of the symbolic value of the Risorgimento, a movement emblematic of the Italians' struggles in the face of foreign domination that echoed fascist Italy's determination to claim its position of prestige in the international political arena. The Risorgimento also materialized the genesis of the modern state, whose natural outcome was manifestly fascist Italy, and the patriotic spirit that

---

Cliché Regroups," *Journal of Modern Italian Studies* 17, no. 4 (2012): 427–36; Mary Ann Smart, "Magical Thinking: Reason and Emotion in Some Recent Literature on Verdi and Politics," *Journal of Modern Italian Studies* 17, no. 4 (2012): 437–47; Mary Ann Smart, "How political were Verdi's operas? Metaphors of progress in the reception of *I Lombardi alla prima crociata*," *Journal of Modern Italian Studies* 18, no. 2 (2013): 190–204.

63   "Aedo del Risorgimento." Luzio, *Per Giuseppe Verdi*, 17.

64   "*Indiscutibilmente nazionale*." Ottavio Tiby, "Verdi e il suo tempo," in *Verdi: Studi e memorie*, 331.

65   "*Le ardite allusioni dell'Ernani, l'eroismo e l'amor di patria in Giovanna d'Arco, gli ardimenti lontani de La Battaglia di Legnano, l'odio e l'ira contro lo straniero ne I Vespri, la gloria delle antiche repubbliche nel Simon Boccanegra, la invocazione all'Italia nell'Attila, sono le voci dell'anima e della fede di questo grande popolano d'Italia dal cuore impetuoso e generoso, di questo eroe del Risorgimento, potente come Garibaldi con la spada sui campi di battaglia.*" The speech was published in the commemorative book *Verdi: Studi e memorie*, edited by the *Sindacato fascista musicisti* and its secretary, Giuseppe Mulè. Roberto Farinacci, "Celebrazione di Verdi," in *Verdi: Studi e memorie*, 11.

motivated the risorgimental upheavals became a catalyst for the process of unification undertaken by the fascists, who intended to strengthen the national identity still fragmented by the country's late unification. The multiplicity of political resonances offered by the Risorgimento helps to comprehend why Verdi, as a key figure of the movement, enjoyed such attention in 1941.

The politicization of Verdi's music and figure increased during the *Anno verdiano*, as the conflict evolved. Verdi became a fighter, referred to as a "man who wins" or a "tireless wrestler,"[66] and the creator of a music depicted in particularly martial terms, endowed, for instance, with "warlike and patriotic tones."[67] Such a terminology echoed the fascist military culture and intended to engage the composer in the war, presupposing his approval of the Duce's foreign policy, as asserted in a commemorative leaflet published in Parma: "Verdi is more relevant than ever in 1941, a year which sees Italy in a fierce struggle against Great Britain. He is among us today, as we fight for Italy's primacy and for its obvious imperial destiny."[68]

Verdi the Man

Portraying Verdi as a fighter allowed to align him with the political, but also ideological fascist agenda; the composer was indeed embedded in a militarist discourse, but he was also at the heart of an anti-modernist rhetoric aiming to depict him as the archetype of an ideal masculinity as defined by the fascist regime. Throughout the *Anno verdiano*, the anti-modernist stance was evidenced by assertions regarding ruralism, anti-urbanism, anti-intellectualism, anti-bourgeoisie, and pronatalism—values essential to Mussolini's doctrine.[69] The dissemination of an anti-intellectual and anti-bourgeois composer emerged prominently at the *mostra*'s inauguration; in his speech, Luzio presented Verdi as a pragmatic artist, who had a "clear vision of human things, psychological acuity, rude authenticity."[70] According to the historian, the correspondence between

---

66   "*L'uomo che vince*"; "*Il lottatore infaticabile.*" Enrico Magni Dufflocq, "Commento alla vita di Verdi," in *Verdi: Studi e memorie*, 24.

67   "*Accenti guerrieri e patriottici.*" Romolo Giraldi, "Dall' 'Oberto' a 'La Battaglia di Legnano,'" in *Verdi: Studi e memorie*, 48.

68   "*Verdi è più che mai attuale in questo 1941 che vede l'Italia in aspra lotta contro la Gran Bretagna. Egli è oggi fra noi, che stiamo combattendo per il primato d'Italia e per il suo certo destino imperiale.*" Teatro Regio: XL Anniversario della morte di Giuseppe Verdi (Parma: Fresching, 1941), 16–17.

69   Sandro Bellassai, "The Masculine Mystique: Antimodernism and Virility in Fascist Italy," *Journal of Modern Italian Studies* 10, no. 3 (2005), 315.

70   "*Limpida visione delle umane cose, acume psicologico, veridicità rude.*" Luzio, *Per Giuseppe Verdi*, 6.

Verdi and Piroli revealed the composer's objection to urbanism, his skepticism towards academics and the "sterility" of universities, and his disappointment in the face of a lack of support for the rural class.[71] These statements aimed at distancing Verdi from intellectualism, perceived under the *ventennio* as a "pathology of masculinity"[72] (although paradoxically Verdi was celebrated prominently at the heart of the fascist intellectual power), as well as from the bourgeoisie, understood by fascism as the result of a masculine identity corrupted by modern civilization. Moreover, Verdi's discontent served to convey the idea of the inadequacy of political liberalism and to reinforce the belief in a democratic immobilism that the fascist regime claimed to tackle upon its rise to power.

Throughout the *ventennio*, fascist anti-bourgeois sentiment was conveyed by exalting the values of the countryside and concomitantly praising the peasant world.[73] Consequently, Verdi's rurality had been frequently exploited during the anniversary, notably at the *mostra*'s opening; Luzio emphasized the composer's love for the land and quoted him when he claimed to Piroli (1878): "I was born and I still remain a peasant, who needs air and complete freedom in all respects!"[74] Through his ruralist depiction of the composer, Luzio also commended Verdi's lifestyle as a landowner, which allowed the historian to address the peninsula's long agrarian tradition (that the fascist regime intended to perpetuate): "Verdi always resorted to Piroli to purchase rustic lands, [...] driven by the healthy love of the land, by an atavistic predilection for agriculture, as a source, not only of national wealth, but also as a nursery of the purest forces of a fruitful people, laborious producer."[75]

Since the peasant was often presented as the quintessence of "natural" or untamed masculinity in fascist discourse, not forgetting that rural population symbolized "an anthropologically purer nucleus of a compact and organic

---

71   "*L'Urbanesimo ebbe in Verdi uno dei primi dichiarati nemici: dei più decisi nel proclamare che troppe sterili lauree dottorali si conquistassero nelle Università; poche proprietari sfruttassero le ricchezze della terra con modernità di metodi, e i reggitori dello Stato a lor volta non discernessero i pericoli che prima o poi dovevano scaturire dall'incuria per l'economia rurale, per i lavoratori di campagna, di città, scuotendo le basi stesse dello Stato.*" Luzio, *Per Giuseppe Verdi*, 7.

72   Bellassai, "The Masculine Mystique," 321.

73   Bellassai, "The Masculine Mystique," 314.

74   "*Io sono nato e mi conservo ancora un contadino, che ha bisogno d'aria e di una completa libertà in tutto e per tutto!*" Luzio, *Per Giuseppe Verdi*, 11–12.

75   "*Al Piroli aveva Verdi sempre parimenti ricorso per gli acquisti di fondi rustici, [...] guidato dal sano amore della terra, da una predilezione atavica per l'agricoltura, qual fonte, non solo di richezza nazionale, sì anche come vivaio delle più pure forze di un popolo fecondo, laborioso produttore.*" Luzio, *Per Giuseppe Verdi*, 6–7.

national community,"[76] portraying Verdi as a rural man aimed at depicting a pragmatic, manual and tied-to-the-soil artisan, therefore, a virile man. This strategy of "de-urbanizing" and, consequently, "de-bourgeoisizing" Verdi (the "bourgeois" symbolizing the well-off urbanized man[77]) was manifested throughout the *Anno verdiano* by writings devoted to the composer's peasant identity, as well as in reports written by authors who visited Verdi's village near Parma and highlighted the bucolic, pastoral, and rural landscape.[78]

The attention paid to the composer's rural identity also served to depict Verdi as an accessible figure. While referring to Verdi's "contact with the sufferings of the humble,"[79] Luzio conveyed a morally exemplary figure (a "model of civil wisdom"[80]) by stressing his kindness and his "profoundly altruistic"[81] nature. Verdi's proximity with ruralism was also related to his origins; having grown up in the small village of Le Roncole, near Parma, the composer was presented as having had a modest, even poor and hard childhood, but who rose to fame thanks to his talent, his determination, and above all his sustained efforts. This narrative allowed to emphasize on the work ethics and its related qualities such as discipline and rigor, while drawing parallels with the demanding, even exhausting—but profoundly virile—lifestyle of the peasants.

Although Verdi had nurtured his peasant identity during his lifetime and portrayed himself as a "simple man" (notably through particularly restrained clothes[82]), the composer was not a *contadino* per se; as an adult, he was a wealthy landowner. He came from a relatively prosperous family, whose parents were not workers of the land but shopkeepers and had been able to provide Verdi with a quality education—a privilege given the high rate of illiteracy at the

---

76   Bellassai, "The Masculine Mystique," 318. The author refers to Pier Giorgio Zunino, *L'ideologia del fascismo: Miti, credenze e valori nella stabilizzazione del regime* (Bologna: Il Mulino, 1985), 309.

77   Bellassai, "The Masculine Mystique," 323.

78   See for instance Giuseppe Adami, "La Casa di riposo per i musicisti," *Scenario* 9, no. 11 (November 1940): 494–96; Carlo Gatti, "Verdi nel 40° anniversario della morte: Ritorno a Sant'Agata," *L'Illustrazione italiana* 68, no. 4 (January 26, 1941): 105–34; Federico Ghisi, "Verdi popolaresco," in *Verdi: Studi e memorie*, 315–23; Remo Giazotto, "Popolo e valutazione artistica: L'arte di Verdi in clima fascista," *Musica d'oggi* 22, no. 8–9 (August–September 1940): 233–35; Tenato Liguori, "Giuseppe Verdi rurale," in *Verdi: Studi e memorie*, 345–48; and Luigi Tonelli, "Una visita ai luoghi verdiani: L'autografo della sinfonia dell'Aida," *Cremona* 12, no. 8–9 (September–October 1940): 369–70.

79   *"Contatto con le sofferenze degli umili."* Luzio, *Per Giuseppe Verdi*, 12.

80   "E tale egli fu [...] modello di sapienza civile." Luzio, *Per Giuseppe Verdi*, 12.

81   "Profondamente altruistica." Luzio, *Per Giuseppe Verdi*, 6, 13.

82   Gerhard, "Verdi-Bilder," 21; Parker, *Leonora's Last Act*, 100.

time.[83] The narrative of a "self-made man" also had been fueled by the composer himself; it had been enhanced under fascism, since it suited the rhetoric of the regime, which fostered male figures in action, but Verdi had always been able to surround himself with resourceful people from which he received assistance to advance his career (such as his greatest patron, Antonio Barezzi[84]).

Staging an accessible figure was also manifested by testifying to the composer's humanness; while recognizing his unique legacy to Italian culture, the commemorators presented Verdi first and foremost as a man, endowed with a fine sensitivity and subject to human sufferings. Throughout the *Anno verdiano*, Verdi's vulnerability was illustrated by the recurrent reference to the death of his two infants, Virginia and Icilio, and his first wife Margherita Barezzi, between 1838 and 1840. Whereas some commemorators underlined the composer's despair, others, including Luzio, insisted on the absence of Verdi's progeny; while Mussolini had undertaken a pronatalist campaign against Italy's declining birthrate, mentioning Verdi's inability to provide a lineage to his homeland showed an even greater fatality.

This episode also served to demonstrate Verdi's moral strength: despite this tragedy, the artist's subsequent success and glory illustrated his resilience and his combativeness, having been able to rise above the misfortunes that overwhelmed him. This archetypal heroic narrative of struggle, overcoming, and triumph was central to the discourse surrounding mythical heroes, such as musicologist Sanna Pederson exemplified with the case of Beethoven.[85] By showing Verdi's "indomitable zeal to overcome the obstacles and reach the summit,"[86] Luzio reinforced a narrative that, according to Pederson's analysis, deepened the composer's masculinity while securing his position at the heart of the Western musical canon.

Verdi the Myth

Verdi's "heroization" also nurtured the cult of the artist as a national myth; exalting Verdi's genius was preeminent throughout the *Anno verdiano*, with pompous depictions that sought to testify to the composer's legendary, even "titanic" or "Olympian" stature. However, the discourse conveyed at the *mostra* was rather contained and not imbued with the strong universalist rhetoric that

---

83   Gerhard, "Verdi-Bilder," 3.

84   Gerhard, "Verdi-Bilder," 6.

85   See Sanna Pederson, "Beethoven and Masculinity," in *Beethoven*, ed. Michael Spitzer (London: Routledge, 2015), 473–91.

86   "*Indomita foga nel superare gli ostacoli per raggiunger la vetta.*" Luzio, *Per Giuseppe Verdi*, 6.

was inherent to the discursive landscape of 1941. Commemorators indeed suggested that Verdi's music, universally understandable (since it was particularly accomplished), addressed all of humanity—an assertion that subtly promoted fascist Italy's cultural expansionism. This topos had not been exploited at the Academy in June 1940, when the discourse revolved around the exaltation of Verdi's national spirit.

These discursive peculiarities could have resulted, on the one hand, from the Duce's attendance; the tributes paid to Verdi probably had to be constrained so that the composer did not overshadow Mussolini—a central figure whose presence was widely publicized. Verdi then had to be depicted as an exemplary figure, but not too flamboyant. On the other hand, the context surrounding the *mostra* may have influenced the discourse; while a great campaign of seduction was deployed to persuade the nation to go to war, presenting Verdi as an Italian, human, and accessible artist may have been deemed more appropriate to establish a connection with the people, to unite the Italians around a common heritage, and to unify the population before the outbreak of hostilities. Since the discourse was directed to the forthcoming home front, universalism was not as essential as it was when Italy became a belligerent.

Verdi under Democracy, Fascist Continuities?

The *mostra verdiana* organized at the Academy did not enjoy great longevity and terminated abruptly on June 15, 1940, in order to protect the potentially endangered exhibits following Italy's entry into the war.[87] Despite its short duration, the *mostra* had nevertheless been a major display of the regime's self-celebration, which took part in an unprecedented propagandistic deployment on the eve of the conflict. According to Paola Cagiano and Susanna Panetta, the *mostra* responded to the need of conveying the image of a strong and united people at a significant and historic moment:

> through the expressive force of the Maestro, [the exhibition] gave an image of Italy's 'power, glory' and reminded the Italians that they belonged to the same nation, to the same culture, to the same tradition. The choice of the

---

87   Cagiano and Panetta, "Giuseppe Verdi e l'Accademia dei Lincei," 442–43.

inauguration date, June 4, 1940, when Italy was only five days away from going to war, could perhaps be interpreted in that sense.[88]

Moreover, the *mostra* could be seen as a tangible expression of Verdi's appropriation by the regime, his "import" at the heart of the fascist intellectual power. This reading contrasted considerably with subsequent commemorations, such as those on the occasion of the fiftieth anniversary of the composer's death in 1951, during which Luigi Einaudi, president of Italy, traveled to Milan and later to Parma to honor Verdi. Drawing a parallel with the 1951 anniversary also brings out numerous post-war resonances and attests that the Verdian mythmaking continued to be manipulated and reinterpreted, but at the service of new political convictions: the celebrations no longer promoted a hegemonic and oppressive regime, but rather supported the return to democracy in a context of political fragility.

Musicologist Harriet Boyd-Bennett has underlined many similarities between the commemorations of 1941 and 1951, which included, on the organizational level, the recurrence of the commemorators, the material (as texts from 1941 were republished in 1951), and the activities (commemorative speeches, exhibitions of memorabilia, musical events, etc.).[89] At the same time, on the discursive level, Boyd-Bennett pointed out that the topoi exploited in 1951 were also surprisingly similar to those emphasized under the fascist regime. For instance, Verdi's quintessential Italianness was still acutely significant in 1951, but rather aimed at rebuilding a fragmented national identity undermined by a conflict that ended in civil war (1943–1945). The universalist rhetoric was also exploited, but no longer to support the expansionist and dominating ambitions of a megalomaniac Duce; they instead sought to make the composer a universal, tolerant, and open-minded figure—an openness that Italy advocated at a time when the country sought to arise from its geopolitical isolation and vouch for the new democratic ideals.

Another major continuity regarded the predominance of the "political" Verdi, a topos that helped to nurture the myth of the composer as an icon of the Risorgimento, a cultural counterpart to Garibaldi. The Risorgimento was also central to post-war historiography and served to establish a national continuity

---

88   "*Una mostra che, attraverso la forza espressiva del Maestro, desse un'immagine di 'potenza, di gloria' dell'Italia e fosse un richiamo per gli italiani di appartenenza alla stessa Patria, alla stessa cultura, alla stessa tradizione. In questo senso, forse, può essere interpretata la scelta della data dell'inaugurazione, il 4 giugno del 1940, quando mancavano soli cinque giorni all'entrata in guerra dell'Italia.*" Cagiano and Panetta, "Giuseppe Verdi e l'Accademia dei Lincei," 442.

89   Harriet Boyd-Bennett, *Opera in Postwar Venice: Cultural Politics and the Avant-garde* (Cambridge: Cambridge University Press, 2018), 74–75.

between the post-fascist Italian State and the unification movement[90]: the struggles that materialized the genesis of the modern state were henceforth paired with the partisan war fought against the Germans from 1943 to 1945, an episode soon described as the "Second Risorgimento."[91] This narrative, which focused on remembering the *biennio* (1943–1945), sought to give weight to the (mainly communist) resistance—and thus reinforce adherence to the relatively strong Communist Party—and to foster, through the risorgimental parallel, the "resurgence" trope reclaimed by the Catholics—who were another predominant political force in post-war Italy.[92] Moreover, the emphasis on the *biennio* allowed to supplant the *ventennio* in the Italian collective consciousness and thus promote a narrative that overshadowed the fascist past.[93] This process of "selective remembering and wilful forgetting"[94] largely contributed to the collective amnesia that marked the post-war Italian attitude.[95] Authorities sought to let fascism fall into oblivion in order to avoid internal divisions and hasten Italy's democratic transition, despite the many continuities it generated in Italian socio-political life.[96] This denial of the fascist past, which was also reflected in music, thus explained the echoes of 1941 found in the 1951 commemorations, as Boyd-Bennett noted: "the fact that the fascist regime had exploited an almost identical strategy only a decade earlier, at the state-sponsored fortieth anniversary celebrations, was conveniently forgotten."[97]

Revealing the numerous continuities in the post-war anniversary bears witness to the ambiguities and ambivalences that impregnated the return to democracy in Italy and illustrates the fact that fascism was not eradicated by the fall of Mussolini's regime. These observations also indicate that the Verdi who was celebrated embodied political ideals both before and after the war.

---

90 Harriet Boyd-Bennett, *Opera in Postwar Venice*, 74–77.
91 Claudio Fogu, "*Italiani brava gente*: The Legacy of Fascist Historical Culture of Italian Politics of Memory," in *The Politics of Memory in Postwar Europe*, ed. Richard Ned Lebow, Wulf Kansteiner, and Claudio Fogu (Durham, NC: Duke University Press, 2006), 149–51.
92 Fogu, "*Italiani brava gente*," 151.
93 Fogu, "*Italiani brava gente*," 150–51.
94 Robert Ventresca, "Debating the Meaning of Fascism in Contemporary Italy," *Modern Italy* 11, no. 2 (2006), 189.
95 Hannah Malone, "Legacies of Fascism: Architecture, Heritage and Memory in Contemporary Italy," *Modern Italy* 22, no. 4 (2017), 448–49, 464–465; Marta Petrusewicz, "The Hidden Pages of Contemporary Italian History: War Crimes, War Guilt and Collective Memory," *Journal of Modern Italian Studies* 9, no. 3 (2004), 270; Ventresca, "Debating the Meaning of Fascism in Contemporary Italy," 196.
96 Ventresca, "Debating the Meaning of Fascism in Contemporary Italy," 196.
97 Boyd-Bennett, *Opera in Postwar Venice*, 74.

Although his figure and his work may have been reclaimed by both democratic and dictatorial powers, the political reappropriation of the composer had fundamentally similar goals: to elicit approval for a political and/or ideological project that was considered legitimate. As Fiamma Nicolodi pointed out, Verdi remained after the fall of the regime "a 'father of the homeland,' a living embodiment (through the examples offered by his art, his life, his character) of the Italian state, henceforth free and united around the new institutional form of the republic."[98] Indeed, Verdi continued and still continues to be put at the service of power, fashioned according to the political forces that celebrate him, whether on the left or on the right, democratic or totalitarian.

References

Published Sources

"Celebrazioni verdiane." Il Musicista 7, no. 11 (August 1940): 168.

"Il 40° anniversario della morte di Giuseppe Verdi." La Stampa, August 23, 1940, 3.

"Il 40° della morte di Verdi: Un ciclo di manifestazioni celebrative." Corriere della sera, August 23, 1940, 4.

"Il Duce inaugura all'Accademia d'Italia la mostra di autografi e cimeli verdiani." Gazzetta di Venezia, June 5, 1940, 5.

"Il Duce inaugura all'Accademia la mostra dei cimeli Verdiani." La Stampa, June 5, 1940, 4.

"Il Duce inaugura la Mostra dei cimeli verdiani." Corriere della Sera, June 5, 1940, 3.

"Il Duce per la celebrazione di Verdi." Gazzetta di Venezia, August 23, 1940, 3.

"Notizie e informazioni." La Rassegna musicale 13, no. 7–8 (July–August 1940): 325.

"Notizie." Musica d'oggi 22, no. 8–9 (August–September 1940): 254.

De Angelis, Alberto. "G. Verdi e il Senatore G. Piroli. Un epistolario inedito." Musica d'oggi 22, no. 3 (March 1940): 59–63.

De Rensis, Raffaello. Mussolini musicista. Mantua: Paladino, 1927.

---

98   "Verdi insomma, anche a regime caduto e a guerra conclusa resta a tutti gli effetti un 'padre della patria,' incarnazione vivente (attraverso gli esempi offerti dalla sua arte, dalla sua vita, dal suo carattere) dello stato italiano, ora libero e unito intorno alla nuova forma istituzionale della repubblica." Nicolodi, "Mitografia verdiana nel primo Novecento," 76.

Farinelli, Arturo. *Giuseppe Verdi e il suo mondo interiore: Discorso per il quarantennio della morte tenuto alla Reale Accademia d'Italia il 19 febbraio 1941–XIX*. Rome: Reale Accademia d'Italia, 1941.

Gatti, Angelo. *L'italianità di Giuseppe Verdi: Discorso per il quarantennio della morte tenuto nella Casa di riposo dei musicisti in Milano il 27 gennaio 1941–XIX*. Rome: Reale Accademia d'Italia, 1941.

Gatti, Carlo. *Verdi nelle immagini*. Milan: Garzanti, 1941.

Luzio, Alessandro, ed. *Carteggi verdiani*. Rome: Reale Accademia d'Italia/Accademia dei Lincei, 1935–47.

———. *Per Giuseppe Verdi: Discorso inaugurale della mostra verdiana alla presenza del Duce nella sede della Reale Accademia d'Italia, 4 giugno 1940–XVIII*. Rome: Reale Accademia d'Italia, 1940.

Mulè, Giuseppe, ed. *Verdi: Studi e memorie*. Rome: Istituto Grafico Tiberino, 1941.

Orestano, Francesco. *Giuseppe Verdi mediterraneo e universale: Discorso per la settimana verdiana di Monaco di Baviera pronunziato il 5 febbraio 1941–XIX nella Münchner Künstlerhaus*. Rome: Reale Accademia d'Italia, 1941.

Teatro Regio: XL Anniversario della morte di Giuseppe Verdi. Parma: Fresching, 1941.

Toni, Alceo. "Mussolini inaugura all'Accademia d'Italia la Mostra dei cimelî verdiani." *Il Popolo d'Italia*, June 5, 1940, 4.

Audiovisual Sources

Istituto nazionale Luce. "Il Duce nella sed dell'Accademia d'Italia inaugura la Mostra dei cimeli verdiani." *Giornale Luce* C0046, June 11, 1940, 1:38.

———. "La gloria di Giuseppe Verdi celebrata a Busseto, città natale del Maestro." *Giornale Luce* C0014, January 31, 1941, 1:02.

———. "Milano—Una visita alla Casa di Riposo per musicisti e cantanti." *Giornale Luce* C0111, January 21, 1941, 2:21.

Secondary Literature

Agnew, John. "'Ghosts of Rome': The Haunting of Fascist Efforts at Remaking Rome as Italy's Capital City." *Annali d'Italianistica* 28 (2010): 179–98.

Allotti, Pierluigi. *Giornalisti di regime: La stampa italiana tra fascismo e antifascismo (1922–1948)*. Rome: Carocci, 2012.

Bardi, Aloma and Mauro Conti, eds. *Teatro comunale di Firenze: Catalogo delle manifestazioni 1928–1997*. Florence: Le Lettere, 1998.

Bellassai, Sandro. "The Masculine Mystique: Antimodernism and Virility in Fascist Italy." *Journal of Modern Italian Studies* 10, no. 3 (2005): 314–35.

Biguzzi, Stefano. *L'orchestra del Duce: Mussolini, la musica e il mito del capo.* Turin: Utet, 2004.

Boyd-Bennett, Harriet. *Opera in Postwar Venice: Cultural Politics and the Avant-garde.* Cambridge: Cambridge University Press, 2018.

Cagiano, Paola and Susanna Panetta. "Giuseppe Verdi e l'Accademia dei Lincei: Percorsi e vicende." In *Verdi e Roma*, edited by Olga Jesurum, 429–56. Rome: Accademia nazionale dei Lincei, 2015.

Capra, Marco. "Tra modernismo e restaurazione: La vita musicale a Parma nel ventennio fascista." *Storia di ieri: Parma dal regime fascista alla liberazione (1927–1945).* Parma: Istituzione biblioteche del comune di Parma, 2011. https://www.comune.parma.it/dizionarioparmigiani/ita/La%20vita%20musicale.aspx?idMostra=49&idNode=380.

———. *Verdi in prima pagina: Nascita, sviluppo e affermazione della figura di Verdi nella stampa italiana dal XIX al XXI secolo.* Lucca: Libreria musicale italiana, 2014.

Chiapparo, Maria Rosa. "Le mythe de la 'Terza Roma' ou l'immense théâtre de la Rome fasciste." *Nuovo rinascimento*, May 17, 2004. https://www.nuovorinascimento.org/n-rinasc/saggi/pdf/chiapparo/roma.pdf.

Fogu, Claudio. "*Italiani brava gente*: The Legacy of Fascist Historical Culture of Italian Politics of Memory." In *The Politics of Memory in Postwar Europe*, edited by Richard Ned Lebow, Wulf Kansteiner, and Claudio Fogu, 147–76. Durham, NC: Duke University Press, 2006.

Ferrarotto, Marinella. *L'Accademia d'Italia: Intellettuali e potere durante il fascismo.* Naples: Liguori, 1977.

Fogu, Claudio. *The Historic Imaginary: Politics of History in Fascist Italy,* Toronto: University of Toronto Press, 2003.

Foro, Philippe. *L'Italie fasciste.* Paris: Armand Colin, 2006.

Gentile, Emilio. *Il mito dello Stato nuovo dall'antigiolittismo al fascismo.* Rome: Laterza, 1982.

———. *Qu'est-ce que le fascisme? Histoire et interprétation.* Paris: Gallimard, 2004.

Gerhard, Anselm. "Verdi-Bilder." In *Verdi Handbuch*, 2nd ed., edited by Anselm Gerhard and Uwe Schweikert, 2–27. Stuttgart: Metzler, 2013.

Giardina, Andrea. "The Fascist Myth of Romanity." *Estudos Avançados* 22, no. 62 (2008): 55–76.

Ginot-Slacik, Charlotte, and Michela Niccolai. *Musiques dans l'Italie fasciste: 1922–1945.* Paris: Fayard, 2019.

Illiano, Roberto, ed. *Italian Music During the Fascist Period.* Turnhout: Brepols, 2004.

Illiano, Roberto and Massimiliano Sala. "The Politics of Spectacle: Italian Music and Fascist Propaganda." *Musikologija/Musicology* 12 (2012): 9–26.

Klauk, Stephanie, Luca Aversano, and Rainer Kleinertz, eds. *Musik und Musik-wissenschaft im Umfeld des Faschismus: Deutsch–italienische Perspektiven.* Sinzig: Studio Verlag, 2015.

Kreuzer, Gundula. *Verdi and the Germans: From Unification to the Third Reich.* Cambridge: Cambridge University Press, 2010.

Malone, Hannah. "Legacies of Fascism: Architecture, Heritage and Memory in Contemporary Italy." *Modern Italy* 22, no. 4 (2017): 445–70.

Nicolodi, Fiamma. "Aspetti di politica culturale nel ventennio fascista." In *Italian Music During the Fascist Period,* edited by Roberto Illiano, 97–122. Turnhout: Brepols, 2004.

———. "Mitografia verdiana nel primo Novecento." In *Verdi Reception,* edited by Lorenzo Frassà and Michela Niccolai, 33–77. Turnhout: Brepols, 2013.

———. "Il sistema produttivo dall'Unità a oggi." In *Storia dell'opera italiana,* edited by Lorenzo Bianconi and Giorgio Pestelli, vol. 4, 167–229. Turin: Edizioni di Torino, 1987.

———. "Musica a Roma nella prima metà del '900." *Analecta musicologica* 45 (2011): 478–98.

———. *Musica e musicisti nel ventennio fascista.* Florence: Discanto, 1984.

Parker, Roger. *"Arpa d'or de' fatidici vati": The Verdian Patriotic Chorus in the 1840s.* Parma: Istituto nazionale di studi verdiani, 1997.

———. "Verdi *Politico*: A Wounded Cliché Regroups." *Journal of Modern Italian Studies* 17, no. 4 (2012): 427–36.

———. *Leonora's Last Act: Essays in Verdian Discourse.* Princeton: Princeton University Press, 1997.

Pauls, Birgit. *Giuseppe Verdi und das Risorgimento: Ein politischer Mythos im Prozess der Nationenbildung.* Berlin: Akademie Verlag, 1996.

Pederson, Sanna. "Beethoven and Masculinity." In *Beethoven,* edited by Michael Spitzer, 473–91. London: Routledge, 2015.

Petrusewicz, Marta. "The Hidden Pages of Contemporary Italian History: War Crimes, War Guilt and Collective Memory." *Journal of Modern Italian Studies* 9, no. 3 (2004): 269–70.

Polo, Claudia. *Immaginari verdiani: Opera, media e industria culturale nell'Italia del XX secolo.* Milan: Ricordi, 2004.

Rosselli, John. *The Life of Verdi.* Cambridge: Cambridge University Press, 2000.

Rostagno, Antonio. "Ouverture e dramma negli anni Settanta: Il caso della Sinfonia di Aida." *Studi verdiani* 14 (1999): 11–50.

Sachs, Harvey. *Music in Fascist Italy.* New York: Norton, 1987.

Smart, Mary Ann. "How political were Verdi's operas? Metaphors of progress in the reception of I *Lombardi alla prima crociata.*" *Journal of Modern Italian Studies* 18, no. 2 (2013): 190–204.

Smart, Mary Ann. "Magical Thinking: Reason and Emotion in Some Recent

Literature on Verdi and Politics." *Journal of Modern Italian Studies* 17, no. 4 (2012): 437–47.

——. "Verdi, Italian Romanticism, and the Risorgimento." In *The Cambridge Companion to Verdi*, edited by Scott L. Balthazar, 29–45. Cambridge: Cambridge University Press, 2004.

Stenzl, Jürg. "Fascismo—kein Thema?" In *Musikforschung Faschismus National-sozialismus: Referate der Tagung Schloss Engers (8. bis 11. März 2000)*, edited by Isolde von Foerster et al., 143–50. Mainz: Are Verlag, 2001.

——. *Von Giacomo Puccini zu Luigi Nono: Italienische Musik 1922–1952: Faschismus, Resistenza, Republik*. Büren: Knuf, 1990.

Tranfaglia, Nicola. *La stampa del regime 1932–1943: Le veline del Minculpop per orientare l'informazione*. Milan: Bompiani, 2005.

Ventresca, Robert. "Debating the Meaning of Fascism in Contemporary Italy." *Modern Italy* 11, no. 2 (2006): 189–209.

Part 3:
(Non-)Democratic Participation in
Popular Music and Performance Cultures

The Intervision Song Contest
Popular Music and Political Liberalization in the Eastern Bloc

Dean Vuletic

Abstract: During the Cold War, Eastern Bloc broadcasting organizations held the Intervision Song Contest (Isc) as an alternative to Western Europe's Eurovision Song Contest (Esc). Staged in Czechoslovakia and Poland between 1964 and 1980, the Isc has usually been depicted in the popular media as merely a belated, fleeting copy of the Esc, with the Isc's failure being a metaphor for the decline of the economic and political systems of communist party-led Eastern Europe. However, unlike with the Esc, there has been little academic research on the Isc. This chapter is based on archival sources from national and international broadcasting organizations, and focuses on the first series of the Isc in Czechoslovakia. It argues that the Isc was conceived by its organizers as a pan-European event that would promote cooperation between the Eastern and Western Blocs, especially in the context of Khrushchev's Thaw and the cultural and political liberalization in Czechoslovakia that culminated in the Prague Spring. The Isc's organizers accordingly introduced innovations that made their contest more internationally open and commercial than the Esc. Furthermore, the staging of the Isc in Czechoslovakia underlined the limits of the Soviet Union's cultural and political influence over Eastern Europe and the role that geopolitics played in the power relations between states within the Eastern Bloc. The Isc was, then, not simply an imitation of the Esc, but rather a product of international political relations that tells us much about the aspirations that some Eastern European artists, politicians, and officials from record companies and television stations had for the democratization of their states.

Dean Vuletic is a historian of contemporary Europe at the Research Center for the History of Transformations (Recet) of the University of Vienna and the author of *Postwar Europe and the Eurovision Song Contest* (London: Bloomsbury, 2018). He received his Ph.D. in history from Columbia University.

The traditional controversies that accompany the voting results in every edition of the Eurovision Song Contest (Esc), one of the world's longest running and most-watched television programs, are widely infamous. As I demonstrate in my book *Postwar Europe and the Eurovision Song Contest*, the first-ever academic monograph on the history of the Esc, such controversies have marked the contest ever since its first edition in 1956. In that year, the Swiss jury allegedly cast the deciding vote that brought Switzerland's entry "Refrain" (sung by Lys Assia) victory in that contest, which was staged in the Swiss city of Lugano. The Swiss jury did so after it voted in place of the Luxembourgish jury, whose members were not able to travel to Lugano to participate in the voting. Since then, voting blocs based on commercial, cultural, geographical, linguistic, and even political connections have been a perennial feature of the Esc.[1] These blocs have been especially controversial since the 1990s, following the entry of states from the former Eastern Bloc and the incorporation of public voting into the contest. In 2009, in response to accusations made mostly by officials from West European national broadcasting organizations that Central and East European public audiences were exacerbating the problem of bloc voting, the public voting component in the final voting results was reduced to fifty percent, with the other half being determined by national expert juries made up of professionals from the music industry. The participation of East European states in the Esc has also been controversial in the post-Cold War era for the involvement of authoritarian governments, such as those of Azerbaijan and Russia. There, the participation of government-controlled national broadcasting organizations in the contest and their hosting of the event, such as in Moscow in 2009 and Baku in 2012, has been used to whitewash the international images of these governments.[2]

Criticisms of Central and East European participants in the Esc by West European commentators have also reflected suspicion over the impact that the integration of states from this region could have on pan-European organizations—not only on the Esc and its organizer, the European Broadcasting Union (EBU), but also, more significantly, on the European Union (EU) and the North Atlantic Treaty Organization (NATO).[3] Yet, these criticisms have highlighted a longer history of West European cultural prejudices against Central and East Europe, prejudices that have considered the latter region to have been, throughout history,

1   Dean Vuletic, *Postwar Europe and the Eurovision Song Contest* (London: Bloomsbury, 2018), 66–74.

2   Vuletic, *Postwar Europe and the Eurovision Song Contest*, 156–59, 194–97.

3   See, for example, the case study on the British Broadcasting Corporation's (BBC) Esc commentator Terry Wogan by Karen Fricker, "'It's Just Not Funny Any More': Terry Wogan, Melancholy Britain, and the Eurovision Song Contest," in*Performing the 'New' Europe: Identities, Feelings and Politics in the Eurovision Song Contest*, ed. Karen Fricker and Milija Gluhovic (Basingstoke: Palgrave Macmillan, 2013), 53–76.

inherently more illiberal, poor, and unmodern than its Western counterpart.[4] Such engrained prejudices have also appeared in popular documentaries and literature that have discussed the popular music industry in Eastern Europe during the Cold War. This has been the case with regard to the Intervision Song Contest (Isc), the Eastern Bloc alternative to the Esc that was staged in Czechoslovakia from 1965 to 1968 and in Poland from 1977 to 1980. As the Isc has received little scholarly attention,[5] it has been clichédly presented in popular media as a fake, feeble, and fleeting, a censored, communist, and controlled, imitation of the Esc.[6] This approach has ignored the connections and similarities between the popular music industries in Eastern Europe and Western Europe in the Cold War era; it has also blinded an understanding of the Isc that is counterintuitive to stereotypical interpretations of the Eastern Bloc as being

---

4   For a seminal study on the cultural construction of such notions of "Eastern Europe," see Larry Wolff, *Inventing Eastern Europe: The Map of Civilization on the Mind of the Enlightenment* (Stanford, CA: Stanford University Press, 1994).

5   The few other academic studies on the Isc mostly focus on the series in Poland, and they include: Mari Pajala, "Intervision Song Contests and Finnish Television Between East and West," in *Airy Curtains in the European Ether: Broadcasting and the Cold War*, ed. Alexander Badenoch, Andreas Fickers, and Christian Henrich-Franke (Baden-Baden: Nomos, 2013), 215–39; Anna G. Piotrowska, "About Twin Song Festivals in Eastern and Western Europe: Intervision and Eurovision," *International Review of the Aesthetics and Sociology of Music* 47, no. 1 (June 2016): 123–35; Yulia Yurtaeva, "Ein schwarzer Rabe gegen Conchita Wurst oder: Wovor hat Russland Angst?" in *Eurovision Song Contest: Eine kleine Geschichte zwischen Körper, Geschlecht und Nation*, ed. Christine Ehardt, Georg Vogt, and Florian Wagner (Vienna: Zaglossus), 111–35; and Yulia Yurtaeva and Lothar Mikos, "Song Contests in Europe During the Cold War," in *New Patterns in Global Television Formats*, ed. Karina Aveyard, Pia Majbritt Jensen, and Albert Moran (Bristol and Chicago: Intellect, 2016), 110–24.

6   For an example of such a presentation, see the television documentary *The Secret History of Eurovision*, dir. Stephen Oliver (Electric Pictures, 2011), which incorrectly asserts that the Esc was not broadcast in the Eastern Bloc during the Cold War and portrays Eastern Europeans as subversively desirous of the Western contest. It also contains the myth that voting in the Isc was done by viewers switching their lights at home on and off and the consequent electricity surges being measured. This myth is also repeated in a non-academic book by Chris West, *Eurovision! A History of Modern Europe Through the World's Greatest Song Contest* (London: Melville House UK, 2017), 97–98. In one of the major English-language media reports on the history of the Isc, which was published by the Bbc, the opening line falsely claims that the Soviet Union set up the Isc: "[w]hen nestled behind the Iron Curtain, the Soviet Union could not take part in the Eurovision Song Contest, so it set up a rival competition—and called it Intervision." Steve Rosenberg, "The Cold War Rival to Eurovision," Bbc (May 14, 2012), https://www.bbc.com/news/magazine-18006446.

backward, closed, and homogenous. Indeed, in my archival research on the Isc that I conducted in the archives of the national broadcasting organizations of the Czech Republic, Germany, Poland, Russia, and Slovakia, I discovered that the contest rather promoted cultural and commercial cooperation between the Eastern and Western Blocs in the 1960s and the 1970s, in light of diplomatic transformations such as the Thaw and the Helsinki Accords. The Isc was the product of liberalization processes in the Eastern Bloc, namely the cultural, economic, and political reforms in the 1960s that accompanied de-Stalinization in Czechoslovakia and culminated in the Prague Spring, or those in Poland in the 1970s that were enacted by the government of Edward Gierek. The Isc's fate in both states was also determined by the ending of these periods of liberalization. Focusing on the first series of the Isc in Czechoslovakia in the 1960s, this chapter will examine what the history of the Isc tells us about the aspirations of Eastern European artists, politicians, and the representatives of record companies and television stations, for the political liberalization of the communist party-led systems in their states, and about the cultural and economic ramifications of liberalizing reforms.

Establishing Eurovision and Intervision

Unlike other international mega events such as the Olympic Games, the Venice Biennale, or the World Cup, the Esc stood out during the Cold War in that it never had representatives from the Western and Eastern Blocs competing against each other. Indeed, it was Cold War division that determined the establishment of Eastern European and Western European international song contests for popular music, as these were based on the membership of the separate international broadcasting organizations that were set up for each of the Blocs. Europe's first international broadcasting organization, the International Broadcasting Union, had been formed in the interwar period, but it never included the Soviet Union due to its diplomatic isolation as the first communist party-led state in the world.[7] In the late 1940s, cooperation among European states in a single international broadcasting organization became unfeasible amidst early Cold War tensions. This resulted in the establishment, in 1950, of separate international broadcasting organizations for each of the Blocs: Western Europe's European Broadcasting Union (Ebu), which was based in Brussels and Geneva, and Eastern Europe's International Broadcasting Organization

---

7   Suzanne Lommers, *Europe—On Air: Interwar Projects for Radio Broadcasting* (Amsterdam: Amsterdam University Press, 2012), 143–44.

(OIR), which was in 1960 renamed the International Radio and Television Organization (OIRT),[8] with headquarters in Prague. Each of these brought together national radio and television broadcasters and promoted cultural and technical cooperation between them, just as each of the Blocs had their own other separate international organizations, like the Council of Europe, the European Coal and Steel Community, Euratom, the European Economic Community, and the NATO for the West, and the Council for Mutual Economic Assistance and the Warsaw Pact for the East.[9] The EBU and the OIRT similarly developed separate networks for program cooperation and exchange among their members. These were called the Eurovision Network (established in 1954) and the Intervision Network (established in 1960), respectively. It was from these that the names of the song contests organized for the members of these organizations were derived.

Following the death of Soviet leader Joseph Stalin in 1953, the beginning of the Thaw under the government of Soviet leader Nikita Khrushchev saw the introduction of de-Stalinization policies that relaxed cultural censorship, including that of Western popular music and other cultural products. As political tensions between Eastern Europe and Western Europe declined, the EBU and the OIR began to cooperate, with the first meeting between their officials being held in Helsinki in 1957. Finland was poised to play a bridging role between the two organizations as it was politically non-aligned, which made its national broadcasting organization, the Finnish Broadcasting Company (Yleisradio Oy, YLE), the only one that was a full member of both the EBU and the OIRT. The cooperation between the EBU and the OIRT was also manifested in the program exchanges between the Eurovision and Intervision networks, with the ESC being one of the earliest examples of these. The ESC was first relayed by the Intervision Network to Eastern European states in 1965. The Intervision Network also received the program for free from the Eurovision Network; this became even more of a political gesture from 1976, when the EBU started requiring a participation fee both from the national broadcasting organizations that entered as well as those that just relayed the contest, but still did not charge OIRT members "to avoid creating misunderstandings between the two Unions."[10] Another symbolic gesture that was made in the ESC towards Eastern Europe was that, after 1965, the hosts of the ESC often mentioned in their introductions to the shows the

---

8   "OIRT" was the abbreviation that was used internationally for the organization, based on its French name "Organisation internationale de radiodiffusion et de télévision," as had also been the case with the OIR.

9   Ernest Eugster, *Television Programming Across National Boundaries: The EBU and OIRT Experience* (Dedham, MA: Artech House, 1983), 39–47.

10   OIRT, "52nd Meeting" (Algiers, May 16–19, 1975), 56 [Archives of the EBU, Concours Eurovision de la chanson, Décisions 1].

states of the Intervision Network in which the contest was being broadcast, thereby underlining to viewers the significance of the Esc as a shared, pan-European, and trans-bloc cultural phenomenon.

Still, there were limits to this cooperation between the Ebu and the Oirt when it came to the Esc and the Isc. Eastern Bloc national broadcasting organizations were, as mentioned above, never allowed to participate in the Esc. Already in 1958, the Oir expressed interest in participating in the song contests organized by other international broadcasting organizations,[11] and it began organizing popular music festivals for its members when it staged the first Festival of Light and Dance Music in Prague. Popular music programs were considered by the Oirt's members to be increasingly important in light of government policies that promoted consumption and entertainment under the liberalizing cultural and economic reforms that marked the Thaw.[12] It was in this context that the Oirt organized a conference of music professionals at the second edition of this festival in 1959 to discuss the development of popular music in the Eastern Bloc.[13] That international song contests played a significant role in fostering cultural cooperation between the Eastern and Western Blocs was also underlined when Oirt officials proposed the joint organization of an international show of popular music between the members of the Eurovision and Intervision networks at a meeting of the representatives of these in Helsinki in 1964. The director general of Czechoslovak Television (Československá televize/Československá televízia, Čst), Jiří Pelikán, subsequently reported that the Ebu officials had rejected the proposal and had instead suggested that the Oirt arrange its own contest and that the two organizations broadcast each other's contests through the Eurovision and Intervision networks.[14] Pelikán did not explain exactly why his Ebu colleagues had rejected the idea for a pan-European song contest, but the answer could lie in a broader disinterest in Western Europe for Eastern European popular cultural products. Through the Western gaze, these were usually considered to be less fashionable and modern than Western ones, as well as being stunted by the continuing censorship that

---

11   Oir, "Resolution" (Moscow, May 21, 1958), 6 [Archives of Czech Television, Oirt, 5/2].

12   Timothy W. Ryback, *Rock Around the Bloc: A History of Rock Music in Eastern Europe and the Soviet Union* (New York: Oxford University Press, 1990), 14–18.

13   Oir, "31st Session of the Oir Administrative Council" (Prague, August 1959), 3–4, [Archives of Czech Television, Oirt, 6/2]; Oirt, "34th Session of the Oirt Administrative Council" (Prague, June 1961), 3–4 [Archives of Czech Television, Oirt, 7/2].

14   Jiří Pelikán, "Předběžná zpráva o setkání s delegacemi Oirt a Uer /Eurovize/a Intervize" (Prague, July 2, 1964), 5, 8 [Archives of Czech Television, Zahraniční styky, 248/27].

was directed at criticisms of communist party rule. So even though the Isc was broadcast in eight Western European states via the Eurovision Network in 1965, there was less public interest for the Isc in Western Europe than for the Esc in Eastern Europe. This was generally the case with the transfer of programs from Intervision to Eurovision members: throughout the Cold War, the national broadcasting organizations from the Eurovision Network always sent more programs to their counterparts in the Intervision Network than vice versa.[15] Although the two sides agreed that the programs involved in the exchange should not be commercially or politically motivated, the Eurovision Network's members often considered the Intervision Network's offerings to be too politicized and uninteresting, while Intervision members also rejected programs from the Eurovision Network that they deemed to be commercial, political, or religious.[16] Still, when it came to the Esc, the only time that Intervision members collectively refused to broadcast it was in 1979, when the contest was staged in Israel, with which almost all Eastern Bloc states—Romania was the only exception—did not have diplomatic relations as they supported the Arab states in the Arab-Israeli conflict. Furthermore, Esc entries were often hits in Eastern Europe when they were recorded in local cover versions: for example, the Czechoslovak singer Helena Vondráčková recorded some Czech-language covers of Esc songs, such as of "Après toi" ("Jak mám spát"/How Can I Sleep) in 1972 and "Save Your Kisses for Me" ("Já půjdu tam a ty tam"/I'll Go There and You There, a duet with Jiří Korn) in 1977. Yet no Isc entry was ever a major success on the Western European charts.

Aspiring to the West

It may seem counterintuitive that communist Eastern Europe was more open to cultural influences from liberal democratic Western Europe than vice versa, especially as the Eastern European national broadcasting organizations were state controlled and therefore promoted the goals and policies of the ruling communist parties. However, as the Isc demonstrated, Western Europe had popular music markets and models that the Eastern European popular music industries increasingly aspired to in the late 1950s and early 1960s. Yet, the

---

15   Thomas Beutelschmidt, *Ost—West—Global: Das sozialistische Fernsehen im Kalten Krieg* (Leipzig: Vistas, 2017), 95-96.

16   ČST, "Rozborová zpráva o činnosti OIRT, Intervize a Eurovize" (Prague, September–October 1965), 30-31 [Archives of Czech Television, Zahraniční styky, 200/1129]; Eugster, *Television Programming Across National Boundaries*, 193-96.

states of the Eastern Bloc did not all experience the Thaw equally. Czechoslo-vakia, for example, had been the most economically prosperous and politically liberal state in the region in the interwar period, when Prague was also a major European center for popular music production with a renowned jazz scene. However, until the early 1960s the Czechoslovak government was slow in instituting cultural, economic, and political reforms, being a relative latecomer to de-Stalinization policies, especially in comparison to Hungary and Poland. The world's biggest statue of Stalin, for example, was demolished in Prague only as late as 1962, while Prague's International Jazz Festival was established in 1964—well after the Sopot Jazz Festival had begun in Poland in 1956. Another early sign of the increasing cultural openness in Czechoslovakia in the early 1960s was the establishment by ČST in 1964 of the Golden Prague international television festival, in which Eastern European and Western European national broadcasting organizations participated. In the context of the second edition of this festival in 1965, the OIRT decided to stage the first edition of the ISC as the Golden Clef Intervision Contest on 12 June, in the Karlín Musical Theatre in Prague. That the ESC was the model for the ISC was underlined by the fact that the rules adopted for the ISC were largely a copy of those for the ESC, a move on the part of the OIRT that the EBU apparently did not oppose, and perhaps even encouraged. However, a major difference between the two contests was that the ISC had just an international jury comprised of musical experts repre-senting each of the participating national broadcasting organizations, with one more from Czechoslovakia as a non-voting chair, and its voting was ostensibly secret.[17] Voting in the ESC, on the other hand, has been done by national juries representing the states participating in the contest, and the results have been presented by each national jury at the end of the show. Whereas the ESC has also always been organized independently by national broadcasting organizations, the preparations for the ISC had more obvious government involvement, reflect-ing the fact that the OIRT's membership was largely based on state-controlled broadcasting organizations. Czechoslovakia's government, namely its Ministry for Culture and Information, accordingly organized the ISC in cooperation with ČST, artists' organizations, concert organizers, and local record companies, and it also approved the selection of Czechoslovak artists for the contest. All of this underlined that the ISC was not just a product of ČST, but also a tool of the state's cultural diplomacy.

Just as the ESC has only allowed entries from states whose national broad-casting organizations were members of the Eurovision Network, the ISC's rules

---

17   ČST, "Statut intervizní 'Soutěže tanečních písní a chansonů' o 'Zlatý klíč'" (Prague, March 10, 1965), 1–5 [Archives of Czech Television, Zahraniční styky, 30/262].

initially only permitted participation in that contest to members of the In-tervision Network. National broadcasting organizations from Czechoslovakia, East Germany, Hungary, Poland, the Soviet Union, and Yugoslavia were rep-resented in the first Isc by two of their most prominent artists, who each performed one song. Karel Gott won this edition of the Isc for Czechoslovakia with the song "Tam, kam chodí vítr spát" (Where the Wind Goes to Sleep). Bulgaria's Lili Ivanova was victorious in the second edition in 1966 with "Adagio," and Czechoslovakia's Eva Pilarová won the 1967 Isc with "Rekviem" (Requiem). In 1966 and 1967, the Isc was incorporated into the first two editions of the Bratislava Lyre festival, which was staged in the Slovak capital to decentralize Czechoslovakia's cultural events, thereby reflecting moves towards the feder-alization of the state. Such cultural events had hitherto been concentrated in Prague, which since 1964 had held both the international television festival and the international jazz festival.[18] During the years that the Isc was staged in Bratislava, the contest expanded to include Bulgaria, Finland, and Romania. This left Albania as the only Eastern European state that was never represented in the Isc, which was the result of that state withdrawing from the Oirt as it opposed the Soviet Union's de-Stalinization policies and took the side of China in the Sino-Soviet split over leadership of the international communist movement. For the rest of the Cold War, Albania remained the Eastern European state that was most closed to Western cultural influences.

From 1966, the organizers of the Isc continued to express an interest in expanding the contest to include Western European entries. This was unlike their Esc counterparts, who were never as open to allowing Eastern Bloc partic-ipants in their contest. The Isc organizers considered either allowing Western European entries to enter the Isc or establishing a contest that would pit songs from the two Blocs against each other.[19] The Isc's connections with the Esc were already apparent in that non-aligned Finland and Yugoslavia—which were the only states that had entries in both the Esc and the Isc from 1965 to 1967 due to their memberships in both the Ebu and the Oirt—were sometimes represented by the same artists in both contests, although, of course, with different songs. Finland's Viktor Klimenko—who was of Cossack origin and had emigrated to Finland from the Soviet Union as a child—and Lasse Mårtenson performed in both the Esc and the Isc in the 1960s. Yugoslavia's Lado Leskovar participated in the Isc in 1966 and the Esc in 1967; Leskovar was preceded as Yugoslavia's entry in the Esc in 1963 and 1965 by Vice Vukov, who went on to compete in the Isc in 1967 and 1968. Further demonstrating how the Esc was

---

18   Ivan Szabó, *Bratislavská lýra* (Bratislava: Marenčin PT, 2010), 17.

19   Jiří Malásek and Ladislav Peprník, "Národní soutěž a Zlatý klíč" (Prague, July 11, 1966), 3 [Archives of Czech Television, Zahraniční styky, 40/311].

a model for the Isc, winners of the Esc were also invited to perform in the Isc, including Udo Jürgens and Sandie Shaw. That the organizers of the Isc sought to make the contest a pan-European event that went beyond Eastern Europe was underlined in internal reports from ČsT that emphasized the cooperation of Western European actors in the Isc. In addition to the performances of the Esc winners, these reports also praised the coverage given to the Isc by Western media outlets and the contracts that Western record companies negotiated with Isc artists, especially Czechoslovak ones like Gott.[20] He went on to develop a prominent career not only in Eastern Europe but also in some Western European states, including Austria and West Germany.

The Prague Spring

Indeed, Gott even became the only resident of an Eastern Bloc state who ever participated in the Esc during the Cold War, when he represented Austria in the 1968 Esc with the song "Tausend Fenster" (A Thousand Windows). Apart from his Czechoslovak nationality, Gott's participation in the Esc was otherwise unremarkable as the contest's rules have never required performers to be citizens of the states that they performed for: Austria was even represented by a Greek singer, Jimmy Makulis, in the 1961 Esc, and, even more politically signif-icant, by the Israeli Carmela Corren in the 1963 Esc. Reflecting Czechoslovakia's increasing cultural openness towards the West in the period of de-Stalinization, the Austrian and Czechoslovak national broadcasting organizations had been developing closer ties in co-productions, live relays, and the exchange of ma-terials since 1964. However, the symbolism of Gott being allowed to perform in the Esc for Austria without censure from the Czechoslovak government—and just months before he went on to represent Czechoslovakia in the 1968 Isc—was heightened by the political context of the Prague Spring. The leadership of the Communist Party of Czechoslovakia had been taken over in January by the reformist Alexander Dubček from Slovakia. With the establishment of the Dubček government, the liberalizing reforms of the Prague Spring began, which included an ending of media censorship that made ČsT more open to cultural and political influences from the West. This also made it most opportune for the Isc's rules to be changed so that Western European entries could be included

---

20   Jaromír Vašta, Jiří Malásek, and Josef Koliha, "Zpráva o přípravě vysílání pořadu 'Vstup volný pro písničku' Intervize—'Zlatý klíč'," (s.l., 1965), 1–2 [Archive of Czech Telvision, Zahraniční styky, 30/262]; Malásek and Peprník, "Národní soutěž a Zlatý klíč," 2–3; ČsT, "Bratislavská lýra 1967" (s.l., 1967), 2–3 [Archives of Czech Television, Zahraniční styky, 40/331].

in the contest in 1968. The Isc consequently became the first international song contest which was open to states that were represented in both the Ebu or the Oirt; this was described in the American music industry magazine *Billboard* as "another step towards open competition and a common market in European pop music."[21]

The 1968 Isc was held in June in the spa resort town of Karlovy Vary, near the borders with East Germany and West Germany, where it was incorporated again into the International Television Festival. Ebu national broadcasting organizations from Austria, Belgium, Finland, Spain, Switzerland, West Germany, and Yugoslavia, together with Oirt ones from Bulgaria, Czechoslovakia, East Germany, Hungary, Romania, Poland, and the Soviet Union, were all represented in the 1968 Isc. The inclusion of Spain reflected the interest of the right-wing dictatorship of Francisco Franco in developing diplomatic relations with Eastern Europe. West Germany's participation was a prelude to the normalization of relations with Eastern European states—with which Bonn mostly still did not have diplomatic relations in 1968—under the *Ostpolitik* (Eastern Policy) that began in 1969. Gott won the Isc again in 1968 with "Proč ptáci zpívají?" (Why do Birds Sing?), while Yugoslavia's Vukov came second and Spain's Salomé, who would be a joint winner of the 1969 Esc, finished third. Yet while the 1968 Isc symbolized the ending of media censorship in Czechoslovakia, it was this media freedom that was among the factors that compelled the Soviet Union and its Warsaw Pact allies to quash the Prague Spring in August 1968. These states had come to believe that the reformist movement would end the communist system in Czechoslovakia and undermine the Eastern Bloc as a whole. As a product of the Prague Spring, and the greater freedom accorded to Čst and its openness to Western cultural and political influences in particular, the Isc was ended after 1968. This occurred in the context of the renewal of media censorship in Czechoslovakia during the "normalization" period, when the reforms of the Prague Spring were mostly reversed. Reformist officials from Čst who had been behind the Isc, such as Pelikán, were accordingly removed from their posts.[22] The careers of some artists who were critical of the Soviet-led invasion of Czechoslovakia were also ended, most notably Marta Kubišová, who had recorded the patriotic song "Modlitba pro Martu" (A Prayer for Marta) just days after and as a protest against the invasion. Kubišová would later become one of the figures of the Charter 77 movement, a group of dissidents who, in 1977, signed a document that criticized the Czechoslovak government's failure to

---

21   Billboard, "Golden Clef Festival for All Europe," *Billboard*, May 11, 1968, 46.
22   Martin Štoll, *Television and Totalitarianism in Czechoslovakia: From the First Democratic Republic to the Fall of Communism* (London: Bloomsbury, 2020), 186, 192–93.

respect human rights and who were consequently subjected to the authorities' repressive measures.[23]

Kubišová had come third in the 1966 Isc with the song "Oh, Baby, Baby," a duet which she performed with Vondráčková. Unlike Kubišová, Vondráčková did not take a political stand against the Czechoslovak government—she was even a part of the pro-government, anti-Charter group that criticized Charter 77—and she went on to win the 1977 Isc for Czechoslovakia with the song "Malovaný džbánku" (The Painted Jug). That was the first time that the Isc had been staged since 1968. This second series of the Isc was a transformation of the Sopot International Song Festival, which had the longest historical tradition of any popular music song festival in the Eastern Bloc, having begun in 1961. As the Polish media was in the 1970s more open to Western cultural influences than most other Eastern Bloc states,[24] the organizers of the Isc from Polish Television (Telewizja Polska, TVP) wanted this new edition of the Isc to include participants from all over the world, and not just communist states or Intervision Network members. They presented the idea of this second series of the Isc in the context of promoting mutual understanding and peaceful cooperation in the "the spirit of Helsinki."[25] This referred to the Helsinki Accords that were concluded among almost all European states in the Finnish capital in 1975, and which included agreements on the inviolability of borders, respect for human rights, and cultural cooperation, including the co-production, exchange, and joint broadcasting of television programs. Indeed, the Isc in its second series was again more international and open than the Esc, which remained closed to any entries from states that were not members of the Ebu. The Polish organizers also introduced an innovation to the Esc model by having a separate international competition for entries submitted by record companies from Eastern Europe and the West, alongside one for entries sponsored by national broadcasting organizations that were mostly members of the Intervision Network.

However, political dissent and social discontent had been growing in Poland in the late 1970s amid an economic crisis. A week before the 1980 Isc, a strike calling for economic, labor, and political reforms began in the Lenin Shipyard in Gdańsk, where the Sopot International Song Festival had first

---

23   Jonathan Bolton, *Worlds of Dissent: Charter 77, The Plastic People of the Universe, and Czech Culture Under Communism* (Cambridge, MA: Harvard University Press, 2012), 154.

24   Sabina Mihelj and Simon Huxtable, *From Media Systems to Media Cultures: Understanding Socialist Television* (Cambridge: Cambridge University Press, 2018), 67–68, 180.

25   Tadeusz Kędzierski, "Sprawozdanie z udziału w 63 Sesji Rady Interwizji" (Warsaw 1979), 2, 4 [Archives of Polish Television, Komitet do spraw radia i telewizji 'Polskie radio i telewizja', 1702/1].

been staged; the strikers capitalized on the already-present media attention for the Isc in nearby Sopot.[26] A week after the 1980 Isc was held, Solidarity (Solidarność), the first independent trade union in the Eastern Bloc, was formed in response to the strikers' requests. As Solidarity became the center of a broader social movement and anti-government protests continued amid worsening economic conditions, the Isc was not held in its usual August slot in 1981: the Polish government's Radio and Television Committee stated in 1981 that "in the current economically and socially tense situation such expenditures would not be approved by the population."[27] The Polish government's further attempt to quell political opposition through the imposition of martial law from December 1981 to July 1983 meant that the Isc would not be held in those years either—and never again revived for the rest of the Cold War, even as the Sopot International Song Festival was restarted in 1984.

Conclusion

The Central and East European members of the OIRT—including the Czech Republic, Poland, and Slovakia, which had all also staged the Isc during the Cold War—joined the EBU in 1993 and went on to enter the Esc. Ironically, considering Czechoslovakia's pioneering role in organizing the Isc, the Czech Republic was the last state from Central Europe to debut in the Esc, doing so only in 2007, even though it had also joined the EBU in 1993. This was in spite of the fact that the Czech Republic was among the states from the former Eastern Bloc that were most successful in their European integration efforts, being among the first of these to enter the Council of Europe, the EU, and NATO. The Esc was perhaps not needed by Czech cultural diplomacy to articulate Prague's Europeanist aspirations as much as the Isc had been a tool for Czechoslovak cultural diplomacy to signify an openness to the West. Even though the Isc was not a Soviet creation, both the Esc and the Isc have figured prominently in Russia's cultural diplomacy since the end of the Cold War. Some Russian politicians—including President Vladimir Putin—have even called for a revival of the Isc, especially as they have criticized the Esc for allegedly being politically biased against Russia or for promoting the visibility of sexual minorities. The Isc has been staged one more time since 1980, in 2008 in Sochi, but that edition only included members from the former Soviet Union

---

26   Rosenberg, "The Cold War Rival to Eurovision."
27   Agence France-Presse, "Kein Geld für Chanson," *Frankfurter Allgemeine Zeitung*, August 15, 1981.

and not from any other state from the former Eastern Bloc.[28] Indeed, that was the first time the Isc was conceived more as a political challenge rather than a cultural opening to the West; it was also the only time that a part of the former Soviet Union ever took the lead in organizing the Isc.[29] In this way, the 2008 Isc was not like the Isc of the Cold War era, which had never been Russian-led or limited to the states of the Soviet Union. The original Isc had been a more internationally open event that reflected the desires of cultural and political actors in Czechoslovakia and Poland for cultural exchange with Western Europe during periods of political liberalization in these two states. Indeed, as an attempt to promote the national popular music industries of the Eastern Bloc, the Isc was modelled not on any Soviet cultural product but on the success of Western Europe's Esc, even though it emerged in the context of Moscow's de-Stalinization policies. Still, the Isc was not simply an imitation of the Esc. Rather, it introduced innovations to the Esc's format that made the Isc more internationally open than its Western European counterpart. That was especially evident in the 1968 Isc that was held during the Prague Spring, and which was the first televised international popular music song contest that included participants from both the Eastern and Western Blocs. Such innovations may seem unexpected when we consider that Eastern Bloc societies were otherwise subjected to greater cultural censorship and travel restrictions than Western European ones were, and that the global trendsetters for popular music during the Cold War were found predominantly in the West and not in the East. Nonetheless, these innovations demonstrate the importance of international song contests in the cultural policies of communist party-led states—especially as symbols of political liberalization, openness towards Western influences, and autonomy from the Soviet Union.

References

Adams, William Lee. "Following Outrage over Conchita, Russia is Reviving its Own Straight Eurovision." Newsweek, July 25, 2014. https://www.newsweek.com/2014/08/01/following-outrage-over-conchita-russia-reviving-its-own-soviet-eurovision-260815.html.

---

28   William Lee Adams, "Following Outrage over Conchita, Russia is Reviving its Own Straight Eurovision," Newsweek July 25, 2014, https://www.newsweek.com/2014/08/01/following-outrage-over-conchita-russia-reviving-its-own-soviet-eurovision-260815.html.

29   During the Cold War, the Soviet Union only once won the Isc, with Alla Pugacheva singing "Vse mogut koroli" (Kings Can Do Anything), in 1978. She went on to represent Russia in the 1997 Esc with the song "Primadonna."

Agence France-Presse. "Kein Geld für Chanson." *Frankfurter Allgemeine Zeitung*, August 15, 1981.

Billboard. "Golden Clef Festival for All Europe." *Billboard*, May 11, 1968.

Bolton, Jonathan. *Worlds of Dissent: Charter 77, The Plastic People of the Universe, and Czech Culture Under Communism*. Cambridge, MA: Harvard University Press, 2012.

Beutelschmidt, Thomas. *Ost—West—Global: Das sozialistische Fernsehen im Kalten Krieg*. Leipzig: Vistas, 2017.

ČST, "Rozborová zpráva o činnosti Oirt, Intervize a Eurovize." Prague, September–October 1965 [Archives of Czech Television, Zahraniční styky, 200/1129].

———. "Statut intervizní 'Soutěže tanečních písní a chansonů' o 'Zlatý klíč.'" Prague, March 10, 1965 [Archives of Czech Television, Zahraniční styky, 30/262].

———. "Bratislavská lýra 1967." s.l., 1967 [Archives of Czech Television, Zahraniční styky, 40/331].

Eugster, Ernest. *Television Programming Across National Boundaries: The Ebu and Oirt Experience*. Dedham, MA: Artech House, 1983.

Fricker, Karen. "'It's Just Not Funny Any More': Terry Wogan, Melancholy Britain, and the Eurovision Song Contest" In *Performing the 'New' Europe: Identities, Feelings and Politics in the Eurovision Song Contest*, edited by K. Fricker and M. Gluhovic, 53–76. Basingstoke: Palgrave Macmillan, 2013.

Kędzierski, Tadeusz. "Sprawozdanie z udziału w 63 Sesji Rady Interwizji." Warsaw, 1979 [Archives of Polish Television, Komitet do spraw radia i telewizji 'Polskie radio i telewizja', 1702/1].

Lommers, Suzanne. *Europe—On Air: Interwar Projects for Radio Broadcasting*. Amsterdam: Amsterdam University Press, 2012.

Malásek, Jiří, and Ladislav Peprník. "Národní soutěž a Zlatý klíč." Prague, July 11, 1966 [Archives of Czech Television, Zahraniční styky, 40/311].

Mihelj, Sabina, and Simon Huxtable. *From Media Systems to Media Cultures: Understanding Socialist Television*. Cambridge: Cambridge University Press, 2018.

Oir. "31st Session of the Oir Administrative Council." Prague, August 1959 [Archives of Czech Television, Oirt, 6/2].

———. "Resolution." Moscow, May 21, 1958 [Czech Television Archives, Oirt, 5/2].

Oirt. "34th Session of the Oirt Administrative Council" (Prague, June 1961) [Archives of Czech Television, Oirt, 7/2].

———. "52nd Meeting." Algiers, May 16–19, 1975 [Archives of the Ebu, Concours Eurovision de la chanson, Décisions 1].

Oliver, Stephen, dir. *The Secret History of Eurovision*. Electric Pictures, 2011.

Pajala, Mari. "Intervision Song Contests and Finnish Television between East and West." In *Airy Curtains in the European Ether: Broadcasting and the Cold War*, edited by Alexander Badenoch, Andreas Fickers and Christian Henrich-Franke, 215–39. Baden-Baden: Nomos, 2013.

Pelikán, Jiří. "Předběžná zpráva o setkání s delegacemi Oirt a Uer /Eurovize/a Intervize." Prague, July 2, 1964 [Archive of Czech Television, Zahraniční styky, 248/27].

Piotrowska, Anna G. "About Twin Song Festivals in Eastern and Western Europe: Intervision and Eurovision." *International Review of the Aesthetics and Sociology of Music* 47, no. 1 (June 2016): 123–35.

Rosenberg, Steve. "The Cold War Rival to Eurovision." Bbc, May 14, 2012. https://www.bbc.com/news/magazine-18006446.

Štoll, Martin. *Television and Totalitarianism in Czechoslovakia: From the First Democratic Republic to the Fall of Communism*. London: Bloomsbury, 2020.

Szabó, Ivan. *Bratislavská lýra*. Bratislava: Marenčin PT, 2010.

Vašta, Jaromír, Jiří Malásek, and Josef Koliha. "Zpráva o přípravě vysílání pořadu 'Vstup volný pro písničku' Intervize—'Zlatý klíč'" (s.l., 1965) [Archives of Czech Telvision, Zahraniční styky, 30/262].

Vuletic, Dean. *Postwar Europe and the Eurovision Song Contest*. London: Bloomsbury, 2018.

West, Chris. *Eurovision! A History of Modern Europe Through the World's Greatest Song Contest*. London: Melville House UK, 2017.

Wolff, Larry. *Inventing Eastern Europe: The Map of Civilization on the Mind of the Enlightenment*. Stanford, CA: Stanford University Press, 1994.

Yurtaeva, Yulia. "Ein schwarzer Rabe gegen Conchita Wurst oder: Wovor hat Russland Angst?" In *Eurovision Song Contest: Eine kleine Geschichte zwischen Körper, Geschlecht und Nation*, edited by Christine Ehardt, Georg Vogt and Florian Wagner, 111–35. Vienna: Zaglossus, 2015.

Yurtaeva, Yulia, and Lothar Mikos. "Song Contests in Europe During the Cold War." In *New Patterns in Global Television Formats*, edited by Karina Aveyard, Pia Majbritt Jensen and Albert Moran, 110–24. Bristol: Intellect, 2016.

"Vodka, Beer, Papirosy"
Eastern European Working-class Cultures Mimicry in Contemporary Hardbass

Ondřej Daniel

Abstract: In this chapter, I discuss the contemporary developments of hard-bass, a predominantly Eastern European electronic dance music style that emerged at the turn of the first decade of the twenty-first century in Russia and spread to different countries of the region and beyond. Specifically, I focus on de-politicized and commodified hardbass in relation to social class and the mutations it underwent in late postsocialism in Eastern Europe, while paying particular attention to contexts of the Czech Republic and Russia. In terms of transnational circulation, I approach hardbass as an element of cultural transfer. The resulting study is based on a multi-site research project focusing beyond Eastern Europe on the specific relationship of hardbass to the Netherlands. I interpret contemporary hardbass music videos in line with mocking colonization by the "normcore" strategies of the "middle class" hipster youth possessing cultural and to certain extent also social and economic capital.

Funding acknowledgment: This study is a result of the research funded by the Czech Science Foundation as the project GA ČR P410/20-24091S "Brave New World: Youth, Music and Class in Czech Post-socialism."

Ondřej Daniel earned his Ph.D. from the Institute of World History of the Faculty of Arts at Charles University with a specialization in postsocialism, nationalism, migration, and popular culture. He is a founding member of the Centre for Study of Popular Culture and is currently based at the Seminar of General and Comparative History, Department of Global History, at the Charles University Faculty of Arts in Prague.

On a late summer day in 2016, the Prague central city square of Václavské náměstí witnessed a rather peculiar meeting. The otherwise commercial and touristy center of the Czech capital became a stage for several dozens of young people, dressed mostly in Adidas tracksuits. Despite the warm afternoon, some of them wore furry hats. Many of these youngsters were squatting on their feet, some were drinking water from vodka bottles, and the others drank beer and maybe even proper vodka. Several packets of sunflower seeds were brought by the mostly local Czech youngsters from one of the many Russian food markets. Some of them were reproducing jump-up electronic rhythms and taking selfies and pictures of others with the help of their smartphones. This carnivalesque flash mob was organized by the Czech Facebook page *Squatting Slavs in Tracksuits* and gathered young people who found their (guilty?) pleasure in the music and dance called hardbass.

I.

In this chapter, I discuss the recent developments in hardbass, a predominantly Eastern European electronic dance music (EDM) style that emerged at the turn of the first decade of the twenty-first century in Russia and spread to different countries in the region and beyond. These developments can be understood as part of a three-stage process in which each phase had a different tone and message: the first phase was satirical, the second was about far-right politics, while contemporary hardbass is increasingly commodified and seemingly de-politicized. The second phase overlapped with the rise of various social movements in the early 2010s and the then-relatively new deployment of Internet memes and viral videos by far-right groups. The masked dancing to hardbass can also be viewed as an East-to-West cultural transfer.[1] My inquiry focuses on hardbass production during the second half of the 2010s and its ties to social class and class mutations in late postsocialist Eastern Europe, with particular attention to the Czech Republic and Russia.[2] I gathered the empirical material for this study in the period between spring 2018 and spring 2020. As part of my research, I followed the YouTube channels and Soundcloud, Instagram, Facebook, and Twitter accounts of several hardbass and related EDM musicians, collectives, and labels such as DJ Blyatman, Blyatsquad, Gopnik McBlyat, Life of Boris, Russian Jump Up Mafia, the Russian Village Boys, the Squatting Slavs in Tracksuits, and Tri poloski. Most of these are semi-professionals and a typical contemporary hardbass product is a music video or a DJ set, which differs substantially from the do-it-yourself (DIY) home video spirit of earlier hardbass.

---

1   Please see a basic Google map here: https://bit.ly/3uzBtoJ.

2   In this chapter, I include under the geographical category of Eastern Europe also postsocialist countries that are otherwise (self-)declared as forming part of Central (Eastern) Europe. The debate about the symbolical geographies of Europe is seemingly endless and goes beyond the scope of this study; see for example Ovidiu Țichindeleanu, "Where Are We, When We Think in Eastern Europe?" in *Art Always Has Its Consequences*, ed. Ivet Ćurlin et al. (Zagreb: WHW, 2010), 85–92.

I was finishing the first manuscript of this study in late March 2020 during the Covid-19 lockdown, at a time when masks were no longer so shocking but dancing in public was forbidden. Due to the cancellation of many hardbass events in the context of the "stay home" policies of late winter and early spring 2020, it was unfortunately not possible to complement the online research with participant observation as was initially planned. I have therefore tried to integrate some other qualitative material, such as online interviews and comments, to at least partly replace this lack. At the same time, it was also an enriching perspective to approach the topic differently, since many hardbass protagonists reacted to the lockdown with an even more massive posting of videos and memes. On the contrary, no home videos of hardbass performances reminiscent of earlier forms were published by the end of March 2020.

Given the transnational character of its cultural references, it is also tempting to approach hardbass through the lens of the traveling concepts theory. I have argued that the far-right leaning version of the genre was in early 2010s a rare example of East-to-West cultural transfer. In reference to the important monograph, "Looking West,"[3] would it make sense to rethink hardbass as a herald of "No More Looking West"? Could one speak of reverse of from "Culturedness-to-Westerness"[4] trajectory? Even if the references to post-Soviet culture and society are central to the joyously uncultured contemporary hardbass, the replies to these questions will most likely need to remain negative and it is more adequate to conceive of it in the terms of transnational circulation. The resulting study is thus based on a multi-site research project focusing beyond Eastern Europe on the specific relationship of hardbass to the Netherlands.

II.

It has been argued that the period that has been not-unproblematically labeled postsocialism has already become history.[5] Historian Philipp Ther has proposed interpreting the postsocialist change with regard to the simultaneous muta-

3   Hilary Anne Pilkington, Elena Omel'chenko, Moya Flynn, and Uliana Bliudina, *Looking West? Cultural Globalization and Russian Youth Cultures* (University Park: Pennsylvania State University Press, 2012).

4   Maria Cristache, "From 'Culturedness' to Westernness: Old and New Consumption Practices in Romanian Postsocialist Homes," in *Proceedings of the History of Consumer Culture Conference 2017* (Tokyo: Gakushuin University, 2018).

5   Martin Müller, "Goodbye, Postsocialism!," *Europe-Asia Studies* 71, no. 4 (2019): 533–50, https://doi.org/10.1080/09668136.2019.1578337.

tions of the West.[6] Also, in the last decade, new interpretations are no longer proposed by scholars predominantly coming from the former West, as was the case at least until the mid-2000s. Urban sociologists Liviu Chelcea and Oana Druta argued that the actors of the neoliberal transition in Eastern Europe thoughtfully used the specter of socialism in order to silence the opposition and push forward anti-socialist policies.[7] Even if this statement might be too strong for all the countries of the region, with a generational distance from the changes of 1989–90, such postsocialist legitimization strategies have gradually eroded. Art critique Marta Dzievańska has called for a revision of the post-Soviet paradigm since the early 2010s.[8] For her and her colleagues, the quest in the aftermath of the post-2008 crisis and the establishment of new populist and authoritarian regimes was to analyze the situation that followed the often problematic and painful neoliberal transitions with new settings of legitimacy and power. This was particularly pertinent for Russia but also for other Eastern European countries, many of which have joined the European Union since the mid-2000s.

Beyond the reference to the socioeconomic and political context of contemporary Eastern Europe, any attempt to treat hardbass should also take into account research on local youth.[9] At least since the mid-1990s, it has been argued that the body of knowledge produced by subcultural studies does not fully mirror the reality of contemporary lifestyle and consumption-based communities in the global core or in postsocialist Europe.[10] Lately, the radicalism of such a post-subcultural approach has been partially revised.[11] Produced in the early 2010s, political hardbass may have overlapped with the agendas

---

6   Philipp Ther, *Die neue Ordnung auf dem alten Kontinent. Eine Geschichte des neoliberalen Europa* (Berlin: Suhrkamp, 2014).

7   Liviu Chelcea and Oana Druţă, "Zombie Socialism and the Rise of Neoliberalism in Post-socialist Central and Eastern Europe," *Eurasian Geography and Economics* 57, no. 4–5 (2016): 521–44, https://doi.org/10.1080/15387216.2016.1266273.

8   Marta Dziewańska, *Post-post-Soviet? Art, Politics & Society in Russia at the Turn of the Decade* (Warsaw: Museum of Modern Art, 2013).

9   Matthias Schwartz and Heike Winkel, eds., *Eastern European Youth Cultures in a Global Context* (London: Palgrave Macmillan, 2016).

10 See for example Andy Bennett, "The post-subcultural turn: some reflections 10 years on," *Journal of Youth Studies* 14, no. 5 (2011): 493–506, and Marta Kolářová, "Hudební subkultury mládeže v současné ČR—postsubkulturní či postsocialistické?," in *Populární kultura v českém prostoru*, ed. Ondřej Daniel, Tomáš Kavka, and Jakub Machek (Prague: Karolinum, 2013), 232–48.

11 Sumi Hollingworth "Performances of Social Class, Race and Gender Through Youth Subculture: Putting Structure Back in to Youth Subcultural Studies," *Journal of Youth Studies* 18, no. 10 (2015): 1237–56, https://doi.org/10.1080/13676261.2015.1039968.

of far-right youth movements in their quest for modernization through the appropriation of different subcultural practices, among which hardbass might be seen alongside football hooliganism, hip hop, graffiti, or skateboarding as one of many. The subcultural dimension of contemporary hardbass should nevertheless be considered in a more nuanced way. In the attempt to problematize the subcultural paradigm, one could try to follow theory of "grey zones" as sketched for the Eastern European context by Alexei Yurchak[12] as well as more recently by the collective of authors led by Ida Harboe Knudsen and Martin Demant Frederiksen.[13] It may be tempting to depict hardbass musicians and fans as not predominantly possessing rigid and die-hard identities. But even playful irony as well as nonsense "eastploitation" aesthetics, both essential qualities of hardbass, have important dimensions of social class.

The issue of class in postsocialism, particularly in relation to popular culture, is not a novel research topic. Scholars have already focused attention on the "new rich" and in particular "new Russians," economic elites who fully profited off of the period during and after the fall of state socialism.[14] Incomparably less has been written about the "middle classes," which in the 1990s were often conceived as a stabilizing factor for local "new democracies."[15] An overview of the local debates about class is presented by Jan Drahokoupil for the case of the Czech Republic in a special issue edited by David Ost, who has also discussed a particular set of approaches to class in the postsocialist Polish academia.[16] Relatively new research tools focusing on the intersection of culture and class have been presented by Dražen Cepić discussing the case of Croatia.[17] Lifestyle, consumption and "culture" have often been distinct markers of the "middle classes."[18] Stephen Crowley, while presenting his account of the

---

12   Alexei Yurchak, *Everything Was Forever, Until It Was No More. The Last Soviet Generation* (Princeton: Princeton University Press, 2006).

13   Ida Harboe Knudsen and Martin Demant Frederiksen, *Ethnographies of Grey Zones in Eastern Europe: Relations, Borders and Invisibilities* (London: Anthem, 2015).

14   For recent summing up of the debate, see Elisabeth Schimpfössl, *Rich Russians: From Oligarchs to Bourgeoisie* (Oxford: Oxford University Press, 2018).

15   See for example Harley Balzer, "Russia's Middle Classes," *Post-Soviet Affairs* 14, no. 2 (1998): 165–86.

16   Jan Drahokoupil, "Class in Czechia: The Legacy of Stratification Research," *East European Politics and Societies and Cultures* 29, no. 3 (2015): 577–587, and David Ost, "Stuck in the Past and the Future: Class Analysis in Postcommunist Poland," *East European Politics and Societies and Cultures* 29, no. 3 (2015): 610–24.

17   Dražen Cepić, *Class Cultures in Postsocialist Eastern Europe* (London: Routledge, 2019).

18   Simon Stewart, *Culture and the Middle Classes* (Farnham: Routledge, 2016). When writing about the "middle class" in my own research, I use quotation

more self-confident "middle classes" in early 2010s Russia, took vital examples of popular beliefs of class relations and struggles from popular culture, in particular from movies.[19] My own research considers popular music as a distinct social class marker, following in the footsteps of Pierre Bourdieu and his notions of cultural and social capital fueling these "distinctions."[20] Consumption and lifestyle can thus be considered as strategies of increasing these forms of capital. Ben Malbon presented a Bourdieu-based concept of "coolness" when treating the EDM "club cultures."[21] So did the already mentioned Maria Cristache[22] and Judit Bodnár,[23] when writing about home decoration as reflections of the shifting class structures in postsocialist Romania and Hungary, respectively. The account of contemporary hardbass at hand aims to merge these scattered debates in discussing a particular social practice mirroring the concepts of youth and class.

III.

In analyzing hardbass as a phenomenon linked with a particular social class, I feel the need to recall the history of the Saint Petersburg rave scene that flourished in the early 1990s due to the relative openness of the late perestroika period and the following decade of changes.[24] Simultaneously, in the Czech

---

marks. Similar to Marxist thinking about the "bourgeoisie," "middle classes" are conceived as an unstable and transitory category, uneasy to describe in a scientific discourse. I therefore follow an emic perspective of the postsocialist Eastern European "middle classes," mostly formed by a neoliberal paradigm and often by self-glorification. On the contrary, I use the reference to lower-income social classes which could be synonymous to Marxist thinking on the "working class" and "lumpenproletariat" without quotation marks.

19   Stephen Crowley, "Russia: The Reemergence of Class in the Wake of the First "Classless" Society," *East European Politics and Societies and Cultures* 29, no. 3 (2015): 698–710.

20   Pierre Bourdieu, *La Distinction. Critique sociale du jugement* (Paris: Minuit, 1979) and "The Forms of Capital," in *Handbook of Theory and Research for the Sociology of Education*, ed. John Richardson (Westport, CT: Greenwood, 1986), 241–58.

21   Ben Malbon, *Clubbing: Dancing, Ecstasy and Vitality* (London: Routledge 1999.

22   Cristache, "From 'Culturedness.'"

23   Judit Bodnár, "Becoming Bourgeois. (Postsocialist) Utopias of Isolation and Civilization," in *Evil Paradises. Dreamworlds of Neoliberalism*, ed. Michael Davis and Daniel Bertrand Monk (New York: New Press, 2009), 140–51.

24   Андрей Владимирович Хаас, *Корпорация счастья. История русского рейва*. Санкт-Петербург: Амфора, 2011 and Алексей Юрчак, "Ночные танцы с ангелом истории. Критические культуральные исследования пост-социализма." In *Культуральные исследования*, ed. Александра Эткинда (Санкт-Петербург: Европейский университет, 2005).

Republic, contact with the United Kingdom's "freetechno" scene was enabled since 1994 through British sound systems exiled in Berlin and profiting off of the Czech Republic's liberal legislation and the unpreparedness of the state security apparatus for the issues that "freeparties" increasingly meant.[25] In the first case, the rave parties were frequented in particular by the university students as well as other parts of the late Soviet intelligentsia. In the second case, "freeparties" were also initially a pastime reserved to the students and other youngsters with ties to the local elites, but they gradually turned into a more trans-class phenomenon.

But the UK rave scene, often understood as a side-product of Thatcherism[26] with its individualism, psychedelic drugs, and corresponding mystical reveries of "temporary autonomous zones,"[27] was neither a unique nor the most important historical predecessor of hardbass. A more direct link can be seen in an already distorted version of rave: a Dutch hardcore techno genre called gabber.[28] In a mid-1990s documentary about gabber,[29] the drugs were also an important reference, but it was not always the same ones as the MDMA-fueled "second summer of love" UK rave scene. Instead, leaning towards the psychedelic trance, a more aggressive and faster rhythms, together with synthetic drugs such as "speed" and an overall dystopic atmosphere fed the seemingly chaotic jump-up *hakken* dancers. Since the early 2010s, hardbass was not alone in the re-appropriation of the long-time démodé gabber. In Poland, Italy, France, and Indonesia, artists and collectives such as Wixapol, Gabber Eleganza, Casual Gabberz, and Gabber Modus Operandi reinvented the gabber influences simultaneously.[30]

---

25   Ondřej Slačálek, "České freetekno-pohyblivé prostory autonomie?," in *Revolta stylem: Hudební subkultury mládeže v České republice*, ed. Marta Kolářová (Prague: Slon, 2011), 83–122, and Rozálie Kohoutová, *CzechTek*, Czech television documentary, 2017.

26   Andrew Hill, "Acid House and Thatcherism: Contesting Spaces in Late 1980s Britain," *Space and Polity* 7, no. 3 (2003): 219–32, and Henry John, "UK Rave Culture and the Thatcherite Hegemony, 1988–94," *Cultural History* 4, no. 2 (2015): 162–86.

27   Hakim Bey, T.A.Z.: *The Temporary Autonomous Zone* (New York: Autonomedia, 1991).

28   Hillegonda C. Rietveld, "Gabber Overdrive—Noise, Horror, and Acceleration," *Turmoil—CTM Magazine* (January 2018), https://openresearch.lsbu.ac.uk/item /869q7.

29   Ari Versluis, "Gabber," *Lola da musica*, season 2, episode 5, aired November 13, 1995 (Vrijzinnig Protestantse Radio Omroep).

30   Joe Muggs, "Gift of the Gabber: The Return of Dance Music's Gloriously Tasteless Subgenre," *Guardian*, January 10, 2020, https://www.theguardian.co m/music/2020/jan/10/gift-of-the-gabber-the-return-of-dance-musics-glo riously-tasteless-subgenre.

Similarly to the first ravers, gabbers were also recruited in the football terraces and many of them shaved their heads. An important reference common to gabber and hardbass is also the link to the far right. One of the skinheads in the documentary greets other visitors of a Dutch gabber party with a Nazi salute,[31] a reference that will be often evoked some seventeen years later when referring to political hardbass. Another common link for gabber and hardbass will also be the shirtless male bodies and sportswear. In the Dutch case, *hakken* dancers were predominantly skinny, while the Eastern European hardbass bodies often foregrounded their carefully built physiques and hardbass verbally rejected drugs.

Exaggerated masculinity is one of the key ingredients of hardbass. In contrast to "freetechno" and similarly to gabber, it is a predominantly male enterprise. Some similarities can also be found with male-dominated spaces in heavy metal concerts, where Jonathan Gruzelier has analyzed the homosociality of moshpits, places that are reserved for hardcore dancers.[32] Interestingly, some of the hardbass performers, such as Gopnik McBlyat, also express their sympathies to metal and hardcore punk.[33] It would surely be tempting to approach hardbass in light of the theory of hegemonic masculinity. The re-traditionalization of gender roles after the fall of state socialism[34] as well as some openly homophobic, sexist,[35] and even misogynist[36] references in its lyrics, could be of importance for such an approach.

On the contrary, the parodic dimension of hardbass, particularly that of détournement of the street (gopnik) culture of lower-income social classes, is a key to the puzzle. Certain specific body techniques, such as squatting, refer to Eastern European street culture[37] and make hardbass undoubtedly part of this reservoir of playful performance. Some similarities in the importance of shock

31   Versluis, "Gabber."
32   Jonathan Gruzelier, "Moshpit Menace and Masculine Mayhem," in *Oh Boy! Making Masculinity in Popular Music*, ed. Ian Biddle and Freya Jarman-Ivens (London: Routledge, 2007), 59–76.
33   Tri poloski, Interview with Gopnik McBlyat, posted March 8, 2020, https://tri -poloski.com/media.
34   Aleksandar Štulhofer and Theo Sandfort, *Sexuality and Gender in Postcommunist Eastern Europe and Russia* (New York: Haworth Press, 2006).
35   To quote one of the many, it seems sufficient to find a correct translation of the Russian word *blyat* used by many of the contemporary hardbass protagonists even as a nickname.
36   Cmh x Gspd x Russian Village Boys "Anti Girl," posted October 20, 2019, https ://www.youtube.com/watch?v=ntxihekLfuM.
37   Asta Vonderau, *Leben im "neuen Europa" Konsum, Lebensstile und Körpertechniken im Postsozialismus* (Bielefeld: transcript, 2010).

can also be found with horrorcore hip hop;[38] others may derive from *chernukha*, a typically perestroika and post-Soviet exploitation genre of cinematography.[39] Such references can also be linked with the aestheticization and de-politicization of earlier hardbass. Images of violent groups teasing other travelers in a post-Soviet metro train,[40] or a general propagation of hate,[41] may come from this aesthetic reservoir. However, hardbass is much more eclectic and beyond the influences discussed above, one can also identify inspirations from trap music,[42] darkwave,[43] Russian *popsa* and *estrada*,[44] as well as from predominantly Dutch happy hardcore rave and continent-wide Eurodance.[45]

IV.

The modernist approach that defined the social class through its production has been distinguished, at least since the global 1960s, by the placement of consumption at the center of understanding social relations.[46] Building upon this argument, I propose to conceive contemporary hardbass through its mocking of the consumption of lower-income social classes. I also propose an interpretation that this rhetorical operation may result from the unachieved ambitions of the Eastern European "middle classes" themselves. This interpretation relates to the strategy of global millennials re-appropriating forgotten lifestyles through so-called "normcore."[47] Simon Reynolds, in his *Retromania*, conceived

---

38   Mikko O. Koivisto, "'I Know You Think I'm Crazy': Post-Horrorcore Rap Approaches to Disability, Violence, and Psychotherapy," *Disability Studies Quarterly* 38, no. 2 (2018), https://dsq-sds.org/article/view/6231/4910.

39   Eliot Borenstein, *Overkill: Sex and Violence in Contemporary Russian Popular Culture* (Ithaca: Cornell University Press, 2008).

40   Russian Village Boys, "Suckcess (prod. Dizelkraft)," posted March 12, 2020, https://www.youtube.com/watch?v=o5JxFkcVQAM.

41   DJ Blyatman & Hвкn, "Eastern Bloc," posted February 12, 2020, https://www.youtube.com/watch?v=7MqS263kA84.

42   DJ Blyatman & Russian Village Boys, "Razjebasser," posted june 19, 2019, https://www.youtube.com/watch?v=yWt3Ko2R1Vg.

43   Russian Village Boys, "Работа," posted September 11, 2018, https://www.youtube.com/watch?v=IUndsLpVx70.

44   Смн & Russian Village Boys, "Диски Вписки," posted January 10, 2020, https://www.youtube.com/watch?v=8TPN0x9NPuM.

45   Gspd, "Евродэнс," posted May 19, 2018, https://www.youtube.com/watch?v=4hV3vaO8W5M.

46   Luc Boltanski and Ève Chiapello, *Le nouvel esprit du capitalisme* (Paris: Gallimard, 1999).

47   Cecilia Winterhalter, "Normcore or a New Desire for Normality: To be Crazy, Be Normal," *Catwalk: The Journal of Fashion, Beauty and Style* 5, no. 1 (2016): 21–42.

such a hipster "back-to-the-future spirit"[48] in terms of a quasi-bohemia present "in any city in the developed world that is large and affluent enough to support a decent-sized upper middle class."[49] "Normsters," as a particular hipster practice, mockingly colonize the particular music and fashion of older generations.

Olga Gurova recently underlined the importance of fashion in the contemporary Russian political debate framed through lifestyle.[50] The key reference in relation to the ready-to-wear brands fetishized by almost all contemporary hardbass protagonists is Adidas. Its "three stripes" (tri poloski) have been the subject of many postsocialist jokes and the importance of the brand in the popular imagination must not be underestimated.[51] In hardbass, the centrality of the reference to Adidas may also be due to the recurring rhyme of the words "hardbass" and "Adidas" in many of the genre's rather rudimentary lyrics. Beyond fashion and Adidas, alcohol and in particular vodka is often referred to. This may be a strategy of (self-)exoticization when communicating with the wider non-Eastern European audience, but it may also function well when communicating among insiders. "Vodka, beer, papirosy," referring to Russian unfiltered cigarettes, in the words of one hardbass lyric, could thus read as a rather ironic "normster" substitution for one's own unachieved ambitions of "Hennessy, champagne, and cigars."

Besides alcohol and fashion, one of the most important references hardbass shares with other EDM and hip hop genres relates to cars. In some of the music videos, we can see hardbass artists driving Mercedes, BMWs, or even Bentleys, but the most referenced and depicted autos are different models of the Soviet and Russian working-class vehicle Lada, which are often refurbished and modified. Most of the vehicles depicted in Russian hardbass music videos have Saint Petersburg or Moscow license plates. Apart from such indirect references to the "two Russian capitals" (and an open one to Amsterdam, as we will see later), other direct geographical references are quite rare in these music videos. What is, on the contrary, not missing is the depiction of different and anonymous working-class neighborhoods, housing estates, and courtyards, often in very

---

48   Simon Reynolds, Retromania: Pop Culture's Addiction to Its Own Past (New York: Faber & Faber, 2011), 174.

49   Reynolds, Retromania: 169.

50   Olga Gurova, Fashion and the Consumer Revolution in Contemporary Russia (London, New York: Routledge, 2015).

51   Caroline Humphrey, "Traders, 'Disorder,' and Citizenship Regimes in Provincial Russia," in Uncertain Transition. Ethnographies of Change in the Postsocialist World, ed. Michael Burawoy and Katherine Verdery (Lanham, MD: Rowman & Littlefield, 1999), 19–52; Liisi Laineste, "Post-Socialist Jokelore: Preliminary Findings and Further Research Suggestions," Acta Ethnographica Hungarica 54, no. 1 (2009): 31–45.

desolate states. Khrushchyovki, as most of these estates are often labelled in the post-Soviet space, were recently brought into the public debate in particular conjunction with the "top-down" gentrification attempts in Moscow.[52] References to such neighborhoods in hardbass music videos should be understood in line with a strategy of mocking the colonization of these spaces by the "normcore," "middle-class" youth.

Similarly, the dilapidated workplaces, such as vast factory halls that constitute the environment for many of these music videos, are all but places where the hardbass protagonists and their audience earn their living. Moreover, the depiction of abandoned infrastructure, such the "no man's land" under bridges, but also deserted streets and roads as well as the desolate public transport where some of these music videos take place, can be seen as an appropriation of the "horrorcore" aesthetics discussed above. While the hardbass far-right football hooligans and activists merrily posed with baseball bats, fighting chains, and iron bars under such concrete structures alongside graffiti of Celtic crosses and "Anti-Antifa" inscriptions in order to frighten their enemies, contemporary hardbass music videos use such surroundings ironically in an attempt to colonize what they perceive as an authentic culture of the lower-income social classes. The problematic dimensions of such seemingly ironically depoliticized approaches to whiteness is something that has been discussed since the beginning of the scholarly debate about hipsters.[53] What is relatively new for hardbass is a dimension of dystopia, with its links to the hedonist and nihilist, synthetic-drug-fueled gabber.

V.

The circle of gabber/hardbass is closed by explicit reference to the Dutch model not only in music but also in visuals, such as Dutch flags worn on the jean jackets of the Russian Village Boys in several of their music videos.[54] The

52   See for example Tom Balmforth, "Moscow's Plan To Raze 'Khrushchyovki' Sparks Anger, Confusion Ahead Of Elections," *Radio Free Europe, Radio Liberty*, May 6, 2017, https://www.rferl.org/a/russia-moscow-khrushchyovki-demolition-ho using-controversy-elections/28471341.html.

53   Mark Greif, "What Was the Hipster?" *New York*, October 24, 2010, http://nyma g.com/news/features/69129/.

54   Russian Village Boys & Mr. Polska "Lost In Amsterdam (Official Music Video)," posted May 24, 2019, https://www.youtube.com/watch?v=DidEz_Tkgo0; DJ Blyatman & Russian Village Boys "Instababe (Official Music Video)," posted November 22, 2018, https://www.youtube.com/watch?v=7114Ojew1ZM; Russian Village Boys & Rät N FrikK "Putindabass," posted January 18, 2019, https://w ww.youtube.com/watch?v=ZLaOStTmRkw.

touristy slogan "Welcome to Netherlands" in one of these music videos also reveals an important dimension of social class, linking contemporary hardbass with those Eastern Europeans affluent enough to travel for pleasure to Western Europe. The feeling of generational dependence on the distribution of wealth is reinforced, however, in one of these music videos by the staged home call (in English) of one of the protagonists, during which his mother advises him by phone to be careful. But the Russian-Dutch trajectory in hardbass should not be seen as a unique vector. To a certain extent, it is also possible to observe "the message delivered back." The professional promoter Tri poloski ("three stripes," referring to Adidas) is based in the Netherlands and acts as a "leading agency for Hardbass artists,"[55] organizing successful and widely visited hardbass parties in the country as well as in neighboring Flanders, according to the audio-visual material presented on the website. At the same time, many East-East collaborations flourish in contemporary hardbass, such as with Mr. Polska in the case of the Russian Village Boys.

Key elements of contemporary hardbass refer to (self-)exoticization strategies, which have long been analyzed in Eastern European and in particular Southeastern European cinema by Dina Iordanova,[56] Tomislav Longinović,[57] or more recently by Andrea Matošević.[58] At this point, it may be particularly fruitful to divert attention to hardbass fans in the Czech Republic, where the fragmented identities deriving from the dominant Czech culture, based on its constant negotiation of allegiance to the West, result in mockingly joyous orientalism of Life of Boris[59] or Squatting Slavs in Tracksuits.[60] Most of the memes posted by these two online projects would be considered xenophobic (and particularly Russophobic) if they had resulted directly from a canon of Czech majority culture. Their central point is the ironic foregrounding of the "unculturedness" of Eastern European societies, and examples from the Czech

---

55   Tri poloski, agency webpage, accessed March 17, 2020, https://tri-poloski.com /agency.

56   Dina Iordanova, *Cinema of Flames: Balkan Film, Culture and the Media* (London: British Film Institute, 2001).

57   Tomislav Z. Longinović, "Playing the western eye: Balkan masculinity and post-Yugoslav war cinema," in *East European Cinemas*, ed. Aniko Imre (New York: Routledge, 2005), 35–48.

58   Andrea Matošević, "(Auto)egzotizacija Balkana i etnografija nositelja značenja u tri primjera sedme umjetnosti," *Narodna umjetnost: hrvatski časopis za etnologiju i folkloristiku* 48, no. 2 (2011): 31–49.

59   Life of Boris, YouTube channel, accessed March 17, 2020, https://www.youtub e.com/channel/UCS5tt2z_DFvG7-39J3aE-bQ.

60   Squatting Slavs in Tracksuits, Facebook page, accessed March 17, 2020, https://www.facebook.com/SquattingSlavs/.

Republic itself are extremely rarely displayed. Instead, a stereotypical meme of Squatting Slavs in Tracksuits could be the body of a Dacia car pulled by horses, i.e., something that would be considered "from the outside" to be just as humorous as a fan of Sasha Baron Cohen's Borat or the French early 2000s humoristic music project, Bratisla Boys.

Given the overall aesthetics of contemporary hardbass, these Czech social media projects mimic the Russian and other Eastern European-based collectives that communicate their class-based "internal orientalism."[61] The East is conceived as somewhere else by the Czech hardbass fans. If it is not somewhere else, it is somebody else who is its bearer, whom Russian and other Eastern European hardbass mimics. Hardbass Czech social media projects at the same time reinforce the aforementioned xenophobic feelings. Beyond their ideological framing of anti-Communism and anti-Russian imperialism, these are often fueled by feelings of endangerment on the part of the Czech urban "middle classes" vis-à-vis the capital of Russia's "middle classes," particularly in the real estate sector.

VI.

Hardbass partly derives from diasporic and global identities. It was argued that emigration from Eastern Europe is particularly pertinent for young people from the "middle classes"[62] who overlap with the population cohort that forms contemporary hardbass fandom. It is a task for the further research to identify the proportion of hardbass fans and performers from Russian and other Eastern European origins in the Netherlands and possibly also in the Czech Republic. Presumably, this is an important but possibly not a central point for explaining hardbass class relations. A lead could also be found in a recurring English-language comment that has been posted under several YouTube hardbass video clips, which runs along the lines of "[that] looks like my babushka's place." The comparison may refer to the villages of traditional Russian wooden houses or the shabby city intersections with their chaotic mix of street signs and

---

61   Michał Buchowski, "The Specter of Orientalism in Europe: From Exotic Other to Stigmatized Brother," *Anthropological Quarterly* 79, no. 3 (2006): 463–82.

62   Anna Amelina, "Hierarchies and Categorical Power in Cross-Border Science: Analysing Scientists' Transnational Mobility between Ukraine and Germany." *Southeast European and Black Sea Studies* 13, no. 2 (2013): 141–55; Sergei Riazantsev, "The New Concept of the Migration Policy of the Russian Federation: Revolution or Evolution?," in *The EU's Eastern Neighbourhood: Migration, Borders and Regional Stability*, ed. Ilkka Liikanen, James W. Scott, and Tiina Sotkasiira (London: Routledge, 2016), 153–68.

advertising, including homemade posters. Contemporary hardbass's mix and switch between English and predominantly Russian and other Eastern European languages has two key consequences: first, the target audience masters the different languages and is drawn from both the East and the West. Second, the mastery of English, albeit an often deliberately broken and heavily accented version, is a sign of social status and a hallmark of young "middle-class" fans.

This analysis of the social complexities that surround contemporary hardbass is refined through a focus on class relations and conflicts. Hardbass's predominantly male fans and song protagonists ironically mimic the cultures of the lower-income social strata in their home countries (predominantly "working class" but also "lumpenproletariat" gopnik cultures) while reinforcing their own positions within the privileged "middle class." While they may lack economic capital in relative comparison to their "middle-class" parents, contemporary hardbass fans and protagonists do have cultural and to some extent also social capital. Their exaggerated "Slavic unculturedness" should be understood as (self-)exoticizing marketing that brings a certain regional specificity to the arena of global EDM club cultures.

References

Amelina, Anna. "Hierarchies and Categorical Power in Cross-Border Science: Analysing Scientists' Transnational Mobility between Ukraine and Germany." *Southeast European and Black Sea Studies* 13, no. 2 (2013): 141–55.

Balmforth, Tom. "Moscow's Plan To Raze 'Khrushchyovki' Sparks Anger, Confusion Ahead Of Elections." *Radio Free Europe, Radio Liberty*, May 6, 2017. https://www.rferl.org/a/russia-moscow-khrushchyovki-demolition-housing-controversy-elections/28471341.html.

Balzer, Harley. "Russia's Middle Classes." *Post-Soviet Affairs* 14, no. 2 (1998): 165–86.

Bennett, Andy. "The Post-Subcultural Turn: Some Reflections 10 Years On." *Journal of Youth Studies* 14, no. 5 (2011): 493–506.

Bey, Hakim, T.A.Z.: *The Temporary Autonomous Zone*. New York: Autonomedia, 1991.

Bodnár, Judit. "Becoming Bourgeois. (Postsocialist) Utopias of Isolation and Civilization." In *Evil Paradises. Dreamworlds of Neoliberalism*, edited by Michael Davis and Daniel Bertrand Monk, 140–51. New York: New Press, 2009.

Bogerts, Lisa and Maik Fielitz. "'Do You Want Meme War?' Understanding the Visual Memes of the German Far Right." In *Post-Digital Cultures of* the Far Right, edited by Fielitz, Maik and Nick Thurston, 137–54. Bielefeld: transcript, 2019.

Boltanski, Luc and Ève Chiapello. *Le nouvel esprit du capitalisme*. Paris: Gallimard, 1999.

Borenstein, Eliot. *Overkill: Sex and Violence in Contemporary Russian Popular Culture*. Ithaca: Cornell University Press, 2008.

Bourdieu, Pierre. *La Distinction. Critique sociale du jugement*. Paris: Minuit, 1979.

———. "The Forms of Capital." In *Handbook of Theory and Research for the Sociology of Education*, edited by John Richardson, 241–58. Westport, CT: Greenwood, 1986.

Buchowski, Michał. "The Specter of Orientalism in Europe: From Exotic Other to Stigmatized Brother." *Anthropological Quarterly* 79, no. 3 (2006): 463–82.

Cepić, Dražen. *Class Cultures in Postsocialist Eastern Europe*. London: Routledge, 2019.

Chelcea, Liviu and Oana Druţă. "Zombie Socialism and the Rise of Neoliberalism in Post-socialist Central and Eastern Europe." *Eurasian Geography and Economics* 57, no. 4–5 (2016): 521–44. https://doi.org/10.1080/15387216.2016.1266273.

Cristache, Maria. "From 'Culturedness' to Westernness: Old and New Consumption Practices in Romanian Postsocialist Homes." In *Proceedings of the History of Consumer Culture Conference 2017*, 128–35. Tokyo: Gakushuin University, 2018. https://www.academia.edu/38167980/From_Culturedness_to_Westernness_Old_and_New_Consumption_Practices_in_Romanian_Postsocialist_Homes.

Crowley, Stephen. "Russia: The Reemergence of Class in the Wake of the First 'Classless' Society." *East European Politics and Societies and Cultures* 29, no. 3 (2015): 698–710.

Daniel, Ondřej. "Hardbass: Intersectionality, Music, Social Media and the Far-Right on the European Periphery." In *(Dis-)Orienting Sounds: Machtkritische Perspektiven auf populäre Musik*, edited by Ralf von Appen and Mario Dunkel, 153–66. Bielefeld: transcript, 2019.

Drahokoupil, Jan. "Class in Czechia: The Legacy of Stratification Research." *East European Politics and Societies and Cultures* 29, no. 3 (2015): 577–87.

Dziewańska, Marta. *Post-Post-Soviet? Art, Politics & Society in Russia at the Turn of the Decade*. Warsaw: Museum of Modern Art, 2013.

Greif, Mark. "What Was the Hipster?," *New York*, October 24, 2010. http://nymag.com/news/features/69129/

Gruzelier, Jonathan. "Moshpit Menace and Masculine Mayhem." In *Oh Boy! Making Masculinity in Popular Music*, edited by Biddle, Ian and Freya Jarman-Ivens, 59–76. London: Routledge, 2007.

Gurova, Olga. *Fashion and the Consumer Revolution in Contemporary Russia.* London, New York: Routledge, 2015.

Хаас, Андрей Владимирович. *Корпорация счастья. История русского рейва.* Санкт-Петербург: Амфора, 2011.

Harboe Knudsen, Ida and Martin Demant Frederiksen. *Ethnographies of Grey Zones in Eastern Europe: Relations, Borders and Invisibilities.* London: Anthem Press, 2015.

Hill, Andrew. "Acid House and Thatcherism: Contesting Spaces in Late 1980s Britain." *Space and Polity* 7, no. 3 (2003): 219–32.

Hollingworth, Sumi. "Performances of Social Class, Race and Gender Through Youth Subculture: Putting Structure Back in to Youth Subcultural Studies." *Journal of Youth Studies*, 18, no. 10 (2015): 1237–56, https://doi.org/10.1080/13676261.2015.1039968.

Humphrey, Caroline. "Traders, 'Disorder,' and Citizenship Regimes in Provincial Russia." In *Uncertain Transition. Ethnographies of Change in the Postsocialist World*, edited by Michael Burawoy and Katherine Verdery, 19–52. Lanham, MD: Rowman & Littlefield, 1999.

Iordanova, Dina. *Cinema of Flames: Balkan Film, Culture and the Media.* London: British Film Institute, 2001.

John, Henry. "UK Rave Culture and the Thatcherite Hegemony, 1988–94." *Cultural History* 4, no. 2 (2015): 162–86.

Kohoutová, Rozálie. *CzechTek*, Czech television documentary, 2017.

Koivisto, Mikko O. "'I Know You Think I'm Crazy': Post-Horrorcore Rap Approaches to Disability, Violence, and Psychotherapy." *Disability Studies Quarterly* 38, no. 2 (2018). https://dsq-sds.org/article/view/6231/4910.

Kolářová, Marta. "Hudební subkultury mládeže v současné ČR—postsubkulturní či postsocialistické?" In *Populární kultura v českém prostoru*, edited by Ondřej Daniel, Tomáš Kavka and Jakub Machek, 232–48. Prague: Karolinum, 2013.

Laineste, Liisi. "Post-Socialist Jokelore: Preliminary Findings and Further Research Suggestion." *Acta Ethnographica Hungarica* 54, no. 1 (2009): 31–45.

Longinović, Tomislav Z., "Playing the Western Eye: Balkan Masculinity and Post-Yugoslav War Cinema." In *East European Cinemas*, edited by Aniko Imre, 35–48. New York: Routledge, 2005.

Malbon, Ben, *Clubbing: Dancing, Ecstasy and Vitality.* London: Routledge, 1999.

Matošević, Andrea. "(Auto)egzotizacija Balkana i etnografija nositelja značenja u tri primjera sedme umjetnosti." *Narodna umjetnost: hrvatski časopis za etnologiju i folkloristiku* 48, no. 2 (2011): 31–49.

Muggs, Joe. "Gift of the Gabber: The Return of Dance Music's Gloriously Tasteless Subgenre." *Guardian*, January 10, 2020. https://www.theguardia

n.com/music/2020/jan/10/gift-of-the-gabber-the-return-of-dance-m
usics-gloriously-tasteless-subgenre.

Müller, Martin. "Goodbye, Postsocialism!" *Europe-Asia Studies* 71, no. 4 (2019): 533–50, https://doi.org/10.1080/09668136.2019.1578337.

Ost, David. "Stuck in the Past and the Future: Class Analysis in Postcommunist Poland." *East European Politics and Societies and Cultures* 29, no. 3 (2015): 610–24.

Pilkington, Hilary Anne, Elena Omel'chenko, Moya Flynn, and Uliana Bliudina. *Looking West? Cultural Globalization and Russian Youth Cultures*. University Park: Pennsylvania State University Press, 2012.

Reynolds, Simon. *Retromania: Pop Culture's Addiction to Its Own Past*. New York: Faber & Faber, 2011.

Riazantsev, Sergei. "The New Concept of the Migration Policy of the Russian Federation: Revolution or Evolution?" In *The EU's Eastern Neighbourhood: Migration, Borders and Regional Stability*, edited by Ilkka Liikanen, James W. Scott, and Tiina Sotkasiira, 153–68. London: Routledge, 2016.

Rietveld, Hillegonda C. "Gabber Overdrive—Noise, Horror, and Acceleration." In: *Turmoil—CTM Magazine*, January 2018. https://openresearch.lsbu.ac.uk/i tem/869q7.

Schimpfössl, Elisabeth. *Rich Russians: From Oligarchs to Bourgeoisie*. Oxford: Oxford University Press, 2018.

Schwartz, Matthias and Heike Winkel, eds. *Eastern European Youth Cultures in a Global Context*. London: Palgrave Macmillan, 2016.

Slačálek, Ondřej. "České freetekno–pohyblivé prostory autonomie?" In *Revolta stylem: Hudební subkultury mládeže v České republice*, edited by Marta Kolářová, 83–122. Prague: Slon, 2011.

Stewart, Simon. *Culture and the Middle Classes*. Farnham: Routledge, 2016.

Štulhofer, Aleksandar and Theo Sandfort. *Sexuality and Gender in Postcommunist Eastern Europe and Russia*. New York: Haworth Press, 2006.

Ther, Philipp. *Die neue Ordnung auf dem alten Kontinent. Eine Geschichte des neoliberalen Europa*. Berlin: Suhrkamp, 2014.

Țichindeleanu, Ovidiu. "Where Are We, When We Think in Eastern Europe?" In *Art Always Has Its Consequences*, edited by Ivet Ćurlin, Ana Dević, Nataša Ilić, Sabina Sabolović, Dóra Hegyi, Zsuzsa László, Magdalena Ziółkowska, and Katarzyna Słoboda, 85–92. Zagreb: WHW, 2010.

Tri poloski. Interview with: GOPNIK MCBLYAT. Posted March 8, 2020. https://tr i-poloski.com/media.

Versluis, Ari. "Gabber." *Lola da musica* Season 2, episode 5. Aired November, 13 1995, on Vrijzinnig Protestantse Radio Omroep (VPRO).

Vonderau, Asta. *Leben im "neuen Europa" Konsum, Lebensstile und Körpertechniken im Postsozialismus*. Bielefeld: transcript, 2010.

Winterhalter, Cecilia. "Normcore or a New Desire for Normality: To be Crazy, Be Normal." *Catwalk: The Journal of Fashion, Beauty and Style* 5, no. 1 (2016): 21–42.

Yurchak, Alexei. *Everything Was Forever, Until It Was No More. The Last Soviet Generation*. Princeton: Princeton University Press, 2006.

Юрчак, Алексей, "Ночные танцы с ангелом истории. Критические культуральные исследования пост-социализма." In *Культуралные исследования*, edited by Александра Эткинда. Санкт-Петербург: Европейский университет, 2005: 1–32.

Disembodiment and South Asian Performance Cultures

Rumya S. Putcha

Abstract: This chapter exposes the role of expressive culture in the rise and spread of late twentieth-century Hindu identity politics. The author examines how Hindu nationalism is fueled by affective logics that have crystallized around the female classical dancer and have situated her gendered and athletic body as a transnational emblem of an authentic Hindu and Indian national identity. This embodied identity is represented by the historical South Indian temple dancer and has, in the postcolonial era, been rebranded as the nationalist classical dancer. The author connects the dancer to transnational forms of identity politics, heteropatriarchal marriage economies, as well as pathologies of gender violence. In so doing, the author examines how the affective politics of 'Hinduism' have functionally disembodied the Indian dancer from her voice and her agency in a democratic nation-state. The author argues that the nationalist and now transnationalist production of the classical dancer exposes misogyny and casteism and thus requires a critical feminist dismantling.

Bibliographical note: Portions of this chapter originally appeared in Rumya S. Putcha, "The Modern Courtesan: Gender, Religion, and Dance in Transnational India," *Feminist Review* 126 (2020): 54–73 and have been reproduced with permission.

Rumya S. Putcha is an assistant professor in the Institute of Women's Studies and the Hugh Hodgson School of Music at the University of Georgia.

Introduction

In 1988, South Indian film director K. Viswanath (b. 1930) released a film entitled "Swarnakamalam" (Golden Lotus). Viswanath cast the beautiful and talented dancer-actress Banupriya (b. 1967) as Meenakshi, the daughter of a high-caste Hindu classical dancer. A product of her father's training, Meenakshi is a gifted performer, but has no interest in leading the life of a classical dancer, which she sees as a dying, anachronistic profession. Her love interest in the film,

Chandrasekhar, however, holds Meenakshi's father in great esteem as a symbol of Indian religious—that is, Hindu—heritage. Throughout the film, this love interest acts as her conscience and encourages Meenakshi to realize that, as her father's daughter, she embodies invaluable cultural knowledge. He implores her to see that modern India needs her to keep Hindu culture "alive"—to keep modernity from erasing cultural memory. By the end of the film, Meenakshi accepts an invitation to move abroad. As she prepares to board a plane and leave India for a new life in the United States, she realizes she is afraid of what she will lose by starting over there—i.e., everything she has ever known, especially her identity as a dancer. Rather than moving to America, she decides at the last second to stay in India, marry Chandrasekhar, and uphold her family's high-caste, Hindu identity by becoming a dancer-teacher, like her father before her.

I was seven years old when *Swarnakamalam* was released and two years into my own initiation into Indian dance and vocal training. *Swarnakamalam*'s dramatization of gendered cultural transmission, symbolized by music, dance, and Brahminical Hindu identity, resonated deeply with my parents, who, like many upwardly mobile and dominant-caste Indians, in the wake of the 1965 Immigration Act,[1] had immigrated to the US. I came to know the film well. Anytime I didn't want to practice dance, my family would plop me in front of the television and make me watch it because, in many ways, *Swarnakamalam* offered me a path to follow, as a first-generation immigrant to the US and a transnational Indian and Hindu woman. Films like *Swarnakamalam*, which connect female dance and daughterhood to homeland, and homeland to upper-caste Hindu identity, are vital in the Indian film industry more broadly since they capitalize on a stabilized understanding of the cultural formations that synonymize a democratic nation-state, Hindu identity, and the gendered body.[2]

---

1   The Hart-Cellar Act, or Immigration and Nationality Act of 1965, phased out the national origins quota system that had been in place since 1921. Whereas previous to the Act, immigration to the US from anywhere besides the United Kingdom, Ireland, and Germany was severely limited, this legislation instituted a preference system that focused on immigrants' skills and family relationships with citizens or residents.

2   See Rachel Dwyer, *Filming the Gods: Religion and Indian Cinema* (New York: Routledge, 2006); Dwyer, *Pleasure and the Nation: The History, Politics and Consumption of Popular Culture in India* (New Delhi: Oxford University Press, 2006); Sangita Gopal and Sujata Moorti, *Global Bollywood: Travels of Hindi Song and Dance* (Minneapolis: University of Minnesota Press, 2008); Ashis Nandy, ed., *The Secret Politics of Our Desires: Innocence, Culpability, and Indian Popular Cinema* (New York: St. Martin's Press, 1998); Madiraju M. Prasad, *Ideology of the Hindi Film: A Historical Construction*, 6th ed. (New Delhi: Oxford University Press, 2001); Jyotika Virdi, *The Cinematic Imagination: Indian Popular Films as Social History* (New Brunswick, NJ: Rutgers University Press, 2003).

Figure 1: Cover of June 26, 2006, Time Magazine featuring an Indian classical dancer as a call-center worker. Source: Time Magazine.

In this chapter, I take a closer look at the affective logics that have crystallized around the now iconic Indian classical dancer. I refer to her as a modern courtesan to capture the gendered and heteropatriarchal imperatives that have situated her as a global emblem of a transnational Indian identity, particularly in democratic and pluralistic North American settings. Culling together ethnography, film and media analysis, and feminist critiques, I trace the cultural formations which connect the romanticized Hindu temple dancer to the modern classical dancer and the fetishization of the female dancer to rape culture.[3] I bring together transnational feminism,[4] queer/affect theory,[5] on the one hand, and a body of work on classical dance by dominant caste Hindus within postcolonial nationalism,[6] gender, caste, democracy, and the Indian nation-state,[7] one the other hand, to critically examine how the affective politics of

---

3   Rape culture, a phrase coined by second-wave feminists in the United States, requires us to see that rape is not simply about sex, but about the normalization of sexism, patriarchy, and heteronormative gendered behavior; see Noreen Connell and Cassandra Wilson, *Rape: The First Sourcebook for Women* (New York: New American Library, 1974); Susan Brownmiller, *Against our Will: Men, Women and Rape* (New York: Simon and Schuster, 1975).

4   See M. Jacqui Alexander and Chandra Talpade Mohanty, eds., *Feminist Genealogies, Colonial Legacies, Democratic Futures* (New York: Routledge, 1997); Inderpal Grewal and Caren Kaplan, *Scattered Hegemonies: Postmodernity and Transnational Feminist Practices* (Minneapolis: University of Minnesota Press, 2006 [1994]); Grewal, *Transnational America: Feminisms, Diasporas, Neoliberalisms* (Durham, NC: Duke University Press, 2005); Saba Mahmood, *Politics of Piety: The Islamic Revival and the Feminist Subject* (Princeton: Princeton University Press, 2012); Chandra Talpade Mohanty, *Feminism without Borders: Decolonizing Theory, Practicing Solidarity* (Durham, NC: Duke University Press, 2003); Jasbir K. Puar, *Terrorist Assemblages: Homonationalism in Queer Times* (Durham, NC: Duke University Press, 2007); Amanda Lock Swarr and Richa Nagar, eds., *Critical Transnational Feminist Praxis* (Albany: SUNY Press, 2010).

5   See Sara Ahmed, *The Cultural Politics of Emotion* (Durham, NC: Duke University Press, 2004); Ahmed, *Queer Phenomenology: Orientations, Objects, Others* (Durham, NC: Duke University Press, 2006); Ahmed, *The Promise of Happiness* (Durham, NC: Duke University Press, 2010); Lauren Berlant, *Cruel Optimism* (Durham, NC: Duke University Press, 2011); Eve Kosofsky Sedgwick, *Touching Feeling: Affect, Pedagogy, Performativity* (Durham, NC: Duke University Press, 2006).

6   See, e.g., Pallabi Chakravorty, *Bells of Change: Kathak Dance, Women, and Modernity in India* (Kolkata: Seagull Books, 2008); Indira Peterson and Davesh Soneji, eds., *Performing Pasts: Reinventing the Arts in Modern South India* (New Delhi: Oxford University Press, 2008); Avanthi Meduri, "Nation, Woman, Representation: The Sutured History of the Devadasi and Her Dance" (Ph.D. diss., New York University, 1996); Janet O'Shea, *At Home in the World* (Middletown, CT: Wesleyan University Press, 2007); Davesh Soneji *Unfinished Gestures: Devadasis, Memory, and Modernity in South India* (Chicago: University of Chicago Press, 2011); Priya Srinivasan, *Sweating Saris: Indian Dance as Transnational Labor* (Philadelphia: Temple University Press, 2012).

7   See Anjali Arondekar, *For the Record: On Sexuality and the Colonial Archive* (Durham, NC: Duke University Press, 2009); Uma Chakravarti, *Thinking Gender, Doing Gender: Feminist Scholarship and Practice Today* (New Delhi: Orient Blackswan, 2016); Partha Chatterjee, "The Nationalist Resolution of the Women's Question," in *Recasting Women: Essays in Indian Colonial History*, ed. Kumkum

twenty-first century postcolonial nationalism have curated and controlled the Indian, that is, female, dancing body.

The larger theoretical intervention I offer in this chapter is that the dancer and her body, even when understood as separable from music, is doing important political work. This work is particularly potent in pluralistic and democratic settings, where the expressive body, becomes a technological[8] metonym for citizenship. First, I lay out a brief history of the rise of postcolonial Hindu identity politics—often glossed as Hindu nationalism or Hindutva—and its bodily discourses through gendered expression like dance, drawing particular attention to the way the body operates within affective attachments based on colonial epistemologies of religion in transnational South Indian dance cultures. I then connect such overdetermined ideologies of identity, religion, and nation, which are often understood to only exist in the Hindi heartland, but have been and continue to be memorialized in Telugu films like *Swarnakamalam* and in visual cultures more broadly, to ethnographic research on classical dance in India as well as the United States. In making these connections between film cultures, visual cultures, and dance studios, I locate myself and my ethnographic access as a transnational Indian woman and dancer. In so doing, I draw on South Asian-American feminist scholarship that engages with South Asian racial formations[9] as well the postcolonial feminist scholarship of Lila Abu-Lughod, Saba Mah-

Sangari and Sudesh Vaid (New Delhi: Kali for Women, 1989), 233–53; Anupama Rao, ed., *Gender, Caste, and the Imagination of Equality* (New Delhi: Women Unlimited, 2018); Sharmila Rege, "The Hegemonic Appropriation of Sexuality: The Case of the *lavani* Performers of Maharashtra," *Contributions to Indian Sociology* 29, no. 1-2 (1995): 23–38; Rajeswari Sunder Rajan, *Real and Imagined Women: Gender, Culture, and Postcolonialism* (London: Routledge, 1993); Sunder Rajan, *Signposts: Gender Issues in Post-Independence India* (New Brunswick, NJ: Rutgers University Press, 2001); Sinha, "Gender in the Critiques of Colonialism and Nationalism: Locating the 'Indian Woman,'" in *Feminism and History*, ed. Joan Wallach Scott (Oxford: Oxford University Press, 1996), 477–504; Sinha, *Specters of Mother India: The Global Restructuring of an Empire* (Durham, NC: Duke University Press, 2006); Tanika Sarkar, *Hindu Wife, Hindu Nation: Community, Religion, and Cultural Nationalism* (Bloomington: Indiana University Press, 2010).

8   Here I am relying in part on Michel Foucault's formulation of "technologies of the self," which "permit individuals to effect by their own means or with the help of others a certain number of operations on their own bodies and souls." *Technologies of the Self: A Seminar with Michel Foucault*, ed. Luther H. Martin, Huck Gutman, and Patrick H. Hutton (Amherst: University of Massachusetts Press, 1988), 88.

9   See Gayatri Gopinath, *Impossible Desires: Queer Diasporas and South Asian Public Cultures* (Durham, NC: Duke University Press, 2005).

mood, Aihwa Ong, and Rajeshwari Sundar Rajan.[10] Taken as a whole, this body of feminist scholarship has lodged a collective critique against cultural relativism and the kinds of Euro-American imperialist intellectual projects that equate orientalized women and their bodies with postcolonial religious nationalism.

To unsettle a facile reading of the Indian classical dancer-as-nation, in this chapter I make a case for viewing visual and performance culture as part and parcel of simultaneously right-wing Hindu nationalist agendas as well as colonial-derived and global North liberal logics. By framing the political and affective economy of the Indian classical dancer as that of a tension between Hindutva or an uncomplicated multiculturalism, I suggest that we understand her as a version of what Sara Ahmed has theorized as a "sticky" symbol, which reveals both religious and patriarchal chauvinism as well as colonial and Orientalist racism.[11] As I expand my lens to think critically about gender, race, and transnational bodies, I am drawing from the kinds of feminist praxis and everyday interventions championed by bell hooks and Sara Ahmed.[12] Indeed, in drawing together ethnographic work, film, and visual culture to think critically and self-reflexively about gender and religion, I take to heart hooks's and Ahmed's respective advice on living a feminist life.

The Female Body in the Postcolonial Indian Archive

In India's case, independent statehood, achieved in 1947, unleashed violent and toxic religious sectarianism. The British, notorious for a divide-and-conquer strategy in colonial administration, championed a brand of religious identitarianism that ultimately amounted to the partition of British India into a Hindu India and a Muslim Pakistan. The affective attachment to the new Indian nation as a Hindu woman and goddess (see Figures 2 and 3) further circumscribes the relationship between religious identity politics, nationalism, and gender,

---

10   See Lila Abu-Lughod, "Do Muslim Women Really Need Saving? Anthropological Reflections on Cultural Relativism and Its Others," American Anthropologist. 104, no. 3 (2002): 783–90; Mahmood, Politics of Piety; Aihwa Ong, "Colonialism and Modernity: Feminist Re-Presentations of Women in Non-Western Societies," Inscriptions 3–4 (1988): 79–93; Ong, "State versus Islam; Malay Families, Women's Bodies, and the Body Politic in Malaysia," American Ethnologist 17, no. 2 (1990): 258–76; Sunder Rajan, Real and Imagined Women (1993).

11   Ahmed,The Cultural Politics of Emotion, 120.

12   bell hooks, Black Looks: Race and Representation, 2nd ed. (New York: Routledge, 2015); Sara Ahmed, Living a Feminist Life (Durham, NC: Duke University Press, 2016).

both in India and in all the spaces and places where India is evoked.[13] The Indian classical dancer and her counterpart in film cultures has animated and mobilized identity politics in ways that have become increasingly urgent with the ascendance of the Hindu nationalist Bharatiya Janata Party (BJP), led by Prime Minister Narendra Modi and his rhetoric of "India First."

Figures 2 and 3: Trans World Air advertisements (1960s) featuring a female Indian classical dancer as a symbol of Indian tourism. Artist credit: David Klein.

In postcolonial India, the Hindu female dancer *is* India (see Figures 2 and 3). Moreover, this iconic and fetishized Hindu dancer emerges from the South Indian context, in the areas known today as Tamil Nadu and Andhra Pradesh, respectively, where she is said to have danced in temples. It is by now a truism among those who study the body in India that the South Indian classical dancer, as an essentialized and visual archetype, exposes dual imperatives of Hindu nationalism and transnationalism that we could not otherwise see. For the role she has played in championing Hindu hegemony in and as India, the figure of the female dancer has loomed large within scholarship on nation, religion, and women in India over the past sixty years. Much of this literature has examined

---

13   Speaking specifically about Bengal, Partha Chatterjee once famously dubbed the gendered identity politics of postcolonial India "The Women's Question"; see Chatterjee, "The Nationalist Resolution of the Women's Question," 233–53.

the nationalist reinvention of the arts and the overdetermination of Sanskrit textual authority to examine the role of the mytho-historical figure of the courtesan, often reduced to the categories of *devadasi* in the South or *tawaif* in the North.[14] Indeed, feminist scholarship from India on dance and music has noted the uneven and reductive historiography of the courtesan from south India in particular as a symbol of a postcolonial and transnational India, and, problematically, a cultural ambassador for a hegemonic and casteist Hindu nation-state.[15]

The modern courtesan, much like her historical counterpart, is an object of desire, but a source of social dystopia. She is saturated with extra-cultural meaning in the transnational and highly mediated spaces in which Indian identity circulates today: from cinema and satellite television[16] to visual culture like advertisements and cosmopolitan standards of beauty. Courtesanship in this equation points to a consolidation of performance training, especially music and dance, steeped as these arts are in a decidedly Hindu identification, into a highly marriageable young woman or daughter in transnational India. Dance training, especially in transnational North American settings, is integral to Indian identity because it signals religious identification as well as regimes of value framed as "beauty" and thus functions as a commodity in marriage economies.[17] Thus, the commodification of the expressive and athletic female

---

14   See, e.g., on South India and the *devadasi*, Avanthi Meduri, "Bharatha Natyam—What Are You?" *Asian Theatre Journal* 5, no. 1 (Spring 1988): 1–22; Amrit Srinivasan, "Temple 'Prostitution' and Community Reform: An Examination of the Ethnographic, Historical and Textual Context of the Devadasi of Tamil Nadu, South India" (Ph.D. diss., Cambridge University, 1984); Srinivasan, "Reform and Revival: The Devadasi and Her Dance," *Economic and Political Weekly* 20, no. 44 (1985): 1869–76; Davesh Soneji, *Unfinished Gestures: Devadasis, Memory, and Modernity in South India* (Chicago: University of Chicago Press, 2011). On North India and the *tawaif*, see Pallabi Chakravorty, *Bells of Change: Kathak Dance, Women, and Modernity in India* (Kolkata: Seagull Books, 2008) and also Shweta Sachdeva, "In Search of the Tawa'if in History: Courtesans, Nautch Girls and Celebrity Entertainers in India (1720s–1920s)" (Ph.D. diss., SOAS, University of London, 2008).

15   See Sharmila Rege, "The Hegemonic Appropriation of Sexuality: The Case of the *Lavani* Performers of Maharashtra," *Contributions to Indian Sociology* 29, no. 1–2 (1995): 23–38.

16   See, for example, Purnima Mankekar, *Screening Culture, Viewing Politics: An Ethnography of Television, Womanhood, and Nation in Postcolonial India* (Durham, NC: Duke University Press, 1999); Mankekar and Louisa Schein, *Media, Erotics, and Transnational Asia* (Durham, NC: Duke University Press, 2012).

17   Women with dance and music training are understood as more marketable on the marriage market. See Reginald and Jamila Massey, *The Music of India* (New Dehli: Abhinav Publications, 1996): 76.

body must be seen as crucial to the Indian identity globally, synonymous as the modern courtesan is with the racial and heterosexual identity she represents visually.

The modern courtesan recasts the rejected qualities of an improperly sexualized woman to new domains of citizenship and choice built on the principles and behaviors of conjugal wifehood. The choice to be appropriately sexual, in particular, is valorized by both young women and the dominant discourses of post-feminism. In South Asia, this "appropriate" behavior is still limited to the confines of patriarchy, and specifically marriage. But as Lucinda Ramberg and Srimati Basu so eloquently observe,

the efficiency of marriage as a unit makes systematic privileges within it invisible; we may only be able to discern these points of fracture such as divorce, which reveals that not only does "gender structured marriage involve women in a cycle of socially caused and distinctly asymmetric vulnerability," but that women "are made vulnerable by marriage itself."[18]

Heteronormative marriage or wifehood were and still are goals for the vast majority of the women with whom I have danced over the past thirty years, in India as well as the United States, even as they acknowledge that marriage will not make them happy. Or as one fellow dancer once exclaimed in exasperation, "I know ninety percent of marriages are unhappy, but we do it anyway!" Affective attachments, especially the expression of pleasure and identification through and by a relationship to the dancing body in popular television and film provide a crucial lynchpin, which explains this "anyway"[19] attitude. In the ethnography I offer below, I examine how, in the dance studio, for example, the comportment of the female body to the rules of heteronormativity is fundamental to the daily experiences of patriarchal order: rape culture. Put another way, the logics of gender in the dance studio require the sidelining of anything resembling choice, much less consent.

The policing of women's bodies as a symptom of rape culture—a hallmark of South Asian feminist critique—has only come under greater scrutiny in the aftermath of the high-profile 2012 rape case, known generally as Nirbhaya, in New Delhi. The argument that has been maintained by many apologists for the rapists involved in the case rests on the widely held belief that there are certain affective behaviors that women, especially young women, can adopt in certain spaces. When such spaces are mutually agreed upon (e.g., a dance stage), rape culture, as a facet of patriarchy, remains intact. This narrow understanding of

---

18   Srimati Basu and Lucinda Ramberg, eds., *Conjugality Unbound: Sexual Economies, State Regulation, and the Marital Form in India.* (New Delhi: Women Unlimited, 2015): 12.

19   A version of Lauren Berlant's *Cruel Optimism.*

affect relies upon what scholars of sexual violence refer to as the "perfect victim" syndrome. In the case of Nirbhaya, the media storm surrounding the case relied on a rhetoric that the victim could have been any Indian woman. Feminists across India have pointed out that Nirbhaya only generated protests because she represented a young woman whom Indians were willing to see as their daughter—that is, a Hindu, high-caste, yet-to-be-married woman.[20] Considering an Indian woman is raped every twenty-two seconds,[21] the flashpoint that Nirbhaya ignited speaks to a very specific and privileged kind of womanhood that sparks outrage. Simply put, Jyoti (the victim's legal name), a Hindu citizen who had every potential of fulfilling a middle-class heterosexual dream of a career, husband, and children, did not deserve to be raped. The fact that she was "punished" by an old India (for this is the euphemism for sexual violence against modern cosmopolitan women) enraged feminists who had championed the very kinds of choices that Jyoti had made so far in her young life.

But this celebration of choice lies at the heart of much of the feminist discourse in and on South Asia and is more generally associated with what are otherwise lumped together as third-wave feminist approaches. An enduring lightning rod in the contemporary global South feminist conversation has been and continues to be the limits of liberal subject formation when it comes to what Mahmood has named in her work as the "politics of piety."[22] In the case of Indian classical dance, it is increasingly important that we interrogate who gets to choose a sovereign gender or sexual identity, and what that might even look like for women within religious affective cultures and their attendant political economies. In posing these questions, I am consciously and carefully avoiding anything resembling judgement on what qualifies as feminist or anti-feminist, especially when women choose to express or abdicate religious identification. Rather, I work towards developing analytical tools, including vocabulary, that can capture "the critical differences between women who are upholders of patriarchal norms and those who fight these norms."[23]

---

20   Krupa Shandilya, "Nirbhaya's Body: The Politics of Protest in the Aftermath of the 2012 Delhi Gang Rape," *Gender & History* 27, no. 2 (2015): 465–86; Mark Phillips et al., "Media Coverage of Violence against Women in India: A Systematic Study of a High Profile Rape Case," BMC *Women's Health* 15, no. 3 (January 22, 2015), https://doi.org/10.1186/s12905-015-0161-x.

21   Calculated based on a standard reporting failure rate of one in ten. See B.L. Himabindu, Radhika Arora and N.S. Prashanth, "Whose Problem Is It Anyway? Crimes against Women in India," *Global Health Action* 7, no. 1 (2014), https://doi .org/10.3402/gha.v7.23718.

22   Mahmood, *Politics of Piety.*

23   Mahmood, *Politics of Piety*, X.

Dance Studios and Sexual Violence

> As I'm leaving class today with my new dance friend Priya and we're walking
> to get an auto, she tells me that I shouldn't get too close to Mastergaru[24]. That
> it looks bad for me to be talking to the "staff" too much. She says that I may
> not have noticed, but everyone was watching when I was asking questions,
> and that the politics are just so bad, I have to be careful about getting too
> close. I'm guessing she's saying this (for my own good, of course; she's a sweet
> kid) because people who talk too much seem like they are kissing up and then
> things get complicated and problems begin when everyone assumes you're
> sleeping with the teacher and then they expect more money. She apparently
> had some sort of bad experience with one of the teachers harassing her. Now
> that I know about her family situation and that she is the only child of a poor
> but Brahmin family, and a daughter at that, it all makes sense why she would
> be so cautious.[25]

I have spent much time over the course of my life training at formal dance
institutes in India, but none with as much nostalgia, for me at least, as the
ones in Chennai. The most prominent Kuchipudi training center in Chennai
(hereafter the KC[26]), was founded with nationalist goals: a commitment to
spreading the message that classical Indian dance was only and always Hindu,
and such history was best articulated by and through gender-normative femininity. As a genre, Kuchipudi historians' particular commitment to Brahminical
propaganda has endured for generations now and has been especially effective
transnationally. [27]

More so than any other dance style that is nominally understood as "classical," Kuchipudi, as an idiom, was developed by and through film cultures.[28] The
most commercially successful South Indian films over the course of the twentieth century featured Kuchipudi choreographers and choreography almost
without exception (see, for example, *Sankarabharanam*).[29] Furthermore, by the
late twentieth century, the films which traveled the farthest were those which
spoke to the mass exodus of South Indians in the post-1965 era and featured

---

24 A term used to address a male guru or teacher. Female instructors are not
    referred to with this honorific.
25 Excerpt from the author's fieldnotes.
26 To protect the privacy of the individuals associated with the dance school I will
    be using pseudonyms.
27 See Rumya Putcha, "Dancing in Place: Mythopoetics and the Production of
    History in Kuchipudi," *Yearbook for Traditional Music* 47 (2015): 1–26.
28 See Katyayani Thota, "Stage to Screen, and Back: A Study of the Dialogue
    between Kuchipudi and Telugu Cinema" (Ph.D. diss., University of Hyderabad,
    2016).
29 *Sankarabharanam*, directed by Kasinadhuni Viswanathan (1980, India).

Kuchipudi in name as well as movement vocabulary. These films, like *Swarnakamalam*, relied on a highly problematic nostalgia for a more hierarchical and more fundamentalist society and, in many cases, named dance schools like the KC in the film itself. Indeed, if one looks at Indian films as a whole, including commercial Hindi films, from the final decades of the twentieth century, there is a distinct pattern of Hindu identity politics and its connections to beautiful, athletic women who are talented dancers that becomes apparent.[30]

Though many have noted the obviously troublesome anti-Muslim and heteropatriarchal aspects of Hindu nationalism that are valorized through film cultures,[31] relatively little has been said about the misogynistic and casteist dynamics that circulate under the banner of classical dance. A number of feminist scholars have critiqued the reproduction of colonial epistemologies of gender in anthropology as a discipline and ethnography as a methodology.[32] What is otherwise known as "participant-observation" exposes certain racialized, gendered, and transnational dynamics that would otherwise remain invisible were it not for the fact that although I am a product of the American academy, I read as an Indian and Hindu woman in the dance studio. It was only after a white female American friend of mine, Erin, came to visit and joined me one day at the KC that I could see how my racial identity, vis-à-vis hers, affected my time in the studio.

Class and rehearsals begin and I'm startled and amused by how Master takes to Erin and, by extension of his obsession with her, how he really drills me

---

30   See Usha Iyer, "Stardom Ke Peeche Kya Hai? / What Is behind the Stardom? Madhuri Dixit, the Production Number, and the Construction of the Female Star Text in 1990s Hindi Cinema," Camera Obscura 30, no. 3 (2015): 129–59, https://doi.org/10.1215/02705346-3160674.

31   See, e.g., Sikata Banerjee, *Gender, Nation and Popular Film in India: Globalizing Muscular Nationalism* (Abingdon: Routledge, 2017); Gopinath, *Impossible Desires*; Sanjeev Kumar, "Constructing the Nation's Enemy: Hindutva, Popular Culture and the Muslim 'Other' in Bollywood Cinema," *Third World Quarterly* 34, no. 3 (2013): 458–69; Madhavi Murty, "Representing *Hindutva*: Nation, Religion and Masculinity in Indian Popular Cinema, 1990 to 2003," *Popular Communication* 7, no. 4 (2009): 267–81.

32   See Lila Abu-Lughod, "Can There Be a Feminist Ethnography?" *Women and Performance: A Journal of Feminist Theory* 5, no. 1 (1990): 6–27; Linda Alcoff, "The Problem of Speaking for Others," *Cultural Critique* 20 (1992): 5–32; Trinh T. Minh-ha, *Woman, Native, Other: Writing Postcoloniality and Feminism* (Bloomington: Indiana University Press, 2009 [1989]); Kirin Narayan, "How Native Is a 'Native' Anthropologist?" *American Anthropologist* 95, no. 3 (1993): 671–86; for a further critique of ethnographic methods and feminist interventions see Kamala Visweswaran, *Fictions of Feminist Ethnography* (Minneapolis: University of Minnesota Press, 1994).

today. He basically gives me his undivided attention. We alternate between dance and talk. His English isn't great so he keeps yelling at me to translate. He makes a huge fuss about my form, especially my aramandi[33] today. He tells me to sit and sit and sit to such a point that I'm on my toes. Now, he doesn't call this by its true name in terms of shastra (textual authority) so I'm pretty confused when he tells me to keep sitting even though my heels have come up. We work through some adavus (basic steps) and I'm totally exhausted. He seems to enjoy Erin's audience and he gets into a bit of a soliloquy with her comparing the East and West. He babbles on about the Vedas and Bharata and generally the history and belief-based systems of the East (India in specific, of course) in comparison to the rational empirical-inquiry driven West. To drive this point home, he gives her, through me, an example. He's holding his stick that he uses to conduct class and puts it behind his back. He says that in India he could keep the stick behind his back and tell someone (a student?) that the stick is there and if he is a person of greater knowledge then he would never have to show the stick to prove its existence. In America, he would need to show the stick to prove it was really there. It's bizarre, it's like he's insulting the West (represented by Erin) in this moment, but uses me as a tool to accomplish that insult. Lesson learned for me, don't bring any more of my White friends along unless I want all kinds of uncomfortable attention.[34]

I had been a student and a Kuchipudi dancer familiar with such spaces for over twenty-five years when the interaction narrated above took place. In that time, I had learned a few important things about how institutional dance spaces operate. I had learned that the men who ran the studio space were generally to be feared, or at the very least, regarded warily. I learned such lessons from a constellation of experiences over the years, ranging from full-on verbal abuse and body shaming to microaggressions that made it clear that dancers from the US were seen as less than those from India. Interestingly though, it was always made abundantly clear that American students were essential to the financial health of a dance institution like the KC. It is common knowledge among dancers that NRI (non-resident Indian) dancers (all American without exception) study at the KC and even perform in productions through a sort of "pay to play" system. As many students know, there are often wealthy parents back in the States who usually bankroll tours in the US, purchasing a lead role for their college-age (or younger) daughter along the way.

My own entry into the KC during my fieldwork, despite my research status at that point, was marked by a collision of patriarchy and payment in a striking and, quite frankly, disturbing manner. A telling example of what I came to see as the marriage of neoliberalism and patriarchy occurred on my very first day.

---

33   Aramandi is loosely understood as a half-sitting baseline posture in most South Indian classical dance forms.

34   Excerpt from the author's fieldnotes.

Now, as a Telugu Brahmin woman, I was at an incredible advantage to move and work in that studio space—I spoke the language and could blend in easily. Yet, the very things that granted me unfettered access also shackled me in some fascinating ways. For example, I was informed I could not enroll myself. Despite being nearly 30 years old at that moment, I required the permission and blessings of either a parent or my husband to enroll in classes. To be fair, this was as much a condition of the dance school as it was one of my natal family. You see, dance studios like the KC have a reputation. Every Telugu family is at least vaguely familiar with the concern that their daughter is going to be manipulated into sex if she is left alone with her male dance guru. The KC has experienced many a scandal over its history and in each case, it is the young dancer who is blamed for "allowing" such sexual indiscretion to occur. Leaving aside the absurdity of holding teenage girls responsible for the sexual predation of the male gurus for the moment, it suffices to say, I was equal parts wary and aghast that I required my father's presence to conduct my research.

My father was mostly there to do his duty, but as is often the case, as a dad, he had very little experience with what happens behind the scenes in dance schools. Mothers are generally the emissaries in such settings, despite patriarchy's stranglehold, but also because of it. My father and I arrived together, ready to formally pay our respects and request my admission to the school as a sishya (student). As is customary, I had brought tambulam (a ceremonial Hindu offering) and was to be formally presented to the guru. I bought a shirt for the guru and fabric for a blouse for his wife, two bananas and one orange, and sandwiched ₹1,116 between the fruit and clothes. After handing the gift over, I touched my new teacher's feet as an act of my obeisance.

The surreptitious gifting of money within the practice of tambulam has always struck me as odd, but it is consistent across nominally Hindu settings. The same practice is observed, for example when one seeks the blessing of a priest. The exchange of currency, though ostensibly meant to curry favor or luck in a temple setting, takes on a very different meaning at an institution like the KC. To be sure, the exchange of money and financial support in general is something that flies under the radar in the transnational and diasporic Hindu classical dance scene. During my time in Chennai, I came to see the impact of Nri wealth as particularly important to any understanding of how religious identity operates for Indian (Hindu) women who consider themselves dancers.

During my time in Chennai, there were larger conversations about who, besides Nris that is, could afford such training and exposure, and what other kinds of social capital could and would be accumulated in the process. A State-side example of how Hindu female bodies signify presented itself clearly to me throughout my training in Houston, since every summer my guru invited artists from India to workshop us on "how to look more Indian." The training we young

American-born Indian women received during such summers was intense and often a test of physical and athletic ability in ways I did not experience during the rest of the year. The takeaway message for those of us who stuck through long eight-hour days in the studio was that dancers in India were better, more athletic; their bodies better trained, more rigorously trained, at the very least. We were encouraged to adjust our diets, to incorporate yoga into our training regimen, and to practice even more.

In 2006, in response to such discourses of relative value, an organization named Yuva Bharati was founded in the Bay Area with the explicit aim of promoting US-based Indian classical dancers. The impetus for the founding of such an organization, as described to me, was to fight the perception that dancers from India were "better" dancers. As one informant and founding member explained, "Our daughters train long and hard here, but they will never be recruited to perform for high-profile events. Those engagements only go to dancers from India. We are trying to create a space that supports dancers trained in the States and stop making them feel like their art is only valued second to the dancers from India."[35] It is important to note that over the decade of programming this organization has presented, the fare has been consistent and homogenous. The only styles of dance presented are those understood as Hindu and classical. To date, there has yet to be a male dancer in their lineup.[36]

I observed how such value judgments worked across transnational borders and within broader Hindu nationalist imperatives in Chennai. "The Season"[37] in Chennai occurs in December and during my fieldwork I had a chance to see how the KC levied its wealth and resources to put its best foot forward during the most prestigious performance time slots on the most hallowed stages, like the Madras Music Academy. During rehearsals, I observed the interactions between the wealthy NRIs and the dancers from India who didn't live in Chennai, but

---

35 Personal correspondence with the author.

36 See http://yuvabharati.org. The amount of NRI wealth that is funneled into representing India in the United States through Indian dance is on the ascent, especially in places like the San Francisco Bay Area. See, for example, Silicon Andhra, a 501(c)(3) organization that supports dance teachers from India to travel to the US and train young women. This organization recently expanded into a degree-granting institution. See https://www.siliconandhra.org/en/.

37 The Season, also referred to as the Music Season, takes place every December in Chennai and lasts about six weeks. During this period, there are increases in international tourism, with many visiting to see the music and dance performances held at local art houses known as *sabhas*. See the newly instituted website for the most recent schedule, http://www.chennaidecemberseason.com, accessed December 29, 2016.

converged upon the stern concrete rehearsal space over the course of the week leading up to the performance.

I was awestruck by the contrast between the two sets of dancers. The dancers from India were lithe: their bodies strong and sinewy and pliable in ways the American dancers were not. I caught myself idealizing the Indian bodies and their aesthetic appeal in a way that reminded me of why Yuva Bharati existed in the first place. My eyes were drawn to one particular dancer and the way she executed one particular movement: a movement which was the cause of much consternation among dancers in my home studio in Houston, Texas.

Figures 4 and 5: Tham-that-tha-din-ha, dancer: Yashoda Thakore, 2020. Photos by Rumya S. Putcha.

The *adavu* or step is colloquially known as sit-stretch, but it's official name or *nadaka* in the KC vernacular is *tham-that-tha-din-ha*.[38] Physically, this movement, as a sequence in the KC training regimen is a test of athletic ability. Only the strongest-bodied dancers can execute the entire sequence in which there are multiple renditions of this movement with differing hand-gestures. This sequence tests core and quadricep strength in a way that dancers know well, but for which we never explicitly train.

That day, as I watched a group of dancers from the United States rehearse alongside a group of dancers from the subcontinent, I could see the distinction between the two sets of bodies. There was a fluidity to the way the female Indian

---

38   There is an equivalent to this *adavu* in Bharatanatyam, though it is executed differently, with a twist.

dancers executed this movement especially in comparison to the way their male counterparts did. The American dancers, I realized, looked more like the men. Their torsos were straighter and the labor and power of their legs was apparent. In other words, the women from the United States read as more masculine in that space because the strength and conditioning of their bodies was visible.

Our *guru*, who was leading the rehearsal, could see the difference too, and began correcting the American dancers, telling them they looked "like men" in their expression of this particular *adavu*. He mocked them and I felt my face grow hot with shame and anger as he looked to the other India-based dancers for support in treating these young women as though their inability to affect a specific femininity was a sign of some great failing. I felt especially for the young dancers in this group, particularly the youngest who was no more than 14. I had gotten to know this young woman well, and I knew that she was not only a dancer, but also a competitive tennis player in the United States. Her body betrayed her tennis training, especially in the way she was able to recruit her quadricep strength and push up from the ground with force. Her athleticism betrayed her dancerly role in that space, and unapologetically demonstrated the sheer muscle strength of her legs. She was a dancer, to be sure, but she was also an American-born sportswoman: her body was powerful and it showed. She looked so confused and hurt in that moment when Master scolded her—she was executing the movement perfectly and she was too young to understand that it was her gender expression that had come under fire.

Dance, Gender, and Religion

Only male bodies are entitled to demonstrate power at the KC; this was something I came to understand well. Despite performing the exact same movements to the exact same tempo, female dancers at the KC are expected to mask the labor taking place by and through their bodies. This masking process is often glossed as *lasyam* or grace, something that is never required of a male body making the same movements. The inverse of *lasyam* in dance vernacular is *tandavam*, which loosely translates as vigor. Put simply, *lasyam* requires all the same movements as *tandavm* but with softened edges.

Functionally, the softening of the body's athletic output is most visible in the initiation of motion and the seamlessness between the start and ending of movement phrases. This masking process extends in ways both subtle and explicit and often includes body shaming against women and commentary like what I heard that day. In the studio, it usually results in telling the American women dancing that they do not dance like Indian women; that their femininity is somehow lacking. Over the course of my life, especially during my time in

Chennai, I came to understand which parts of my body needed to be leveraged more or less to mark my gender identity and, in turn, how this gender work translated to heteronormative Hindu affect.

In Chennai, the part of the body that indexed gender and sexuality most acutely was my hips. The positioning of my hips demonstrated my gender and the movement of my hips did the work of eliciting sexuality. Male dancers are not expected to over-exaggerate their hips, but in a fascinating and revealing performance at an annual tourism festival, I observed a male guru of mine dancing with a woman in unison. During this performance, as in many others where a man and a woman dance together (see below), the male body position mirrors the female.

I didn't think much of their synchronicity at the time; if anything, such an aesthetic was to be expected. Female body comportment is the default setting in nominally Hindu dance styles, especially Bharatanatyam and Kuchipudi. After the performance, however, as I congratulated my guru, he asked me quietly, betraying a sense of shame and self-consciousness, "do I look too much like a woman when I dance?" Shocked at the vulnerability of his question at the time, I did what I thought would seem most supportive and batted away his concern. I quickly and overzealously reassured him that his masculinity remained fully intact and that he needn't worry about seeming emasculated. His dance was graceful and beautiful and that was what made him a man.

Yet, that question undeniably raised a number of questions about what kinds of work gender is doing in spaces that are so fully saturated with sexual affect and religiosity inscribed on cis-gendered female bodies. His concern was particularly paradoxical since the style he was presenting, Kuchipudi, is best known for its tradition of female impersonation. This legacy, known as *stri vesam*, connects across performance idioms and, as many scholars of theatre and dance have noted, is a symptom of hyper-patriarchy, Brahminism, and homo/transphobia under the logics of Hindu nationalism.[39] The practice of female impersonation is central to narratives of Kuchipudi's contribution to Indian cultural memory and relies on an axiom in Hindu nationalism: Brahmin men adjudicate on how female bodies should look and act. In the process of such legislation, cis-gender female comportment becomes codified and stylized. I, like a generation of dancers before me, learned how to affect womanhood

---

39   See, i.e., Kathryn Hansen, "Stri Bhumika: Female Impersonators and Actresses on the Parsi Stage," *Economic and Political Weekly* 33, no. 35 (1998): 2291–300; Hansen, "Making Women Visible: Gender and Race Cross-Dressing in the Parsi Theatre," *Theatre Journal* 51, no. 2 (1999): 127–47; Davesh Soneji, "Performing Satyabhama: Text, Context, Memory and Mimesis in Telugu-Speaking South India" (Ph.D. diss., McGill University, 2004).

Figure 6: M.V.N. Murthy and Priya Sunderesan. Photo Courtesy: Avinash Pasricha.

from women who learned from men who built their artistic careers seducing audiences as women. The KC maintains this kyriarchical pedagogy, particularly in the affecting of cis-female heterosexuality. These structures of oppression, especially around the idea of what kinds of behavior translate into desirable dancerly affect, reveal a great deal about what kinds of work gender performance does on and off stage. Simply put, classical dance cultures, by virtue of their primary gendered affective purpose, are, by definition, examples of religious nationalism and its transnational consequences. Furthermore, the concomitant discourses of aspirational Hindu womanhood à la wifehood, which appear through performance cultures, require us to see the production and control of sexuality as legitimated sex work.[40] Wifehood, by virtue of its implication in institutional dance cultures, is simply a destination and the journey is for sale.

Conclusion

As a way to bring my own web of cogitation on dance, womanhood, and religion to a close, I returned to what, in many ways, started it: I watched *Swarnaka-malam* again. This time as a grown woman, an academic who has slowly disaggregated a lifetime of dance training from its ethnographic potential, and the heuristics of diasporic film-viewing from the nostalgia and desire it used to (and sometimes does still) evoke. At the end of the film, before Meenakshi decides to forgo a life abroad with all the chances and risks it offers, she reads a letter that Chandrasekhar has written her. In it, he exhorts her to "be happy." All he asks is that if she ever thinks of him when she dances, that she remembers who she really is. The message, that happiness is achievable, but at odds with an intact sense of identity, while somehow romantic at an earlier time in my life, now only speaks to a deep and abiding sense of pressure that many women—not only dancers—experience under the reductive and intractable identity politics of postcolonial and transnational forms of nationalism. We are offered two options, to adhere to or to abdicate, both of which require us to understand a Hindu identification and its expression through dance as something forced upon us.

Sara Ahmed once observed how happiness is used to justify oppression and that feminist work over the past century has primarily attempted to disabuse us of the idea that working towards happiness leads to it. If being a happy Indian woman means training one's body and emotions to look and feel and uphold Hindu heteropatriarchy, so goes the narrative at least, what kinds of feminist interventions are available to us? I am reminded and indebted here to Saba Mahmood's work, which has demonstrated that women can and do find personal and political ways to resist, even under extreme conditions. And so I have come to see the Indian dancer as an athlete and her athleticism as a form of resistance to Hindu nationalist imperatives, on the one hand, and a symptom of challenging uncomplicated notions of democratic plurality in transnational settings, on the other. The standard framings of her athletic body as a sexualized

---

40   See Subir K. Kole, "From 'Veshyas' to 'Entertainment Workers': Evolving Discourses of Bodies, Rights, and Prostitution in India," *Asian Politics & Policy* 1, no. 2 (2009): 255–81; Jyoti Puri, Woman, Body, Desire in Post-Colonial India Narratives of Gender and Sexuality (New York: Routledge, 2002).

icon can and do lead to new forms of rape culture and objectification, this is true, but for the women I have danced with over the years, both in India and in the US, dance and its physicality provides a powerful sense of bodily autonomy for the individual who, like the tennis-player-dancer I met in Chennai, relishes the feeling of her body and its power. In the end, this is how body endures as a site of resistance for the individual, in spite of, or perhaps precisely because of, broader and often contradictory political imperatives.

References

Abu-Lughod, Lila. "Can There Be a Feminist Ethnography?" *Women and Performance: A Journal of Feminist Theory* 5, no. 1 (1990): 6–27.
———. "Do Muslim Women Really Need Saving? Anthropological Reflections on Cultural Relativism and its Others." *American Anthropologist* 104, no. 3 (2002): 783–90.
Ahmed, Sara. *The Cultural Politics of Emotion.* Durham, NC: Duke University Press, 2004.
———. *Queer Phenomenology: Orientations, Objects, Others.* Durham, NC: Duke University Press, 2006.
———. *The Promise of Happiness.* Durham, NC: Duke University Press, 2010.
———. *Living a Feminist Life.* Durham, NC: Duke University Press, 2016.
Alexander, M. Jacqui, and Chandra Talpade Mohanty, eds. *Feminist Genealogies, Colonial Legacies, Democratic Futures.* New York: Routledge, 1997.
———. "Cartographies of Knowledge and Power: Transnational Feminism as Radical Praxis." In *Critical Transnational Feminist Praxis*, edited by Amanda Lock Swarr and Richa Nagar, 23–45. Albany: SUNY Press, 2010.
Alter, Joseph. *Yoga in Modern India: The Body Between Science and Philosophy.* Princeton: Princeton University Press, 2004.
Alcoff, Linda. "The Problem of Speaking for Others." *Cultural Critique* 20 (1992): 5–32.
Arondekar, Anjali. *For the Record: On Sexuality and the Colonial Archive.* Durham, NC: Duke University Press, 2009.
Banerjee, Sikata. *Gender, Nation and Popular Film in India: Globalizing Muscular Nationalism.* Abingdon: Routledge, 2017.
Basu, Srimati, and Lucinda Ramberg. *Conjugality Unbound: Sexual Economies, State Regulation, and the Marital Form in India.* New Delhi: Women Unlimited, 2015.
Berlant, Lauren. *Cruel Optimism.* Durham, NC: Duke University Press, 2011.
Brownmiller, Susan. *Against Our Will: Men, Women and Rape.* New York: Simon and Schuster, 1975.

Chakravarty, Uma. *Gendering Caste Through a Feminist Lens*. Calcutta: Stree, 2003.

———. *Thinking Gender, Doing Gender: Feminist Scholarship and Practice Today*. New Delhi: Orient Blackswan, 2016.

Chakravorty, Pallabi. *Bells of Change: Kathak Dance, Women, and Modernity in India*. Kolkata: Seagull Books, 2008.

Chatterjee, Partha. "The Nationalist Resolution of the Women's Question." In *Recasting Women: Essays in Indian Colonial History*, edited by Kumkum Sangari and Sudesh Vaid, 233–53. New Delhi: Kali for Women, 1989.

Connell, Noreen and Cassandra Wilson. *Rape: The First Sourcebook for Women*. New York: New American Library, 1974.

Dwyer, Rachel. *Filming the Gods: Religion and Indian Cinema*. New York: Routledge, 2006.

———. *Pleasure and the Nation: The History, Politics and Consumption of Popular Culture in India*. New Delhi: Oxford University Press, 2006.

Foucault, Michel. *The History of Sexuality, Vol. 1*, translated by Robert Hurley. New York: Vintage Books, 1990 [1976].

Foucault, Michel, Luther H. Martin, Huck Gutman, and Patrick H. Hutton. *Technologies of the Self: A Seminar with Michel Foucault*. Amherst: University of Massachusetts Press, 1988.

Gopal, Sangita, and Sujata Moorti, eds. *Global Bollywood: Travels of Hindi Song and Dance*. Minneapolis: University of Minnesota Press, 2008.

Gopinath, Gayatri. *Impossible Desires: Queer Diasporas and South Asian Public Cultures*. Durham, NC: Duke University Press, 2005.

Grewal, Inderpal. *Transnational America: Feminisms, Diasporas, Neoliberalisms*. Durham, NC: Duke University Press, 2005.

Grewal, Inderpal, and Caren Kaplan. *Scattered Hegemonies: Postmodernity and Transnational Feminist Practices*. Minneapolis: University of Minnesota Press, 2006 [1994].

Hansen, Kathryn. "Stri Bhumika: Female Impersonators and Actresses on the Parsi Stage." *Economic and Political Weekly* 33, no. 35 (1998): 2291–300.

———. "Making Women Visible: Gender and Race Cross-Dressing in the Parsi Theatre." *Theatre Journal* 51, no. 2 (1999): 127–47.

Himabindu, B.L., Radhika Arora and N.S. Prashanth. "Whose Problem Is It Anyway? Crimes against Women in India." *Global Health Action* 7, no. 1 (2014). https://doi.org/10.3402/gha.v7.23718.

hooks, bell. *Black Looks: Race and Representation*. 2nd ed. New York: Routledge, 2015.

Iyer, Usha. "Stardom Ke Peeche Kya Hai? / What Is behind the Stardom? Madhuri Dixit, the Production Number, and the Construction of the Female

Star Text in 1990s Hindi Cinema," *Camera Obscura* 30, no. 3 (2015): 129–59. https://doi.org/10.1215/02705346-3160674.

Kole, Subir K. "From 'Veshyas' to 'Entertainment Workers': Evolving Discourses of Bodies, Rights, and Prostitution in India," *Asian Politics & Policy* 1, no. 2 (2009): 255–81.

Kumar, Sanjeev. "Constructing the Nation's Enemy: Hindutva, Popular Culture and the Muslim 'Other' in Bollywood Cinema," *Third World Quarterly* 34, no. 3 (2013): 458–69.

Mahmood, Saba. *Politics of Piety: The Islamic Revival and the Feminist Subject.* Princeton: Princeton University Press, 2012.

Mankekar, Purnima. *Screening Culture, Viewing Politics: An Ethnography of Television, Womanhood, and Nation in Postcolonial India.* Durham, NC: Duke University Press, 1999.

Mankekar, Purnima, and Louisa Schein. *Media, Erotics, and Transnational Asia.* Durham, NC: Duke University Press, 2012.

Massey, Reginald, and Jamila Massey. *The Music of India.* New Dehli: Abhinav Publications, 1996.

Meduri, Avanthi. "Bharatha Natyam—What Are You?" *Asian Theatre Journal* 5, no. 1 (Spring 1988): 1–22.

———. "Nation, Woman, Representation: The Sutured History of the Devadasi and Her Dance." Ph.D. diss., New York University, 1996.

Minh-ha, Trinh T. 2009. *Woman, Native, Other: Writing Postcoloniality and Feminism.* Bloomington: Indiana University Press, 2009 [1989]

Mohanty, Chandra Talpade. *Feminism without Borders: Decolonizing Theory, Practicing Solidarity.* Durham, NC: Duke University Press, 2003.

Murty, Madhavi. "Representing Hindutva: Nation, Religion and Masculinity in Indian Popular Cinema, 1990 to 2003." *Popular Communication* 7, no. 4 (2009): 267–81.

Nandy, Ashis. *The Secret Politics of Our Desires: Innocence, Culpability, and Indian Popular Cinema.* New York: St. Martin's Press, 1998.

Narayan, Kirin. "How Native is a 'Native' Anthropologist?" *American Anthropologist* 95, no. 3 (1993): 671–86.

Ong, Aihwa. "Colonialism and Modernity: Feminist Re-Presentations of Women in Non-Western Societies." *Inscriptions* 3–4 (1988): 79–93.

———. "State Versus Islam; Malay Families, Women's Bodies, and the Body Politic in Malaysia." *American Ethnologist* 17, no. 2 (1990): 258–76.

O'Shea, Janet. *At Home in the World.* Middletown, CT: Wesleyan University Press, 2007.

Peterson, Indira, and Davesh Soneji, eds. *Performing Pasts: Reinventing the Arts in Modern South India.* New Delhi: Oxford University Press, 2008.

Phillips, Mark, Mostofian, Fargol, Jetly, Rajeev, Puthukudy, Nazar, Madden, Kim, and Bhandari, Mohit. "Media Coverage of Violence against Women in India: A Systematic Study of a High Profile Rape Case." Bᴍᴄ *Women's Health* 15, no. 3 (January 22, 2015). https://doi.org/10.1186/s12905-015-0161-x.

Prasad, Madiraju M. *Ideology of the Hindi Film: A Historical Construction.* 6th ed. New Delhi: Oxford University Press, 2008.

Puar, Jasbir K. *Terrorist Assemblages: Homonationalism in Queer Times.* Durham, NC: Duke University Press, 2007.

Puri, Jyoti. *Woman, Body, Desire in Post-Colonial India Narratives of Gender and Sexuality.* New York: Routledge, 2002.

Putcha, Rumya S. "Between History and Historiography: The Origins of Classical Kuchipudi Dance." *Dance Research Journal* 45, no. 3 (2013): 1–20

———. "Dancing in Place: Mythopoetics and the Production of History in Kuchipudi." *Yearbook for Traditional Music* 47 (2015): 1–26.

Qureshi, Regula Burckhardt. "In Search of Begum Akhtar: Patriarchy, Poetry, and Twentieth-Century Indian Music." *World of Music* 43, no. 1 (2001): 97–137.

Ramaswamy, Sumathi. *The Goddess and the Nation: Mapping Mother India.* Durham, NC: Duke University Press, 2010.

Rao, Anupama, ed. *Gender, Caste, and the Imagination of Equality.* New Delhi: Women Unlimited, 2018.

Rege, Sharmila. "The Hegemonic Appropriation of Sexuality: The Case of the lavani Performers of Maharashtra." *Contributions to Indian Sociology* 29, no. 1–2 (1995): 23–38.

Sachdeva, Shweta. "In Search of the Tawa'if in History: Courtesans, Nautch Girls and Celebrity Entertainers in India (1720s–1920s)." Ph.D. diss., SOAS, University of London, 2008.

Sarkar, Tanika. *Hindu Wife, Hindu Nation: Community, Religion, and Cultural Nationalism.* Bloomington: Indiana University Press, 2010.

Sedgwick, Eve Kosofsky. *Touching Feeling: Affect, Pedagogy, Performativity.* Durham, NC: Duke University Press, 2006.

Shandilya, Krupa. "Nirbhaya's Body: The Politics of Protest in the Aftermath of the 2012 Delhi Gang Rape." *Gender & History* 27, no. 2 (2015): 465–86.

Sinha, Mrinalini. "Gender in the Critiques of Colonialism and Nationalism: Locating the 'Indian Woman.'" In *Feminism and History,* edited by Joan Wallach Scott, 477–504. Oxford: Oxford University Press, 1996.

———. *Specters of Mother India: The Global Restructuring of an Empire.* Durham, NC: Duke University Press, 2006.

Soneji, Davesh. "Performing Satyabhama: Text, Context, Memory and Mimesis in Telugu-Speaking South India." Ph.D. diss., McGill University, 2004.

———, ed. *Bharatanatyam: A Reader.* New Delhi: Oxford University Press, 2010.

———. *Unfinished Gestures: Devadasis, Memory, and Modernity in South India.* Chicago: University of Chicago Press, 2011.

Srinivasan, Amrit. "Temple 'Prostitution' and Community Reform: An Examination of the Ethnographic, Historical and Textual Context of the Devadasi of Tamil Nadu, South India." Ph.D. diss., Cambridge University, 1984.

———. "Reform and Revival: The Devadasi and Her Dance." *Economic and Political Weekly* 20, no. 44 (1985): 1869–1876.

Srinivasan, Priya. *Sweating Saris: Indian Dance as Transnational Labor.* Philadelphia: Temple University Press, 2012.

Sunder Rajan, Rajeswari. *Real and Imagined Women: Gender, Culture, and Postcolonialism.* London: Routledge, 1993.

———. *Signposts: Gender Issues in Post-Independence India.* New Brunswick, NJ: Rutgers University Press, 2001.

Swarr, Amanda Lock, and Richa Nagar, eds. *Critical Transnational Feminist Praxis.* Albany: SUNY Press, 2010.

Thota, Katyayani, "Stage to Screen, and Back: A Study of the Dialogue between Kuchipudi and Telugu Cinema." Ph.D. diss., University of Hyderabad, 2016.

Virdi, Jyotika. *The Cinematic Imagination: Indian Popular Films as Social History.* New Brunswick, NJ: Rutgers University Press, 2003.

Visweswaran, Kamala. *Fictions of Feminist Ethnography.* Minneapolis: University of Minnesota Press, 1994.

Filmography

Sankarabharanam, 1980, directed by Kasinathuni Viswanath. Distributed by Poornodaya Movie Creations.

Swarnakamalam, 1988, directed by Kasinathuni Viswanath. Distributed by Poornodaya Movie Creations.

Part 4:
Sonic Implications of Political Changes

Music Activism in Serbia
at the Turn of the Millennium
Counterpublics, Citizenship, and Participatory Art

Milena Dragićević Šešić and Julija Matejić

Abstract: This paper explores subaltern cultural counterpublics in Serbia in the last three *decades*, through different forms of performative and participatory music activism: from radio activism, public noise, and performances in public spaces during the 1990s, to self-organized choirs in the 2000s and 2010s. By referring to the concept of citizenship, it emphasizes the importance of the relationship between politicality and performance in the public sphere. Analyzed case studies have shown how subaltern counterpublics brought together aesthetical, ethical, and intellectual positions, challenging principles imposed by the state and the church. Through music activism, cultural counterpublics addressed different social anomies: nationalism, xenophobia, social exclusion, hatred, civil rights, and social justice, becoming a focal point of civil resistance, a discursive arena that provokes and subverts mainstream politics. An interdisciplinary research framework has been achieved through linking music and cultural studies with political sciences and performance studies, then applied to the data gathered from the empirical ethnographic research covering several case studies.

Milena Dragićević Šešić is former President of the University of Arts in Belgrade and a professor of Cultural Policy & Management. A guest lecturer at numerous universities worldwide, Dragićević Šešić has published twenty books and 250 essays, which have been translated in seventeen languages. An expert for Unesco, EU, and the CoE, Dragićević Šešić was named a Commandeur dans l'Ordre des Palmes Academiques in 2002.

Julija Matejić is a Ph.D. candidate and teaching assistant at the University of Arts in Belgrade. Following her career as a pianist, Matejić has developed into a professional in the field of arts management. Her research interests include performativity in music, art in public space, post-memory, and sustainable development in the field of culture.

Buka u modi! (Noise in Fashion!)[1]

Introduction

This paper explores different forms of dissent and performative music activism in Serbia in the last three decades, developed in response to the breakup of Yugoslavia, the rise of nationalism, a series of armed conflicts during the 1990s, economic sanctions, and hyperinflation, as well as democratic changes and the never-ending transition to a market economy in the 2000s. This period is bordered by the first mass civic protest against Slobodan Milošević's oppressive regime (March 9, 1991) at its beginning and a series of Ne da(vi)mo Beograd (loosely translated: Don't Let Belgrade D(r)own)[2] manifestations and protests against the Belgrade Waterfront project[3] and the authoritarian rule of the current President Aleksandar Vučić and his governing Serbian Progressive Party (Sns) at its end. The authors mostly focus on music activism, public noise, and performances in public spaces during the 1990s, perceived as counterpublic participatory activist actions. The main research question is whether the dissenting intellectuals and artists succeeded in creating a parallel discursive and performative realm—so-called cultural counterpublics. This study is one of the rare examples of exploring and encompassing music within the counterpublic realm, given that most of the research in Serbia relating to counterpublics has been published in the fields of theatre, performance studies, or visual arts. Furthermore, the research focusing on music activism so far has been mostly conducted in the sphere of musicology; therefore, this paper is an attempt at making an interdisciplinary analysis by linking musical studies with political sciences and cultural studies.

---

1   A forceful and influential song by the Serbian new-wave and post-punk band *Disciplin A Kitschme* from 1990.

2   Don't Let Belgrade D(r)own advocates sustainable city development, urban and cultural policies, and citizens' participation in urban development, thus fighting against the appropriation of public spaces in a non-transparent manner for private interests.

3   An urban project designed by the Abu-Dhabi-based Eagle Hills, currently transforming the centrally located Savamala district into Serbia's Dubai. The project has sparked the revolt of a large number of experts and citizens since 2014.

Context

We may say that the musical chronotope[4] of Serbia in the 1990s was embedded in the dissolution of the country (with hundreds of thousands of people killed and exiled), as well as the transformation of the ex-Yugoslav republics into new independent states, which resulted not only in redefining separate national identities and developing staunch pacifist and anti-nationalist movements, but also in rethinking the concepts of civil society and citizenship as such. While the government created a new state—the Federal Republic of Yugoslavia[5]—it was set on maintaining the Yugoslav identity. At the same time, it was looking for ways to integrate the Montenegrin identity into a "wider" Serbian, as if it was a part of Serbian identity.

The civil society was polarized between two distinctive worlds. On one side, nationalist movements (even paramilitary forces) were calling for the eradication of the Yugoslav, therefore, the formation of the Serbian identity which had to include all ethnic Serbs living across the former Yugoslavia. On the other side, the pacifist independent cultural scene, with its cosmopolitan *urbazona*, introduced the art of protest and rebellion in the public sphere based on the concept of citizenship by questioning the official policies and practices imposed by the state. Oppositional intellectuals, artists, and civil-society organizations—often labeled as Other Serbia—were predominantly excluded from public institutions and media. Consequently, they had a crucial role in creating an alternative space for civic resistance and dissent.

In the field of music, the breakup(s) of Yugoslavia(s) sparked the so-called music war, bearing in mind that the "hierarchy of musical differences that was constructed as a tool of racial/cultural separation from the common state" heavily contributed to it.[6]

Turbo-folk, as a musical genre combining traditional *melos*, Greek, and Oriental musical elements (already existing in neo-folk music) with technological advances and electronic sounds, emerged in Serbia in the 1990s and has

---

4   Mikhail Bakhtin, "Forms of Time and of the Chronotope in the Novel," in *The Dialogic Imagination*, ed. Michael Holquist (Austin: University of Texas Press, 1981), 84–258.

5   The *Savezna Republika Jugoslavija* was a federation of two constituent republics, Serbia and Montenegro, created in 1992 that claimed to be the only successor state to the Socialist Federative Republic of Yugoslavia (today often referred to as *ex-Yugoslavia*), with its six constituent republics (Bosnia and Herzegovina, Croatia, Macedonia, and Slovenia, in addition to the two above).

6   Tomislav Longinović, "Music Wars: Blood and Song at the End of Yugoslavia," in *Music and the Racial Imagination*, ed. Ronald M. Radano and Philip V. Bohlman (Chicago: University of Chicago Press, 2001), 629.

provoked numerous controversial theories. However, the majority of social theorists deal with turbo-folk as a socio-political phenomenon close to the regime,
neglecting music activism and musical counterpublics. Turbo-folk has usually
been linked to the pro/anti Milošević dichotomy, to the disintegration of the
state, war(s), nationalism, kitsch, and moral downfall. The official policy imposed
by the state through the public radio and television system not only praised
and promoted this genre,[7] but also introduced the Warrior Chic iconography[8]
and presented pop music "in a different, Westernised light [...]. Pop and rock
music became engrafted into seemingly innocuous representations of Serbian
patriotism, or 'civic nationalism.'"[9]

Even though we could say that the ideological conflicts triggered by popular music reached their peak during the 1990s, this phenomenon was not
unique, neither for this particular timeframe, nor for Serbia as a geographic
context.[10] The modernization of society (through its historical processes of
socio-economic liberalization, industrialization, and urbanization) was usually
equated with the erasure of the oriental heritage targeted by the European-
oriented urban elite.[11] The development of the music industry in Serbia in the
1970s only intensified this division; popular (pro-Western) music was promoted
as something urban, as music intended for the high and upper middle class,

---

7   Milena Dragićević Šešić, "Media war and hatred: the role of media in preparation
     of conflicts," *Kultura* 93/94 (1994): 191–207; Dragićević Šešić, *Neofolk kultura:
     publika i njene zvezde* (Novi Sad: Izdavačka knjižarnica Zorana Stojanovića, 1994);
     Eric Gordy, *The Culture of Power in Serbia: Nationalism and the Destruction of Al-
     ternatives (Post-Communist Cultural Studies)* (University Park, PA: Pennsylvania
     State University Press, 1999); Ivana Kronja, *Smrtonosni sjaj: masovna psihologija
     i estetika turbo-folka* (Belgrade: Tehnokratija, 2000); Stef Jansen, "The Streets
     of Belgrade. Urban Space and Protest Identities in Serbia," *Political Geography*
     20 (2001): 30–55; Radovan Kupres, *Sav taj folk* (TV documentary, Belgrade:
     Television B92, 2004).
8   Ratka Marić, "Značenje potkulturnih stilova—istraživanja omladinskih potkultu-
     ra" (Ph.D. diss., University of Belgrade Faculty of Political Science, 1996).
9   Srđan Atanasovski, "Recycled Music for Banal Nation: The Case of Serbia 1999–
     2010," in *Relocating Popular Music: Pop Music, Culture and Identity*, ed. Ewa
     Mazierska and Georgina Gregory (London: Palgrave Macmillan, 2015), 84.
10   The continuous and constant tension between Eastern-Asian and Western-
     European influences in Serbian music culture can be traced since the mid-
     nineteenth century in different historical settings, starting with the liberation
     from the Ottoman Empire through the Kingdom of Serbs, Croats, and Slovenes
     and the Socialist Federal Republic of Yugoslavia (especially after the "Tito-Stalin
     split" and the opening of the country to the West).
11   Miša Đurković, "Ideološki i politički sukobi oko popularne muzike u Srbiji,"
     Filozofija i Društvo 25 (2004): 274–75.

while a Yugoslav neo-folk (the pop-folk style that preceded turbo-folk) was considered primitive, as music of the lower middle class, working class, and rural population.[12] What is more, turbo-folk is to be understood only as a Serbian version of a Balkan-wide musical phenomenon and post-socialist trend.[13]

Therefore, theorists usually do not define turbo-folk as a music genre, but as an ideological determinant. According to Miša Đurković, there are three different standpoints on turbo-folk: 1) the traditionalists, nationalists, and cultural conservatives (such as composer Zoran Hristić, singer Pavle Aksentijević, and singer Miroslav Ilić), who perceive turbo-folk as an Islamic attack on Serbian spiritual traditions; 2) the so-called globalists and cosmopolitans (such as journalist Petar Luković, sociologist Eric Gordy, and Milena Dragićević Šešić) who also see turbo-folk as a threat to Serbian culture, (mis)used by Milosević's government for nationalist mobilization; and 3) the new Trotskyist leftists gathered around the Center for History and Theory of Culture (Citok) and the magazine *Prelom*, according to whom turbo-folk is just another example of "globalism," while the first two groups are considered cultural racists bothered by its oriental elements.[14] A group of younger theorists gathered around *Prelom* has considered turbo-folk as "populaire," citizen-driven, and authentically subversive towards the socialist neo-folk music, even though it is controlled by the official music industry.[15]

Having in mind that the "culture wars" triggered by music are usually only ideological—as an infighting between the advocates of different musical subcultures—we strongly believe and would like to stress that such conflicts in Serbia during the 1990s progressed into truly political music activism (which will be demonstrated in the examples hereinafter).

On the one hand, turbo-folk as the most broadcasted music genre was (mis)used by Milošević's regime as a means for holding on to power. Such

---

12 Đurković, "Ideološki i politički sukobi oko popularne muzike u Srbiji," 277.

13 Archer perceives Balkan pop-folk styles as an Ottoman cultural legacy linked to the wider discourse of Balkanism and otherness opposed to a "European" and cosmopolitan society; Rory Archer, "Assessing Turbofolk Controversies: Popular Music between the Nation and the Balkans," *Southeastern Europe* 36 (2012): 178. He argues that there have emerged numerous different pop-folk styles across the Balkan Peninsula, all being criticized by cultural elites on similar grounds—including *muzika popullore* in Albania, *muzică orientală* or *manele* in Romania and *chalga* in Bulgaria (Archer, 201). See also Todorova, Bakić-Hayden, Bjelić and Savić; cited in Archer.

14 Đurković, "Ideološki i politički sukobi oko popularne muzike u Srbiji," 280–82.

15 Branislav Dimitrijević, "Ovo je savremena umetnost: turbofolk kao radikalni performans," *Prelom, Journal for Images and Politics* 2/3 (2002): 94–101; Boris Buden, "Kad budem ustaša i Jugoslaven," in *Barikade* (Zagreb: Arkzin, 1997), 266–71.

an approach was excessively supported by newly established private media stations (TV Pink, TV Palma, Radio Košava) and nightclubs (e.g. Madona, owned by Milošević's son), as well as diaspora-driven private music companies, such as Gastarbeiter and refugee music markets,[16] that soon became the significant financiers investing in this phenomenon. Conversely, turbo-folk was also rejected by the democratic opposition, upper-middle-class counterpublics, and urban radio stations due to its vulgarity and banality of both music and lyrics.

This cultural and political polarization in Serbia was evident in the field of music much more than in other art forms. Emerging civil society organizations (such as the Center for Cultural Decontamination or Czkd and the Rex Cultural Center) and few public cultural institutions (including the Cultural Center of Belgrade and House of Youth)[17] gathered around the Belgrade Circle[18], Radio B92, the daily newspaper Borba, and the two radio stations that were repeatedly gaining and losing their independence (Radio Index and Radio Studio B), forming a counterpublic realm known for its performative, participative, and carnivalesque actions.[19]

During particular periods of media censorship introduced after the protests in March 1991, and especially during the ban on broadcasting talk formats on the radio, music genres gained an "informative role" (mostly Western rock and punk), being the only messenger of the voices of dissent. Throughout the Nato airstrikes on Serbia in 1999, when the Radio B92 was deprived of its broadcasting equipment, the internet had already become an alternative space for the censored radio stations and the Association of Independent Electronic

---

16   Ljerka Vidić Rasmussen, "The Southern Wind of Change: Style and the Politics of Identity in Pre-war Yugoslavia," in *Retuning Culture: Musical Changes in Central and Eastern Europe*, ed. Mark Slobin (Durham, NC: Duke University Press, 1996), 99–117.

17   At least until 1993 when the re-étatisation of the cultural system definitively abolished the remnants of Yugoslav participatory governance (the self-government model that enabled as much autonomy from the party as cultural workers were brave enough to take). See V.K. Ćurgus, *Kultura vlasti—indeks smena i zabrana. The Culture of the Power—An Index of Suspensions and Prohibitions* (Belgrade: Radio B92, 1994).

18   The Belgrade Circle is an Ngo founded in Belgrade in 1992 by a group of dissident intellectuals gathered against the nationalism, xenophobia, and politics of the war during the 1990s. It hosted lectures of renowned Serbian and international intellectuals, including Jacques Derrida, Christopher Norris, and Richard Rorty.

19   See Mikhail Bakhtin, *Rabelais and His World* (Bloomington: Indiana University Press, 1984); Milena Dragićević Šešić, "The Street as Political Space: Walking as Protest, Grafitti, and the Student Carnivalization of Belgrade," *New Theatre Quarterly* 17, no. 1 (2001): 74–86. https://doi.org/10.1017/S0266464X00014342.

Media (ANEM) to disseminate information and music, with the support of the European media activist community.[20]

Theoretical Framework:
Art, Citizenship, and Cultural Counterpublics

In this paper we would like to offer an interpretation of subaltern cultural counterpublics[21] as a specific artistic chronotope in Serbia at the turn of the millennium that used different participatory artistic practices as the primary means of their expression and public spaces as places of their representation. Thus, we use the multi-perspectivist approach[22] by combining notions and concepts from different disciplines: political sciences and concepts of citizenship, public sphere, and urban commons,[23] geopolitics,[24] counterpublics and subaltern cultural counterpublics,[25] through performance studies interconnecting body, movements, performances, citizenship, and participation,[26]

---

20 Robin Hamman, "Radio B-92 in Belgrade Harnesses the Power of a Media Activist Community During the War to Keep Broadcasting Despite Terrestrial Ban," in *Community Informatics: Enabling Communities with Information and Communications Technologies*, ed. Michael Gurstein (London: Idea Group Publishing, 2000), 561–67.

21 Nancy Fraser, "Rethinking the Public Sphere: A Contribution to the Critique of Actually Existing Democracy," in *Habermas and the Public Sphere*, ed. Craig J. Calhoun (Cambridge: MIT press, 1992), 109–42; Michael Warner, "Publics and Counterpublics," *Public Culture* 14, no. 1 (2002): 49–90.

22 Douglas Kellner, "Toward a Multiperspectival Cultural Studies," *Centennial Review* 36, no. 1 (1992), 5–41, https://www.jstor.org/stable/23739831.

23 Engin F. Isin and Patricia K. Wood, *Citizenship and Identity* (London: Sage Publications, 1999); Jens Kimmel, Till Gentzsch, and Sophie Bloemen, *Shared Spaces: New Paper on Urban Commons* (a research project and report by Commons Network & raumlaborberlin, 2018), https://www.commonsnetwork.org/wp-content/uploads/2018/11/SharedSpacesCommonsNetwork.pdf.

24 Dominique Moïsi, *The Geopolitics of Emotion: How Cultures of Fear, Humiliation, and Hope are Reshaping the World* (New York: Anchor Books, 2010).

25 Fraser, "Rethinking the Public Sphere"; Warner "Publics and Counterpublics."

26 Janelle Reinelt, "Performance at the Crossroads of Citizenship," in *The Grammar of Politics and Performance*, ed. Shirin Rai and Janelle Reinelt (New York: Routledge, 2015), 34–50; Bishnupriya Dutt, Janelle Reinelt, Shrinkhla Sahai, eds., *Gendered Citizenship: Manifestations and Performance* (London: Palgrave Macmillan, 2017) and particularly Shirin Rai, "The Dilemmas of Performative Citizenship," in *Gendered Citizenship: Manifestations and Performance*, 25–44; Patrice Pavis, *Dictionnaire de la performance et du theatre contemporain* (Paris: Armand Colin, 2014).

music activism,[27] urban studies,[28] memory studies,[29] and, finally, Bakhtin's concepts of chronotope and carnival that are so important for understanding the counterpublic realm and its performative, participative, and carnivalesque character. At the same time, this research takes into account numerous cultural, sociological, and musical studies related to the phenomena of art and activism in the 1990s in Serbia, from turbo-folk[30] to resistance and cultural dissent.[31]

In political theory, citizenship and identity are often perceived as antinomic principles; however, we need to recognize "the rise of new identities and claims for group rights as a challenge to the modern interpretation of universal citizenship."[32] This was also an issue in Serbia, from the standpoint of both government and civil society. During the 1990s, Other Serbia, a civil society cultural counterpublic, was a sort of "parallel discursive arena"[33] that advocated a kind of responsible, critical, "practicing" citizenship: "Citizenship is not an unmarked, universal status or role which can be equally possessed by all people. Rather, in our view, citizenship is a practice, and as such, it is

---

27   Mark Mattern, *Acting in Concert: Music, Community, and Political Action* (New Brunswick, NJ: Rutgers University Press, 1998); Žak Atali, *Buka: ogled o političkoj ekonomiji muzike* (Belgrade: Biblioteka XX vek, 2007).

28   Christian Borch and Martin Kornberger, eds., *Urban Commons: Rethinking the City* (Abingdon: Routledge, 2015); Peter J.M. Nas, ed., *Cities Full of Symbols: A Theory of Urban Space and Culture* (Leiden: Leiden University Press, 2011); Greg Richards and Robert Palmer, *Eventful Cities, Cultural Management and Urban Revitalisation* (Kidlington: Elsevier Science, 2010).

29   Pierre Nora, *Realms of Memory* (New York: Columbia University Press, 1996–1998).

30   Srđan Atanasovski, "Turbo-folk as 'Bad Music': Politics of Musical Valuing," in *Böse Macht Musik. Zur Ästhetik des Bösen in der Musik*, ed. Sara R. Falke and Katharina Wisotzki (Bielefeld: transcript, 2012), 157–72; Atanasovski "Rhythmanalysis of the Policescape: The Promise of an Ecological Turn in the Practice of Soundscape Studies," *Musicological Annual* 52, no. 2 (2016): 11–23; Dimitrijević, "Ovo je savremena umetnost"; Ljerka Vidić Rasmussen, "The Southern Wind of Change"; Đurković, "Ideološki i politički sukobi oko popularne muzike u Srbiji;" Archer, "Assessing Turbofolk Controversies."

31   Ćurgus, *The Culture of the Power*; Jana Dolečki, Senad Halilbašić, and Stephan Hulfeld, eds., *Theatre in the Context of the Yugoslav Wars* (London: Palgrave Macmillan, 2018); Rajko Maksimović, *Tako je to bilo 3: autobiografska sećanja (1990–2002), "Godine koje su pojele bubašvabe"* (Belgrade: Author's Edition, 2002); Marić, "Značenje potkulturnih stilova—istraživanja omladinskih potkultura"; Ana Hofman, *Novi život partizanskih pesama* (Belgrade: Biblioteka XX vek, 2016).

32   Isin and Wood, *Citizenship and Identity*, 4.

33   Fraser, "Rethinking the Public Sphere," 123.

embodied, enacted and performed through a range of actions and in a variety of settings."[34]

By introducing the concept of citizenship in performance theory—as an essential and constantly evolving component of democracy, underling its aspects of belonging, exclusion, role-playing, performing, representing, and social agency—Janelle Reinelt has emphasized the importance of the relationship between politicality and performance in the public sphere.[35] That is exactly how counterpublics in Serbia perceived citizenship: not as documents confirming their ethnic identity in a form of "a critical materiality of citizenship,"[36] but as a continuous practice of questioning and contestation realized within the public realm. Thus, numerous forms of alternative art were created in a dialogue with different social movements, as methods and tools of social struggle.

Increasingly, these alternative artistic practices and narratives went not only beyond genre boundaries but also outside of traditional cultural institutions. Civil and student protests in 1991, 1996–97, and 2000 were the most dramatic (both forceful and theatrical) examples of social activism through the arts—the so-called artivism in recent Serbian history.[37]

It is important to underscore that such artistic actions demanded not only reflexivity,[38] but also "interdisciplinary scholarship, creative practice and activism."[39] They embodied (mostly middle-class) cultural counterpublics that soon started feeling subaltern due to experienced repression, exclusion, and censorship (the so-called blacklists within the media and public institutions). Accordingly, the Serbian subaltern cultural counterpublic was a space "where members of subordinated social groups invent and circulate counter discourses to formulate oppositional interpretations of their identities, interests, and

---

34   Dutt et al., "Introduction," in *Gendered Citizenship*, 1.
35   Reinelt, "Performance at the Crossroads of Citizenship."
36   Rai, "The Dilemmas of Performative Citizenship," 26.
37   Aleksandar Brkić, *Cultural Policy Frameworks (Re)constructing National and Supranational Identities: The Balkans and The European Union* (Amsterdam: European Cultural Foundation, 2014), 164; Milena Dragićević Šešić, Julija Matejić and Aleksandar Brkić, "Mobilizing Urban Neighbourhoods: Artivism, Identity, and Cultural Sustainability," in *Cultural Sustainability in European Cities: Imagining Europolis*, ed. Svetlana Hristova, Milena Dragićević Šešić, and Nancy Duxbury (Oxon: Routledge, 2015), 193–205.
38   "Key to performance is reflexivity: to perform is to be aware of the act of doing something, and to show doing it. Performance always bears the traces of this reflexivity—it 'knows' it shows. Not all performance is confined to individual subjects—institutions also perform [...] [and] all performances are transactional—between the performers and the spectators or recipients of the act." Rai and Reinelt, eds., *The Grammar of Politics and Performance*, 4.
39   Dutt et al., "Introduction," in *Gendered Citizenship*, 2.

needs,"[40] succeeding in formulating a parallel public sphere that was influential in spite of all repression.

Citizens' activism through the arts was a new phenomenon, especially in Serbia. Even though the concept of civil society as an agent of democracy had been introduced in political theory and political movements already in the 1980s,[41] cultural/performance/music studies in Europe introduced the notion of citizenship and the role of civil society only in the 1990s. Understandably, in an environment of ethnic nationalist conflicts and social stumbling, with Serbian political and cultural authorities clamoring for at least *l'art pour l'art*, if not "patriotic" artistic contributions, opposition artists openly started to relate their profession to their civic responsibility.

Various artistic subaltern counterpublics have brought together the aesthetical, ethical, and intellectual positions that challenged the principles officially imposed by both the state and the church in the 1990s, including nationalism, xenophobia, patriarchal values, hate speech, and media manipulation. As the "strive for independence" temporarily silenced the Croatian and Slovenian scenes, a particularly strong counterpublic front emerged in Serbia, aggravated by the air attacks on Dubrovnik and Osijek in 1991. Only three days after the first bombing of Dubrovnik, the protest in front of the Presidency of Serbia on October 9, 1991, spawned the NGO Women in Black, one of the key anti-war organizations that has been leading protests in public spaces ever since, often in cooperation with the Dah theatre and other artists.

Apart from such direct political engagement against Serbian politics, cultural and music activism were (and still are) also aimed at different global social anomies of a present-day world: from consumerism and the "spectacularization" of society (including the festivalization of music life) to xenophobia and hatred towards the others (migrants, the LGBT population, women, etc.) as well as the denial of human rights in different regions of the world.

Both in theory and in practice, the concepts of artistic participation and countercultural artistic practices of rebellion emerged in the United States of America in the 1960s, comprising community art projects, murals, underground film productions, and processions led by the politically active Bread and Puppet Theatre, as well as diverse forms of the Theatre of the Oppressed (Augusto Boal). In Europe, artistic participation was developed mostly within the scope of public cultural policies (the democratization of culture, later cultural democracy)—e.g., through the process of the *animation socio-culturelle* in France, as well as community art in the United Kingdom (urban furniture, murals, mosaics, etc.).

---

40   Fraser, "Rethinking the Public Sphere," 123.
41   This initiated changes within youth political culture in Yugoslavia, particularly Slovenia, through such journals as *Mladina*, *Problemi*, etc.

The notion of (cultural) participation in socialist Yugoslavia was mostly linked to festivities, rituals, or certain types of well-planned state or city ceremonies. Ever since the Congress of Yugoslav Writers banned socialist realism in 1952, the direct instrumentalization of art was not so common. The attempts at dissent through the arts were sporadic in the 1960s and the 1970s and were mostly linked to the Yugoslav Black Wave film movement or the "ethnic rights" movements of the Croatian, Slovenian, and Serbian nationalist dissidents.[42]

In a more recent context, Patrice Pavis has described participation as an action aimed at a spectator that participates in the creation of scenic or social event, leaving behind his or her status of a passive observer.[43] The participatory process within artistic and cultural projects diminishes the distance between a spectator on one side and an artist on the other; once only a witness, a spectator becomes a participant and a co-creator.[44] According to Pavis, with the development of political theatre and happenings, audience participation has become more political, as artists engage spectators in order to help them become more independent, self-assured, critically aware, and socially responsible. As a result, participatory art practices are increasingly present in everyday life, depending on the contributions and even co-creation of random passers-by.

Whereas participatory art projects are common in theaters and museums—using the devised theatre methods, or with people often being invited to exhibit their own artifacts (as is the case with the Museum of Broken Relationships in Zagreb and the Museum of Yugoslavia in Belgrade)—participatory projects in the field of music are infrequent, most probably due to the widespread stereotype that people need to be musically educated in order to participate.

However, numerous philosophers, theorists, and political scientists have been pointing out the political dimensions of music. This assumption is based on countless empirical examples of both the uses and misuses of music for

---

42   The first book that raised such issues in Yugoslavia was *Mixed Media* by Bora Ćosić. Published in 1972, the book was praised in certain underground circles yet was never acknowledged in academia or the broader cultural public. However, it was one of the triggers for the creation of cultural counterpublics that in the 1980s included a few theaters (Glej and SMG in Ljubljana, Atelje 212 in Belgrade), student cultural institutions (including the Student Cultural Center—SKC in Belgrade), and Black Wave film directors (Vučićević, Makavejev, Žilnik, etc.), as well as youth press and student radio stations.

43   Pavis, *Dictionnaire de la performance et du theatre contemporain*, 169–70.

44   Needless to say, the type and degree of participation differs from one artform to another; for example, in multimedia, even a distant "spectator" becomes a participant, by using new digital technologies to interfere and react without any physical interaction (see Pavis, *Dictionnaire*, 170). However, such individual experience is not connected to a community, which is the *sine qua non* of participatory art projects (especially scenic performances).

political purposes—in political criticism, propaganda, environmental and con- sciousness-raising statements, etc. Even though music activism may or may not eventually result in democratic changes, the political significance of music may include much more than the aforementioned explicit examples—"its impact on human identity and capacity, its role in defining or destroying communities, and its part in cultural revitalization and self-determination."[45] Building on Plato, Luther, John Dewey, and Antonio Gramsci, political scientist Mark Mattern has developed the concept of "acting in concert": community-based political action through music that has the power to mobilize people who might otherwise remain silent.

Music activism is often linked to the phenomenon of art in public space accessible to everyone.[46] As a place of social interaction, public space embodies individual experiences of coming together with other people here and now. Therefore, music in public space cannot be neutral—it contributes to the place- making and meaning-making of shared acoustical sites, influencing people and their emotional and social behavior to a certain extent. It can also encourage communication, social interaction, and social mixing, as well as intercultural and social inclusion, in formal and informal ways.[47]

Since the 1960s, citizens have started to appropriate public spaces world- wide for both protests (against the war in Vietnam, student protests in 1968, etc.) and for artistic and musical performances. Furthermore, many cities have declared themselves "free cities" (Amsterdam, San Francisco), exempting street artists from paying city taxes. Over time, the need to use public spaces has arisen from both bottom-up initiatives (such as community art projects encour- aging citizens to appropriate their own neighborhoods[48]) as well as top-down

---

45   Mattern, *Acting in Concert*, 5.

46   The use of public space has been changing throughout history. Squares and streets have had their social role as a stage for spectacles ever since the Roman Empire and the Caesars' triumphal returns from the wars. In more recent history, nation-state representation was perfected through specially designed public spaces suitable for processions and military parades (e.g., the Champs de Mars and the Avenue des Champs-Élysées in Paris, Red Square in Moscow, etc.). Nevertheless, celebrations of the dates linked to the workers' and feminist movements usually occur at places of special significance, places of memory— *lieu de memoire* (Nora, *Realms of Memory*) or urban symbol bearers (Nas, *Cities Full of Symbols*; e.g., Place de la Bastille in Paris, Slavija square in Belgrade, etc.).

47   Julija Matejić, "Music in Public Space" (Master's thesis, University of Arts in Belgrade, 2009), 107.

48   Public art projects in the 1960s and 1970s can be classified by their relation towards: 1) the—natural, urban, or artistic—environment, 2) audience partici- pation, and 3) social engagement—activism through performances, happenings, theater of the oppressed, theater of social intervention, socio-cultural animati-

(competitive city-branding policies leading towards creative, smart, and event-ful cities[49]). Increasingly, citizens are called upon to design their own public spaces as shared spaces of urban commons[50] through different everyday prac-tices of so-called "listening against" and strategies for controlling sonic (sound) spaces as spaces of listening, as well as "fighting" against the consumeristic *horror vacui/silentii*—the "fear of the empty/silent space."[51] This strict sepa-ration and, at the same time, overlapping of private and public realms (however contradictory it seems) have had significant implications on the ways music is practiced in everyday life and consumed during "festivities" and consumeristic spectacles. With a foreign aid (mostly from the Open Society Foundation), the civic realm in Serbia has developed different platforms for hosting varied actors (professionals, amateurs, interested citizens, passers-by, etc.), without the risk of being controlled. Sadly, only few of them have survived, such as the CZKD.

Counterpublics in Serbia could relate neither to the music canonized by schools and academia nor to turbo-folk or omni-popular Western pop music, but to music activism mostly rooted in rock and punk music genres, aiming at social justice, the culture of memory, civil rights, and freedom. The difference was not only in the musical language itself but also in places of inscenation and interaction with audiences. Instead of concert halls and stadiums, activism through music requires public spaces and direct audience participation, while disregarding "excellence" as the ultimate demand of music performance.

Thus, in the last decade of the twentieth century, millions of people throughout Serbia brought their voices together as a direct reaction to long-term exposure to repression, nationalism, xenophobia, devastation, and the collapse of not only the country itself but also of its common core values. By examining these voices and focusing on music activism and its role in the socio-political turmoil in recent Serbian history, we are not outlining a retrospective account of all the phenomena that occurred; instead, we choose to discuss only

---

on, etc.; see Milena Dragićević Šešić, *Umetnost i alternativa* (Belgrade: Institut za pozorište, film, radio i televiziju, Fakultet dramskih umetnosti, Clio, 2012), 79–80. The terminological evolution from *open spaces* to *public spaces*, from *social engagement* to *activism* and *artivism*, from *audience participation* to *citizen participation*, emphasizes the changes in approach and in the socio-political context. The more that open spaces in cities were privatized, the more the citizens needed to fight for the "public sphere" and for the possibility of using common space for community projects.

49 See Richards and Palmer, *Eventful Cities, Cultural Management and Urban Revitalisation.*

50 See Borch and Kornberger, *Urban Commons: Rethinking the City*; Kimmel, Gentzsch, and Bloemen, *Shared Spaces: New Paper on Urban Commons.*

51 Atanasovski "Rhythmanalysis of the Policescape."

the most influential ones. By presenting several case studies, we distinguish different types of music activism: not only individual and collective, professional and amateur, but also "activism within music" and "activism through music."

Sounds of Democracy—Sounds of Counterpublics

Following their own beliefs, members of both art and popular music elites contributed (directly and indirectly) to the overall fight for civil rights and freedom in Serbia during the 1990s. Numerous singers, members of pop, rock, and punk bands, composers, musicians, and professors in music schools and on the university level actively participated in civil and student protests, in numerous concerts of support, increasingly criticizing the political situation in their lyrics, writings, screenplays, and scripts, as well as unfailingly portraying complex relationships within the society in their own musical language.

When it comes to the culture of dissent, counter-discourses, and activism in the field of music, we differentiate numerous types of social and political engagement in the Serbian public sphere over the last three decades. For the purpose of this paper, however, we will focus only on those that undoubtedly crossed with more significant civil society movements, contributing to the counterpublic realm. These include:

a)   Concerts of art, rock, and pop music in traditional venues, with the spirit of protests being integrated into the music performed—both in the musical language itself and in the lyrics;[52]

b)   Direct political engagements, public speeches during the protests, and manifestations against the regime (symbolically calling on then-President Slobodan Milošević to resign);[53]

---

52   This includes concerts by the prominent songwriter Đorđe Balašević, which were symbolically organized as part of counterpublics and the culture of dissent. Another example is a concert by the eminent Serbian violinist Mateja Marinković held at the Ilija M. Kolarac Endowment concert hall in April 1998, during the conflicts in the province of Kosovo; in his piece called *Call from Tombs*, Marinković used rhythmic patterns commonly known from the street protests of 1996–97.

53   Probably the most detailed testimonies of such events are given in the 2002 memoirs of composer Rajko Maksimović, one of the most present and active musicians in the dramatic events of the 1990s; see Maksimović, *Tako je to bilo 3: autobiografska sećanja (1990–2002)*, "*Godine koje su pojele bubašvabe*" (Belgrade: Author's Edition, 2002). Other examples include composer Milan Mihajlović's speech at the opening of the First International Review of Composers held in Sremski Karlovci and Novi Sad in May 1992, as well as an open letter to

c)   Radio broadcasts of music as a symbol of dissent;[54]
d)   Participatory "music" and noise-making civic performances organized and implemented during different mass protests in the winter of 1996–97;[55]
e)   Insurgent concerts on main public squares;
f)   Ephemeral participatory artistic actions, often in the form of multimedia performances;[56]
g)   Permanent troupes and self-organized art collectives gathered around different cultural platforms.[57]

---

the public by composers, musicologists, and music artists against isolation, harassment, torture, and killing of people based on their nationality, religious, or political beliefs; the public "kneeling" of approximately fifty composers invited by composer Vuk Kulenović and the Composers' Association of Serbia on June 14, 1992; and composer Dejan Despić's public speech at the Vidovdan convocation of Democratic Serbia held on June 28, 1992. At that time, the Composers Association of Serbia was greatly politically engaged. According to Milan Mihajlović, then-president of the Association: "We reacted at a time when it was critical, when our members were also affected. I continue to believe that our primary role is to pursue the profession and to promote our creativity. But also, when something that I think threatens our work happens, I think the Association should react, and no one has the right to keep our mouths shut." See Dubravka Savić, "Svet nas još uvek sluša" *Večernje novosti* (June 5, 1994).

54 See Dragićević Šešić, "B-92 urbani radio—politika, alternativa, rok."
55 This includes the protests against the electoral fraud attempted by then-President Slobodan Milošević and his party that erupted in November 1996 and lasted for four months, gathering thousands of people on the streets daily throughout Serbian cities. Artists contributed with their wittiness and imagination, creating a carnivalesque atmosphere on the streets, stimulating citizens to join and contribute with their own creativity. This phenomenon was documented in numerous films, including Radivoje Andrić's *January River* (1997), Želimir Žilnik's *Do jaja* (1997), and Goran Marković's *Kordon* (2002).
56 Such as *Potop* (*Flood*), a performance by the Led Art collective (Novi Sad, October 16, 1993), with the New Art Forum contemporary music ensemble wearing Saša Marković Mikrob's masks and performing the "Tuba Mirum" from the Mozart's Requiem, and the musical *Armatura* (authored by Ana Karapešić), performed by Škart, Mikrob, URGH! on November 8, 1993, at the Faculty of Architecture in Belgrade. These two events indeed crossed disciplinary boundaries and contributed to the creation of cultural counterpublics. Not only a common denominator of these two actions, Mikrob's masks were soon to be seen everywhere—on the markets, at railway stations, in clubs, shops, etc.—offered by the artist himself to passers-by.
57 Primarily self-organized choirs, which are analyzed in more detail further in this chapter. Additionally, numerous events were organized by independent cultural centers and private clubs as part of Belgrade's fluid club scene. Independent cultural centers introduced extraordinary music programs: CZKD had organized the "drum symposium" Prestup on February 29, 1996, a year before the drums

Musical counterpublics reflect different socio-political contexts in distinct genres. As composer Milan Mihajlović has emphasized, every work of art reflects the time in which it is created, as is the case with the titles of some of his compositions written during the 1990s—*Eine kleine Trauermusik* (A *Little Grieving Music*, 1990) and *Memento* (1993), the contents of which, as he himself admits, "are probably not accidental."[58] Mihajlović has further elaborated on the impact of social reality on his personal poetics: the symbolism of *Memento*, for example, lies in a horrible war environment—an environment of primitivism that surrounds us all: "We must not neglect the feelings of the exiled and the humiliated. We must not forget the dead. Because of this whole situation, I have been terribly upset for a long time, so it makes sense that all of this is reflected in my music."[59]

Similarly, horrified by the war and the refugee convoys in Bosnia (especially the Jewish refugee convoys that had left Sarajevo at the very beginning of the war), composer Ivana Stefanović tried to translate her attitude toward these circumstances into the musical language of her radiophonic piece *Lacrimosa* (1993). It includes not only quotes from Pergolesi, Mozart, Verdi, Penderecki, Britten, and Sephardic songs, but also sounds from the streets of Sarajevo (May 1992) and Belgrade (June 1992). This cathartic piece points to the loss of the sound map of the city under the booms of cannons from the surrounding hills. As a true example of program music, it grasps the composer's outcry: "Full of tears—say the texts of all the prayers of the world... It is full of tears this musical prayer of mine, dedicated to a friend from Sarajevo."[60]

There are not that many examples of explicit and visible political engagement in art music within the walls of traditional concert halls. Some may say that an individual professional (artistic) contribution to music activism seems to be somewhat hidden in personal poetics. However, even though it is perceived as "activism within music" (and is therefore not easily comprehensible

---

became a symbol of civic protests (the word *prestup*, meaning "violation," also refers to the leap year), whereas conductor Premil Petrović introduced music theater in Cinema Rᴇx and Beton hala Theater (performing Mozart's *Bastien and Bastienne*, 1996; Manuel de Falla's *El retablo de maese Pedro*, 1997; Arnold Schoenberg's *Pierrot Lunaire*, 1998; and Igor Stravinsky's *Histoire du Soldat*, 2000).

58   Ivana Stefanović, "Susreti sa savremenicima: Milan Mihajlović; Posebna, tvrdoglava sorta," *Politika*, November 3, 1993, 17.

59   Maja Smiljanić, "Milan Mihajlović, kompozitor i dobitnik nagrade Stevan Mokranjac. Muzika bez predumišljaja," *Borba*, April 21, 1994, 15.

60   Dragićević Šešić, *Umetnost i kultura otpora*, 197; Ana Kotevska, *Isečci s kraja veka: Muzičke kritike i (ne)kritičko mišljenje (1992-1996)* (Banja Luka: Besjeda; Belgrade: Clio, 2017), 36.

by everyone), such a professional contribution is of great importance since it is written/recorded as a trace of a zeitgeist for generations to come.[61]

In a way, a similar, yet slightly different approach to social activism within music can be seen in numerous theatrical performances and films, produced both in the country and abroad, as a reaction to the madness of national-ism and the wars. As explained by undoubtedly the most active and socially engaged composer in the field of applied music at that time—Zoran Erić—"it is active music that is not just a mere décor but participates equally in the plot, and its absence would be noticed."[62] Some of the most significant theater plays and films interwoven by his music, (directly or indirectly) referring to the atrocious social reality, include *Mother Courage and her Children* (Bertolt Brecht/Lenka Udovički, 1992), *Der Prozeß* (Franz Kafka/Sonja Vukićević, 1998), *Ubistvo s predumišljajem* (*Premeditated Murder*, Gorčin Stojanović, 1995), and *Stršljen* (*Hornet*, Gorčin Stojanović, 1998), all of them expressing either the dreadfulness of the wars or covering a wide range of complex and appalling socio-political actualities in the region.

Due to the political and social circumstances, music activism "grew" from the individual to the collective (mass), from the professional to more amateur, spontaneously moving the stage from concert halls into the public space so that the impact would be more effective and efficient.

Music activism in public space in Serbia owes its character to the programs and activities of Radio B92, one of few genuinely free media outlets in Belgrade, which gained both political and generational credibility in March 1991 when, despite the ban on broadcasting talk formats, it continued to fight against the regime by spreading its political messages through music.[63] As a result, its

---

61   In addition to the art music pieces already mentioned, we also single out Svetlana Kresić's *Klinički kvartet* (*Clinical Quartet*, 1991), Vojin Komadina's *Tužne pjesme* (*Sad Songs*, for voice and piano, 1992), Dejan Despić's *Dies irae* (for oboe, violin, viola, cello and piano, 1992), Vuk Kulenović's *Boogie* (for piano and orchestra, 1993), Zoran Erić's *Images of Chaos IV—I Have not Spoken* (for alto saxophone, bass mouth harmonica, actor and mixed choir, 1995), Srđan Hofman's *Nokturno beogradskog proleća 1999* (*A Nocturne of Belgrade Spring 1999*, for chamber ensemble, live electronics and audio tape, 1999–2000), Ivan Jevtić's *Izgon* (*Exodus*, 2001), and Aleksandra Vrebalov's *...hold me, neighbour, in this storm...* (2007). See Melita Milin, "Art Music in Serbia as a Political Tool and/or Refuge During the 1990s," *Musicological Annual* 47, no. 209 (2011), 209–17, https://doi.org/10.4312/mz.47.1.209-217.

62   Biljana Lijeskić, "Kompozitor Zoran Erić, dobitnik specijalne nagrade na Bijenalu scenskog dizajna: Inspiraciju čuvam kao izvor čiste vode," *Glas javnosti*, September 19, 2000, 14.

63   Dragićević Šešić, *Umetnost i kultura otpora*, 53.

Figure 1: Led Art collective, New Art Forum ensemble for contemporary music, and Mikrob, Potop (Flood), 1993, performance, Novi Sad. Photo by and courtesy of Vesna Pavlović.

radio audience increased significantly, and people realized that anyone could contribute.

In 1992, a supergroup named Rimtutituki brought together members of the then most influential rock and roll bands and musicians (Partibrejkersi, Električni orgazam, and Ekatarina Velika—Ekv) for the purpose of signing the petition against the mobilization.[64] At first, without a permit for a public performance, they started their fight against the futility and folly of the war from a truck, by performing live on the streets of Belgrade, spreading slogans such as "Mir brate, mir!" ("Peace brother, peace!"); "Nećemo da pobedi narodna muzika" ("We do not want the folk music to win"), and "Ispod šlema mozga nema" ("There is no brain underneath a helmet").[65] Once permission to perform was obtained, a concert called "Sos peace or do not count on us" was organized at the Republic Square on April 6, 1992, against the Serbian government's involvement in the civil war in Bosnia and Herzegovina. Its slogan was an anti-war message addressed to Serbia's generals and government as a direct paraphrase of the famous song from 1978: "You can count on us!" ("Računajte na nas!") by the rock

---

64   Even the name of the group is a form of a protest, as it is directed to those in power and loosely translated from an argot understandable throughout the former Yugoslavia as "up yours!"

65   Električni Orgazam Official, "Rimtutituki Uzivo Na Kamionu [1992]," music video, 53:16, posted March 8, 2016, https://www.youtube.com/watch?v=OJU yhL3dRbU.

band Rani Mraz (*Early Frost*), a patriotic song that glorified Yugoslavism. The concert gathered between 30,000 and 50,000 citizens.[66]

Over four months of civic and student protests during the winter of 1996–97, citizens throughout Serbia gathered daily and organized mass protest walks against the election rigging, which entirely changed the profile of the public space: "this type of spatial emancipation in the city center determined rebellious freedom of movement, and as such definitely opened new horizons for street freedoms."[67] We would agree that the streets of Belgrade succeeded in staging life itself, with sound, noise, and music having a significant role. Protest rallies advanced into a mobile sound force, often including orchestras, drummers (grouped around Dragoljub Đuričić), trumpets, ravers, and other kinds of innovative, creative, and witty handmade noisemaking instruments. The sound-base of these protests was music, particularly rock and punk, known for their subversive drive. Such a "culture and art of resistance," with the use of performativity in public space, aimed at direct criticism and a change of government and its apparatus.[68]

These protests were not static gatherings; they were defined by walking (symbolizing the effort to exercise the freedom to move throughout the city) and noise (*Noise in Fashion!*—action based on the eponymous aforementioned song), conceived as a noise production during the broadcast of State Television News at 7:30 PM, in front of government and media buildings. Obviously, the choice of institutions was not random; if French economic and social theorist Jacques Attali is to be trusted, the fear of noise is particularly noticeable in totalitarian systems, as nothing essential happens in the absence of noise and there is no real power without the control of noise.[69] That is precisely why it is not surprising that the initiative was massively accepted by the citizens, with their inventiveness best seen in the production of noise, with instruments made from drainpipes, found objects, wires, and kitchen pots. Those who could not join the walks contributed from their balconies (by placing banners and speakers on their windows, producing noise, or throwing confetti and balloons), and we would say that this inter-stimulation of the events on the streets and the facades created a specific ambiance in the city as never before in the Balkans.[70] Over time, this noise advanced into music, culminating with the mass

---

66   Električni Orgazam Official, "Rimtutituki—Mir brate mir—Ne Racunajte Na Nas [Live 1992]," music video, 5:59, posted March 9, 2016, https://www.youtube.co m/watch?v=S-TobTR5NdY.

67   Miroslava Lukić-Krstanović, "Belgrade Street Drama of the 1990s: (Re)constructing History and Memory," *Prace Etnograficzne*, no. 2 (2018), 27–48.

68   Dragićević Šešić, *Umetnost i kultura otpora*, 26.

69   Atali, *Buka: ogled o političkoj ekonomiji muzike*, 10–12.

70   Dragićević Šešić, "B-92 urbani radio—politika, alternativa, rok," 277.

Figure 2: Student protests, 1996, Belgrade. Photo by and courtesy of Vesna Pavlović.

performance of the *Symphony for Whistles, Trumpets, and Drums* directed by the composer Zoran Hristić in the closing ceremony of the civil and student protests.[71]

---

71   Gordana Suša and Voja Donić, *Pištaljka jača od pendreka* (Belgrade: Vin Production, 1996), video, 1:08:07, posted November 19, 2016, by "N1," https://www.youtube.com/watch?v=Y3tQ-RDN8L0, 0:00–2:50.

These protests were also marked by popular, rock, and punk bands that were staunch opponents to the regime, and were not afraid to send a clear message, including Električni orgazam, Partibrejkersi, Eyesburn, Love Hunters, Atheist Rap, Kanda, Kodža i Nebojša, Darkwood Dub, Del Arno Bend, Rambo Amadeus, and others. One of the largest rock concerts in recent Serbian history—the concert for New Year's Eve 1997—was organized by the members of the student protest marketing team and non-governmental/non-profit association Šta hoćeš ("What Do You Want"). It was attended by more than 500,000 people, with Đorđe Balašević, Partibrejkersi, Familija, Love Hunters, and Darkwood Dub performing on stage, with Prodigy, Sting, Harvey Keitel, Emir Kusturica, Patriarch Pavle of the Serbian Orthodox Church, and others greeting people via a video link.

Rock music has been identified as urban, cosmopolitan, and dissident music of engagement and rebellion, as opposed to the folk, neo-folk and turbo-folk music that was widely used for state propaganda. Therefore, rock music was a cultural vehicle not only for political changes but also for collective identity construction and the deprovincialization of society: "as a genre that expressed cosmopolitanism and individualism, rock provided not only a discourse but a set of shared practices for identity construction, [...] stories within which Serbian students of middle-class, professional backgrounds could locate themselves and through which they could narrate their desired participation in a European civil society." What is more, rock music was "a soundtrack for the story that students told of their collective resistance."[72]

Various groups of artists and individuals (professionals, students, and amateurs) participated in the protests in many different ways, through artistic actions, happenings, provocations, performances, and interventions, mostly in partnership with non-governmental community organizations. Therefore, it is not easy to classify particular actions within particular branches of art because of the conscious violation of all traditional art conventions and forms, as well their ritual form of expression and specific process of realization. Of course, it was not all about "festivity, music, and fun," as an oblivious reader might assume—the fight against the regime brought people together in dangerous settings (which are not the subject of this paper). Even though they were unsafe, city streets were deliberately chosen as places where citizens could demonstrate their disobedience, intellectual superiority, creativity, progressive

---

72   Marc W. Steinberg, "When Politics Goes Pop: On the Intersections of Popular and Political Culture and the Case of Serbian Student Protests," *Social Movement Studies* 3, no. 1 (2004), 3–29, https://doi.org/10.1080/1474283042000194939, 19–22.

ideas, cynicism, wittiness, dignity, and pride as instruments of rebellion against the regime, wars, dictatorship, and autocracy.

Probably the most striking example of music artivism was the performance of the ballet *Macbeth/It* (William Shakespeare/Sonja Vukićević, Belgrade, 1996), produced by Czkd. Ballerina, choreographer, and director Sonja Vukićević and actor Slobodan Beštić passionately and violently performed to music composed by Zoran Erić in front of a police cordon in Kolarčeva Street, surrounded by protestors, almost naked and splashed by water in the middle of a freezingly cold night. It was a real example of an art performance as a medium for spreading radical artistic ideas.

Figure 3: Sonja Vukićević and Slobodan Beštić, Macbeth/It, 1996, performance, Belgrade. Photo by and courtesy of Vesna Pavlović.

We would agree that the politicization of art during the protests was beneficial in two ways: not only did it help to mobilize student and citizen support, but it mostly prevented the protests from escalating to violence (though, unfortunately, not always). As rationalized by Đorđe Tomić: "it was much more difficult for the police to use force against protesters who were sharing flowers or reading poetry aloud in front of the police cordon."[73] Unlike the aforementioned "activism within music," this is an extreme example of political "activism through music" and performance, which could be considered "confrontational," since

---

73 Đorđe Tomić, "Ulične studije—odsek: protest! Studentski protesti tokom ere Milošević," in *Društvo u pokretu. Novi društveni pokreti u Jugoslaviji od 1968. do danas*, ed. Đorđe Tomić and Petar Atanacković (Novi Sad: Cenzura, 2009), 214.

"music helps assert the claims of the community, which are believed to stand in direct opposition to the claims of others."[74]

Such carnivalization of a city[75] imposes the idea of a "city-as-action," which involves not only political struggle as such but also its dramaturgy and its *mise-en-scène*. As defined by Silvija Jestrović, "it involves the construction, decomposition, and re-creation of the city through action—through dynamic self-design—suggesting the idea of space as a palimpsest in which both synchronous and diachronic elements of the city are seen. The theatricality of protest is a strategic, conceptual, deliberately thought-out aspect of counter-spectacle."[76]

After an era of fear and hopelessness, and a culture of humiliation during the 1990s, democratic changes and socio-political events in the 2000s brought a culture of hope.[77] But the sense of togetherness and community belonging was short-lived. The culture of hope was soon replaced by the culture of disappointment, especially after the assassination of Serbia's first democratic prime minister, Zoran Đinđić, in 2003. As a result, in the following years, different artivistic initiatives attempted to bring back the sense of connectedness to the community through bottom-up artivism and civic imagination aiming at raising awareness, introducing critical thinking, as well as promoting peace and an inclusive society.

That is when alternative choirs, orchestras, and self-organization as the way of operating came to the forefront. Horkeškart (in Serbian, *hor* meaning "a choir," and *škart*—"a discard") was the first self-organized choir within the territory of the former Yugoslavia. It was founded in 2000 by the members of the art group Škart to perform the song "Svete krave" (Holy cows, by Croatian singer Arsen Dedić) at Czkd, alluding to the fact that, even after the democratic changes, specific individuals in the society were still untouchable (such as criminals and politicians). Open for everyone to join, led by professional conductors, and with rehearsals held in different cultural centers (Czkd, Rex, the Parobrod and City cultural centers) and private flats, the collective was centered around the concepts of self-organization, equality, social activism, non-profit engagement, and unrestrained "expression of both personal opinion and of course talent."[78] With diverse repertoire (from the socially engaged and

---

74   Mattern, *Acting in Concert*, 25.
75   Dragićević Šešić, *Umetnost i kultura otpora*, 275.
76   Silvija Jestrović, "Grad-kao-akcija," in *Umetnost i kultura otpora* by Milena Dragićević Šešić (Belgrade: Institut za pozorište, film, radio i televiziju, Fakultet dramskih umetnosti, Clio, 2018), 411.
77   Moïsi, *The Geopolitics of Emotion*.
78   Marija Macić, "The Alternative Choir as a Creative Platform," in *Equal Yet Different: Self-Organisation of an Alternative Choir and Orchestra*, exhibition catalogue (Belgrade: UK Parobrod, 2015), 34–35.

revolutionary re-actualization of partisan and workers' songs to their own songs), Horkeškart performed in public spaces, village schools, orphanages, refugee camps, festivals, art galleries, museums, and markets, often wearing pajamas or workers' uniforms. Over the years, the collective has become divided: while some members had a growing ambition for the collective to become a well-rehearsed rock and roll band, others wanted it to be more socially engaged. Consequently, the group Škart left the choir in 2006, with its name being changed into Horkestar (from *orkestar*—"an orchestra"). During the twenty years of its existence and through music activism enriched by humor, the "Horke" phenomenon has been raising awareness of the importance of both individual and social responsibility.

Similar choirs were also formed throughout the region, including the lesbian-feminist choir Le zbor in Croatia in 2005, Prrrroba made of ex-Horkeškart members in Belgrade in 2007, the female choir Kombinat in Slovenia in 2008, Raspeani Skopjani in Macedonia in 2009, the lesbian-feminist choir Le wHore in 2010, and the anti-fascist choir Naša pjesma (Our Song) in 2016 in Belgrade. These self-organized collectives have been more than choirs; as creative platforms, they have been carrying and spreading socially engaging messages, calling for solidarity and humanity, stressing the importance of musical association and the (out-)loud expression of resistance and social criticism.

Figure 4: Horkestar on regional tour: Festival of self-organized choirs, 2018, performance, Zagreb. Source: Courtesy of Horkestar.

The wider general public got to know the work of Horkeškart/Horkestar through different actions aimed at collective mobilization, such as "Nazad" (Back!) in 2006, with the choir performing the song "Back!" in front of the building of the Government of the Republic of Serbia, the Supreme Court, the University of Belgrade, the Serbian Academy of Science and Arts, and the Patriarchate of the Serbian Orthodox Church, as a direct critique of the slowing down of country's path toward European integration, as well as certain regressive occurrences in the society, if not created by then at least not prevented by those institutions. Within the program of the Belgrade International Week of Architecture (BINA) in 2014, and in direct interaction with citizens, Horkestar created lyrics and music on the theme of public spaces, aiming to preserve Belgrade's public spaces and point out their shortcomings. The same year, Horkestar not only performed songs previously censored by the Belgrade Youth Center in front of the very institution, on the occasion of its fiftieth anniversary, but also performed in front of Zvezda cinema, privatized under suspicious circumstances, yet occupied by a group of activists (students, filmmakers, and other cultural workers) for the purpose of screening films for free to citizens of Belgrade. Since 2014, Horkestar has been most socially active in support of the Don't Let Belgrade D(r)own) movement, by participating and performing in their mass protests against the Belgrade Waterfront project. Horkestar's cover of the anti-fascist revolutionary "¡Ay Carmela!" became the anthem of the movement.[79]

As acts of social engagement and protest against the public reality, such examples of music activism and new genre public art situated outside conventional art spaces are dialogical, based on dialogue and participation, forging "a provisional sense of collectivity."[80] Therefore, we would agree that "Horke" phenomenon has offered "a positive and unique influence on the lives of individuals."[81]

Conclusions

The cultural domain, especially the field of music, brings to the fore social and political dichotomies. Musical counterpublics have used different means to send a message and to achieve their goals in different historical and socio-

---

79   Ne da(vi)mo Belgrade, "Čiji grad? Čiji glas? [2016]," music video, 2:13, posted June 7, 2016, https://www.youtube.com/watch?v=5Swh69bhW0U.

80   Grant Kester, "Conversation Pieces: The Role of Dialogue in Socially-Engaged Art," in *Theory in Contemporary Art Since 1985*, ed. Zoya Kucor and Simon Leung (Oxford: Blackwell, 2005), 76–88.

81   Momir Josipović, "The Trajectory of Horkestar Members' Social Circles," in *Equal Yet Different*, 39.

political contexts. Specific musical genres were considered mainstream in one *hic et nunc* and musical chronotope, while at the same time being regarded as dissenting and rebellious in another.[82]

As the study of Serbian musical chronotope(s) in the last thirty years has shown, after more than a decade of an unfinished transition and democratic changes (2000–10), certain specificities of the 1990s reemerged in the 2010s, such as a disjunction of public and counterpublic realms in the field of music. Such polarization in musical circles is based on a musical genre and its status within society (public and counterpublic spheres). Even though the polarization implies that musical literacy and taste are often regarded as critical elements of social and cultural identity constructions, it does not suggest that contemporary art music cannot be heard in both spheres—rather, that the manner and place of performance of a particular piece of music determine its contextual meaning. On the one hand, the official, public music realm (constructed by the public music education system) shapes apolitical performers (regarded as "music professionals") and implies traditional concert venues for a high-culture audience profile qualified to comprehend (art) music. On the other hand, musical counterpublics use collaborative and socially engaged community-driven practices, advocating for the values that are not only cultural but also sociopolitical and ideological. Therefore, the subaltern counterpublic realm often imposes a dislocation from traditional concert venues, demands direct and outspoken politicality and the joint production of both knowledge and artistic practice, the reintroduction of alternative, (experimental) exploratory research and creative practices, forgotten (socialist, but also other) traditions, and inter/transdiciplinarity, including new media, as well as uncommon ways of music production and dissemination.[83]

---

82 Even listening to a certain type of music can proclaim an affiliation to either public or counterpublic realms; however, this paper focuses on socially engaged civic practices and not on passive listeners and particular audiences.

83 This claim was recently confirmed when, after two months of the global COVID-19 pandemic and lockdown, the first Ars vs. Corona music concert outside of the virtual space was organized by cultural counterpublics, including the NGO BUNT (an acronym meaning "rebellion," standing for *Beogradska umetnička nova teritorija*—Belgrade Artistic New Territory). The concert was organized in a symbolic place of today's cultural counterpublics—a space of the academic cultural and artistic society Ivo Lola Ribar (named after the antifascist national hero, one of the leaders of the youth and student revolutionary movement in Yugoslavia, killed during World War II). As it seems, the public cultural system was not ready (or not brave) enough to take an action in such turbulent and risky times, while musical counterpublics and their loyal audience—experienced in tough situations—have found the strength to make such a significant act. Created in 2013 by the prominent Serbian flutist Ljubiša Jovanović and composer

Thus, if we discuss the musical chronotopes in Serbia in the 1990s and today, we may conclude that some of the elements from the 1990s have been reinstalled in recent times, yet the carnivalesque spirit and forms of artivism have changed. Though the "carnival as the subversive undercurrent in modernity 'discovered' by Bakhtin"[84] was the key form of artivism and resistance during the citizens' and students' protests in the 1990s, it has lost its subversive force over time, due to its overuse by the political parties in power, organizing top-down public manifestations in different populist formats. However, sparks reminiscent of the 1990s are certainly visible in the protests of the Don't Let Belgrade D(r)own movement. It seems that Bruegel's painting *The Fight Between Carnival and Lent*, which inspired Jacques Attali's analysis of the political economy of music, might be appropriate to denote the contemporary Serbian carnivalesque musical chronotope. Although the dichotomy (between an inn and a church as symbols of two societal poles) cannot be directly applied, we can imagine the dichotomy between the two types of the carnival itself—a populist-consumeristic one in the official public cultural realm on one side, and a participatory-activist one self-organized within cultural counterpublics on the other. Although Bruegel foresaw a well as a space for gathering the whole community, the two aforementioned realms in Serbia do not share a common space where the two carnivals could meet. As we have shown, the music sphere in Serbia is much more complicated, organized in separate and utterly different realms (value chains) that rarely intersect. Nevertheless, we dare to imagine a symbolic well, created through numerous actions forming the counterpublics' places and platforms of cultural and social engagement, such as CZKD—Belgrade's epicenter of civil resistance.

In that sense, we believe that music activism in Serbia has developed within civil society movements to form a discursive arena of cultural counterpublics and the culture of dissent, mostly represented by the aforementioned social and pacifist movements and artistic NGOs active on the so-called independent scene. These groups have been subverting mainstream local politics since the 1990s, fighting for democratic values in Serbia, but also developing solidarity across the borders throughout the region. Thus, practices of dissent and citizenship within and through participatory civic musical actions at the turn of the

---

Ivana Stefanović, BUNT organizes an annual alternative music festival of the same name.

84 Nele Bemong, Pieter Borghart, Michel De Dobbeleer, Kristoffel Demoen, Koen De Temmerman, and Bart Keunen, eds., *Bakhtin's Theory of the Literary Chronotope: Reflections, Applications, Perspectives* (Gent: Academia Press, 2010), iii, http://library.um.edu.mo/ebooks/b28005533.pdf.

millennium have been resonating ever since, as the sounds of counterpublics and sounds of democracy that still have their *raison d'être* today.

References

Archer, Rory. "Assessing Turbofolk Controversies: Popular Music between the Nation and the Balkans." *Southeastern Europe* 36 (2012): 178–207.

Atali, Žak. *Buka: ogled o političkoj ekonomiji muzike.* Belgrade: Biblioteka XX vek, 2007.

Atanasovski, Srđan. "Turbo-folk as 'Bad Music:' Politics of Musical Valuing." In *Böse Macht Musik. Zur Ästhetik des Bösen in der Musik*, edited by Sara R. Falke and Katharina Wisotzki, 157–72. Bielefeld: transcript, 2012.

———. "Recycled Music for Banal Nation: The Case of Serbia 1999–2010." In *Relocating Popular Music. Pop Music, Culture and Identity*, edited by Ewa Mazierska and Georgina Gregory. London: Palgrave Macmillan, 2015.

———. "Rhythmanalysis of the Policescape: The Promise of an Ecological Turn in the Practice of Soundscape Studies." *Musicological Annual* 52, no. 2 (2016): 11–23.

Bakhtin, Mikhail. *Rabelais and His World.* Bloomington: Indiana University Press, 1984.

———. "Forms of Time and of the Chronotope in the Novel." In *The Dialogic Imagination*, edited by Michael Holquist. Austin: University of Texas Press, 1981.

Bemong, Nele, Pieter Borghart, Michel De Dobbeleer, Kristoffel Demoen, Koen De Temmerman, and Bart Keunen, eds. *Bakhtin's Theory of the Literary Chronotope: Reflections, Applications, Perspectives.* Gent: Academia Press, 2010. http://library.um.edu.mo/ebooks/b28005533.pdf.

Borch, Christian and Martin Kornberger, eds. *Urban Commons: Rethinking the City.* Abingdon: Routledge, 2015.

Brkić, Aleksandar. *Cultural Policy Frameworks (Re)constructing National and Supranational Identities: The Balkans and The European Union.* Amsterdam: European Cultural Foundation, 2014.

Buden, Boris. "Kad budem ustaša i Jugoslaven." In *Barikade*, 266–71. Zagreb: Arkzin, 1997.

Ćosić, Bora. *Mixed Media*, Belgrade: Author's Edition, 1972.

Ćurgus, V. K. *Kultura vlasti—indeks smena i zabrana. The Culture of the Power— An Index of Suspensions and Prohibitions.* Belgrade: Radio B92, 1994.

Dimitrijević, Branislav. "Ovo je savremena umetnost: turbofolk kao radikalni performans." *Prelom, Journal for Images and Politics* 2/3 (2002): 94–101.

Dolečki, Jana, Senad Halilbašić, and Stephan Hulfeld, eds. *Theatre in the Context of the Yugoslav Wars*. London: Palgrave Macmillan, 2018.

Dragićević Šešić, Milena. "Media War and Hatred: The Role of Media in Preparation of Conflicts." *Kultura* 93/94 (1994): 191–207.

———. *Neofolk kultura: publika i njene zvezde*. Novi Sad: Izdavačka knjižarnica Zorana Stojanovića, 1994.

———. "B-92 urbani radio—politika, alternativa, rok." *Zbornik radova Fakulteta dramskih umetnosti* 1, no. 1 (1997): 352–71.

———. "The Street as Political Space: Walking as Protest, Grafitti, and the Student Carnivalization of Belgrade." *New Theatre Quarterly* 17, no. 1 (2001): 74–86. https://doi.org/10.1017/S0266464X00014342.

———. *Umetnost i alternativa*. Belgrade: Institut za pozorište, film, radio i televiziju, Fakultet dramskih umetnosti, Clio, 2012.

———. *Umetnost i kultura otpora*. Belgrade: Institut za pozorište, film, radio i televiziju, Fakultet dramskih umetnosti, Clio, 2018.

Dragićević Šešić, Milena, Julija Matejić and Aleksandar Brkić. "Mobilizing Urban Neighbourhoods: Artivism, Identity, and Cultural Sustainability." In *Cultural Sustainability in European Cities: Imagining Europolis*, edited by Svetlana Hristova, Milena Dragićević Šešić, and Nancy Duxbury. Routledge Studies in Culture and Sustainable Development, 193–205. Oxon: Routledge, 2015.

Dutt, Bishnupriya, Reinelt, Janelle, Sahai, Shrinkhla, eds. *Gendered Citizenship: Manifestations and Performance*. London: Palgrave Macmillan, 2017.

Đurković, Miša. "Ideološki i politički sukobi oko popularne muzike u Srbiji." *Filozofija i Društvo* 25 (2004): 271–84.

Električni Orgazam Official. "rimtutituki - mir brate mir - ne racunajte na nas [live 1992]." Music video, 5:59, posted March 9, 2016. https://www.youtube.com/watch?v=S-TobTR5NdY.

———. "rimtutituki uzivo na kamionu [1992]." Music video, 53:16, posted March 8, 2016. https://www.youtube.com/watch?v=OJUyhL3dRbU.

Fraser, Nancy. "Rethinking the Public Sphere: A Contribution to the Critique of Actually Existing Democracy." In *Habermas and the Public Sphere*, edited by Craig J. Calhoun, 109–42. Cambridge: MIT Press, 1992.

Gordy, Eric. *The Culture of Power in Serbia: Nationalism and the Destruction of Alternatives (Post-Communist Cultural Studies)*, University Park, PA: Pennsylvania State University Press, 1999.

Hamman, Robin. "Radio B-92 in Belgrade Harnesses the Power of a Media Activist Community During the War to Keep Broadcasting Despite Terrestrial Ban." In *Community Informatics: Enabling Communities with Information and Communications Technologies*, edited by Michael Gurstein. Hershey, 561–67. London: Idea Group Publishing, 2000.

Hofman, Ana. *Novi život partizanskih pesama*. Belgrade: Biblioteka XX vek, 2016.

Isin, Engin F., and Patricia K. Wood. *Citizenship and Identity*. London: Sage Publications, 1999.

Jansen, Stef. "The Streets of Belgrade. Urban Space and Protest Identities in Serbia." *Political Geography* 20 (2001): 30–55.

Jestrović, Silvija. "Grad–kao–akcija." In *Umetnost i kultura otpora* by Milena Dragićević Šešić, 409–422. Belgrade: Institut za pozorište, film, radio i televiziju, Fakultet dramskih umetnosti, Clio, 2018.

Josipović, Momir. "The Trajectory of Horkestar Members' Social Circles." In *Equal Yet Different: Self-Organisation of an Alternative Choir and Orchestra*. Exhibition catalogue, 38–39. Belgrade: UK Parobrod, 2015.

Kellner, Douglas. "Toward a Multiperspectival Cultural Studies." *The Centennial Review* 36, no. 1 (1992): 5–41. https://www.jstor.org/stable/23739831.

Kester, Grant. "Conversation Pieces: The Role of Dialogue in Socially-Engaged Art." In *Theory in Contemporary Art Since 1985*, edited by Zoya Kucor and Simon Leung, 76–88. Oxford: Blackwell, 2005.

Kimmel, Jens, Till Gentzsch, and Sophie Bloemen. *Shared Spaces: New Paper on Urban Commons*. A research project and report by Commons Network & raumlaborberlin, 2018. https://www.commonsnetwork.org/wp-content/uploads/2018/11/SharedSpacesCommonsNetwork.pdf.

Kotevska, Ana. *Isečci s kraja veka: Muzičke kritike i (ne)kritičko mišljenje (1992–1996)*. Banja Luka, Belgrade: Besjeda, Clio, 2017.

Kronja, Ivana. *Smrtonosni sjaj: masovna psihologija i estetika turbo-folka*. Belgrade: Tehnokratija, 2000.

Kupres, Radovan. Sav taj folk, TV documentary, Belgrade: Television B92, 2004.

Longinović, Tomislav. "Music Wars: Blood and Song at the End of Yugoslavia." In *Music and the Racial Imagination*, edited by Ronald M. Radano and Philip V. Bohlman, 622–643. Chicago: University of Chicago Press, 2001.

Lijeskić, Biljana. "Kompozitor Zoran Erić, dobitnik specijalne nagrade na Bijenalu scenskog dizajna: Inspiraciju čuvam kao izvor čiste vode." *Glas javnosti*, September 18, 2000.

Lukić-Krstanović, Miroslava. "Belgrade Street Drama of the 1990s: (Re)constructing History and Memory." *Prace Etnograficzne*, no. 2 (2018): 27–48.

Macić, Marija. "The Alternative Choir as a Creative Platform." In *Equal Yet Different: Self-Organisation of an Alternative Choir and Orchestra*. Exhibition catalogue, 34–35. Belgrade: UK Parobrod, 2015.

Maksimović, Rajko. Tako je to bilo 3: autobiografska sećanja (1990–2002), "*Godine koje su pojele bubašvabe*." Belgrade: Author's Edition, 2002.

Marić, Ratka. "Značenje potkulturnih stilova—istraživanja omladinskih potkultura." Ph.D. diss., Belgrade: Fakultet političkih nauka, 1996.

Matejić, Julija. "Music in Public Space." Master's thesis, University of Arts in Belgrade, 2009.

Mattern, Mark. *Acting in Concert: Music, Community, and Political Action*. New Brunswick, NJ: Rutgers University Press, 1998.

Milin, Melita. "Art Music in Serbia as a Political Tool and/or Refuge During the 1990s." *Musicological Annual* 47, no. 209 (2011): 209–17. https://doi.org/10. 4312/mz.47.1.209-217.

Moïsi, Dominique. *The Geopolitics of Emotion: How Cultures of Fear, Humiliation, and Hope are Reshaping the World*. New York: Anchor Books, 2010.

Nas, Peter J.M., ed. *Cities Full of Symbols: A Theory of Urban Space and Culture*. Leiden: Leiden University Press, 2011.

Ne da(vi)mo Belgrade. "Čiji grad? Čiji glas? [2016]." Music video, 2:13, posted June 7, 2016. https://www.youtube.com/watch?v=5Swh69bhW0U.

Nora, Pierre. *Realms of Memory*. New York: Columbia University Press, 1996–1998.

Paunović, Žarko. "Mirovne aktivnosti u Srbiji: između inicijativa i pokreta." *Filozofija i društvo* no. 7 (1995): 107–25.

Pavis, Patrice. *Dictionnaire de la performance et du theatre contemporain*. Paris: Armand Colin, 2014.

Rai, Shirin. "The Dilemmas of Performative Citizenship." In *Gendered Citizenship: Manifestations and Performance*, edited by Bishnupriya Dutt, Janelle Reinelt, Shrinkhla Sahai, 25–44. London: Palgrave Macmillan, 2017.

Reinelt, Janelle "Performance at the Crossroads of Citizenship." In *The Grammar of Politics and Performance*, edited by Shirin Rai and Janelle Reinelt, 34–50. New York: Routledge, 2015.

Richards, Greg, and Robert Palmer. *Eventful Cities, Cultural Management and Urban Revitalisation*. Kidlington: Elsevier Science, 2010.

Savić, Dubravka. "Svet nas još uvek sluša." *Večernje novosti*, June 5, 1994.

Smiljanić, Maja. "Milan Mihajlović, kompozitor i dobitnik nagrade Stevan Mokranjac. Muzika bez predumišljaja." *Borba*, April 2, 1994.

Stefanović, Ivana. "Susreti sa savremenicima: Milan Mihajlović; Posebna, tvrdoglava sorta." *Politika*, November 3, 1993.

Steinberg, Marc W. "When Politics Goes Pop: On the Intersections of Popular and Political Culture and the Case of Serbian Student Protests." *Social Movement Studies* 3, no. 1 (2004): 3–29. https://doi.org/10.1080/1474283 042000194939.

Suša, Gordana, and Voja Donić. *Pištaljka jača od pendreka*. Video, 1:08:07. Belgrade: VIN Production, 1996. Posted November 19, 2016, by "N1." https://www.youtube.com/watch?v=Y3tQ-RDN8L0.

Tomić, Đorđe. "Ulične studije—odsek: protest! Studentski protesti tokom ere Milošević." In *Društvo u pokretu. Novi društveni pokreti u Jugoslaviji od 1968. do danas*, edited by Đorđe Tomić and Petar Atanacković, 184–231. Novi Sad: Cenzura, 2009.

Vidić Rasmussen, Ljerka. "The Southern Wind of Change: Style and the Politics of Identity in Pre-war Yugoslavia." In *Retuning Culture: Musical Changes in Central and Eastern Europe*, edited by Mark Slobin, 99–117. Durham, NC,: Duke University Press, 1996.

Warner, Michael. "Publics and Counterpublics." *Public culture* 14, no. 1 (2002): 49–90.

Expanding Musical Inclusivity
Representing and Re-presenting Musicking in Deaf Culture through Hip Hop

Katelyn E. Best

Abstract: Products such as headphones, music streaming platforms, and learning assessments foster a hearing-centric realization of music that places auditory senses at the forefront of musical experience. Yet within the context of Deaf culture, a linguistic minority defined by the use of sign language, music takes on new meaning as musical experience is expanded to other senses of the body. Despite this relative construction, music in Deaf culture has been subjugated to a hegemonic ideology that undermines and marginalizes Deaf experiences of sound. However, Deaf musicians have been able to work toward subverting the ideological limitations that have been placed on their music, and by extension their bodies, by adapting musical structures produced by mainstream society and realigning them toward Deaf priorities. Using ethnographic methods including artist interviews, this chapter investigates how Deaf rappers have created a style of hip hop that prioritizes Deaf experiences of sound over hearing ones and considers how, through performance, they subvert hegemonic control over Deaf musical expression and promote the inclusion of Deaf forms of musicking.

Katelyn E. Best is a Teaching Assistant Professor in Musicology at West Virginia University and Co-director of the Society for Ethnomusicology Orchestra. She is also co-editor of *At the Crossroads of Music and Social Justice*, which will be published in Indiana University Press's Activist Encounters in Folklore and Ethnomusicology series. Her work traces the development of dip hop (sign language rap) in the United States and examines the sociocultural mechanisms that have historically colonized d/Deaf experiences of music. She has contributed articles to *Lied und populäre Kultur/Song and Popular Culture* and *The Journal of American Sign Languages and Literatures*, a peer reviewed journal with publications in American Sign Language.

> "To build democracy is to include the least amongst us
> and society at large does a poor job of bringing others to the table,
> so we'll have to bring our own chairs and build a bigger table."
>
> Connell Crooms, Deaf activist and former artist[1]

In 1967, the Music Educators National Conference hosted a symposium on "Music in American Society" to discuss the state of music education in the United States.[2] Known as the Tanglewood Symposium, this meeting brought together a diverse group of people with a wide range of professional backgrounds to participate in an event that "sought to reappraise and evaluate basic assumptions about music in the 'educative' forces and institutions of [US] communities—the home, the school, peer cultures, professional organizations, church, community groups, and communications media."[3] The documentary report from this symposium not only provided a record of the proceedings, but also included a declaration for greater representation of musical diversity in curricula.

Over the years, music institutions have become more interdisciplinary and mindful of expressive forces that lie within and beyond the margins of dominant musical thought, exploring musical diversity at the intersections of race, disability, sexuality, gender, and class, among other categorical crossroads. At the same time, educative forces remain sites of production that shape musical hierarchies as they determine what forms of music are represented, to what extent they are represented, how they are represented, and who represents them. Music production, practice, learning, dissemination, and consumption naturalize and embed basic assumptions of music within society that place ideological restrictions on what constitutes music and how music should be experienced, learned, and evaluated. This results in the production of a musical know-how that upholds certain elements as fundamental to music, generating measurements of musical quality and standards that determine musical inclusion or exclusion.

While musical meaning is relatively shaped and determined, music in Deaf culture, a linguistic minority defined by the use of sign language, has been subjugated to mainstream manifestations that undermine and marginalize Deaf experiences of sound.[4] Products such as headphones designed to transmit

---

1   Connell Crooms, email correspondence with the author, February 21, 2020.
2   The Music Educators National Conference (MENC) is a US-based organization known today as the National Association for Music Education (NAfME).
3   Robert A. Choate, "Documentary Report of the Tanglewood Symposium," *Music Educators National Conference* (Washington, DC: Library of Congress, 1968), iii.
4   I am employing the practice of differentiating Deaf culture from the condition of being deaf through the use of a capitalized "D," a convention proposed by James

music exclusively to the ear, music streaming platforms programmed solely for audio file formats, and learning assessments in the form of aural exams, implemented within classrooms to assess musical skill and development, foster a hearing-centric realization of music that places auditory senses at the forefront of musical experience.[5] This ideology, when projected onto music in Deaf culture, delegitimizes the culture because it constructs a reality in which deafness functions as an impediment to musical experience instead of as a component that shapes it. However, Deaf musicians have been able to work toward subverting ideological limitations that have been placed on their music and by extension their bodies. Some musicians have done this by adapting musical structures produced by mainstream society and realigning them toward Deaf priorities.

While music within Deaf culture encompasses a diversity of forms and is not limited to one particular style, some artists have used hip hop as a foundation to express music that is culturally localized, challenging stereotypes of deafness through their work and subverting hearing-centric constructions of music in the process. This chapter investigates how Deaf rappers have created a style of hip hop that prioritizes d/Deaf experiences of sound over hearing ones and considers how, through performance, they subvert hegemonic control over Deaf musical expression and promote the recognition and inclusion of Deaf forms of musicking.

Situating Myself

My own understanding of music has been dominated by my experience as a hearing person. I grew up in a musical household, where singing around the piano was a frequent family activity and vocal tonality was prized. I consumed music through technology that catered to my body and listening practices. I studied music in academic institutions whose music instruction and assessment were designed in ways that were accessible to me and inclusive of my musical experiences. These systems privileged my perspective of music and, in turn, validated my body through the "musical ability" acquired and demonstrated by it. It wasn't until I began graduate studies in ethnomusicology at

---

Woodward in 1972. See Carol Padden and Tom Humphries, *Deaf in America: Voices from a Culture* (Cambridge, MA: Harvard University Press, 1988), 2.

5   Katelyn E. Best, "Musical Belonging in a Hearing-Centric Society: Adapting and Contesting Dominant Cultural Norms through Deaf Hip Hop," *Journal of American Sign Languages and Literatures*, August 6, 2018, trans. Carla Shird, 5, http://journalofasl.com/deaf-hiphop/.

Florida State University in 2008 that I became critically aware of the musical bias embedded within them and myself.

I first began researching Deaf music in 2011 and, in 2012, I began conducting fieldwork on the development of dip hop in the United States, a style of hip hop that employs the technique of rapping in signed language.[6] I became involved in this research because I was interested in learning more about this style of music, its development, and practitioners, but also because there was a dearth of research on Deaf music that employed ethnomusicological modes of investigation to examine a culturally relative construction of music in Deaf culture.

As a community whose members reside in various geographical locations, Deaf culture is translocalized—existing in transient spaces that extend across localities, and its ethnomusicological study subsequently extends beyond geographical spaces as field locations become transient and realized in both physical and virtual domains.[7] As Deaf scholar Joseph J. Murray points out, "The major features of the new Deaf cultural landscape consist of gatherings at designated public or private spaces situated both in physical, geographical space and at virtual sites that exist only in moments of active creation and consumption."[8] When conducting fieldwork at physical sites such as Deaf festivals, ASL slams, open mic nights, and concerts, I used more traditional means of documentation including written observations, informal interviews, photography, and audio/visual recording. On the other hand, virtual sites, like Twitter, Facebook, SoundClick, and YouTube, became both ethnographic and archival sites of investigation as the electronic spaces in which artists and their followers interact became indefinitely preserved within online platforms. In addition to this, many of my interviews with artists took place virtually, both synchronously and asynchronously, through means of Skype, Facebook messaging, email correspondence, etc. in order to facilitate scheduling, online access, and communication through a shared written language.

---

6   A significant portion of this early fieldwork was published in "That's so Def: Redefining Music Through Dip Hop, the Deaf Hip Hop Movement in the United States," Ph.D. diss., Florida State University, 2015.

7   Clemens Greiner and Patrick Sakdapolrak, "Translocality: Concepts, Applications and Emerging Research Perspectives," Geography Compass 7, no. 5 (2013): 373–74.

8   Joseph J. Murray, "Coequality and Transnational Studies: Understanding Deaf Lives," in Open Your Eyes: Deaf Studies Talking, ed. H-Dirksen L. Bauman (Minneapolis: University of Minnesota Press, 2008), 105.

Sound in Deaf Culture

"Strobe lights are Damn Noisy"
Shannon Dean Marsh, Deaf educator and former Asl *instructor*[9]

Within Deaf culture, deafness is a way of life informed by a shared language, community, and sensory experience of the world; in this context, music takes on new meaning as musical experience is expanded to other senses of the body. Although agreement is complicated by different degrees of deafness, subsequent ranges of auditory perception, and ages of onset, along with a host of socio-cultural factors, a culturally relative construction of music in Deaf culture stems from an intersensory experience of sound that decentralizes an aural-centric framework. Musicologist Jeannette DiBernardo Jones notes, "In a deaf musical experience, the whole body becomes the membrane. Both deaf and hearing people can feel sound vibrations, but hearing people tend to focus only on the auditory perception of these sound vibrations."[10] While deafness naturally subverts the dominance of auditory input over other sensory domains within sonic experience, Deaf cultural practices further shape and determine interpretations of sound. As sound studies scholar Tom Rice reminds, "rather than being a universal set of sensory aptitudes, ways of listening are an aspect of 'habitus,' a set of culturally informed bodily and sensory dispositions."[11] In this regard, culturally acquired ways of knowing, participating in, and navigating the world produce shared realizations of sound within Deaf culture that deviate from traditional associations with the ear.

While the word "sound" is conventionally defined in acoustic terms, sound in Deaf culture is signified across sensory modalities. As Mara Mills observes, "The history of deaf communication makes clear that sound is always already multimodal."[12] Given the form, practice, and centrality of sign language within Deaf culture, words commonly associated with sound in oral language, such as "speaking" and "listening," are applied to other sensory domains. In her book, *Staring How We Look* Rosemarie Garland-Thomson uses the phrase "visual listening" when describing communication in sign language. She remarks, "This kind of visual listening can exceed the range of hearing communication, as when

9   Shannon Dean Marsh, Facebook message to the author, February 3, 2020.
10 Jeannette DiBernardo Jones, "Imagined Hearing: Music-Making in Deaf Culture," in *The Oxford Handbook of Music and Disability Studies*, ed. Blake Howe et al. (New York: Oxford University Press, 2015), 58.
11 Tom Rice, "Listening," in Keywords in Sound, ed. David Novak and Matt Sakakeeny (Durham, NC: Duke University Press, 2015), 101.
12 Mara Mills, "Deafness," in *Keywords in Sound*, ed. David Novak and Matt Sakakeeny (Durham, NC: Duke University Press, 2015), 52.

a Deaf person 'overhears' a conversation across a room or chats with signers far out of auditory range."[13] Since sign language is communicated manually, the reality of "speaking" applies to bodily movement and "listening" to visual reception. In this regard, conversations can be "heard" in environments that do not facilitate aural reception, for instance through windows, crowded spaces, or underwater. As discussed by Jeannette DiBernardo Jones in her chapter titled "Imagined Hearing: Music-Making in Deaf Culture," this concept of visual listening is realized within American Sign Language through the sign LISTEN placed by the eyes instead of the ears, the latter of which would denote aural listening. d/Deaf educator and former American Sign Language instructor Shannon Marsh explains that for the past decade, the ASL community has tried to differentiate between listening in terms of hearing and seeing by using the number "3" handshape and twitching the fingers beside the eyes instead of the ears.[14] This change in placement indicates that the act of "listening" is being executed by the eyes but also signifies a move towards liberating words that have been colonized by hearing priorities and reassigning them to constitute Deaf ones.[15] Marsh attributes the prior use and implementation of LISTEN signed beside the ears to oralism and the Milan Convention, which led to changes in deaf education that discriminated against Deaf culture, linguistic practices, and ways of life by imposing hearing practices and values onto Deaf bodies. Forced adoption of oral communication in place of manual was the most prominent form of oppression that resulted from the Convention.[16] Marsh notes that after the Convention, "The focus on [the] ability to hear and speak was so pervasive in education for the deaf." He further remarks,

> "Listen." That was a word that was preached upon deaf school kids, focusing on using our ears [...] as time went on, we realized "Well, listen[,] how do we listen? With our eyes! Not our ears!" So, we modified the signs that were

13   Rosemarie Garland-Thomson, *Staring: How We Look* (Oxford: Oxford University Press, 2009), 121.

14   Shannon Dean Marsh, Facebook message to the author, February 3, 2020.

15   This is not to say that the sign LISTEN placed by the ears is meaningless to Deaf people. As musicologist Jessica Holmes notes in her article that theoretically examines d/Deaf listening experiences, "Many d/Deaf people, including those who are profoundly deaf, have residual hearing [...]. The significance and function of residual hearing is, however, necessarily individual." See Holmes, "Expert Listening beyond the Limits of Hearing: Music and Deafness." *Journal of the American Musicological Society* 70, no. 1 (2017): 175.

16   Leila Monaghan. "Deaf Education History: Milan 1880," in *The SAGE Deaf Studies Encyclopedia*, ed. Genie Gertz and Patrick Boudreault (London: Sage Publications, 2016), 173–78.

centered around ears to eyes [...]. How we process language [and] input information really is ultimately [with] our eyes, not ears.[17]

Rapper and actor, Darius "Prinz-D the First Deaf Rapper" McCall, describes implementing this practice within his performance. For instance, he explains that if he's rapping the phrase "Listen, hear me out," he would sign "hear me out" beside his eyes to reflect how his Deaf audiences "hear" him.[18] Within this example, he attributes the eyes with processes of listening. While the adoption of this practice is not ubiquitous within the Deaf community or consistent among Deaf rappers, its structure and application reflect culturally constituted listening practices that also contribute towards decentralizing the ideological pervasiveness of associations with the ear.

According to Deaf scholars Carol Padden and Tom Humphries,

> There are two ways to think about sound. The most familiar is that sound is a change in the physical world that can be detected by the auditory system [...]. But what is often overlooked is that sound is also an organization of meaning around a variation in the physical world.[19]

Within this construction of "sound as variance," sound can be manifested through patterns of light, colors, motions, or frequencies. While these manifestations can be directly related to acoustic sound patterns, they can also exist outside of them. Musicologist Jessica Holmes discusses this in terms of "imagined sound." In her broad analysis of d/Deaf experiences of sound, Holmes suggests "Through the synchronization of visual cues with corresponding imagined sounds, the image and its movement thus serve as an index of sorts; the visual cue automatically triggers the 'sound.'"[20] This is representative, for example, in switching lights on and off. While this is a culturally accepted way to get someone's attention in the Deaf community, it is also considered "noisy" within some contexts. As Marsh explains from his own experience, "Visual lights that are jarring [are] extremely noisy for me."[21] Here, Marsh uses the word "noisy," one that has been linguistically tied to audible productions of sound to describe disruptive visual input and in doing so extends sonic meaning. These sonic formations and linguistic extensions can be compared to Garland-Thomson's application of "visual listening" but applied to sound to refer to "visual sounding." "Visual sounding" is used here to denote the production

---

17   Shannon Dean Marsh, Facebook message to the author, February 26, 2021.
18   Darius McCall, M4a audio correspondence with the author, April 6, 2020.
19   Carol Padden and Tom Humphries, *Deaf in America: Voices from a Culture* (Cambridge, MA: Harvard University Press, 1988), 92.
20   Holmes, "Expert Listening beyond the Limits of Hearing," 188.
21   Shannon Dean Marsh, Facebook message to the author, February 3, 2020.

of visual stimuli that are processed as rhythmic and spatial patterns and, in essence, metaphorically "sound."

The sonic landscape shaped by culturally informed realizations of sound re-determines musical meaning based on Deaf aesthetics. As Deaf studies scholar Summer Loeffler remarks, "Deaf people operate in a different sensory universe and thus have formed a unique take on music, one which encompasses visual and tactile forms."[22] When song lyrics are expressed in sign language, music becomes extremely visual. When incorporated, lyrics in sign language become a fundamental musical component, one that is "sonically" visual. At the same time, visual musical elements are not limited to linguistic expression. In her study on music in Deaf culture ethnomusicologist Miriam Gerberg notes,

> David Spayne of Colchester England also spoke of "seeing" music. He says: "I 'see' music in movement, the conductor's baton moving, the violin bows going up and down. Also on the beach, the waves lapping the shore and the trees blowing in the wind. It's the same way I lip read."[23]

In this description, Spayne first provides an example of a traditional musical setting, but focuses on visual stimuli (i.e., the movements of the baton and the violin bows). The latter is directly tied to the production of sound whereas the former prompts it. In instances of acoustic silence within this setting, the conductor's baton still visually sounds. In the second example, Spayne experiences music in unconventional contexts. Here, he describes aspects of nature, which visually sound around him, as musical (i.e., the movement of water and trees).

In their article, Jody Cripps and Ely Lyonblum describe "signed music," which they use to classify musical expression originating from within Deaf culture, as encompassing compositions that incorporate lyrics as well as those that incorporate non-lyrics. They explain that "Non-lyrics do not include language in an explicit manner, but musicians who produce these sounds are expected to possess the necessary language and cultural knowledge."[24] Through their example of a non-lyric signed song, "Eyes" composed and performed by J. E. Cripps, they highlight how the music of the song is sounded visually, noting "She [J. E. Cripps] performed using hand and facial movements in an abstract way [...] [and] successfully produced what is visually perceived as music from

22 Summer Loeffler, "Deaf Music: Embodying Language and Rhythm," in *Deaf Gain: Raising the Stakes for Human Diversity*, ed. H-Dirksen L. Bauman and Joseph J. Murray (Minneapolis: University of Minnesota Press, 2014), 438.

23 Miriam Gerberg, "Falling on Deaf Ears: Musical Meaning and Experience in the American Deaf Community," unpublished manuscript, 2007, 14.

24 Jody Cripps and Ely Lyonblum, "Understanding the Use of Signed Language for Making Music," *Society for American Sign Language Journal* 1, no. 1 (2017): 79.

beginning to end."[25] In A *Deaf Way II Anthology: A Literary Collection by Deaf and Hard of Hearing Writers*, Melissa Whalen discusses her experience of visual elements intertwined with acoustic ones, writing, "At the Deaf school, we had a special music room in which flashing colored lights represented the different musical tones. When the stereo was turned on, the room became a disco, a kaleidoscope of colors flashing around the walls."[26] While this example employs music that was created outside of the Deaf community, the incorporation of visual components dislodged the centrality of aurality within Whalen's musical listening experience. Similarly, Deaf artist and rapper Sean Forbes provides another perspective of this kind of interrelation through a video clip he posted of his band's drummer, Nick King, playing a drum kit engineered to illuminate with each percussive hit. Adding the tag "visual drummer" to the post, he writes, "Can you feel the rhythm just from seeing this?"[27] By adding the descriptor "visual" to "drummer," Forbes identifies drumming with visual components and correlates the sense of feeling through seeing within his question referring to the rhythmic patterns played by King. These examples, provided by Whalen and Forbes, depict visual musical elements while also demonstrating cross-modal components that amplify an intersensory experience of music.

Music in Deaf culture, as Loeffler noted earlier, can also encompass tactile components which shape musical contour. While, according to anthropologists Michele Friedner and Stefan Helmreich, "phenomenologies of vibration are not singular," tactility can contribute to and function as another component of musical experience.[28] As rapper and Deaf activist Warren "Wawa" Snipe explains, "Letting the music take over has a mysterious way to allow you to enjoy beats or tingling sensations that some deaf cannot hear but feel."[29] Wawa highlights the variation of deaf experience but also indicates towards shared practices of feeling within Deaf culture. Yet, as Holmes remarks,

> The feasibility of touch/vibration as a listening strategy depends on a host of logistical variables, such as the material properties of a given acoustical

25 Cripps and Lyonblum, "Understanding the Use of Signed Language," 86.

26 Melissa Whalen, "The Noisy House," in *The Deaf Way II Anthology: A Literary Collection by Deaf and Hard of Hearing Writers*, ed. Tonya M. Stremlau (Washington, DC: Gallaudet University Press, 2002), 24.

27 Sean Forbes. "Sean Forbes on Facebook Watch." Facebook Watch. Sean Forbes, April 26, 2019. https://www.facebook.com/deafandloud/videos/34860875267 7084/.

28 Michele Friedner and Stefan Helmreich, "Sound Studies Meets Deaf Studies," *Senses and Society* 7, no. 1 (2012): 77.

29 Katelyn E. Best, "'We Still Have a Dream:' The Deaf Hip Hop Movement and the Struggle Against the Socio-Cultural Marginalization of Deaf People," *Lied und Populäre Kultur/Song and Popular Culture* 60/61 (2015–16): 72.

space, instrumental register, the degree and method of amplification, and music's precise expressive function.[30]

Rapper and founding member of Silent Mob James "Def Thug" Taylor III articulates challenges of not always being able to experience this musical component, noting, "If the music is low I won't be able to feel the beats or vibrate [and] I get frustrated."[31] Prinz-D also describes variables that inhibit this experience, explaining,

> I would love to have speakers on the stage that are facing me. That way I can hear my voice and kind of hear the beat a little better and just kind of feel it more [...] having speakers, like floor speakers pointed towards me, I can really get into the feel of it. Because the audience will feel it [either way]; however, I won't feel it as much without them [speakers], but I can still make it rock![32]

Here, McCall highlights the importance of being able to audibly hear acoustic elements and kinesthetically feel vibrational components of his compositions, thus emphasizing the intersensory experience of his music and performance. Within Deaf culture, vibration functions as another component that can be used to shape musical experience. While, as Def Thug and Prinz-D observe, the amplification and directionality of speakers can enhance the acuteness of vibrations, these experiences can also be heightened through tactile interfaces. As Wawa describes,

> With your head on the piano and feeling it—it channels. It heightens your sense, where you know exactly where you want the feeling. I've had a couple of people call me telling me "you know Wawa, the way you hear music is different [from] how we do it but it's addictive." [...] I like to use anything to take the sound [...] I like to take it apart and find something that gets my interest and zoom in on it. Then I put it all together again and it's like a whole new thing. And people were like "What did you just do?" "Well, I just took the groove." "No, that wasn't there before." "Yes, it was." "No way! How did you know?" "Well I felt it." "You felt it?"[33]

In his description, Wawa not only shows the impact of the tactile components and interfaces that play a role within his musical composition, expression, and performance, but also expands musical experience beyond normative notions. Loeffler observes, "Many Deaf people in history have shown that music has a different meaning for them and thus have reframed the way Deaf people perceive

---

30   Holmes, "Expert Listening beyond the Limits of Hearing," 209.
31   James L. Taylor III, email correspondence with the author, December 12, 2014.
32   Darius McCall, M4a audio correspondence with the author, April 6, 2020.
33   Warren Snipe, Skype interview with the author, August 22, 2013.

and enjoy music."[34] While a Deaf realization of sound employs visual and tactile sensory modes, this is not to say that aurality is entirely disregarded. Rather, aural elements share a more equitable role, or in some instances, a lesser role in relation to other sensory domains. These characteristics and intersensory experiences of sound represent a Deaf acoustemology that integrates aural, visual, and kinesthetic modes of sonic exploration.

Hip Hop as a Platform

> "I [was] born where Rap [was] Born at
> and In The South Bronx where I Grew up we always play loud Musics."
> *James "Def Thug" Taylor III, rapper, writer, and founding member of Silent Mob*[35]

Musically, hip hop[36] possesses characteristics that appeal to culturally informed experiences of sound in Deaf culture. Sean Forbes describes the structural appeal of hip hop, explaining, "When I first heard rap music, it really spoke to me because the beats and the bass lines and everything was just very groove driven especially the G-funk stuff from Dr. Dre and other west coast stuff."[37] Prinz-D also remarks, "I am a huge hip hop head. I like any genre that has a lot of boom in the bass drums."[38] Here, Forbes and Prinz-D highlight the unintended predisposition for hip hop music to register with Deaf experiences of sound. For example, pronounced bass beats can trigger a tactile response in a way that higher frequencies do not. The emphasis on the rhythm section in hip hop music, dating back to DJ Cool Herc's practices of isolating and looping the break beat, creates a musical environment that facilitates an intersensory experience.[39] Although a product of a hearing community, hip hop is a rhythmically driven style of music that does not necessarily heighten melodic elements that would otherwise ideologically restrict Deaf experiences to hearing-centric limitations.

Given its DIY origins and grass-roots aesthetics, hip hop offers a democratizing musical landscape that has provided Deaf rappers with tools to actualize music from a Deaf perspective. As African American Studies scholars

---

34   Loeffler, "Deaf Music," 440.

35   James L. Taylor III, email correspondence with the author, December 12, 2014.

36   Within this chapter, when using the term "hip hop," I am referring to the overall musical style generally comprised of "rapping" (the vocal or lyrical content) and "DJing" (the accompanying instrumentals), unless otherwise specified.

37   Sean Forbes, live performance recorded by the author, March 6, 2014.

38   Darius McCall, email correspondence with the author, December 20, 2014.

39   Jeff Chang, *Can't Stop Won't Stop: A History of the Hip-Hop Generation* (London: St. Martin's Press, 2007), 78–9.

Marcyliena Morgan and Dionne Bennett note, "hip-hop culture is based on a democratizing creative and aesthetic ethos. [...] Because most hip-hop artists are self-taught or taught by peers in the hip-hop community, hip-hop has empowered young people of all socioeconomic backgrounds all over the world to become artists in their own right."[40] As such, hip hop culture and the ethos surrounding it has provided an outlet that does not ideologically constrict Deaf people to relying on hearing people for "musical access," but rather allows them to assert and create music on their own terms. According to American journalist and historian Jelani Cobb, "At its core, hip hop's aesthetic contains three components: music, or 'beats,' lyrics, and 'flow'—or the specific way in which beats and lyrics are combined."[41] Drawing from these fundamental elements, dip hop utilizes heavy bass and low frequency patterns for the beats and incorporates the technique of rapping in sign language, producing an intersensory flow that is tactile and visual at its structural core.

In addition to providing a framework that appeals to culturally relative constructions of music in Deaf culture, hip hop also facilitates representation. Since its inception, hip hop has provided a platform for marginalized voices, creating a musical space that amplifies counter-hegemonic narratives and social critique. This is not to say that all hip hop functions in this way. As Craig Meyer and Todd Snyder point out,

> For some, hip-hop music is misogynistic, homophobic, and promotes violence and drug use among America's youth. For others, hip-hop music is voice as action: a genre of music that exemplifies the oppressed voices of an often overlooked and disenfranchised American demographic.[42]

While hip hop is inhabited in many places and exists in dichotomous ways, within this context, it functions as an educative force where "what is represented," "how it is represented," and "who represents it" can be self-determined, subsequently reshaping and renegotiating politics of representation. According to Morgan and Bennett, hip hop "transcends and contests conventional constructions of identity, race, nation, community, aesthetics, and knowledge."[43]

---

40   Marcyliena Morgan and Dionne Bennett, "Hip-hop and the Global Imprint of a Black Cultural Form," *Daedalus* 140, no. 2 (2011): 177.

41   William Jelani Cobb, *To the Break of Dawn. A Freestyle on Hip-Hop* (New York: New York University Press, 2007), 14.

42   Craig A. Meyer and Todd D. Snyder, "The New Political Rhetoric of Hip-Hop Music in the Obama Era" in *Sounds of Resistance: The Role of Music in Multicultural Activism*, ed. Eunice Rojas and Lindsay Michie (Santa Barbara: Praeger, 2013), 229.

43   Morgan and Bennett, "Hip-hop and the Global Imprint of a Black Cultural Form," 177.

In this regard, hip hop has been an outlet for some people within the Deaf community to present themselves on their own terms and through their own language, subsequently breaking down stereotypes of deaf people in the process. While hip hop exists in paradoxical ways, capitalized within a commercial market on the one hand and originating from the peripheries on the other, its contradictory existence opens up opportunities for dip hop artists, along with others originating from the margins, to work their way toward breaking down barriers in the music industry and, by extension, mainstream society.

As a musical genre and broader culture that embraces the underrepresented, the illicit, and the taboo, hip hop embodies an ethos of rebellion that facilitates agency. Within this setting, Deaf rappers claim a musical space that redetermines ways music is realized and empowers a Deaf perspective. Hip hop storytelling techniques facilitate exposure that allows Deaf rappers to move beyond a rhetoric of stigmatization and disability naturalized within discourse on "music" and "deafness" and instead create a new picture based on their experience and cultural reality. Within their discussion on the globalization of hip hop and the development of African styles, African studies scholars Msia Kibona Clark and Mickie Mwanzia Koster remark, "African hip hop groups emerged, and many were inspired to express hip hop culture from African perspectives, thus indigenizing and localizing hip hop to be their voice for social protest."[44] In a similar way, Deaf rappers have gravitated toward hip hop and, in doing so, have been able to participate on their own terms as members of mainstream society—to be represented, included, and heard—while "indigenizing" hip hop to embody Deaf musical aesthetics and constructions of sound.

Dip Hop Performance

> "Dip hop is really hip hop through Deaf eyes—through Deaf culture [...]
> You're learning sign language; you're seeing things through Deaf eyes
> —their view, how they view the world."
> Warren "WAWA" Snipe, rapper, actor, and founder of SLYKI Entertainment[45]

While sign language, coupled with heavy rhythmic bass patterns and the technique of rapping, serves as the primary foundation for dip hop, each performer embodies this style of music in their own way. In order to encompass the diversity of sound experiences within Deaf culture and also express their voices

---

44   Msia Kibona Clark and Mickie Mwanzia Koster, "Introduction," in *Hip hop and Social Change in Africa: Ni Wakati*, ed. Shaheen Ariefdien, et al. (Washington, DC: Lexington Books, 2014), xiii.
45   Warren Snipe, Skype interview with the author, August 22, 2013.

within mainstream culture, some rappers have made their music both bi-lingual and bi-musical.[46] Bi-lingual in this context consists of the inclusion of manual and oral languages. Employing ethnomusicologist Mantle Hood's concept of bi-musicality, bi-musical within this setting refers to the incorporation of Deaf musical aesthetics coupled with hearing aesthetics that may not necessarily be valuable to a Deaf experience of sound but would appeal to a hearing audience. While not a fundamental component of dip hop music and performance, many rappers compose and perform their music in bi-musical ways, making their music accessible to hearing audiences. For some, this also speaks to their bi-musical identity, as well as the position of this musical style within the larger traditions of hip hop and signed music.[47]

These performance structures can take on many forms. Some rappers perform to a pre-recorded track of their music that they record ahead of time in the studio, while others employ d/Deaf or hearing DJs, and there are also those who perform with a live band or include dancers. Depending on the performance venue and travel logistics, many dip hop artists have employed various combinations of these structures within their performances at one point or another. In terms of performing bi-lingually, some rappers perform their lyrics in both languages simultaneously, others hire a hearing vocalist to interpret the lyrics from sign language, and many others perform in sign language to a pre-recorded track of their lyrics so they can focus their attention on performing in sign language instead of trying to concentrate on rapping in two different languages that employ different grammatical and rhyming structures. While many Deaf rappers perform their songs in both oral and manual languages in order to make their music accessible for hearing people, and by extension market to a larger audience, these translations of lyrics are not a necessary component.[48] At the same time, some rappers, especially those who did not acquire sign language at an early age, do not consider the incorporation of oral lyrics to be a translation since the language is very much a part of their bi-lingual identity.

Other practitioners of dip hop, particularly grassroots rappers and dip hop groups, perform primarily for Deaf audiences and do not incorporate the use of oral language or bi-musical elements. For example, Silent Mob, an early grassroots rap group originating from the Bronx, N.Y., has performed most of

---

46   Mantle Hood, "The Challenge of 'Bi-musicality,'" *Ethnomusicology* 4, no. 2 (1960): 55–9.

47   When using "signed music" here, I am referring to Cripps and Lyonblum's definition of the term that classifies it as "original lyric and/or non-lyric musical performances done by native deaf signers" (Cripps and Lyonblum, "Understanding the Use of Signed Language," 78).

48   Best, "'We Still Have a Dream,'" 74.

their music solely in sign language. Def Thug explains, "I play beats with no voices. That Was My plan, [and] I keep it that way because that's where we started rap, with our hands first, not voices."[49] Instead of incorporating oral and manual languages—for example ASL with English—Def Thug describes creating a mixture of ASL, home signs, and street signs. He comments,

> We have [our] own "Street Sign Language" [...] I'm from South Bronx from the Project, and Of course I use street language. So I mixed it with ASL. It's like magic [−] will make your eyez hypnotize. Not only that, I learned from other Deaf Thugs from all Over The Bronx, Harlem, Brooklyn, Queen[s], and [a] few [other] states. They have their own street sign languages so I used it sometime[s].[50]

While performing in an oral language is not a fundamental requirement of dip hop, practitioners agree that if a performance does not include sign language it is not dip hop.[51] While each rapper employs different performance techniques and embodies dip hop musically in their own way, collectively, they have used hip hop as a foundation in which to express and promote a culturally relative style of music.

Some practitioners of dip hop self-identify in different ways. Some instances include "deaf rapper," "ASL rapper," or "signsong rapper," emphasizing the fundamental component of rap incorporated within this style. Some of these artists apply the term "dip dop" to classify their music, while others use "hip hop," "deaf hip hop," or "sign language rap." However, the term "dip hop," which was coined by Wawa in 2005, functions as a way to identify this style of music while facilitating the formation of a musical category that is comprised of Deaf musical elements, one unassociated with words that may evoke etic stereotypes of music and deafness.[52] Furthermore, the creation of the sign DIP HOP also serves to classify a new musical style that is created by and for members of the Deaf community. The sign DIP HOP consists of the ASL letter "F" handshape and is a compound sign, one that combines two signs together. As Marsh notes,

> Wawa's "dip hop" [sign] is an "F" handshape and it's unique... I'd suggest that it is a combination of "find/pick/discover" for the first half of the sign, then sideways movement with the same handshape makes me think of "free," or something a conductor for an opera would do. [...] So basically, it's like "Find

49 James L. Taylor III, email correspondence with the author, December 12, 2014.
50 James L. Taylor III, email correspondence with the author, December 12, 2014
51 Best, "'We Still Have a Dream,'" 74.
52 Best, "'We Still Have a Dream,'" 73.

and be Free." ...he [Wawa] managed to "Morph" those two separate signs and their facial expressions/cues into one.[53]

The following figure, which is based on a video by Wawa, demonstrates the handshape and movement of the sign.[54]

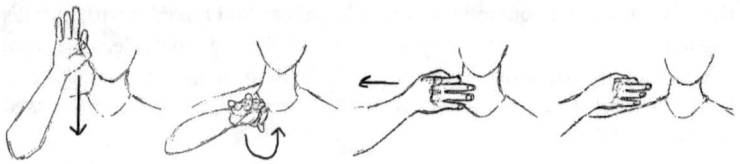

Figure 1: Anne Wood Drysdale, original sketch of Asl sign "Dip Hop," 2021, original drawing. Photo: Anne Wood Drysdale. Courtesy of the artist.

As Marsh notes, the movement of the sign is similar to that of a conductor, traveling downwards in motion but instead of moving outward, it dips inward and then out to the side.

Dip hop is brought to life through live performance. Within this space, dip hop artists create a musical landscape that heightens intersensory experiences of sound and promotes alternative modes of musicking based on Deaf aesthetics. Given this, the musical elements, structures, and tools incorporated within dip hop performances are designed to communicate and appeal across sensory modalities. According to Deaf studies scholar H-Dirksen Bauman, "The traditional parsing out of senses in the West is a bit of a folk belief that links each sense with a particular organ, instead of seeing perception as a more malleable synesthetic process."[55] In order to enhance cross-modal sensory perception within performance settings, some musicians and artists within the Deaf community have creatively implemented and adapted different instruments, media, and technology. For example, musician Myles de Bastion, founder of CymaSpace, draws from cymatics in order to develop new technologies that expand sensory perception within performance contexts. He explains,

---

53   Shannon Marsh, Skype interview with the author, December 21, 2014. When asked about the creation of the sign and Marsh's analysis, Wawa confirmed and said that it was "on point" (Warren Snipe, Facebook message to the author, March 2, 2021).

54   Warren Snipe, .Mov audio/visual correspondence with the author, December 14, 2014.

55   Joseph N. Straus, Extraordinary Measures: Disability in Music (New York: Oxford University Press, 2011), 169.

Our events can be experienced using all the senses. Our team (develop & invent) multi-sensory technologies. For example[,] furniture such as chairs and couches that react to the music and vibrate. And lighting fixtures, guitars and drums are a variety of instruments we make.[56]

Inventions such as these and adaptations of musical structures and tools have been utilized within dip hop concerts, subsequently enhancing the musicking experience across sensory domains. In a virtual performance streamed on February 20, 2021, Sean Forbes called attention to this aspect of their performance, remarking,

Nick showing up with that light up drum set... really what happened was, we performed in Kentucky for the Kentucky Deaf Festival. The best Deaf Festival out there. And Nick was like "I need to get a drum set that lights up." So, he came back home [to Detroit] and bought one. So, Nick. Thank you.[57]

The use of this kind of technology is not ubiquitous within dip hop performance, nor is it limited to this musical style; however, it represents new technologies and experimentations that are being explored to facilitate intersensory experiences.

Through their expression of lyrics, performers embody and "sound" visual musical elements that expand musical dimension. When rapping in sign language, musical contour becomes manifested within a spatial dimension that moves beyond vertical and horizontal trajectories.[58] The placement of signs, the pace of signing, and features of the movement, along with other visual cues, shape musical dynamics, accent, and tone. When asked about the use of dynamics within conversational communication, Marsh commented that

[A] form of whisper is when you sign really small. [...] As for shouting. Sign way big! When I get excited. During a lecture. Or. A conversation. I really

---

56 Myles de Bastion, "D-PAN Interview: Myles de Bastion- Musician." YouTube, dpanvideos, uploaded on 4 March 2015, https://www.youtube.com/watch?v=brTeroQTRwc.

57 Sean Forbes, Live virtual performance recorded by the author, February 20, 2021.

58 Anabel Maler has analyzed this in her own work on sign language song translations; see Maler, "Songs for Hands: Analyzing Interactions of Sign Language and Music," *Music Theory* Online 19, no.1 (2013) and "Musical Expression Among Deaf and Hearing Song Signers," in *The Oxford Handbook of Music and Disability Studies*, 73–91. This section focuses on the space used by dip hop artists, based on ethnographic research and accounts from its practitioners, and, as such, does not provide a musical analysis of dip hop performances but rather explores a musical epistemology through this research.

sign a lot bigger, take up more space. More extreme facial expressions. Lots more. Moving around. Just claiming a bigger space. So that's shouting.[59]

When applied to performance contexts, rappers are able to play with these dynamics, along with other characteristics that shape the "sounding" of the signs. Prinz-D notes the difference of rapping versus conversing in sign language, explaining,

> Rapping in sign language is so much different to speaking in sign language. [...] it [singing] is much easier to rehearse because, with rap, I rap a little faster because the pace of the lyrics [is] much faster. The instrumental, the beat, is also as fast.[60]

Prinz-D describes often simplifying his signs in order to be able to rap at a faster speed. He does this through a process of recording himself practicing a song and then going back and cutting material until the flow is just right. He also describes how he works with the space on stage and alters his signing in performance contexts, stating,

> I use the stage to my advantage. I like to be closer to the audience to be able to showcase my acting skills [...] I'm theatrical and I want people to draw attention towards my signs and my emotions. In the softer moments, I'm signing in smaller spaces closer to my body [...] A lot of times people know I'm doing an emotional song when I start to look down and my head is looking at the signs and they're much closer to my body towards my chest. I get closer to the audience but I slow down the ASL so people can understand it better because it is confined to a small space on my chest.[61]

Here, Prinz-D points out characteristics of his own performance style based on his affinity for acting but also calls attention to how his body positioning, sign placement, and size of movement musically conveys the mood of a song. He uses larger signs on his choruses to signal group "singing" or participation. While each rapper fashions their own style and performance techniques, Prinz-D's account demonstrates that the use of sign language, which is foundational to dip hop performances, conveys visual elements that are likewise integral to the music.

Since hip hop is a rhythmically driven style of music, rhythm plays a fundamental role within dip hop music and is manifested in different ways within the context of performance. When rapping in sign language, artists embody rhythm through the duration and movement of signs while emphasizing an underlying rhythmic beat with their bodies. As Prinz-D explains,

---

59   Shannon Dean Marsh, Facebook message to the author, February 5, 2020.
60   Darius McCall, M4a audio correspondence with the author, April 6, 2020.
61   Darius McCall, M4a audio correspondence with the author, April 6, 2020.

a lot of times with beats, I would try to sign towards the beat—sign towards the line. [...] My signs would match that rhythm. Also, I would just shake my body, just like "uh, uh, uh." I would just snap my shoulders side to side. [...] So just imagine, if you can just visualize, you can actually see me shuffle, almost doing like a Harlem shake. [...] [On certain beats] you can actually kind of visualize my shoulders and head doing a circle motion and my signs go that way too.[62]

Here, Prinz-D demonstrates sounding the rhythm with his body, as it is directly related to the movement of his signing. Cognitive neuroscientist Frank Russo describes a beat as "a pattern of *perceptual* accents that occur at equally spaced time intervals across a rhythmic sequence" noting that "by invoking the notion of a perceptual accent, the beat is ultimately a psychological construct."[63] He explains further, stating,

There are several reasons for considering the beat in this manner. First, the perceptual accents need not be physically prominent (i.e., louder or longer). Second, the beats of a rhythm do not always coincide with events of a rhythm. Third, the feeling of the beat can persist even after the music stops.[64]

In this regard, the beat embodied by Prinz-D visually "sounds," and continues to persist even if it is not always visible, for instance in moments when he stops rapping or if his body is paused or executing other rhythms. This process of neural entrainment is also realized through other visual, tactile, and aural patterns within dip hop performance that activate multi-sensory experiences of rhythm not associated with linguistic structures. De Bastion comments, "I have experimented with changing sound into light! I connect the sound intensity with the color of light. The human brain is exceptionally good at pattern recognition."[65] As noted by de Bastion's statement, cross-modal sensory experiences associated through patterns are not restricted to rhythmic elements but can apply to melodic ones as well.

Dip hop performances can also include other visual and tactile components that contribute to expanding sensory experiences of music while broadening musical arrangement and structure. Some rappers use video screens to project their lyrics, adding another musical aspect to their performance that visually illustrates both rhythmic and melodic elements. The text on the screen strengthens the visual experience of music through variations in movement,

62   Darius McCall, M4a audio correspondence with the author, April 6, 2020.
63   Frank A. Russo, "Music Beyond Sound: Weighing the Contributions of Touch, Sight, and Balance," *Acoustical Society of America* 16, no. 1 (2020): 39.
64   Russo, "Music Beyond Sound," 39.
65   De Bastion, "D-PAN Interview."

illustration, size, and placement. For example, musical accents can be conveyed through different colors of words that emphasize or isolate a section of a word or phrase. Word painting can be employed visually through placement manipulation or color signification. Dynamics can also be expressed through alterations in font size. Adrian Mangiardi, who has directed music videos for Sean Forbes as well as other rappers like Wawa, has been a pioneering artistic leader in this medium. He describes his initial experience filming and editing his first music video, "I'm Deaf" by Sean Forbes, explaining,

> At that time there were no words. It was just Sean signing with a white background. I was watching it with my cochlear implants on and then suddenly they died. I was lost. I couldn't follow the beat. So, I got in touch with Sean […] and we both thought it would be good to put the words in the video.[66]

In addition to demonstrating the ways sound is visually realized through film, the inclusion and illustration of lyrics within music videos and screens also provide linguistic access to deaf audience members who do not speak sign language or who, for instance, speak British Sign Language instead of American Sign Language, or vice versa, but share a common written language.

Although prominent components, the incorporation of sign language and video screens, if employed, are not the only ways in which rappers decentralize aural experiences and expand music to other senses. Lights can be used to express musical components and rhythmic patterns, as in de Bastion's work with CymaSpace for instance. Unless the artists travel with instruments or gear, however, the incorporation of this component is largely determined by performance venues and local production engineers. Beyond logistical challenges, some dip hop artists choose not to include lights in their performances because they either find them too distracting or feel that they detract from the primary focus. At the same time, lights remain a component used by some rappers in their performances and/or a feature of performance venues. In addition, the incorporation of live instruments can also provide another visual layer. For example, Jake Bass, Sean Forbes's producer, collaborator, and band member, is often seen playing the keytar within live performances since it produces a more visual experience of the patterns of his movements, which would ordinarily be obscured if he was playing an electric piano.

While these techniques emphasize visualizations of rhythm and melody, tactile components also contribute toward enhancing alternative experiences

---

66   Adrean Mangiardi, "D-Pan Interview: Adrean Mangiardi—Video Director." YouTube, dpanvideos, uploaded on 7 February 2013, https://www.youtube.com/w atch?v=hYhceJGM6hc.

Figure 2: Mark Levin (left), Sean Forbes (middle), and Jake Bass (right), video screens and keytar at Performance in Pittsburgh, 2014, digital image, Pittsburgh, PA. Photo: Katelyn Best.

of music. Vibrations of heavy rhythmic bass patterns function as a significant tactile component within dip hop performances. As Russo explains, "Cities around the world host Deaf raves—giant parties where dancers feel the music through powerful subwoofers and bass shakers connected to floorboards."[67] Deaf Rave, an organization founded in England by Troi "DJ Chinaman" Lee, which includes rappers Kevin "Signkid" Walker and Matthew "MC Geezer" Taylor, has used experimental tactile audio technology, produced by SUBPAC, that is designed to heighten the sensitivity of low bass frequencies through wearable packs. Not Impossible Labs is another business that has produced similar technology for artists' use in the US. In addition to these experimental technologies, tactile interfaces and other vibrotactile stimuli have also been incorporated or provided by some rappers within the context of dip hop performances. According to Loeffler,

> Deaf people do take advantage of architectural surroundings to enhance tactile communication and to embody materials to fit Deaf bodies and needs. [...] Deaf people, likewise, have applied architectural materials and

---

67   Russo, "Music Beyond Sound," 37.

objects to enhance their appreciation for music. Examples include using balloons [...] and sitting on top of speakers at concerts.[68]

When Marko "Signmark" Vuoriheimo, a Finnish based rapper, performed in Florida during his 2012 US tour, balloons were provided to contribute to a multi-sensory experience. Some dip hop artists have also traveled with subwoofers and vibrating floors that further enhance tactile musical components.

While technical production components such as lights, screens, visual projections, and subwoofers are not limited to dip hop concerts or used by all practitioners of this style, these performance settings draw attention to elements that redefine what is musical. Within this context, rappers heighten musical experiences that decentralize aural components, subsequently subverting hearing-centric constructions of music that have restricted what music is and can be within Deaf culture. Although musical perception varies from person to person, audiences within dip hop performances become immersed in a performance space where music, culturally defined, is enhanced, Deaf aesthetics are prioritized, and musical elements can be experienced across sensory domains, subsequently, providing a more inclusive performance experience.

Figure 3: Signmark (left), Brandon Bauer (middle), and DJ Weirdness (right), audience member waves balloon at performance in Lake Mary, FL, 2012, digital image, Lake Mary, FL. Photo: Katelyn Best.

---

68   Loeffler, "Deaf Music," 451.

Representing and Re-presenting

"My music is very emotional. It's insightful. It's story based, and it's based off of my experiences as a deaf person growing up."

Prinz-D, rapper, actor, and former member of the Helix Boyz[69]

Using hip hop as a foundation, deaf rappers have developed a musical style that provides an inclusive performance experience that represents music from a Deaf perspective. Through performance presence, lyrical content, and word play, dip hop artists create a stage in which to reposition deafness on their own terms and break down stereotypes proliferated by an etic perspective.

As Wawa observes,

> We're coming to a point where people are having a hard time believing that we are deaf or hard of hearing cause some of these folks think, "You're not supposed to be able to talk, you're not supposed to even be able to hear the music, how is this?" So, this is our teaching moment, our educating moment.[70]

Within the context of dip hop performance, Deaf rappers negotiate attitudes and misrepresentations through their own voice while expressing their individual and collective identity. Through their music, dip hop artists reclaim their Deaf identity, address discrimination and oppression based on deafness, and raise awareness to the inherent value of Deaf ways of being. This can be observed within the song titles alone, for instance, "We No Hear" by Wawa, "Listen with Your Eyes" by Signkid, "I'm Deaf" by Sean Forbes, "Diamanthände" (Diamond Hands) by DKN, "Deaf Man Dem in the Deafhood" by MC Geezer, "Our Life" by Signmark, and "Story Ya Ma Champion" by Lal Daggy. As Wawa noted,

> Sean Forbes talks about Deaf culture in his work. Signmark was the heaviest person to really talk about Deaf culture in his work. [...] I'm more of a storyteller but I have a punch line that can draw you in. The kind of thing where people are like "whoa."[71]

Together through their work and the expressive techniques they each individually employ, dip hop artists create a space within mainstream society to educate and raise awareness while empowering other d/Deaf people through their example. Commenting on his music, Prinz-D notes,

> It [my music] appeals to other deaf and hard of hearing audience members, especially the ones who don't know ASL because they can relate to when

---

69   Darius McCall, email correspondence with the author, April 6, 2020.
70   Warren Snipe, Skype interview with the author, August 22, 2013.
71   Warren Snipe, Skype interview with the author, August 22, 2013.

parents neglected them because "Oh, they're deaf. Oh, he can't hear, She can't do this. Oh, I'll just have her sit where she is or stay where he is and we'll take care of it." They feel like they have to depend on people. People have told them "No" or they can't do this or do that because they're deaf. I have to show, not show, but I have to prove it. [...] I can do this.[72]

Through representation, Prinz-D and other dip hop artists subvert ideological constructions of deafness that have historically undermined their identities and stigmatized their bodies while paving the way for other Deaf voices. While not every rapper or every song composed and performed by Deaf artists focuses on Deaf identity, their performance counters ideological Othering and exclusion as they present experiences and perspectives that extend across the deaf and hearing divide.

Drawing from the political and subversive nature of socially conscious hip hop, dip hop artists empower a Deaf musical identity through self-representation while claiming a musical space that is at once representative of individual as well as cultural identity. Deaf activist Connell Crooms addresses the intersectionality of Deaf identity, calling attention to the experiences of Black-Deaf rappers, remarking,

> Hip hop is the story of struggle and triumph in black culture, the documentation of The Black Experience. For Black-Deaf individuals we experience just as much racism and marginalization, deaf hip hop allows us the creative space to express those grievances. We will see more of our own stories being told and the impact that we can have in building democracy by advocating language accessibility and equity in education and the workplace. That's just one issue that both white and black deaf people share in common.[73]

In the hip hop spirit of "keepin' it real," deaf rappers have employed storytelling techniques that represent a Deaf way of life while also illustrating intersectionality. Lyrics, in this regard, provide a platform to creatively address and tackle challenges shared collectively by the Deaf community as well as those experienced at the intersections of individual identity through a style of hip hop that is, in itself, a manifestation of intersectional expression. Within this context, rappers express a voice shaped by culture, race, ethnicity, and class through their own language within a space where it can be amplified. In this way, they represent their Deaf cultural identity and experience of deafness while contributing to a broader representation of the Deaf community. In addition to this, through the musical expression of their own experiences, rappers are able

72   Darius McCall, M4a audio correspondence with the author, April 6, 2020.
73   Connell Crooms, email correspondence with the author, February 21, 2020.

to speak to other people's experiences, creating a space in which their voices are not only recognized but shared. As Prinz-D explains,

> I'll never forget this. I was doing one of my early songs, and there was this one fan. And, the fan was just right by the stage lip syncing every single word of the song—and just knew it from front to back—and came up to me and said "Dude, I really relate to that, your music, because everything that you wrote, you've written about, pretty much happened in my life." And, I believe that's the reason why I wrote music, because there's somebody out there that feel[s] the way I felt growing up. And, if I'm able to touch people and make them feel like someone thinks that they matter too [...]. To be honest, that's the most beautiful thing ever in the world.[74]

Figure 4: Prinz-D (left) and Sho'Roc (right), Signing to "Stand Up" at the Mississippi Deaf Festival, 2014, digital image, Jackson, MS. Photo: Katelyn Best.

Through dip hop performance, rappers not only cultivate cultural recognition and respect, but also decolonize hegemonic control of music in Deaf culture by performatively re-presenting "music" and "deafness" through the use of musical structures shaped by Deaf experiences of sound. While hearing-centric constructions of music have situated deafness as an obstacle limiting musical access, dip hop artists have demonstrated how deafness plays an integral role in shaping musical expression through their use of hip hop.

---

74   Darius McCall, M4a audio correspondence with the author, April 6, 2020.

Within this context, they produce and perform music on their own terms, fostering new ways of musicking—Deaf ways of musicking that expand beyond normative practices so heavily embedded and naturalized within mainstream society. In this regard, dip hop artists are able to subvert power structures that have dominated and limited music in Deaf culture. Through their performance, rappers disrupt singular notions of music, destabilizing musical structure and "know-how" produced by educative forces and embedded within society. While tedious, those that compose and perform bi-lingually and bi-musically foster a musicultural space that is accessible to both deaf and hearing audiences, which generates a wider reach for their music and a more inclusive setting for both d/Deaf and hearing audiences. As Warren Churchill points out when discussing one of Signmark's performances,

> One need not be proficient in ASL to engage with the music; nor do DHH individuals need any special accommodations to experience it [...]. Rather, it suggests something more communal and celebratory. Marko [Signmark], his band mate, and the audience join together in shared *aural* and *visual* gestures of musicking that affirm Deaf cultural pride.[75]

Figure 5: Wawa (front) and audience members, teaching audience members at the Kentucky DeaFestival, 2014, digital image, Louisville, KY. Photo: Katelyn Best.

---

75   Warren Churchill. "Deaf and Hard-of-Hearing Musicians: Crafting a Narrative Strategy." *Research Studies in Music Education* 37, no. 1 (2015): 31.

Within this setting, Deaf culture is brought to the forefront and hearing audience members become immersed in an environment where they are in need of access and oral interpretation, illuminating the importance of linguistic access and equality that is not always represented within hearing musicking spaces. This positioning reinforces cultural ownership of the musical space produced by Deaf rappers, empowering Deaf authority. As Clark and Koster remark, "Globally, hip hop artists have been important agents for social change, directly impacting shifts in behavior and attitudes toward social institutions and traditions." While the content of dip hop music varies and some songs are more socially oriented than others, dip hop artists ultimately invite their audience to become immersed in their world, acting as agents of social change while fostering inclusion and recognition of music based on Deaf aesthetics.

Little Victories

> "I love what I do. I love the community that I grew up in.
> And, I love the way that I experience music.
> Sean Forbes, Rapper and Co-founder of D-PAN (Deaf Professional Artist Network)[76]

Just a week after its release, on February 28, 2020, Sean Forbes's EP, Little Victories, ranked number one in the hip hop genre on iTunes and number one for all categories on Amazon Music, making him the first Deaf musician to make it to the Billboard 200 chart. Coming in at ninety-three for top album sales, Forbes had the support of the Deaf community who rallied behind him to help him achieve this historic goal. As Forbes commented in an interview with the Fox affiliate in Detroit, "The only reason why I'm number one on the charts right now is the Deaf community. Without the Deaf community that would not be possible."[77] From fans to famous icons within and outside of the Deaf community, people shared videos and posts promoting the release of Forbes's album in endeavors to help him achieve recognition within the music industry, in a heightened capacity, for his work as a deaf musician. While the album was released in mp3 format, this medium functions as a way to raise awareness of music in Deaf culture within mainstream popular culture, promoting the work of dip hop artists by extension. This achievement signifies a considerable victory for the Deaf community and demonstrates their combined

---

76 Forbes, February 20, 2021.
77 Fox 2 Detroit, "Deaf Detroit Area Rapper Sean Forbes Makes History, Shoots up the Charts," 29 February 2020, https://www.fox2detroit.com/news/deaf-detr oit-area-rapper-sean-forbes-makes-history-shoots-up-the-charts.

power to break down institutional barriers, self-represent, promote inclusion, and, ultimately, amplify Deaf voices.

In the epigraph that opened this chapter, Crooms stated, "To build democracy is to include the least amongst us and society at large does a poor job of bringing others to the table, so we'll have to bring our own chairs and build a bigger table."[78] Together, dip hop artists are building a bigger table as they break down ideological divisions between "music" and "deafness" that have and continue to suppress experiences of musicking in Deaf culture. With performance as a platform, dip hop artists raise cultural awareness and expand the hegemonic limits of what music is and can be. As Sean Forbes's uncle once told him "you need to create your own path, create your own world. We have Eminem, we have Kid Rock […]. Do something different."[79] In following a different path, dip hop artists have explored music based on culturally relative terms. Even though music has historically been considered by members of both hearing and Deaf communities as a cultural product of a hearing society, Deaf artists are finding more ways to acquire musical meaning based on Deaf aesthetics. Brought together through their unconventional experience of sound shaped by shared cultural aesthetics, dip hop artists as well as other musicians within the Deaf community continue to push conventional musical boundaries. Through their work, they represent music in Deaf culture as they re-present it through new forms of musicking.

References

Aplin, Christopher. "Urban Beats, Religious Beliefs, and Interconnected Streets in Indigenous Hip-Hop: North American Indian Influences in African American Music." In *Sounds of Resistance: The Role of Music in Multicultural Activism*, edited by Eunice Rojas and Lindsay Michie, 85–112. Santa Barbara: Praeger, 2013.

Asante Jr., M. K. *It's Bigger Than Hip Hop: The Rise of the Post-Hip-Hop Generation*. New York: St. Martin's Press, 2008.

Bauman, H-Dirksen L. "Audism: Exploring the Metaphysics of Oppression." *Journal of Deaf Studies and Deaf Education* 9, no. 2 (2004): 239–46.

———, ed. *Open Your Eyes Deaf Studies Talking*. Minneapolis: University of Minnesota Press, 2008.

78　Connell Crooms, email correspondence with the author, February 21, 2020.
79　Sean Forbes, interview with the author, March 6, 2014.

Berdayes, Vincent, Luigi Esposito, and John W. Murphy, eds. *The Body in Human Inquiry: Interdisciplinary Explorations of Embodiment*. Cresskill: Hampton Press, 2004.

Best, Katelyn E. "Musical Belonging in a Hearing-Centric Society: Adapting and Contesting Dominant Cultural Norms through Deaf Hip Hop." *Journal of American Sign Languages and Literatures*, August 6, 2018. Translated by Carla Shird. http://journalofasl.com/deaf-hiphop/.

———. "That's so Def: Redefining Music Through Dip Hop, the Deaf Hip Hop Movement in the United States." Ph.D. diss., Florida State University, 2015.

———. "'We Still Have a Dream:' The Deaf Hip Hop Movement and the Struggle Against the Socio-Cultural Marginalization of Deaf People." *Lied und Populäre Kultur/Song and Popular Culture* 60/61 (2015–16): 61–86.

Cachia, Amanda. "Loud Silence: Turning Up the Volume on Deaf Voice." *The Senses & Society* 10, no. 3 (2016): 321–40.

Chang, Jeff. *Can't Stop Won't Stop: A History of the Hip-Hop Generation*. London: St. Martin's Press, 2007.

Choate, Robert A. *Documentary Report of the Tanglewood Symposium*. Washington, DC: Library of Congress, 1968.

Churchill, Warren. "Deaf and Hard-of-Hearing Musicians: Crafting a Narrative Strategy." *Research Studies in Music Education* 37, no. 1 (2015): 21–36.

Clark, Msia Kibona, and Mickie Mwanzia Koster. "Introduction." In *Hip hop and Social Change in Africa: Ni Wakati*, edited by Shaheen Ariefdien, et al., ix–xxviii. Washington, DC: Lexington Books, 2014.

Cobb, William Jelani. *To the Break of Dawn. A Freestyle on Hip-Hop*. New York: New York University Press, 2007.

Cripps, Jody. "Ethnomusicology & Signed Music: A Breakthrough." *Journal of American Sign Languages and Literatures*, August 6, 2018. Translated by Kathleen Roberts Jarashow. https://journalofasl.com/ethnomusicology/.

Cripps, Jody and Ely Lyonblum. "Understanding the Use of Signed Language for Making Music." *Society for American Sign Language Journal* 1, no. 1 (2017): 78–95.

Darrow, Alice-Ann, and Diane Loomis. "Music and Deaf Culture: Images from the Media and Their Interpretation by Deaf and Hearing Students." *Journal of Music Therapy* 36, no. 2 (1999): 88–109.

de Bastion, Myles. "D-Pan Interview: Myles de Bastion—Musician." YouTube, dpanvideos. Uploaded on 4 March 2015. https://www.youtube.com/watch?v=brTeroQTRwc.

Erlmann, Veit, ed. Hearing Cultures: Essays on Sound, Listening and Modernity. Oxford: Berg Publishers, 2004.

Forbes, Sean. "Sean Forbes on Facebook Watch." *Facebook Watch*. Accessed

November 20, 2019. https://www.facebook.com/deafandloud/videos/34 8608752677084/.

Fox 2 Detroit. "Deaf Detroit Area Rapper Sean Forbes Makes History, Shoots up the Charts." Accessed March 1, 2020. https://www.fox2detroit.com/n ews/deaf-detroit-area-rapper-sean-forbes-makes-history-shoots-up-th e-charts.

Friedner, Michele, and Stefan Helmreich. "Sound Studies Meets Deaf Studies." *Senses and Society* 7, no. 1 (2012): 72–86.

Garland-Thomson, Rosemarie. *Staring: How We Look.* Oxford: Oxford University Press, 2009.

Gerberg, Miriam. "Falling on Deaf Ears: Musical Meaning and Experience in the American Deaf Community." Unpublished manuscript, 2007.

Harrison, Anthony Kwame, and Craig E. Arthur. "Hip-Hop Ethos." *Humanities* 8, no. 1 (2019): 1–14. https://doi.org/10.3390/h8010039.

Holmes, Jessica A. "Expert Listening beyond the Limits of Hearing: Music and Deafness." *Journal of the American Musicological Society* 70, no. 1 (2017): 171–220.

Hood, Mantle. "The Challenge of 'Bi-musicality.'" *Ethnomusicology* 4, no. 2 (1960): 55–59.

Janzen, John M. Ngoma: *Discourses in Healing in Central and Southern Africa.* Berkeley: University of California Press, 1992.

Jones, Jeannette DiBernardo. "Imagined Hearing: Music-Making in Deaf Culture." In *The Oxford Handbook of Music and Disability Studies*, edited by Blake Howe et al., 54–72. New York: Oxford University Press, 2015.

Ladd, Paddy. *Understanding Deaf Culture: In Search of Deafhood.* Bristol: Multilingual Matters, 2003.

Leppänen, Taru. "Unfolding Non-Audist Methodologies in Music Research: Signing Hip Hop Artist Signmark and Becoming Deaf with Music." In Musical Encounters with Deleuze and Guattari, edited by Pirkko Moisala et al., 33–49. New York: Bloomsbury Publishing, 2017.

Listman, Jason et al. "Deaf Musicality and Unearthing the Translation Process." *Journal of American Sign Languages and Literatures*, August 6, 2018. Translated by Kathleen Roberts. http://journalofasl.com/deaf-musicality-and-unearthing-the-translation-process/.

Loeffler, Summer. "Deaf Music: Embodying Language and Rhythm." In *Deaf Gain: Raising the Stakes for Human Diversity*, edited by H-Dirksen L. Bauman and Joseph J. Murray, 436–56. Minneapolis: University of Minnesota Press, 2014.

Maler, Anabel. "Musical Expression Among Deaf and Hearing Song Signers." In *The Oxford Handbook of Music and Disability Studies*, edited by Blake Howe et al., 73–91. New York: Oxford University Press, 2015.

Mangiardi, Adrean. "D-Pan Interview: Adrean Mangiardi—Video Director." You-

Tube, dpanvideos. Uploaded on 7 February 2013. https://www.youtube.co m/watch?v=hYhceJGM6hc.

Meyer, Craig A. and Todd D. Snyder. "The New Political Rhetoric of Hip-Hop Music in the Obama Era." In *Sounds of Resistance: The Role of Music in Multicultural Activism*, edited by Eunice Rojas and Lindsay Michie, 229–49. Santa Barbara: Praeger, 2013).

Mills, Mara. "Deafness." In *Keywords in Sound*, edited by David Novak and Matt Sakakeeny, 45–54. Durham, NC: Duke University Press, 2015.

Minestrelli, Chiara. *Australian Indigenous Hip Hop: The Politics of Culture, Identity, and Spirituality*. New York: Routledge, 2016.

Monaghan, Leila. "Deaf Education History: Milan 1880." In *The SAGE Deaf Studies Encyclopedia*, edited by Genie Gertz and Patrick Boudreault, 173–78. London: Sage Publications, 2016.

Morgan, Marcyliena, and Dionne Bennett. "Hip-hop and the Global Imprint of a Black Cultural Form." *Daedalus* 140, no. 2 (2011): 176–96.

Padden, Carol, and Tom Humphries. *Inside Deaf Culture*. Cambridge, MA: Harvard University Press, 2005.

———. *Deaf in America: Voices from a Culture*. Cambridge, MA: Harvard University Press, 1988.

Perry, Imani. *Prophets of the Hood: Politics and Poetics in Hip Hop*. Durham, NC: Duke University Press, 2004.

Rice, Tom. "Listening." in *Keywords in Sound*, edited by David Novak and Matt Sakakeeny, 99–111. Durham, NC: Duke University Press, 2015.

Robinson, Octavian. "Deafening Music: Transcending Sound in Musicking." *Journal of American Sign Languages and Literatures*, August 6, 2018. http s://journalofasl.com/transcending-sound/.

Rose, Tricia. *Black Noise: Rap Music and Black Culture in Contemporary America*. Hanover, CT: Wesleyan University Press, 1994.

Rosen, Russell S. "Representations of Sound in American Deaf Literature." *Journal of Deaf Studies and Deaf Education* 12, no. 4 (2007): 552–65.

Russo, Frank A. "Music Beyond Sound: Weighing the Contributions of Touch, Sight, and Balance." *Acoustical Society of America* 16, no. 1 (2020): 37–45.

Silver, Ann. "My Experience as an Artist—Vis-à-Vis Deaf Art." Visual Anthropology Review 15, no. 2 (1999): 37–46.

Small, Christopher. *Musicking: The Meanings of Performing and Listening*. Hanover, CT: Wesleyan University Press, 1998.

Straus, Joseph N. *Extraordinary Measures: Disability in Music*. New York: Oxford University Press, 2011.

Whalen, Melissa. "The Noisy House." In *The Deaf Way II Anthology: A Literary Collection by Deaf and Hard of Hearing Writers*, edited by Tonya M. Stremlau, 11–28. Washington, DC: Gallaudet University Press, 2002.

About mdwPress

The Open Access University Press of the mdw

mdwPress is the open access academic publisher of the mdw – University of Music and Performing Arts Vienna. With this press, the mdw aims to increase the visibility of its research in all its diversity and contribute to the development of a global, resource-saving open access infrastructure. Free from commercial motives, mdwPress makes research results freely accessible and reusable for the interested public.

The quality and academic freedom of mdwPress are ensured by an academic board whose regularly rotating internal and external members are characterized by distinguished academic achievements. Each proposal for a publication project, including a suggestion for the peer reviewing procedure of the entire manuscript, is discussed and determined by this board.

mdwPress is open to all academic publication formats, including journals and innovative formats, and welcomes inter- and transdisciplinarity. mdwPress complies with the current technical and ethical standards for publishers and participates in the further development of these standards. Where necessary, mdwPress relies on external partnerships. For the production and distribution of printed books, mdwPress cooperates with transcript.

About this Volume

This anthology gathers contributions based on keynotes and conference papers presented at isaScience 2018, August 10–14, in Reichenau/Rax, Austria. The editors invited selected presenters as well as additional authors whose research matches the book's thematic focus to submit chapters that were subject to two written assessments based on a standardized form, following a regular double-blind peer review process. In total, eighteen independent invited reviewers were involved. The mdwPress coordination and the editors supervised the review process. The mdwPress academic board was not involved, since it was only installed at the end of this quality assurance process.

GPSR Authorized Representative: Easy Access System Europe, Mustamäe tee
50, 10621 Tallinn, Estonia, gpsr.requests@easproject.com